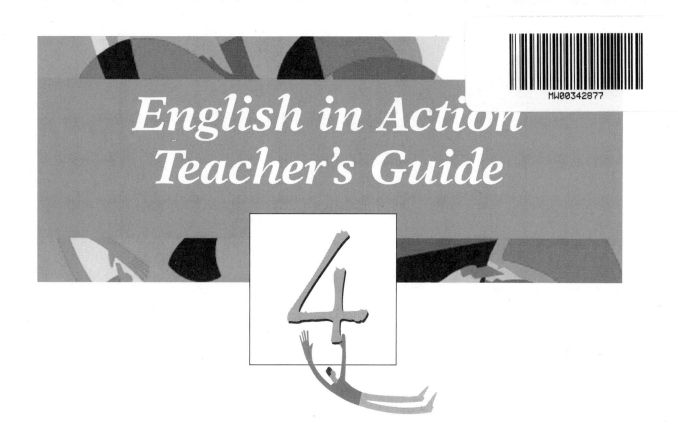

English in Action
Teacher's Guide

4

Barbara H. Foley

Elizabeth R. Neblett

John Chapman

THOMSON

™

HEINLE

Australia • Canada • Mexico • Singapore • Spain • United Kingdom • United States

English in Action 4, Teacher's Guide

by Barbara H. Foley, Elizabeth R. Neblett, and John Chapman

Publisher, Adult and Academic ESL: *James W. Brown*
Senior Acquisitions Editor: *Sherrise Roehr*
Director of Development: *Anita Raducanu*
Development Editor: *Sarah Barnicle*
Assistant Editor: *Audra Longert*
Editorial Assistant: *Katherine Reilly*
Senior Marketing Manager, Adult ESL: *Donna Lee Kennedy*
International Marketing Manager: *Eric Bredenberg*
Director, Global ESL Training & Development:
 Evelyn Nelson
Senior Production Editor: *Maryellen Killeen*
Senior Frontlist Buyer: *Mary Beth Hennebury*

Project Manager: *Tünde A. Dewey*
Compositor: *Pre-Press Co., Inc.*
Text Printer/Binder: *West Group*
Text Designer: *Sue Gerould*
Cover Designer: *Gina Petti/Rotunda Design House*
Photo Researcher: *Jill Engebretson*
Photography Manager: *Sheri Blaney*
Cover Art: *Zita Asbaghi* / **Unit Opener Art:** *Zita Asbaghi*
Illustrators: *Scott MacNeill; Ray Medici;*
 Glen Giron, Roger Acaya, Ibarra
 Cristostomo, Leo Cultura of Raketshop
 Design Studio, Philippines

ISBN: 0-8384-5201-9

For permission to use material from this text or product contact us:
Tel: 1-800-730-2214
Fax: 1-800-730-2215
Web: www.thomsonrights.com

International Division List

ASIA
Thomson Learning
5 Shenton Way
#01-01 UIC Building
Singapore 068808
Tel: 65-6410-1200
Fax: 65-6410-1208

AUSTRALIA / NEW ZEALAND
Nelson Thomson Learning
102 Dodds Street
South Melbourne
Victoria 3205
Australia
Tel: 61-(0)3-9685-4111
Fax: 61-(0)3-9685-4199

BRAZIL
Thomson Pioneira Ltda
Rua Traipú, 114-3° Andar
Perdizes
01235-000 - São Paulo - SP
Brasil
Tel: 55 11 3665-9900
Fax: 55 11 3665-9901

CANADA
Nelson Thomson Learning
1120 Birchmount Road
Scarborough,
Ontario M1K 5G4
Canada
Tel: 416-752-9448
Fax: 416-752-8102

JAPAN
Thomson Learning
Nihonjisyo Brooks Bldg. 3-F
1-4-1 Kudankita
Chiyoda-ku
Tokyo 102-0073
Japan
Tel: 81-3-3511-4390
Fax: 81-3-3511-4391

KOREA
Thomson Learning
Suite 301 Richemont Building
114-5 Sung San-Dong Mapo-ku
Seoul 121-250
Korea
Tel: 82-2-322-4926
Fax: 82-2-322-4927

LATIN AMERICA
Thomson Learning
Séneca 53
Colonia Polanco
11560 México D.F.
México
Tel: 52-55-5281-2906
Fax: 52-55-5281-2656

SPAIN / PORTUGAL
Paraninfo Thomson Learning
Calle Magallanes 25
28015 – Madrid
España
Tel: 34-(0)91-446-3350
Fax: 34-(0)91-445-6218

TAIWAN
Thomson Learning
12F, No. 10 Heng Yang Road
Taipei, Taiwan, R.O.C.
Tel: 886-2-2375-1118
Fax: 886-2-2375-1119

EUROPE / MIDDLE EAST/AFRICA
Thomson Learning
High Holborn House
50 / 51 Bedford Row
London WC1R 4LR
United Kingdom
Tel: 44-20-7067-2500
Fax: 44-20-7067-2600

Acknowledgments

We would like to acknowledge the many individuals who helped, encouraged, and supported us during the writing and production of this series. In keeping with an open-ended format, we would like to offer a matching exercise. Please be advised, there is more than one correct "match" for each person. Thank you all!

Jim Brown
Eric Bredenberg
Sherrise Roehr
Sarah Barnicle
Maryellen Killeen
Audra Longert
Tünde A. Dewey
All the Heinle sales reps
The students at Union County College
The faculty and staff at UCC
Our families

- for your creative eye for art and design.
- for your enthusiasm and support.
- for your support, patience, and humor while guiding this project.
- for your faith in the authors.
- for your smiles and your stories.
- for your encouragement, comments, and suggestions.
- for putting up with us!
- for your understanding of the needs of teachers and programs.
- for your keeping us all on schedule.
- for your help with research.

The authors and publisher would like to thank the following reviewers and consultants:

Linda Boice
Elk Grove Unified School District, Sacramento, CA

Rocio Castiblanco
Seminole Community College, Sanford, FL

Jared Erfle
Antelope Valley High School, Lancaster, CA

Rob Kustusch
Triton Community College, River Grove, IL

Patricia Long
Old Marshall Adult School, Sacramento, CA

Kathleen Newton
New York City Board of Education, Bronx, NY

Alberto Panizo
Miami-Dade Community College, Miami, FL

Eric Rosenbaum
Bronx Community College, Bronx, NY

Michaela Safadi
South Gate Community, South Gate, CA

Armando Valdez
Huantes Learning and Leadership Development Center, San Antonio, TX

Contents

Contents

To the Teacher

Many years ago, I attended an ESL workshop in which the presenter asked a full audience, "How many of you read the **To the Teacher** at the front of the text?" Two participants raised their hands. Since that time, I have begged my publishers to release me from this responsibility, but have always been overruled.

As a teacher, you can form a clear first impression of this book. Flip through the pages. Will the format appeal to your students? Look carefully through the table of contents. Are most of the structures and contexts that your program has established included in the text? Thumb slowly through a few units. Will the activities and exercises, the support, the pace be appropriate for your students? If you wish, you can even read the rest of **To the Teacher** below.

English in Action is a four-level core language series for ESL/EFL students. It is a comprehensive revision and expansion of *The New Grammar in Action*. The popularity of the original edition delighted us, but we heard the same requests over and over: "Please include more readings and pronunciation," and "Could you add a workbook?" In planning the revision, our publisher threw budgetary concerns to the wind and decided to produce a four-color, redesigned version. The revision also allowed us, the authors, an opportunity to refine the text. We are writers, but we are also teachers. We wrote a unit, then immediately tried it out in the classroom. Activities, tasks, and exercises were added, deleted, and changed in an ongoing process. Students provided daily and helpful feedback.

This fourth book is designed for high-intermediate level students. Students at this level already have good control of the basic tenses and structures of English and can apply them in meaningful communication. The units in this text gradually expand the students' ability to use more complex language to discuss high-interest, universal topics.

Units are completely contextualized and gradually build around topics such as leisure activities, sports, job performance, business and industry, and country music. Throughout each unit, there is support in the form of clearly illustrated situations, vocabulary boxes, grammar notes, and examples. As students move through the unit, they engage in situations and activities in which they can see, hear, and practice English. Listening is a key component of the unit. Initially, students are asked to listen for the structures in individual sentences. As the unit

develops, the structure is incorporated into dialogues and longer narratives. The pronunciation section additionally reinforces the structure, providing practice with elements such as contractions and tense contrast.

Active Grammar

Each unit opens with an illustration or photo and discussion questions to introduce the topic and to draw the students into the unit. The following six to seven pages of exercises integrate the context and the new grammar. As students progress through this section, they will find a wide variety of both controlled and open-ended activities. There are pictures to discuss, opportunities to interview their teachers and their classmates, conversations to develop, stories to enjoy, dictations for students to present to a partner, and even a few traditional fill-in-the-blank exercises to complete. We encourage you to try them all.

The directions are clear and there are examples for each exercise. Artwork and photos illustrate the context clearly. For many of the exercises, the entire class will be working together with your direction and explanations. Other exercises show a pairwork icon 👥 —students can try these with a partner or in a small group. You should walk around the classroom, listening to students and answering questions. With this variety of activities, this book should appeal to every learning style.

Pronunciation

Within the **Active Grammar** section is an exercise that focuses on pronunciation. These are specific pronunciation points that complement the grammar or vocabulary of the lesson, such as contractions, syllable stress, reductions, and linking.

The Big Picture

This is our favorite section, integrating listening, vocabulary, and structure. A large, lively picture shows a particular setting or situation, such as obtaining a driver's license, speaking to a school counselor, or gossiping about friends. After listening to a short narrative or conversation, students answer questions, fill in information, review structures, or complete conversations.

Reading

In the fourth book, the reading feature has been significantly expanded and is now a two-page spread. Each reading is longer and is directly related to the context of the unit. There are new vocabulary words and structures that have never been introduced. Teachers can help ESL readers learn that understanding meaning is primary. It is not necessary to master or look up every new word. Each reading is followed by exercises that help to develop reading skills, such as scanning for information, reading for details, taking a multiple choice test, understanding vocabulary in context, and understanding the pros and cons of a topic.

Writing Our Stories

The writing section has also grown into a two-page format. The first page provides a writing model and some form of brainstorming, such as a checklist, discussion questions, fill-in sentences, or a chart. The writing tasks usually ask students to write about their lives or opinions. For variety, other units may direct students to describe a process, write street directions, or write an opinion letter. Each section also practices or develops one writing point, such as using transition words, using quotation marks, or organizing ideas before writing. Several teachers have told us about the creative ways they share student writing, including publishing student magazines, designing a class Web page, and displaying stories and photos taken by their students. Included at the end of the writing page is a new feature entitled *Looking at the Internet*. If your school has a computer lab or students have Internet access at home, these short suggestions will provide a starting point for follow-up activities on the Internet.

Practicing on Your Own

Some teachers ask students to do the exercises in class. Another suggestion for homework is the audio component. Ask students to listen to it three or four more times, reviewing the vocabulary and the exercises they did in class. Our students tell us that they often write the story from the Big Picture as a dictation activity.

Grammar Summary

Some teachers wanted this summary at the beginning of the unit; others were pleased to see it at the end. Use this section if and when you wish. Some students like to see the grammar up front, having a clear map of the developing grammar. We have found, though, that many of our students at the intermediate level are confused with long grammar explanations at the beginning of a unit. There are small grammar charts as needed throughout the unit. The ending summary brings them together.

Teacher's Guide

We have developed the *English in Action 4 Teacher's Guide* to be a support to teachers of all levels of experience. New teachers will benefit from the clear, step-by-step instructions on using the Student Book, while more experienced teachers will find creative and fun ideas for expanding on the Student Book material. Each **Teacher's Guide** page includes a reduced Student Book page, along with guidelines for effectively teaching and expanding on the activities on that page. At the bottom of many of the **Teacher's Guide** pages are audio scripts for the listening activities on that page. These audio scripts are for listening activities that do not already appear on the Student Book page. The audio scripts are also included at the end of the Student Book. The audio scripts allow teachers who do not have access to the audio to read aloud to their students the audio portion of the listening activities.

The **Teacher's Guide** also features a helpful grammar section in the appendices. This section, the **Grammar Summary Expansion,** is designed to give teachers more information about the grammatical structures and points taught in each Student Book unit.

I am sure we will be revising the text again in three or four years. We will be gathering your input during that time. You can always e-mail us at **www.heinle.com** with your comments, complaints, and suggestions.

Liz and I both work at Union County College in Elizabeth, New Jersey. We teach at the Institute for Intensive English, a large English as a Second Language program. Students from over 70 different countries study in our classes. Between us, Liz and I have been teaching at the college for over 40 years! When Liz isn't writing, she spends her time traveling, taking pictures, and watching her favorite baseball team, the New York Mets. Liz took many of the pictures in the texts, for which our students eagerly posed. In the warm weather, I can't start my day without a 15- or 20-mile bicycle ride. My idea of a good time always involves the outdoors: hiking, kayaking, or simply working in my garden.

Barbara H. Foley
Elizabeth R. Neblett

Photo Credits

This page constitutes an extension of the copyright page. We have made every effort to trace the ownership of all copyrighted material and to secure permission from copyright holders. In the event of any question arising as to the use of any material, we will be pleased to make the necessary corrections in future printings. Thanks are due to the following authors, publishers, and agents for permission to use the material indicated.

All photos courtesy of Elizabeth R. Neblett with the following exceptions:

p. 2, top left: Phil Borden/Photo Edit
p. 2, top right: Liba Taylor/CORBIS
p. 2, bottom left: Table Mesa Prod./Index Stock Imagery
p. 2, bottom right: Jan Halaska/Index Stock Imagery
p. 4, bottom left: Phil Cantor/Index Stock Imagery
p. 4, bottom right: Tom Carter/Index Stock Imagery
p. 30, left: Roman Soumar/CORBIS
p. 30, right: Kevin Fleming/CORBIS
p. 36, top: Bill Lai/Index Stock Imagery
p. 36, bottom: IT STOCK INT'L/Index Stock Imagery
p. 62: Grant Heilman Photography/Index Stock Imagery
p. 63: Patricia Barry Levy/Index Stock Imagery
p. 75: Table Mesa Prod./Index Stock Imagery
p. 76, top right: Stephen Umahtete/Index Stock Imagery
p. 76, center left: Bud Freund/Index Stock Imagery
p. 76, center middle: Martin Fox/Index Stock Imagery
p. 76, center right: Raenne Rubenstein/Index Stock Imagery
p. 76, bottom left: Antonio Mendoza/Index Stock Imagery
p. 76, bottom middle: Yvette Cardoza/Index Stock Imagery
p. 76, bottom right: PhotoDisc/Getty Images
p. 88: Joe Bator/CORBIS
p. 107, top left: Sam Greenwood/IPN/AURORA
p. 107, top right: Duomo/CORBIS
p. 107, bottom left: Reuters NewMedia Inc./CORBIS
p. 107, bottom right: Reuters NewMedia Inc./CORBIS
p. 110: AFP/CORBIS
p. 116: Owen Franken/CORBIS
p. 127, center: Frank Siteman/Index Stock Imagery
p. 127, bottom: Ellen Skye/Index Stock Imagery
p. 128: Christian Peacock/Index Stock Imagery
p. 132, top left: Royalty-Free/CORBIS
p. 132, top right: Stephen Derr/Getty Images
p. 132, bottom left: Orion Press/Index Stock Imagery
p. 132, bottom right: Morton Beebe/CORBIS
p. 138: Kareem Black/Stone
p. 142: Digital Vision/Getty Images
p. 158, top: Andy Sacks/Stone
p. 158, center: Ted Wilcox/Index Stock Imagery

p. 158, bottom: Rob Lewine/CORBIS
p. 190: Dennis Brack/IPN/AURORA
p. 192, top: Myrleen Cate/Index Stock Imagery
p. 192, bottom: PhotoDisc/Getty Images
p. 206, top: Royalty-Free/CORBIS
p. 212, top left: PhotoDisc Green/Getty Images
p. 212, top second from left: John Luke/Index Stock Imagery
p. 212, top second from right: photolibrary.com/Index Stock Imagery
p. 212, top right: GOLDBERG DIEGO/CORBIS SYGMA
p. 212, center left: Spencer Grant/Photo Edit
p. 212, center second from left: Eyewire/ Getty Images
p. 212, center second from right: Allen Fredrickson/Index Stock Imagery
p. 212, center right: PhotoDisc/Getty Images
p. 212, bottom left: Randy Lorentzen/Index Stock Imagery
p. 212, bottom second from left: PhotoDisc/Getty Images
p. 212, bottom second from right: Ryan McVay/PhotoDisc/Getty Images
p. 212, bottom right: Courtesy of Dieceland
p. 214: Bettmann/CORBIS
p. 228, top left: Jeff Albertson/CORBIS
p. 228, top middle: AP Photo/Hussein Malla
p. 228, top right: Reuters NewMedia Inc./CORBIS
p. 228, center left: AFP/CORBIS
p. 228, center middle: AP Photo/Reed Saxon
p. 228, center right: Manuel Zambrana/ CORBIS
p. 228, bottom left: Reuters NewMedia Inc./ CORBIS
p. 228, bottom middle: AFP/CORBIS
p. 228, bottom right: Abilio Lope/CORBIS
p. 230: Reuters NewMedia Inc./CORBIS
p. 233, top: Reuters NewMedia Inc./CORBIS
p. 233, bottom: Reuters NewMedia Inc./CORBIS
p. 236, top left: AP Photo/John Russell
p. 236, top right: David McNew/Getty Images
p. 236, bottom: AP Photo/Mark Humphrey
p. 238, top: Evan Agostini/Liaison/Getty Images
p. 238, bottom: AP Photo/Luca Bruno

Unit 1
Education

Discuss what the person in the unit title art is doing. Ask:

• *What do you see next to the number 1?* (An upside-down man with a pencil in his hand)
• *What is he doing?* (He's filling in an answer on a test paper.)
• *What does this picture have to do with the unit?* (Part of getting an education is learning how to do well on tests.)

A. High school.

• Point to the four photographs and ask students to describe what each room looks like and what activities are taking place. Then, help them identify the country where each photo might have been taken. For example:

T: *What does the classroom look like in picture one?*
S1: *There are a lot of desks in long rows.*
T: *What are the students doing?*
S2: *They are sitting and writing in their notebooks.*
T: *What country do you think this is?*
S3: *Is it Japan?*
S4: *Maybe it's Korea.*

• After discussing all four pictures, ask students to take turns saying which one (or ones) look the most like a high school classroom in their native country. Encourage them to tell what specific things about the classroom setup and the student activities are the same in their country.

B. Schools are different from country to country.

Students complete the activity individually. Then, they compare answers in small groups. Review the responses with the whole class.

1 Education

A. High school. Which picture best describes a high school classroom in your native country?

1.    2.

3.    4.

B. Schools are different from country to country. Answer or complete the following statements about high school in your native country. Then, compare your answers with a group of classmates. (Answers will vary.)

1. The school year begins in _____ (month) and ends in _____ (month) .
2. The school day begins at ___ : ___ (time) and ends at ___ : ___ (time) .
3. School **meets / does not meet** on Saturdays.
4. High school students **choose / do not choose** some of their own courses.
5. Students **type / do not type** their papers for their classes.

6. All students **study / do not study** the same subjects in school.

7. Students **study / do not study** with students of the same ability.

8. The teacher **changes / does not change** classrooms.

9. The teacher **gives / does not give** oral tests.

10. Most students **work / do not work** after school.

11. Families **pay / do not pay** for books.

12. Students **wear / do not wear** uniforms.

13. There **are / are not** after-school clubs for the students.

14. What kind of tests do high school students take in your native country?
    (Circle) all correct answers.

    a. multiple-choice

    b. true / false statements

    c. essay (write compositions)

    d. oral tests

    e. other _____

15. High school students are required to study the following subjects.
    (Circle) all correct answers.

biology	foreign languages
physics	literature
chemistry	typing
psychology	secretarial skills
sociology	physical education
cooking	woodworking
art	sewing
music theory	mathematics
musical instruments	Latin or Greek
drama	geography
history	government

Suggestion

If you feel that many students in your class may need extra help with the vocabulary in Exercise B, divide the class into small groups as they begin this activity. Ask students to read through the 15 questions without trying to answer them. Just have them circle any words or phrases they don't understand. Review the words by writing each new item on the board and discussing the meaning with the whole class. Then, have students complete the exercise individually and compare answers in small groups.

☀ Active Grammar:
Present Continuous Tense

A. Look at the pictures.

- Review the grammar chart at the top of the page. Ask students to describe the formation of present continuous sentences. For example:

  T: *What comes first in a present continuous statement?*

  S1: *A noun or a pronoun.*

  T: *What comes next?*

  S1: *The verb "be" in the present tense. You can also have the negative form of "be."*

  T: *What comes last?*

  S1: *The base form of the main verb followed by "-ing."*

- Have students read the instructions. Answer any questions they may have. Point out the sample answer. Then, explain the time limit and have students begin writing. Announce how much time remains after five minutes and one minute before the time is up. Students compare sentences with a partner.

B. *Yes/No* questions.

- Review the grammar chart at the bottom of the page. Following the format used in Exercise A, have students describe the formation of present continuous tense *Yes/No* questions.
- Review the list of questions with the class. Answer any questions they may have. Then, have students ask and answer the questions about the pictures in small groups. Review the answers with the whole class.

☀ Active Grammar: Present Continuous Tense

A. Look at the pictures. In your notebook, write as many sentences as you can in ten minutes. Compare your sentences with a partner.

A student *is talking* on the telephone.

Be Statements		
I	am am not	
He She	is is not	studying.
We You They	are are not	

1.

2.

3.

4.

B. *Yes/No* questions. Answer the questions about the photos in Exercise A. *(Answers may vary. Suggested answers below.)*

Photo 1

1. Are the students taking a test? Yes, they are.
2. Are they working together? Yes, they are.
3. Are they listening to a tape? No, they aren't.

Yes/No Questions		
Am	I	
Is	he she	studying?
Are	we you they the students	

Photo 2

4. Are some students working on computers? Yes, they are.

5. Are they working in the library? No, they aren't.

6. Are they using the printer right now? No, they aren't.

Photo 3

7. Is the young woman concentrating on her work? Yes, she is.

8. Is the student behind her talking? No, he isn't.

9. Are the students taking a test? Yes, they are.

Photo 4

10. Are the students playing soccer? No, they aren't.

11. Is everyone wearing a uniform? Yes, they are.

12. Are they playing in bad weather? No, they aren't.

Write two more questions about the photos. Ask a classmate your questions.

13. _____?

14. _____?

C. Your classroom. Look around your classroom and answer the following questions. Write your answers on the blanks. (Answers will vary.)

Present Continuous Tense: *Who**		
Who	is	studying English? reading a novel? writing an essay? talking to you?
Who* takes the *singular* verb form.		

Present Continuous Tense: *Wh-* Questions			
What Where Why	am	I	studying? reading? writing? doing?
	is	he she	
	are	we you they the students	

1. Who is sitting next to the door? _____

2. Who is talking to the teacher? _____

3. What are the students doing? _____

4. Where is the teacher standing? _____

5. Who is wearing a suit? _____

6. What are you wearing? _____

7. Where are you sitting? _____

8. What language are the students speaking? _____

Education **5**

Write two more questions about the photos.

Give students two or three minutes to write out two more questions. You may wish to have them work in pairs. Then, ask them to read the questions aloud. Answer each one, explaining any new words in either the question or the answer.

C. Your classroom.

• Review the forms presented in the two grammar charts by having students take turns making up sentences using the words in the chart. Call on a second student to give a possible answer. For example:
S1: *What is he studying?*
S2: *He's studying math.*

• Read and discuss the instructions. Then, have students write their answers individually. Review the answers with the class. Elicit several true and grammatically correct answers for each question. For example, correct answers to question 1 might include: *I am, Gina and Carlo are, Kenji is,* and *No one is.*

Suggestion

If appropriate for your class, provide additional oral practice. Have students close their books. Then, ask different students to take turns asking one of the questions and calling on a classmate to answer. If students are able to do this with a fair degree of accuracy, you might invite volunteers to make up original present continuous *Wh-* questions to ask each other.

Active Grammar: Simple Present Tense

A. Your school.

• Point out the simple present tense statements in the grammar box and review how affirmative and negative statements are formed. For example:

T: *Which pronouns are followed by a verb with an -s ending?*
S1: He *and* she.
T: *Which pronouns are followed by a verb with no -s ending?*
S2: I, we, you, *and* they.

• Then, discuss the negative forms. Ask:

T: *Which pronouns use do not or don't?*
S1: I, we, you, *and* they.
T: *Which pronouns use does not or doesn't?*
S2: He *and* she.

• Ask students to complete the activity on their own. Review the answers with the whole class.

B. Adverbs of frequency.

• Discuss the meaning of the adverbs of frequency in the box at the right. Then, review the placement of adverbs of frequency within a sentence as explained at the top of the box.
• Read the instructions and call on individuals to use the cues to make up sentences about you that are true.

Suggestion

For additional practice with adverbs of frequency, ask students to take turns adding one to each of the sentences in Exercise A. Check to see that they place the adverb of frequency before the verb. Explain that some sentences cannot take an adverb of frequency if they are true facts that don't generally change. See item 7 in Exercise A. Another example might be: My notebook is blue.

Active Grammar: Simple Present Tense

(Answers will vary.)

A. Your school. Complete the sentences about your school. Use the verbs in parentheses.

I We You They	study do not study don't study	English.
He She	studies does not study doesn't study	

1. I ___study / don't study___ (study) in the morning.
2. Students ___pay / don't pay___ (pay) tuition for classes.
3. A typical student ___goes / doesn't go___ (go) to classes every day.
4. Students ___live / don't live___ (live) in dormitories.
5. I ___call / don't call___ (call) my teachers by their first names.
6. Our school ___has / doesn't have___ (have) good computer facilities.
7. There ___is / isn't___ (be) a library in my school building.
8. The school ___offers / doesn't offer___ (offer) after-school activities for the students.
9. Teachers ___give / don't give___ (give) many tests during the semester.
10. My classmates and I ___take / don't take___ (take) class trips.

B. Adverbs of frequency. Talk about your teacher, using adverbs of frequency.

speak loudly
My teacher *almost always* speaks loudly.

1. speak softly
2. (be) on time
3. give quizzes
4. use a tape recorder
5. write on the chalkboard
6. give spelling tests
7. show videos
8. use red ink to correct our papers
9. give homework on the weekends
10. _____

Place adverbs of frequency **after the** verb *to be* and **before all other verbs.**

He **is** *never* on time.
He *always* **comes** to school late.

always	100%
usually	90%
almost always	
frequently often	70–80%
sometimes	50%
rarely seldom	10–20%
almost never	5%
never	0%

C. Study habits. How do you study? Read each statement and check (✓) *always*, *sometimes*, or *never* about your own study habits. Then, listen to your partner describe his or her study habits. (Answers will vary.)

	Me			My partner		
	always	sometimes	never	always	sometimes	never
1. I do my homework.						
2. My homework is neat.						
3. I ask questions in class.						
4. I read a newspaper in English.						
5. I try to speak English outside of class.						
6. I ask for extra help when I need it.						
7. I speak English in class.						
8. I study in a quiet place.						
9. I study an hour or more a day.						
10. I get to class on time.						

Complete these sentences about you and your partner. Use the adverbs in parentheses. (Answers will vary.)

1. My partner ——————————————————. (always)

2. I ——————————————————. (always)

3. My partner ——————————————————. (never)

4. I ——————————————————. (sometimes)

5. My partner ——————————————————. (sometimes)

6. My partner and I ——————————————————. (always)

7. My partner and I ——————————————————. (sometimes)

8. My partner and I ——————————————————. (never)

C. Study habits.

• Review the statements in the left-hand column and answer any questions about vocabulary that students may have. Then, have them complete the "Me" part of the chart on their own.

• Students then work with partners. They take turns listening to each other describe their study habits in full sentences. For example: *I always do my homework.* The listener records the partner's statements on the "My Partner" part of the chart.

Complete these sentences about you and your partner.

Have students refer to the chart, fill in their answers on their own, and then, check answers with their partner. Call on several students to read their answers to the class.

☀ Active Grammar: Simple Present Tense Questions

ᵃᵼ **A. Roommates.** Sophie and Lizzy are college roommates, but they have very different schedules, habits, and interests. Listen to the two roommates, complete the questions with "Do" or "Does," and then, answer the questions. (Answers for Sophie and Lizzy belo⟩

Yes/No **Questions**

Do you work?	Yes, I **do**.	No, I **don't**.
Does she work?	Yes, she **does**.	No, she **doesn't**.

1. __Does__ Sophie take all of her courses in the morning? ___Yes, she does___ .
2. __Do__ you take your English class in the morning? ___Answers will vary___ .
3. __Does__ Sophie keep her side of the room neat? ___Yes, she does___ .
4. __Does__ Sophie get up early? ___Yes, she does___ .
5. __Do__ you get up early? ___Answers will vary___ .
6. __Does__ Sophie study in the room? ___Yes, she does___ .
7. __Do__ you study in your bedroom? ___Answers will vary___ .
8. __Does__ Lizzy take all of her courses in the afternoon? ___Yes, she does___ .
9. __Does__ Lizzy keep her side of the room neat? ___No, she does___ .
10. __Do__ you keep your home neat? ___Answers will vary___ .
11. __Does__ Lizzy hand in her papers on time? ___No, she does___ .
12. __Do__ you hand in your homework on time? ___Answers will vary___ .

Are you more like Sophie or Lizzy? Explain. (Answers will vary.)

8 UNIT 1

A. Roommates. (CD1, Track 1 through CD1, Track 2)

• Point to the picture and ask students to comment on the differences between the two roommates. Accept all reasonable answers and repeat each one in full-sentence form.

• Ask students to listen to the tape as Sophie and Lizzy talk about themselves. What differences can the students remember? Review the 12 questions at the bottom of the page.

• Review the contents of the *Yes/No* Questions box.

• Point out the helping verb blank at the beginning of each sentence and the short answer blank after each one. Have students fill in the helping verbs on their own. Review the completed questions with the class.

• Play the audio again and have the students write the appropriate short answer at the end of each sentence. Review the correct answers with the whole class.

Are you more like Sophie or Lizzy?

Invite several students to describe how they are like Sophie or Lizzy. Encourage students to give specific examples from their own lives.

Audio Script

A. Roommates. Sophie and Lizzy are college roommates, but they have very different schedules, habits, and interests. Listen to the two roommates, complete the questions with *Do* or *Does,* and then, answer the questions.

(CD1, Track 1)

Sophie: Hi, I'm Sophie, and I'm a morning person. When the sun comes up, I feel great. I get a lot of things done in the morning, so I take courses early in the morning. I'm finished with my classes by noon. I like to keep everything neat and in order. If things are out of place, I go crazy! My favorite subjects are science and math, so I think I'm going to major in chemistry or computer science. I really like computers and I do all of my work on my computer. I almost never write by hand. Oh, and I always hand in my class work on time. But, my roommate, Lizzy, is completely different from me. We get along well, though.

(Audio Script continues on page 251.)

B. *Wh-* **questions.** Work with a small group of students. Interview each other about your daily schedules and habits. *(Answers will vary.)*

	Wh- Questions		
What Where Why How How much	do does	I we you they he she	study English? work? eat?

Question	You	Partner 1	Partner 2
1. What time do you get up?			
2. What do you eat for breakfast?			
3. What time do you leave your home?			
4. Where do you eat lunch?			
5. How do you get to school?			
6. How long does it take?			
7. What hours do you work?			
Write three more questions to ask your partners.			
8.			
9.			
10.			

 C. Pronunciation: Linking: */do you/.* Listen and repeat each question.

1. What do you do?
2. Where do you work?
3. When do you get up?
4. How do you get home?
5. Where do you live?
6. Why do you study here?
7. What do you do on weekends?
8. When do you do your homework?
9. What time do you leave for school?
10. Where do you shop for food?

Practice asking and answering the questions with a partner.

D. *Who* **questions.** Answer these *who* questions about students in your class.

1. Who always arrives on time?
2. Who wears a baseball cap to class?
3. Who often arrives late?
4. Who always has a pencil sharpener?
5. Who goes to work after class?

Write three more *Who* questions.

(Answers will vary.)

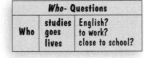

	Who- Questions	
Who	studies goes lives	English? to work? close to school?

B. *Wh-* **questions.**

• Review the grammar chart at the top of the page. Ask students to describe the formation of present tense *Wh-* questions. For example:

  T: *What comes first in a present tense* Wh- *question?*
  S1: *A* Wh- *word, like* what, where, *or* how.
  T: *What comes next?*
  S1: *The helping verb* do *or* does.
  T: *And then?*
  S1: *A pronoun like* I *or* we.
  T: *And what's at the end?*
  S1: *The base form of the main verb.*

• Review the seven examples and answer any questions students may have. Then, have them write three more questions at the bottom of the chart. Ask some students to read their questions to the class. Correct as necessary.
• Students form groups, ask two other people the questions, and record their answers in the chart.

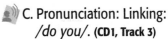 **C. Pronunciation: Linking:** */do you/.* **(CD1, Track 3)**

Play the audio once while students only listen. Point out that the words *do* and *you* are linked together and pronounced almost as if they were a single word. Then, play the audio again and have students repeat each question.

Practice asking and answering the questions with a partner.

Pairs take turns asking and answering the questions.

D. *Who* **questions**

Have individuals read one question at a time and name another student to answer the question.

Write three more who questions.

Have students write three questions on their own. Then, as with Exercise D, have individuals read one question at a time and choose another student to answer their question.

☀ Active Grammar: Nonaction Verbs

Review the nonaction verb chart at the top of the page. Give examples of correct and incorrect use of some verbs. For example: *"Linda appears tired"* is a correct sentence. We don't say, *"Linda is appearing tired."*

👥 A. Ask and answer the questions with a partner.

- Read the instructions and remind students to use only the simple present form. Point out the example and have a pair of students read it aloud.
- Then, have partners work their way through all eight questions, taking turns asking and answering them. Review the exercise by inviting a pair of students to ask and answer the questions in front of the whole class.

Suggestion

For additional practice, have students write out some or all of the questions and answers. Ask them to check each other's work.

B. The Student Center.

- Discuss the picture on page 10 with the class. Ask students to point out Lana, Bill, Lee, and Jamal and tell what each one is doing.

☀ Active Grammar: Nonaction Verbs

The following verbs usually take the simple present form.

appear	have	like	own	sound
believe	hear	look	prefer	taste
feel	hope	love	see	understand
hate	know	need	smell	want

👥 A. Ask and answer the questions with a partner. Use the simple present form.

(Questions and answers may vary.)

Do you believe in UFOs?
No, I don't.

1.

you / believe in
Do you believe in UFO's?

2.

you / like
Do you like icecream?

3.

which / you / prefer
Which cup do you prefer?

4.

your teacher / have
(bird/turtle/cat)
Does your teacher have a...?

5.

you / own
Do you own a house?

6.

your teacher /
know how to speak
Does your teacher know
how to speak French?

7.

what kind of /
your teacher / have
What kind of car does
your teacher have?

8.

you / want to / take
Do you want to
take a plane?

B. The Student Center.

Student Center

CAFE   PIZZA

LANA   BILL   LEE   JAMAL

Use the cues to write sentences about the students in the picture on page 10. Many of the verbs are nonaction verbs. Write the sentences in your notebook.
(Answers may vary.)

1. Students / like / to meet / student center
   Students like to meet at the student center.
2. They / need to relax / between classes
   They need to relax between classes.
3. Two students / play / video games
   Two students are playing video games.
4. Some students / study / together
   Some students are studying together.
5. Some music / play / in the background
   Some music is playing in the background.
6. Students / hope to pass / their exams
   Students hope to pass their exams.
7. They / (not) hear / the noise
   They don't hear the noise.
8. Lana and her boyfriend / watch / TV
   Lana and her boyfriend are watching TV.
9. Bill / look / bored
   Bill looks bored.
10. He / (not) like / daytime dramas
    He doesn't like daytime dramas.
11. Two students / buy / pizza
    Two students are buying pizza
12. The pizza / smell / good
    The pizza smells good.

C. The chess players. Read this story about the two chess players in the picture. Fill in the correct form of the verbs in parentheses. Use the present continuous or the simple present form.

Lee and Jamal are juniors in the computer science department. They (always / study) _____always study_____ hard, but every afternoon, they (take) _____take_____ a break to play their favorite game — chess. Lee and Jamal both (belong) _____belong_____ to their school's chess team, and they (be) _____are_____ two of the best players on the team. They (prefer) _____prefer_____ the chess team to any of the other teams at the school. Lee and Jamal (play) _____play_____ chess almost every afternoon at 3:00 in the Student Center. It's 4:00 now, and as usual, they (play) _____are playing_____ a game. Right now, Lee (think) _____is thinking_____ about his next move, and Jamal (smile) _____is smiling_____ because he (know) _____knows_____ that he is about to win this game. Even though the Student Center is noisy, and students (talk) _____are talking_____, music (play) _____is playing_____, and the TV (be) _____is_____ on, Lee and Jamal (hear / not) _____don't hear_____ the noise. They (concentrate) _____are concentrating_____ on their game. Lee (want) _____wants_____ to win because Jamal has won their last two games.

Write a paragraph in your notebook about another student or students in the picture. Use the simple present and the present continuous forms.

B. The Student Center.
(continued)

• Read the instructions. Remind students that some of the sentences will require the present continuous tense and some the simple present tense. Suggest that they refer back to the box at the top of page 10 if they aren't sure which to use.

• Students complete the sentences on their own and check their answers with a partner. Then, review all answers by having different students write one sentence each on the board. Correct errors as you review the sentences with the class.

C. The chess players.

Students read the story and fill in the answers individually. Review the correct answers orally with the whole class.

Write a paragraph in your notebook about another student or students in the picture.

Have students look at the picture on page 10. Begin by eliciting from the class a few possible statements that use the simple present and the present continuous. Then, have students complete their paragraphs on their own. Collect the paragraphs and mark any errors before returning them to the students.

Suggestion

Choose some sentences from student papers that contain errors in the use of the two tenses and write them on the board, drawing a blank line in place of the incorrect verb form. Ask different students to say the sentence with the correct verb form.

The Big Picture:
The University of Texas at San Antonio

☼ **A. Listen to the description of this university. (CD1, Track 4)**

- Ask students what information they think is important in choosing a college to attend. Tell students that there are over a thousand colleges in the U. S., and that students have difficulty deciding where to apply.
- Direct students to read numbers 1 to 11 before they listen. Ask about any new words or information.
- Play the audio and ask students just to listen the first time through. Then, play it again and ask them to circle the correct information and fill in the blanks as they listen a second time. Play the audio a third time for them to confirm their answers. Review the correct answers with the whole class.

☼ The Big Picture: The University of Texas at San Antonio

☼ **A. Listen to the description of this university. As you listen, complete and circle the correct information.**

1. Location: urban   (suburban)   rural
2. Degrees: two-year   (four-year)
3. Type of university: (public)   private
4. Number of full-time students: __12,034__ Part-time students: __5,391__
   Graduate students: __3,000__
5. Number of faculty: __963__
6. Application fee: $ __25__ Online application available: (Yes) No
7. Recommendations for high school applicants:
   - __4__ years of English   __2__ years of a social science
   - __2__ years of a foreign language   __2__ years of a lab science
   - __3__ years of math   __1__ years of fine arts
8. Minimum SAT score required: __1000__   (Answers may vary.
9. Three possible majors: __accounting__ __art history__ __biology__
10. Number of computers on campus: __800__
11. Services available for students:
    a. __Learning centers__ for students who need extra help __athletic teams, dram__
    b. Examples of student activities: __and theater, science organizations__
    c. Programs for freshman students: __orientation programs__

Audio Script

A. Listen to the description of this university. As you listen, complete and circle the correct information. (CD1, Track 4)

The University of Texas is a large university with many campuses all over Texas. This is a description of the University of Texas at San Antonio, which is located in southeastern Texas.

The University of Texas at San Antonio, or U.T.S.A., is a four-year public university with three campuses. U.T.S.A.'s main campus is located on a suburban campus, 15 miles from downtown San Antonio. The university has a large undergraduate population. It enrolls 12,034 full-time students and 5,391 part-time students. In addition, three thousand students attend the graduate school that offers masters and doctoral degrees. The university employs 963 faculty.

Students who want to attend U.T.S.A. have to follow the same procedures that most college applicants do. First of all, there's an application fee of $25. All students must mail a high school transcript that has all of their grades. All students must complete an application, which they can do online if they want to. The university recommends that students complete four years of English, two years of a foreign language, three years of math, two years of a social science, and two years of a lab science, such as biology or chemistry. The university also recommends prospective students to have one year of fine arts, such as music or art. Most students take the SAT, or Scholastic Aptitude Test, and have total scores of 1000 or above.

(Audio Script continues on page 251.)

B. True or False. Read each statement. Then, circle *T* for *True*, or *F* for *False*.

1. The University of Texas at San Antonio is a four-year university. **(T)** F
2. U.T.S.A. is a private university. T **(F)**
3. The main campus is in downtown San Antonio. T **(F)**
4. The university has two campuses. T **(F)**
5. U.T.S.A. has a graduate school. **(T)** F
6. U.T.S.A. employs about eight hundred faculty. T **(F)**
7. Students pay $15 for the application fee. T **(F)**
8. The university recommends two years of a foreign language. **(T)** F
9. The university recommends a lab science. **(T)** F
10. Most future students take the SAT. **(T)** F

C. Listen and write short answers to the questions about the university.

Yes, it is.	Yes, there is.	Yes, it does.	Yes, they do.	Yes, there are.
No, it isn't.	No, there isn't.	No, it doesn't.	No, they don't.	No, there aren't.

1. No, it isn't.
2. No, it doesn't.
3. Yes, there is.
4. Yes, it does.
5. No, they don't.
6. No, it isn't.
7. Yes, there are.
8. No, they don't.
9. Yes, there are.
10. Yes, there is.

D. University life. Fill in the correct present tense form of the verbs in parentheses.

1. The University of Texas at San Antonio _____has_____ (have) many campuses.
2. About 9,400 students _____study_____ (study) at U.T.S.A.
3. Future students _____pay_____ (pay) an application fee.
4. Students _____take_____ (take) standardized tests before they go to U.T.S.A.
5. U.T.S.A. _____has_____ (have) a learning center with tutors and counselors for the students.
6. The university _____gives_____ (give) the students free career counseling.
7. Students _____go_____ (go) to the employment service when they _____need_____ (need) to find jobs.

Audio Script

C. Listen and write short answers to the questions about the university.
(CD1, Track 5)

1. Is the university a two-year university?
2. Does the university have only one campus?
3. Is there a graduate school at the university?
4. Does the university require students to pay an application fee?
5. Do future students need three years of a foreign language?
6. Is it a private university?
7. Are there computers on campus for the students?
8. Do students who need academic help pay for the tutoring at the learning center?
9. Are there opportunities for women to participate in sports?
10. Is there an orientation for new students?

B. True or False.

Ask students to answer all of the questions, even if they aren't absolutely sure they are correct. Then, review the correct answers with the class.

Suggestion

If appropriate for your class, you may wish to have students complete only the Exercise B answers they are sure of the first time around. Then, play the Exercise A audio again and have them fill in the rest of the answers.

C. Listen and write short answers to the questions about the university.
(CD1, Track 5)

• Point out the short answers in the chart. Ask different students to make up a possible question to go with each short answer. For example:

T: *What question could you ask to get the answer "Yes, they do?"*
S1: *Do they have a football team?*
T: *Right.*
S2: *Do many students study chemistry?*
T: *Right.*

• Then, play the audio and have students write their answers. Review the correct answers orally with the class.

D. University life.

Students complete the exercise individually and check their answers with a partner. Review the correct answers with the class.

Reading:
New Jersey Institute of Technology (N.J.I.T.)

A. Before You Read.

- Read the instructions. Explain that scanning means that you don't read every single word of a passage. With scanning, you look over the paragraphs very quickly, trying to find the answer to a specific question.
- Practice how to scan for specific information. Read question 1 and ask students what kinds of words they would look for to find this information. (They might look for the name of the school or the name of a city.)
- Call attention to the other five questions. Ask students to read each question, think about what kinds of words they would look for to find this information, and then scan the article quickly.

Note

Answer to Exercise A, page 14 and Exercise B, page 15 is marked in the Student Book reading. The remaining circled numbers and underlines are the answers to Exercise B, page 15 only.

A. Before You Read. Scan the reading to find the answers to the following questions.

1. Where is the school located?
2. Does N.J.I.T. have a graduate school?
3. How much is the application fee?
4. What is the minimum SAT score?
5. What is the minimum grade average that N.J.I.T. accepts?
6. Does the school offer evening classes?

Note: Numbered and underlined answers are for page 15, exercise B.

New Jersey Institute of Technology, or ① N.J.I.T., is located in Newark, New Jersey, ten miles from New York City. It is a four-year public university

and technical college. The college offers bachelor's degrees in science, engineering, computer science, architecture, management, technology, and many other fields. N.J.I.T. also has graduate programs in many subjects, in addition to programs for educators. Ninety percent of the students come from New Jersey and ②70 percent commute between home and school. ③The average age of entering students is eighteen.

In addition to an application, students who are interested in applying to N.J.I.T. need to prepare the following materials for admission:

- the application fee; in 2002, the fee was $35
- an official high school transcript of grades
- official SAT (Scholastic Aptitude Test) scores; ④the recommended score is 1000 total or above
- for ⑤non-U.S. citizens, students must send a photocopy of visas or permanent resident cards

The college requires all interested students to have a strong math and science background. Students must have a B average, four years of high school English and two years of science, including one of a laboratory science. ⑥Different majors, such as management, require three years of high school mathematics.

N.J.I.T. has a comprehensive program available for students who prefer distance learning, or ⑦learning on their computers. N.J.I.T. offers bachelor and master degree programs and graduate certificates online. ⑧Students who want to take a course or two without getting a degree or certificate can take noncredit courses online. ⑨Online courses are designed for students who need flexibility. Maybe they have demanding jobs that require overtime during the week, so they cannot take classes during the week. Maybe they have an odd work shift. Some students may have disabilities, which do not permit them to go to classes in person. Distance-learning courses may be right for these types of students who want to study from home.

In addition to day classes and online classes, N.J.I.T. offers many evening and early morning classes. It also has a summer session. ⑩Students who need extra preparation get special instruction, English as a second language classes, or tutoring. Like many other colleges today, a computer is a necessary requirement for N.J.I.T.'s students, so N.J.I.T. gives each student a personal computer for use until graduation. The students can purchase computers at graduation.

On campus, there are dormitories for the students who prefer to live on campus or who live too far away to commute. There is also fraternity housing for students who are members of one of the fraternities. For fun, students can participate in the many clubs and organizations that N.J.I.T. offers. For example, ⑪there are organizations for the variety of ethnic groups such as the Korean Student Association, the Polish Student Association, and the Caribbean Student Organization. For students interested in media, there is a theater group, a radio station, and a newspaper. Finally, there are many organizations for students in different majors.

If you think you might be interested in this college, look at its Web site on the Internet for more information.

B. Reading for details. Number and underline the answers to the following questions.

1. Where is N.J.I.T. located?

   (See pages 14 and 15 for numbered and underlined answers.)

2. What percent of the students commute to the campus?

3. What is the average age of entering students?

4. What is the minimum SAT score for applicants?

5. Does the college accept foreign students?

6. Do all majors require three years of high school mathematics?

7. What is *distance learning*?

8. Who takes online courses?

9. Why do students like online courses?

10. What type of services are available for students who need more preparation?

11. What kinds of clubs and organizations can students join?

- Ask students to read the questions to themselves and ask about anything they don't understand. Then, have them use the scanning method, (see Teacher's Guide, page 14) to locate the information, underline and number the answers, using circled numbers.

- Review the answers by reading each question aloud and calling on a student to tell which paragraph the answer is located in. Then, have the student read his/her underlined answer to the class.

Writing Our Stories: My Schedule

A. Read.

Ask students to read the story to themselves. When they finish, invite them to ask about anything they don't understand and to make any comments they wish about the student's schedule.

B. In your notebook, describe your weekly school schedule and your classes.

• Read the instructions and review the list of questions to be sure students understand all of them.

• Tell students they can use the list of questions to organize their descriptions.

Suggestion

You may wish to ask students to outline the information they are going to use in their descriptions before they start writing them. For example, you might have them make brief notes about class times, study times, the kinds of tests they take, and so forth. This way they will have all the necessary facts, vocabulary, and spelling figured out ahead of time and will be better able to focus on other aspects of correct language usage as they begin writing.

Writing Our Stories: My Schedule

A. Read.

I am a student at N.J.I.T. This is my freshman year, and my major is computer engineering. I have a very full schedule.

I'm taking six courses this semester. On Mondays, Wednesdays, and Fridays I have Introduction to Computer Science from 9:00 to 9:50. Then, I go to English class until 10:50. We read literature and write papers. At 11:00, I go to Calculus II. (I took calculus in high school, so I received credit for Calculus I.) At 12:00, I have a physical education class. I play soccer in that class. Finally, I have a lunch break at 1:00. After lunch I have my freshman seminar. This course helps freshman students adjust to their first year in college. We talk about how to take notes and how to arrange our time so that we can do all of our work. We also talk about social life on campus. Tuesdays and Thursdays are my light days. I only have one class—history—at 10:00. Then, I'm free for the rest of the day, so I have time to work part-time at my uncle's store. I work from 12:00 to 6:00, and I also work on weekends. I do my homework in the evening.

Tarsem

B. In your notebook, describe your weekly school schedule and your classes. Try to answer the following questions in your description: (Answers will vary.)

• What school do you attend?
• Are your classes difficult, easy, or just right?
• What's your favorite class? Why?
• When and where do you study? How many hours do you study a week?
• What kind of tests do you have?
• Do you like your school? Why or why not?

C. *Such as.* Complete each sentence with appropriate examples.
(Answers will vary. Sample responses below)

> *Such as* introduces examples. When you write a paragraph, it is important to include examples. Give two or three examples after *such as.*
> The university offers many fine arts majors *such as* art history and studio art.
> Some colleges *such as* junior colleges and community colleges offer two year programs.

1. My classmates come from different countries such as ____Japan____, ____Brazil____, and ____Morocco____.

2. In our English class, we are studying many things such as ____reading____ and ____writing____.

3. Computers are useful for many things such as ____writing compositions____ and ____writing letters____.

4. A medical student has to study subjects such as ____biology____ and ____chemistry____.

5. Languages such as ____Chinese____ and ____Russian____ are difficult to learn.

D. Edit. There is one underlined mistake in each sentence. Correct each mistake.

1. The Division of Physical Education offer͡s many recreational programs.

2. N.J.I.T. is develop-ing many programs to attract women and minority students to engineering and the sciences.

3. U.T.S.A.'s campuses provides opportunities for many students.

4. Some students ~~are preferring~~ to study from their own homes, using computers.

5. What kind of exams do students usually take?

6. The students ~~leave~~ rarely their classes without a homework assignment.

Looking at the Internet

Most colleges and universities have Web sites that describe their programs, activities, and admission procedures. Their URLs (Internet addresses) end in **.edu**, which stands for education. Here are two examples: New York University's URL is www.nyu.edu. The University of Texas at San Antonio's URL is www.utsa.edu. Click on **Search** and enter the name of a college or university that interests you.

Education **17**

C. *Such as.*

• Review the *such as* explanation at the top of the page. Then, ask students to make up original examples of their own. You might give them cues to get them started. For example:

T: *Foods you like.*
S1: *I like desserts such as ice cream, cake, and cookies.*
T: *Things you can buy in a department store.*
S1: *In a department store you can buy many different types of clothing such as pants, shoes, and hats.*

• Have students complete the sentences and check their answers with a partner. Review the exercise by calling on several different students to read their answers to each question.

D. Edit.

Have students complete the activity on their own and then compare answers with a partner. Go over the answers and explain any that students are not sure of.

Suggestion

Explain that editing is an important part of writing. Encourage students to always edit their own work. Suggest that they also exchange papers with a classmate when they have time so they can practice editing each other's work.

Looking at the Internet

• If there is a computer in your classroom, use it to demonstrate the activity. Invite students to suggest a college or university for you to research.
• Have students continue their own searches at home, in the library, or in the school's computer lab and report back during the next class session.

☀ Practicing on Your Own

A. Complete this story.

Ask students to do the activity individually and check their answers with a partner.

B. In your notebook, write 10 questions about the story.

Read the instructions and point out the sample questions and answers. As students write their ten questions, have them include some that require *yes* answers and some that require *no* answers.

Suggestion

You can use the students' questions for oral review in class. Have different students read one of their questions aloud and call on another student to answer.

☀ Practicing on Your Own

A. Complete this story. Use the simple present or the present continuous tense.

Joe is the manager of the student center, and this is his twentieth year working there. Joe _____knows_____ (know) the names of almost all of the students who _____visit_____ (visit) the center every day. He _____likes_____ (like) to talk to the students, and he _____misses_____ (miss) them during vacations.

Today is the beginning of final exams, so the student center _____isn't_____ (negative–be) as busy as usual. A few students _____are taking_____ (talk) in a corner, soft music _____is playing_____ (play), and a group of students _____are discussing_____ (discuss) a final project. Many students _____are studying_____ (study) in the library this week and _____are typing_____ (type) their papers in the computer centers. Today, Joe _____Japan_____ (prepare) some special treats for the students because he _____understands_____ (understand) that exam time is very stressful. The students _____don't have_____ (negative–have) a lot of free time during exam weeks, and they _____often miss_____ (miss–often) their meals at the dining hall. It's 11:30 P.M., and Joe _____is making_____ (make) some cookies, and pizzas _____are baking_____ (bake) in the ovens. The center _____smells_____ (smell) wonderful. Students _____are looking_____ (look) up from their books and _____are getting_____ (get) ready to take a study break.

B. In your notebook, write 10 questions about the story.
(Questions may vary. Some possible questions and answers below.)

> Does Joe know the names of almost all of the students? Yes, he does.
> Are some students talking? Yes, they are.

Does he like to talk to the students? Yes, he does.
Does Joe miss them during vacation? Yes, he does.
Is the student center busy today? No, it isn't.
Are students talking? Yes, they are.
Do students have a lot of free time? No, they don't.

Grammar Summary

▶ **1. Present continuous tense**

   a. Use the present continuous to talk about an action that is happening now.

   b. Time expressions such as *now, right now, at the moment,* and *at this moment* are often used with the present continuous.

Are you **using** the computer?	No, I**'m not.** I**'m talking** on the phone.
Is she **buying** her books?	Yes, she **is.**
What **are** you **doing**?	I **am studying.**
Who **is drinking** a cup of coffee?	The students **are.**
Where **are** they **studying**?	They **are studying** in the library.
Why **is** he **talking** to the counselor?	He **is talking** to the counselor about a course.

▶ **2. Simple present tense**

   a. Use the simple present tense to describe a routine, a schedule, or a repeated action.

   b. These time expressions are often used with the simple present tense:

every day	**on the weekends**	**in the summer**
every year	**on Mondays**	**in the fall**

Do you **study** in the morning?	Yes, I **do.**	No, I **do not.**
Do the students **speak** English in class?	Yes, they **do.**	No, they **do not.**
Does she **work** part-time?	Yes, she **does.**	No, she **does not.**
Does he **take** any science courses?	Yes, he **does.**	No, he **does not.**
Where **do** you **study**?	I **study** in the library.	
How often **do** they **speak** English?	They **always speak** English.	
When **does** she **work**?	She **works** three evenings a week.	
How much **does** it **cost**?	It **costs** $250 per course.	

▶ **3. *Who* questions**   *Who* takes a singular verb form.

Who **speaks** English in class?	I do.
Who **arrives** on time?	All of the students do.
Who **has** an extra pencil?	She does.

▶ **4. Adverbs of frequency**

Place adverbs of frequency **after** the verb *to be,* but **before** all other verbs.

They **are always** on time.	He **always arrives** late.

▶ **5. Nonaction verbs**   Nonaction verbs usually take the present tense form.

This class is easy. I **know** all the answers.

She's studying hard because she **wants** to do well on the exam.

The students **like** the class because it is interesting and fun.

Grammar Summary

• Review the five grammar explanations and sample sentences with the class. Invite students to make up alternate sentences for each example in the chart. For example, in place of *Who is drinking a cup of coffee?*, a student might ask, *Who is wearing a red shirt?*

• Answer any questions students may have about the grammar items.

• See the Grammar Summary Expansion on page 258 for a more complete explanation of these grammar points.

Unit 2
Colonial Times
(1607-1776)

Discuss what the person in the unit title art is doing. Ask:

• *Who is sitting next to the number 2?* (A woman)
• *What is she doing?* (She's stirring a pot over a fire. She's cooking something.)
• *What does this have to do with the unit?* (In colonial times people didn't have stoves. They cooked over open fires.)

A. Colonial America.

• Discuss the map with the class. Ask questions to orient them to the map and to help them make use of what they already know. For example:

T: *Where is north?*
S1: (pointing) *The top of the map is north.*
T: *Where is the Atlantic Ocean?*
S2: (pointing) *It's here in the east—on the right side of the map.*

Suggestion

Ask students to locate this area on the map of the U.S. on page 278 (Student Book). Compare this map to a world map.

• Ask students to read through the questions and ask about anything they don't understand. Then, discuss the answers to the questions as a whole class.

Suggestion

Discuss what a colony is. Ask students who come from countries which were formerly colonies to tell who managed the territory before it became independent. In some cases there may have been several different colonial rulers over a long period of time.

Colonial Times
(1607-1776)

A. Colonial America. Look at the map of colonial America and answer the questions.

New Hampshire
Maine (part of Mass.)
PLYMOUTH
Massachusetts
New York
Rhode Island
Connecticut
Pennsylvania
New Jersey
Maryland
Delaware
Virginia
JAMESTOWN
N.Carolina
Atlantic Ocean
S.Carolina
Georgia
THE 13 COLONIES

1. What is a colony? A place outside of a country but considered part of that country
2. Who is a colonist? A person who lives in that place outside their country.
3. How many original colonies were there in the United States? 13
4. What country were the colonists from? England
5. Which colony was the farthest south? Georgia
6. What ocean bordered the colonies to the east? The Atlantic Ocean
7. Where was the colony of Jamestown? Virginia
8. Where was the colony of Plymouth? Massachusetts

A. Read about the first English settlements in the United States.

The colonial period in the United States **lasted** from 1607 to 1776. Most early colonists **were** men and women from England who **decided** to start a new life in the United States. The colonists **settled** along the eastern coast of what is now the United States, from Georgia to New Hampshire. Many people **made** the difficult trip across the Atlantic Ocean to find religious freedom. Other people **came** for political freedom. The new country **offered** other families the opportunity to own land and to earn a living in farming, trade, or fishing.

The first settlements **were** small and life **was** very difficult. In 1607, three shiploads with 105 settlers **arrived** in what is now Virginia and **started** the colony of Jamestown. Life **was** difficult in the new land and over half the settlers **died** in the first two years from the cold, disease, and lack of food. The colonists **learned** about tobacco and smoking from Native Americans and **discovered** that tobacco **grew** well in Virginia. The tobacco crop finally **gave** the colonists a way to earn money as pipe smoking **became** popular in Europe.

In 1620, another settlement **began** in Plymouth, in the state that is now Massachusetts. In England, everyone **had** to practice the same religion. The Pilgrims **wanted** religious freedom. More than 100 men, women, and children **made** the long trip across the Atlantic Ocean on the *Mayflower*. Unfortunately, they **landed** in America in late November and **did not have** time to plant crops. The Wampanoag Indians **helped** them through the winter. Even though the Indians **showed** them how to hunt and fish, half the settlers **died** that first winter. In the spring, the Indians **gave** them seeds of native plants and **showed** the Pilgrims how to plant corn, beans, and squash. The Pilgrim settlement **survived** and **grew** slowly.

B. Answer these questions using the past tense. (Answers may vary. Suggested answers below.)

1. When was the colonial period in the history of the United States?
   It was from 1607 to 1776.
2. What country were most early colonists from?
   They were from England.
3. Why did people come to the new land?
   They came for religious and political freedom and opportunity to own land and earn money.
4. What part of the United States did the first colonists settle in?
   They settled in Virginia.
5. Why was life so difficult in the colonies?
   The colonists died from cold, disease, and lack of food.
6. Were the colonists the first people in the United States?
   No, they weren't. The Native Americans (or Indians) were.
7. How did the people in Jamestown finally earn a living?
   They grew tobacco.
8. Where did the Pilgrims land?
   They landed in America (in Plymouth).
9. Why did they come to the new land?
   They wanted religious freedom.
10. Who helped them through the first winter?
    The Wapanoag Indians did.
11. How did they help them?
    They showed them how to hunt and fish.
12. About 100 men, women, and children landed in Plymouth. How many were alive one year later? Half were alive one year later.

Active Grammar: Past Tense

A. Read about the first English settlements in the United States.

• Ask students to complete the reading on their own and discuss what they have read with a partner. Suggest that they underline any words or phrases they don't understand. Then, invite students to write those sentences on the board. Use simple explanations, paraphrasing, and examples to help clarify the meaning of each sentence.

• Have students read the passage a second time. When they finish, call their attention to the past tense verbs in boldface type. Call on different students to give the base form of each past tense verb.

B. Answer these questions using the past tense.

Call on a different student to answer each question. Prompt them to use the verbs in bold-face type in their answers. Repeat each answer, correcting any errors or omissions. Then, call on another student to repeat the answer.

☀ Colonial Life

☀ Colonial Life

A. Look at the pairs of pictures and listen to the comparison between life in colonial times and life today. (CD1, Track 6)

- Invite students to point to different sets of pictures and tell what they see. Explain anything they don't understand about the pictures.
- As you play the audio the first time, ask students to look at the pictures and point to the one that is being talked about. Play the tape a second time, pausing after each section that describes a pair of pictures. Ask students to repeat the statement about this pair of pictures using their own words, or to make up a new statement about the pair of pictures.

B. Look at each picture.

Ask students to work together as they point to the pictures and describe what life was like in colonial America. Review the answers by calling on different students to compare different pairs of pictures.

C. Write the past tense forms of these verbs.

Students complete this exercise individually and check their answers with a partner.

A. Look at the pairs of pictures and listen to the comparison between life in colonial times and life today.

B. Look at each picture. Describe life in colonial America.
(Answers will vary.)

C. Write the past tense forms of these verbs.

Regular verbs

call	called	talk	talked
cook	cooked	travel	traveled
milk	milked	use	used
play	played	watch	watched

Irregular verbs*

buy	bought	make	made
drive	drove	read	read
go	went	sleep	slept
grow	grew	write	wrote

*****Note**: See the chart of irregular verbs on page 273.

Audio Script

A. Look at the pairs of pictures and listen to the comparison between life in colonial times and life today. (CD1, Track 6)

The colonial period in the United States lasted from 1607 to 1776. Most early colonists were men and women from England who decided to start a new life in North America. They settled along the eastern coast of what is now the United States, from Georgia to New Hampshire. Life at that time was very different from today. Most people lived on small farms and were self-sufficient for most of their needs. People grew all of their own food and cooked it over open fires. They didn't go to supermarkets or cook on stoves. When they needed milk, they milked their own cows. They didn't go to the supermarket and buy a carton of milk. Houses functioned without modern conveniences or electricity. Instead of electric lights, people read and worked by candlelight. They didn't sleep on mattresses with box springs. They used to sleep on feather beds. In the evening, instead of watching TV, they read to each other and played games. When people wanted to communicate with friends or relatives far away, they used to write letters. They didn't have telephones or e-mail. For transportation, the people used horses and wagons; they didn't drive cars. Life was slower and simpler, but people worked hard from sunup to sundown.

D. **Complete these sentences about life in Colonial America.** Write a past tense verb from Exercise C. (Answers will vary. Suggested answers below)

Simple Past Tense	
I	watched TV.
You	didn't watch TV.
He	drove a car.
She	didn't drive a car.
We	
They	

1. People ___didn't go___ to supermarkets.
2. They ___grew___ their own food.
3. People ___cooked___ over open fires.
4. They ___didn't use___ stoves.
5. People ___milked___ their own cows.
6. They ___didn't buy___ milk at the supermarket.
7. Families ___used___ candles for light.
8. People ___didn't sleep___ on mattresses.
9. At night, families ___didn't watch___ TV.
10. They ___read___ and ___played___ games.
11. People ___didn't call___ one another on the telephone.
12. They ___wrote___ letters to one another.
13. People ___traveled___ by horse and wagon.
14. They ___didn't drive___ cars.

E. **Ask and answer these questions about your first year in the United States.**

(Answers will vary.)

1. When did you arrive in the United States?
2. How did you travel here?
3. Why did you come to the United States?
4. What did you bring with you?
5. Who did you live with at first?
6. Did you speak any English?
7. When did you begin to study at this school?
8. Where was your first job?
9. How did you find your first job?
10. Was your first year in the United States difficult?

D. Complete these sentences about life in Colonial America.

Students complete the sentences individually. Then, have then check their answers with a partner.

E. Ask and answer these questions about your first year in the United States.

Have students take turns asking each other the questions. Move around the room as they work, offering language support as needed.

Suggestion

If it's appropriate and there's enough class time, invite several students to share their answers to each of the questions with the whole class.

F. What's wrong with this picture?

• Have students read the instructions. Then, read aloud the two sample answers. Divide the class into pairs or groups of three and have them see how many other wrong things they can find. Set a time limit (perhaps ten minutes).

• Then, call on different students to point to and describe the errors in the picture. Next, have them check their answers against the list printed upside down at the bottom of page 35.

F. What's wrong with this picture? There are 16 things wrong with this picture. In a group of two or three students, see how many you can find. Check your answers on page 35.

> Children **didn't play** with toy trucks.
> Houses **didn't have** air conditioners.

 Past Tense: *Be*

I He/She It	was	difficult.
You We They	were	young.

There	was	no kitchen.
There	were	few schools.

A. ***Was/Were.*** Complete these sentences with *was* or *were*.

1. Life _____was_____ very difficult for the first settlers in the New World.
2. The first homes _____were_____ small buildings made of wood and mud.
3. There _____was_____ no kitchen in the house.
4. There _____was_____ no bathroom, either. There _____was_____ a small outhouse in the back.
5. Windows _____were_____ small because no glass _____was_____ available.
6. The first settlers _____weren't_____ (negative) farmers or hunters, so they _____were_____ often hungry.
7. At first, there _____were_____ few schools in the colonies.
8. Many girls _____were_____ married by the age of 16.
9. The newspaper _____was_____ an important source of information.
10. By 1776 the population of the colonies _____was_____ over three million.

B. Now and then. The sentences in the first column tell about life today. Use the information in the second column to talk about life in the late 1700s.

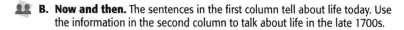
The president is _____.
The first president was George Washington.

Today	**1790**
1. The president is _____.	1. George Washington
2. The president's salary is $400,000 a year.	2. $25,000
3. The capital is in Washington, D.C.	3. New York
4. There are fifty states.	4. thirteen states
5. The largest state is Alaska.	5. Virginia
6. The population is about 280 million.	6. about four million
7. The average family size is three people.	7. eight people
8. Life expectancy is about 77.	8. 32
9. Cars are the main form of transportation.	9. horses and wagons
10. The largest city is New York.	10. Philadelphia

 Past Tense: *Be*

A. *Was/Were.*

- Review the grammar charts at the top of the page. Then, ask:

  T: *Which past form of* be *is used with plural subjects like* we *and* they?
  S1: *Were.*
  T: *What form is used with singular subjects like* I, he, *and* she?
  S2: *Was.*
  T: *Which subject pronoun is both singular and plural?*
  S3: *You.*
  T: *Why?*
  S3: *Because sometimes* you *represents one person and sometimes two or more people.*

- Have students complete the sentences individually and compare their answers with a partner.

B. Now and then.

- Read and discuss the instructions and sample response. Then, have students work in pairs, taking turns reading statements from the first column, and responding with past tense statements containing the information from the "1790" column.

A. Pronunciation: *Used to*
(CD1, Track 7)

Play the audio several times as students just listen. Then, have them practice repeating the pronunciation of *used to* in isolation several times. (It sounds like "you stuh.") Play the audio again and have students repeat the sentences.

B. Talk about life in colonial times using *used to.*

• Read the instructions. Then, review the meaning of the words in the vocabulary box. Use brief explanations, pictures in the book, and simple drawings on the board to clarify the meaning of any items students aren't sure of.

• Have pairs of students take turns reading the sentences and responding with *used to* statements. Be sure both students have a chance to practice all the *used to* sentences. Remind them to think about correct pronunciation.

C. Complete these sentences about life in your country.

Students complete the sentences on their own. Then, they read their work to a partner. If time permits, encourage students to read to more than one other student.

Suggestion

If students have difficulty pronouncing the shortened form of *used to*, write a simply spelled pronunciation on the board. For example: *Used to = you stuh.* Explain that in this case the letter *o* in the word *to* sounds like the letter *u* in the word *up.* Say the words *used to* in isolation several times and ask students to repeat, paying careful attention to the sound of the words.

Used to

A. Pronunciation: *Used to.* Listen and repeat.

1. Today, people drive cars. In colonial times, they used to drive horses and wagons.
2. Today, people cook on stoves. They used to cook over open fires.
3. Today, people buy food in supermarkets. They used to grow their own food.
4. Today, people take medicine when they are sick. In colonial times, they used to take herbs.
5. Today, people write e-mails to their friends. They used to write letters.

B. Talk about life in colonial times using *used to.* Read each sentence about life today. Use the vocabulary box to talk about life in colonial America. Be careful of your pronunciation. (Answers may vary.)

wooden mugs	candlelight	one-room schoolhouses
read to each other	cloaks	spoons and their fingers
long dresses	almost everyone	leather boots

1. Today, girls wear jeans or dresses or skirts.
   In colonial times, girls used to wear long dresses.
2. Today, people wear coats in the winter.
3. Today, people eat with forks, knives, and spoons.
4. Today, people drink from glasses.
5. Today, most children study in large public schools.
6. Today, most families watch TV at night.
7. Today, children wear sneakers.
8. Today, people read by electric lights.
9. Today, some people go to church every Sunday, but others never go.

cloak

wooden mug

C. Complete these sentences about life in your country. Then, read your sentences to a partner. (Answers will vary.)

1. When I lived in _____, I used to _____.
2. My family and I used to _____ every summer.
3. My friends and I used to _____ on Saturday nights.
4. I used to _____ TV _____ hours a day.
5. I _____ typical foods such as _____ and _____.
6. I never used to _____.

26 UNIT 2

☀ Past Tense Questions

Where When	did	I you she he we they	work? live? play?

A. Interview. Listen to Eric speak about his childhood in Peru. Complete the questions. Then, ask and answer the questions with a partner.

1. Where _did he grow up_____? (grow up)
2. How many brothers and sisters _____did he have_____? (have)
3. Where _____did he live_____? (live)
4. What ____did____ his family _____own_____? (own)
5. How _____did he get_____ to school? (get)
6. What _____did he do_____ after school? (do)
7. What _____did he do_____ in the summer? (do)
8. _____Did he go_____ on vacation? (go)
9. Where ____did he_____ sometimes _____go_____ in the summer? (go)
10. What ____did____ his grandmother always _____make_____? (make)

B. Ask your partner about his/her childhood. Use these cues. (Suggested questions below.)

1. Where / grow up? **Where did you grow up?**
2. have a big family? **Did you have a big family?**
3. How many brothers and sisters / have? **How many brothers and sisiters did you have?**
4. live / in the city? **Did you live in the city?**
5. How / get to school? **How did you get to school?**
6. like school? **Did you like school?**
7. What / do / after school? **What did you do after school?**
8. spend time / grandparents? **Did you spend time with your grandparents?**
9. go on vacation? **Did you go on vacation?**
10. study English in school? **Did you study English in school?**
11. play a sport? **Did you play a sport?**
12. work when you were in high school? **Did you work when you were in high school?**

Colonial Times (1607–1776)   **27**

☀ Past Tense Questions

ⓐ A. Interview. (CD1, Track 8)

• Play the audio and ask students to just listen the first time through. Then, read the instructions and go over the questions and cue words with the class.

• Play the audio again and ask students to complete the questions. Remind them to use the grammar box at the top if they need help with the word order for the questions. Have students check their answers with a partner.

• Play the audio a third time, pausing after each line that contains an answer to one of the questions, and call on a student to respond. Confirm correct answers and correct any wrong answers.

B. Ask your partner about his/her childhood.

Have students take turns asking each other the questions. Encourage them to add information after any *yes/no* responses. For example, instead of just saying *Yes, I did* in response to question 2, suggest that they add a sentence such as, *There were six of us living in our house.*

Suggestion

If time permits, have students switch partners several times so that they have a chance to practice the questions and answers more than once.

Audio Script

A. Interview. Listen to Eric speak about his childhood in Peru. Complete the questions. Then, ask and answer the questions with a partner. **(CD1, Track 8)**

Oscar: Eric, where were you born?
 Eric: I was born in a small town in Peru. On the coast.
Oscar: How many brothers and sisters did you have?
 Eric: There were four boys—I was the youngest.
Oscar: Did your grandparents live in the same town?

 Eric: My grandparents, my two aunts, my five uncles. We all lived in the same town. And I had lots of cousins.
Oscar: Did you live in the city or the country?
 Eric: In the country. My family owned a small farm. In the winter, I had to get up early and milk our cow.
Oscar: How about school? Did you walk to school or take the bus?
 Eric: In our town, there were no school buses. I used to ride my bike to school.
Oscar: What did you do after school?

(Audio Script continues on page 251.)

☀ The Big Picture: Benjamin Franklin

ᴵᴵᴵ A. Listen. (CD1, Track 9)

- Explain that Benjamin Franklin was an American who lived in Philadelphia, Pennsylvania, in colonial times. Tell them that they will be hearing a story about who he was and some of the things he did.
- Point out the pictures of Franklin's inventions and discuss briefly what each one is used for.

An *odometer* measures the distance a person or vehicle travels.

A *lightning rod* protects a building by carrying the electrical charge away from the building and into the earth where it doesn't cause any damage.

A *Franklin stove* is cleaner and produces more heat than a fireplace.

Bifocals are glasses with two different lenses so that the wearer can see clearly up close and far away.

- Read the instructions and play the audio. Ask students to mark their answers. Then, play the audio a second time so they can check their work. Review the correct answers with the class.

ᴵᴵᴵ B. Note taking. (CD1, Track 10)

- Explain that note taking involves writing down the most important ideas in a very simple form. People do not usually use complete sentences when they take notes.
- Play the audio and ask students to just listen the first time through. Then, play it again and ask them to complete the notes in their books. You may wish to play the audio several times, or you may want to pause the audio after each lettered section. Give students time to review notes. Correct completions with the class.

☀ The Big Picture: Benjamin Franklin

ᴵᴵᴵ A. Listen. Which invention is each sentence describing? Write the number of the correct sentence under each invention.

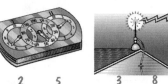 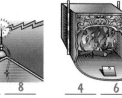

 2   5   3   8   4   6   1   7

ᴵᴵᴵ B. Note taking. Listen and complete this outline about the life of Benjamin Franklin.

A. Early life
1. Born in _____Boston_____ on ___January 17, 1706___
2. Attended school for __2__ years
3. Trained to become a _____printer_____
4. Moved to ___Philadelphia___
5. Opened a ___printing shop___

B. Franklin helped to improve life in the city of Philadelphia.
1. Started the first ___public library___
2. Helped to organize the first ___fire department___
3. Served as ___post master___ and set up ___routes for delivery of mail___
4. Convinced city officials to pave the ___streets___

C. Four inventions
1. _____stove_____
2. _____odometer_____
3. _____bifocals_____
4. ___lightening rod___

D. Contributions as a leader
1. Signed the Declaration of ___Independence___ and the Constitution.
2. Served as minister to ___France___

E. Death
1. Died on ___April 17, 1790___

28 UNIT 2

Audio Script

A. Listen. Which invention is each sentence describing? Write the number of the correct sentence under each invention. (CD1, Track 9)

1. The top half of this invention helps a person to see distance; the bottom half helps a person to see things close up.
2. With this device, you can measure distance.
3. Before this invention, lightning sometimes struck houses and caused fires.
4. Before this invention, people used to have open fires inside their homes.
5. Franklin used this device to map mail routes for towns.
6. This appliance helped people heat their homes safely and with less wood.
7. Franklin cut two pairs of glasses in half and joined them together.
8. This device protects buildings from lightning. It directs lightning into the ground.

(Audio Script for Exercise B appears on page 252.)

C. Look at your outline and answer these questions.

1. Where was Benjamin Franklin born? Boston, MA
2. How long did he attend school? 2 years
3. What trade did he learn? Printing
4. What city did he move to? Philadelphia
5. What business did he open? Printing shop
6. What service did Franklin help to start? Public library
7. How else did he help the city of Philadelphia? Organized first fire department
8. What did he invent to measure distance? Odometer
9. What important documents did he sign? Declaration of Independence and the Constitution
10. When did he die? April 17, 1790

D. Complete. Write the questions to the answers.

1. When _____ was Benjamin Franklin born _____?
   He was born in 1706.
2. _____ Did he graduate _____ from high school?
   No, he didn't graduate from high school.
3. How many languages _____ did he speak _____?
   He spoke five languages.
4. What _____ did he do _____ when he was postmaster?
   He set up the mail routes for the city.
5. What _____ did he experiment _____ with?
   He experimented with electricity.

E. Proverbs. Listen and complete these famous sayings of Ben Franklin. Then, discuss their meanings.

1. A penny _____ saved _____ is a penny _____ earned _____.
2. Time is _____ money _____.
3. Early to _____ bed _____, early to rise, makes a man _____ healthy _____, _____ wealthy _____, and wise.
4. Fish and _____ visitors _____ smell in three days.
5. An _____ apple _____ a day keeps the _____ doctor _____ away.
6. Well done is _____ better than _____ than well said.
7. There was never a good _____ war _____ or a bad _____ peace _____.

C. Look at your outline and answer these questions.

Call on individuals to consult their notes and answer the questions orally. Rephrase any incorrect responses and ask the student to repeat them.

D. Complete.

Ask students to complete the questions individually and check their answers with a partner. Then, call on a different student to repeat each question. Write the missing words on the board and have students correct their own work.

E. Proverbs. (CD1, Track 11)

• Review what a proverb is by asking students to give examples of English language proverbs they already know.
• Have students just listen the first time you play the audio. Then, play it a second time and have them fill in the missing words. Write the missing words on the board and discuss the meaning of each proverb and give an example of each.

Suggestion

Invite students to translate favorite proverbs from their first language into English and explain what they mean.

Audio Script

E. Proverbs. Listen and complete these famous sayings of Ben Franklin. Then, discuss their meanings. **(CD1, Track 11)**

1. A penny saved is a penny earned.
2. Time is money.
3. Early to bed, early to rise, makes a man healthy, wealthy, and wise.
4. Fish and visitors smell in three days.
5. An apple a day keeps the doctor away.
6. Well done is better than well said.
7. There was never a good war or a bad peace.

A. Before You Read.

Point to the pictures, read the captions, and invite students to comment. Ask:
Were the Pilgrims' homes large or small?
What did the homes look like?
Where do you think the Pilgrims got their food?

Name one historic area in your country. Why is it famous?

• Call on several different students to answer.
• Discuss the prereading question with the class. Ask:

What is one historical place in your country?
What is this place famous for?
When people visit this place, what do they see?

Match each vocabulary word with its definition.

• Have students match each word with the correct definition. If necessary, paraphrase the definitions. For example:

a. *An object that someone finds in the ground that was left there thousands of years ago.*
b. *an imitation object that looks exactly the same as the real object.*
c. *someone who looks at very old objects to learn about the period of history they came from.*

Review the correct matches with the class.

• Ask students to read the story to themselves. When they finish, invite them to ask about any sentences they don't understand. Try to avoid spending a lot of time defining and discussing individual words. Explain that they only need to understand the main idea of each sentence. Restate problem sentences in simple English.

A. Before You Read.

This house is a reproduction of a pilgrim home from 1627.

Notice the clothing of the woman. She is a museum staff member dressed as a colonial woman from 1627.

Name one historic area in your country. Why is it famous? (Answers will vary.)

Match each vocabulary word with its definition.

____c____ **1.** archaeologist   **a.** an item or piece of item from the past. It is often dug from the ground.

____a____ **2.** artifact   **b.** a copy or reproduction of an original item

____b____ **3.** replica   **c.** a person who studies artifacts to learn about the past

    Plymouth, Massachusetts, about forty-five miles south of Boston, is a popular tourist attraction. Plymouth was the site of the second colony in America. On November 11, 1620, a small ship of English settlers landed there and started a colony, looking for a better life and religious freedom.

    One of the most popular attractions in Plymouth is Plimouth Plantation. Plimouth Plantation was the dream of Henry Hornblower II. When he was a boy, Hornblower read and heard stories about the pilgrims who lived in Plymouth. When he was older, he worked with archaeologists in Plymouth for many years. They found more than 350,000 artifacts from the time of the colonists. At the same time, historians studied pilgrims' journals and writings to learn about the lives of the early colonists. In 1945, Henry Hornblower's father gave $20,000 to the Pilgrim Society, allowing it to begin the reconstruction of Plimouth Plantation. The Society made reproductions of the clothes, tools, furniture, and houses of the 1620s. The museum opened in 1947, with just one reproduction of a colonial home.

Today, Plimouth Plantation brings to life the original settlement of 1627. It is a living museum of more than twenty homes, shops, and gardens. Visitors can walk through the colonial town where each house on the main street looks exactly like a house of the 1620s. The village is not just a collection of exhibits to look at. The museum staff are the "colonists," and they dress, talk, and carry out the activities of colonial America. They wear the same kinds of clothes that the Plymouth colonists used to wear. The women cook in open fireplaces and follow colonial recipes. The men raise the same vegetables and care for the same kinds of animals that were present in colonial times. Everyone uses the same kinds of tools that the pilgrims used almost four hundred years ago. When visitors talk to the "colonists," the "colonists" answer with the same English and the same accent that the colonists had.

Over the years, Plimouth Plantation has expanded. Today, it is also possible to visit a replica of the Mayflower II, the ship the pilgrims sailed from England to Plymouth. There is also a reproduction of a Wampanoag homesite, which introduces visitors to the life of the Indian tribe who helped the colonists survive their first years in their new country. A trip to Plimouth Plantation is a trip back in history.

B. Check your comprehension. (Suggested answers below.)

1. When did the pilgrims come to America? They came in 1620.
2. Was Plymouth, Massachusetts, the first colony? No, it wasn't wasn't. It was the second.
3. Why did the pilgrims leave England?
   They were looking for a better life and religious freedom.
4. How did Henry Hornblower find out about the pilgrims at Plymouth?
   He read and heard stories about the pilgrims.
5. What did archaeologists find at the site?
   They found artifacts from the time of the pilgrams.
6. How did historians reproduce the plantation?
   They studied pilgrim journals and writings.
7. Why is Plimouth Plantation a living museum?
   It is a reproduction of the original settlement with museum staff as "colonists."
8. What do the "colonists" wear?
   They wear the same kind of clothes that colonists used to wear.
9. What do the "colonists" do?
   The woman cook in open fireplaces, and the men raise vegetables
10. What language do the "colonists" speak? and care for animals.
    They speak the same English with the same accent the colonists had.
11. What else can visitors at Plimouth Plantation see?
    They can see a reproduction of the Mayflower II and a Wampanog home site.

C. Place these events in chronological order.

3	a.	Reconstruction of the settlement began.
5	b.	The museum expanded to include the larger settlement.
2	c.	Henry Hornblower I donated money to begin the reconstruction of Plymouth
6	d.	Visitors can now see a replica of the *Mayflower II* and an Indian homesite.
4	e.	The museum with just one building opened to the public.
1	f.	Archaeologists and historians began to study Plymouth.

B. Check your comprehension.

Ask students to complete the activity individually and check their answers with a partner. As you correct the exercise with the class, ask students to read aloud the sentence or sentences from the story that prove the answer is correct.

C. Place these events in chronological order.

Ask students to try to complete the activity while looking back at the story.

☀ Writing Our Stories: Growing Up in Bangladesh

A. Read Mahmuda's story about growing up in Bangladesh.

Ask students to read the story on their own. Suggest that they read it straight through without stopping. Ask students if any of Mahmuda's experiences were similar to their own school experiences. What experiences were different?

A. Read Mahmuda's story about growing up in Bangladesh.

I grew up in Dhaka, the capital of Bangladesh. I was the second oldest of five children. We lived in a small house in a busy area of the city. I smile as I remember growing up in my country.

I started school when I was five years old. In elementary school, I used to walk to school with my brothers and sisters. The classes at our school were large, usually with 50 to 70 students. Boys and girls attended the same classes; however, boys sat on one side of the room and girls sat on the other. The girls wore a blue and white uniform to school. My pants were white and over them I wore a large, comfortable blue shirt called a *camis*. The girls covered their hair with white head scarves.

In high school, I took public transportation to school. Girls attended classes in the morning, from 8:00 to 12:00, and boys attended classes in the afternoon from 12:30 to 4:30. We studied Bengali, our language, and English, Arabic, history, science, geography, and math. Our teachers were very strict. If we talked in class or didn't do our homework, they hit our hands or shoulders with a stick.

The school year began in January and ended in December. We also had a few weeks off in the summer. At that time, my family visited my grandparents, who lived in a small village. They had a large rice paddy. We played, swam in the pond, and ran after the cows and chickens.

After school, we had to be creative in order to entertain ourselves. Like most families, we didn't have a telephone. Until I was in eighth grade, we didn't have a television, either. In the afternoon, I did my homework, helped my mother, took care of my younger brothers and sisters, and played with my girlfriends. We told stories, sewed, jumped rope, and, like students all over the world, gossiped about our teachers and the other students in our class.

Mahmuda

B. Brainstorming. (Answers are checked below.)

Before writing, it is helpful to think about your topic. Many writers brainstorm for five or ten minutes, writing down all ideas that come to mind. They don't write sentences, just words and phrases. They then choose several of these ideas to include in their stories.

Before writing, Mahmuda brainstormed for ten minutes. Which of her ideas did she use in her story?

Elementary School	High School	Vacation	Ramadan	After School
walked ✔	tuition	school: Jan to Dec.✔	Feb. or March	no telephone ✔
50–70 students ✔	bus (✔)	summer ✔	celebration	no TV ✔
uniform ✔	girls—a.m. ✔	grandparents ✔	special food	homework ✔
head scarves ✔	boy—p.m. ✔	rice paddy ✔	gifts	help at home ✔
	teachers—strict ✔	play ✔		girlfriends ✔
	sports			

C. My childhood
Brainstorm about your childhood for ten minutes, writing down all ideas that come into your mind. Choose two or three of your ideas and write a composition about growing up.

D. Edit. Find and correct the mistakes.

1. I ~~not~~ (did) live with my parents. I lived with my grandparents.
2. I use(d) to play with my friends after school.
3. Before I went to school, I milk(ed) the cow.
4. We didn't ~~had~~ (have) a telephone.
5. When I ~~am~~ (was) eight years old, we moved to the city.
6. What ~~you did~~ (did you do) after school?
7. After I came home from school, I played soccer with my friends.
8. How old ~~you were~~ (were you) when you started school?
9. Did you work when you ~~are~~ (were) in high school?
10. How many brothers and sisters ~~you had~~ (did you have)?

Looking at the Internet

Historical Sites. Click on **Search.** Enter the name of your state and the phrase "historical sites." You will find the names of several parks, forts, museums, churches, early houses, and other sites in your state with historical significance. Read about one of these places. Tell your class the name of the historical site and show its location on a map of your state. Give the following information.

1. What can you see and do at this site? (Answers will vary.)
2. When is it open?
3. How much is the admission?

B. Brainstorming.

- Ask students to read the definition of brainstorming. Discuss any questions they have about the process.
- Ask students to look at Mahmuda's notes and circle the items that she included in her story. Review the correct answers by having five students write on the board all the items that she used from one of the columns.

C. My childhood.

- Remind students to write down whatever ideas come to mind, even if they seem silly or unrelated. Explain that doing this will help them come up with a greater number of useful ideas. Announce how much time remains after five minutes, and again two minutes before the time is up.
- Suggest that students choose two or three key ideas from their brainstormed list as the basis of their compositions. The writing can be done as homework or in class.

D. Edit.

Have students complete the activity on their own and then compare answers with a partner. Go over the answers and explain any that some students are not sure of.

Looking at the Internet

- Before asking students to complete this assignment, you may wish to locate a site and show it to students during class if possible. You might also wish to give students a list of possible sites to get them started.
- During the next class, have students share their findings with the rest of the class.

A. Jamestown: The first English settlement.

Students can complete this exercise on their own. Suggest that they use the list on page 273 (or a dictionary) if they need help with any of the past tense irregular verbs. Review the correct answers with the class.

B. Past questions.

Ask students to do the activity individually. As they work, students can check the list of past tense verbs on page 273 if necessary. Have students check their answers with a partner.

Suggestion

For further practice, ask students to make up past question exercises similar to Exercise B based on the notes on Benjamin Franklin on page 28. For example:

1. *How long* _____?
   Two years
2. *What* _____?
   A printing shop

(Answers: How long did he attend school? What kind of business did he open?)

Students exchange papers and complete the questions. Then, they return the papers to the writer, who checks the work.

A. Jamestown: The first English settlement. Write the past tense form of the verbs in parentheses.

In January 1607, three small ships _____ left _____ (leave) England for America. Four months later, they _____ arrived _____ (arrive) in America. Several of the men on the ship _____ didn't survive _____ (negative—survive) the long, stormy journey. The men _____ chose _____ (choose) an area on the James River that is now in the state of Virginia. They _____ began _____ (begin) to build a fort. The men _____ were _____ (be) "gentlemen" and _____ weren't _____ (negative—be) used to working with their hands. Their purpose in America _____ was _____ (be) to hunt for gold and to start a small colony for England.

But there _____ wasn't _____ (negative—be) any gold. The winter _____ came _____ (come) and there _____ wasn't _____ (negative—be) enough food. Many men _____ got _____ (get) sick. By the end of the first winter, only forty men _____ were _____ (be) still alive.

Over the next three years, more settlers _____ arrived _____ (arrive), but they _____ weren't _____ (negative—be) farmers, so the first few years of the colony _____ were _____ (be) very difficult. Disease, starvation, and Native Americans _____ killed _____ (kill) most of the settlers. Eventually, the colonists _____ learned _____ (learn) more about farming and the weather. They _____ made _____ (make) peace with the Indians. Tobacco, not gold, _____ produced _____ (produce) the real wealth of the new colony. As the years _____ went _____ (go) by, more and more settlers _____ arrived _____ (arrive), and many small towns _____ grew _____ (grow) along the river.

B. Past questions. Complete these questions about life in colonial times. (Answers may vary)

1. What _____ did the colonists grow _____? Vegetables.
2. Where _____ did they live _____? In wooden houses.
3. What _____ did the woman wear _____? Long dresses.
4. How _____ did they travel _____? By horse and wagon.
5. Where _____ did they sleep _____? On feather beds.
6. What _____ did thet eat _____ in the winter? Bread and meat.
7. How _____ did they spend free time _____? They read to one another.

Grammar Summary

▶ 1. Past tense

We use the simple past tense to talk about actions that happened in the past time.
Regular past verbs end in **-ed**.
The chart of irregular past verbs is on page 273.

▶ 2. Past time expressions

yesterday	a few minutes ago	last night	in 1750
the day before yesterday	a few days ago	last week	in 1995
	a few weeks ago	last year	

▶ 3. Past tense: *be*

Jamestown **was** the first English settlement.
Many settlers **were** very religious.
Was the voyage long and difficult? Yes, it **was**.
Were the settlers farmers? No, they **weren't**.
Where **was** the first settlement? It **was** in Jamestown.

▶ 4. Past tense verb forms

Regular verbs	Irregular verbs
Colonial people **worked** hard.	Colonial women **wore** long dresses.
They **lived** on farms.	Colonial families **had** gardens.
Families **didn't live** in cities.	Houses **didn't have** bathrooms.
Did children **attend** school?	**Did** children **wear** sneakers?
Yes, they **did**.	No, they **didn't**.
Where **did** colonial people **live**?	When **did** the first colonies **begin**?
They **lived** on farms.	They **began** in the 1600s.

▶ 5. *Used to* *Used to* shows habitual or repeated actions in the past.
The action was true in the past, but not any longer.

People **used to milk** their own cows.	(Now people buy milk in the supermarket.)
I **used to live** near the beach.	(Now I live in the city.)

Answers for Exercise F on page 24.

Note: You should have the same ideas, but your sentences may be different.

1. Children didn't play with toy trucks.
2. Houses didn't have air conditioners.
3. People didn't fly helicopters.
4. People didn't smoke cigarettes.
5. Girls didn't wear short skirts.
6. People didn't wear sneakers.
7. Wagons didn't have rubber tires.
8. Farmers didn't use tractors.
9. Streets didn't have traffic lights.
10. Towns didn't have paved streets.
11. Women didn't cook on barbecue grills.
12. People didn't have electricity.
13. There were no TVs.
14. People didn't have portable tape players.
15. People didn't wear wristwatches.
16. Houses didn't have doorbells.

Grammar Summary

- Review the five grammar explanations and sample sentences with the class. Invite students to make up alternate sentences for each example in the chart. For example, in place of *I used to live near the beach*, a student might say, *I used to live in Mexico City*.
- Answer any questions students may have about the grammar items.
- See the Grammar Summary Expansion on page 259 for a more complete explanation of these grammar points.

Unit 3
Family Matters

Discuss what the person in the unit title art is doing. Ask:

• *Who do you see next to the number 3?* (A man and woman with a child between them)
• *What are they doing?* (The man is holding one of the child's hands and the woman is holding the other.)
• *What does this have to do with the unit?* (It shows a father and mother both caring for a child.)

A. Marriage and divorce statistics.

• Ask students to look at the two pictures and explain the difference between the two couples. (One couple look like they are in love and the other couple looks very unhappy.) Discuss the meaning of the word *divorce* and ask students how common divorce is in their countries.

• Have students read through the list of statistics and discuss the information with a partner. Then, discuss the statistics with the class. Ask questions such as:

Why do you think the average age of marriage is going up? Why do you think so many marriages end in divorce? Why do you think second marriages are more likely to fail than first marriages?

• Read aloud the two questions under the list of statistics and invite several different students to answer them.

3 Family Matters

A. Marriage and divorce statistics. Read this information about marriage and divorce in the United States. Then, discuss the questions. (Answers will vary.)

• Over two million couples are married each year in the United States.
• The average age at marriage is rising. Currently, the average age at marriage is 26 for women and 29 for men.
• Forty-three percent of first marriages end in divorce within 15 years.
• The older a woman is at marriage, the longer the marriage will last. Teenagers who marry are more likely to get divorced than couples who are older.
• Massachusetts has the lowest divorce rate in the United States. Nevada has the highest divorce rate.
• The divorce process takes about one year.
• Over 75% of women and 80% of men who get divorced remarry within five years.
• Second marriages have a greater chance of failure than first marriages.

1. Were you surprised by any of these statistics?

2. How does this information compare with marriage and divorce in your native country?

Active Grammar: Future Tense

A. The divorce. Read Tom's account of his marriage and divorce. <u>Underline</u> all future tense verbs.
(Highlighted words are the answers.)

> **Child support** is money that one parent pays for child expenses, such as food, clothing, and housing.
>
> **Alimony** is money that one spouse pays to the other spouse for support.

Amy and I got married twelve years ago. At first, we were really happy together, but after a few years, we began to have problems. I don't really know what happened. We went to marriage counselors, we made promises, and then we broke them. We argued about everything. Even though we tried to work things out, we couldn't. Finally, we decided to get a divorce. I'm not worried about Amy or myself because we're adults, but I'm worried about the kids. We have two children, Carly and Jason. Carly is seven; Jason is ten. Amy and I have agreed on joint custody of the children. I'm packing now because <u>I'm going to move</u> to an apartment in the next town. Amy <u>is going to stay</u> here in the house. The children will live with her during the week, and they <u>will live</u> with me on the weekends. They will still go to the same school and be with all their friends. In the summer, they will live with me in July and with Amy in August. That way we can plan vacations and time with the kids.

Amy and I are working on the arrangements with our lawyers. I'm going to pay child support and I'm going to pay alimony for three years. Amy was a homemaker and she stayed home with the children for ten years. She's going to need a job now. Before we got married, she finished one year of college. She'll go back to school part-time and study accounting.

Life is going to be very different for all of us.

Future: *Be + going to* + verb			
Amy Tom	is isn't		find a job.
I	am am not	going to	move.
You We They	are aren't		get a divorce.

Future: *Will*		
I She He We You They	will will not won't	find a job. get married. go to school.

B. Answer these questions about Tom and Amy. Try not to look back at the story.

1. How long were Tom and Amy married? They were married 12 years.
2. How did they try to work out their problems? They went to marriage counselors.
3. When is Tom going to leave? Soon. Tom is packing now.
4. Where is he going to live? He's going to live in an apartment in the next town.
5. Who will the children live with?
   The children will live with Amy during the week and Tom on weekends.
6. What is joint custody?
   Sharing responsibility for the children.
7. Where are the children going to live in the summer?
   They are going to live with Tom in July and Amy in August.
8. How long is Tom going to pay alimony?
   He's going to pay alimony for 3 years.
9. Does Amy have a job?
   No she doesn't have a paying job. She was a homemaker.
10. What is she going to study?
    She's going to study accounting.
11. How will life be different for this family?
    (Answers will vary.)

Family Matters **37**

Active Grammar: Future Tense

A. The divorce.

• Students complete the reading and underlining activity individually. Correct the underlining activity by reading the passage aloud and asking students to raise their hands when you get to a future tense verb.

• Review the definitions in the box at the top of the reading. Then, ask students if there are any other words or phrases they don't understand. Use simple explanations, paraphrases, and synonyms to clarify meaning.

• Review the grammar charts at the middle of the page. Explain that both *going to* and *will* can be used to talk about future plans.

B. Answer these questions about Tom and Amy.

Have students answer the questions individually and check their answers with a partner. Review the correct answers with the whole class.

C. Amy's plans.

Read the instructions and ask a student to read aloud the sample answer. Have students work with a partner to complete the rest of the sentences. Review the correct answers with the whole class.

D. Tom's plans.

• Review the explanation of present continuous with future meaning in the box. Then, give several examples of pairs of sentences that mean the same thing even though one uses *is going to* and the other uses the present continuous. (*I am going to have lunch at 12:00 today. I'm having lunch at 12:00 today.*) Ask students to make up similar pairs of sentences.

• Call on different students to say one of the exercise sentences each. Invite the class to listen for and correct any errors.

C. Amy's plans. Complete these sentences about Amy's plans using the future tense. Some of the sentences are negative. (Answers may vary.)

| hire | join | study | be | stay | get |
| attend | register | cover | ✓look | help | start |

1. Amy _____is going to look_____ for a job.
2. Amy _____is going to register_____ for college next semester.
3. Amy _____will attend_____ school part-time.
4. She _____will study_____ accounting.
5. She _____won't stay_____ home all day anymore.
6. When the children come home from school, Amy _____will be_____ at work.
7. Amy _____is going to hire_____ a babysitter for the children in the afternoon.
8. Amy's mother _____will help_____ her when the children are sick and when they have a day off from school.
9. Amy _____will get_____ medical benefits from Tom's employer for one year. After that, his company _____will cover_____ only the children.
10. Amy _____is going to join_____ a group for single parents.
11. She _____will start_____ dating if she meets someone special.

D. Tom's plans. Tom is going to move this weekend. Use the cues to describe his future plans in the present continuous tense.

> **Present Continuous: Future Meaning**
> If a specific time in the future is stated or understood, the present continuous tense can show future meaning.
> **Tom is moving** tomorrow.

1. pack / tonight   Tom is packing tonight.
2. rent a van / this weekend   He is renting a van this weekend.
3. move / Sunday   He is moving (on) Sunday.

4. his brother / help him move **His brother is helping him move.**

5. sign a lease / for a year **He is signing a lease for a year.**

6. take / his stereo system **He is taking his stereo system.**

7. keep / the computer **He is keeping the computer.**

8. buy / new furniture / next week **He is buying new furniture next week.**

9. telephone company / install his phone / Monday
   The telephone company is installing his phone (on) Monday.
10. see / his lawyer / next week
   He is seeing his lawyer next week.

E. My plans. What are your plans after class? What are your plans for tomorrow? Using the present continuous, write your plans on the lines. *(Answers will vary.)*

_____

_____

_____

_____

F. Find someone who . . . Walk around the room and ask your classmates these questions about their future plans. Use *be + going to* or *will*. Try to find someone who answers *Yes* to an item. Write that student's name on the line.
(Answers will vary.)

Are you going to change jobs? No, I'm not. (Continue to ask other students.)

Are you going to change jobs? Yes, I am. (Write that student's name on the line.)

1. get married? _____

2. move? _____

3. visit your native country? _____

4. buy a house? _____

5. see a lawyer? _____

6. attend a wedding? _____

7. change jobs? _____

8. take a vacation? _____

9. start a business? _____

10. graduate from college? _____

E. My plans.

Have students write their answers individually. Then, call on volunteers to present their sentences to the class.

F. Find someone who . . .

• Read the instructions and answer any questions about how to do the activity. Point out the sample language and ask a pair of students to read the dialogues aloud. Remind students to write only the student's name in the blank, not a full-sentence answer.

• Set a time limit (perhaps ten minutes) for students to complete the activity.

Suggestion

For additional oral practice with the *going to* future, ask students to tell the rest of the class some of the things they learned about their classmates. For example: *Ali is going to get married next month.* Then, encourage students to tell other things they are going to do in the near future.

Active Grammar:
Will—Promises and Predictions

A. Offers to help.

• Have students read the instructions. Review the expressions in the box at the right to make sure students know what all of them mean. Then, have two students role-play the problem and the offer of help in the box at the top of the exercise.

• Call on different students to read aloud each problem. Have the reader choose another student to make the offer of help. After the offer is made, invite other students to confirm the answer if it is right, or to offer a different answer if they think the original one was wrong.

B. Predictions.

• Have students complete their predictions individually. Then, have them share their responses with a small group and practice giving a reason for each choice. Provide an example of an explanation for the first item:

> *I don't think families will have more children. Prices are going up all the time. Parents are going to have smaller families because they won't have enough money to support a large family.*

• Call on different students to tell the class whether they agree or disagree with each prediction and give their reason(s). After each presentation, invite a student who feels the opposite to give his or her reason(s) for feeling differently.

Active Grammar: *Will*—Promises and Predictions

A. Offers to help. You are a helpful person. Offer to help each person. Use the expressions in the box to help you. You will need to use one of the expressions two times. (Answers may vary.)

> Who will take my children to school if it's raining?
> Don't worry. I'll drive them.

1. I don't understand this homework.
2. My car broke down and I don't have a ride to school.
3. I can't find my keys.
4. I don't know how to use my new DVD player.
5. I just moved in and I don't know anyone around here.
6. How do you get to the mall?
7. I wrote this report, but I need someone to read it over for me.
8. I received a letter in English, but I don't understand it.
9. My car has a flat tire.
10. My income taxes are due, but I don't know how to fill out the form.

> introduce you
> give you directions
> help you
> ✓ drive them
> help you find them
> show you how
> translate it
> check it
> change it
> give you a ride

B. Predictions. Sit in a group and read these predictions about the future of family life in the next 20 years. Check (✓) *Agree* or *Disagree*. Explain the reason for your choice. (Answers will vary.)

	Agree	Disagree
1. Families will have more children.		
2. The number of divorces will increase.		
3. There will be more single mothers.		
4. More women will stay home and take care of their children.		
5. More people will work from home offices.		
6. More men will stay home with their children.		
7. Men will help more with household chores.		
8. Women will receive the same pay as men.		
9. More companies will offer day-care facilities.		
10. More grandparents will live with their children.		

C. Changes. How will life change for each of these people? Make four predictions about each person or couple. (Sample answers below. Answers may vary.)

1.

They will get married.

2.

She will graduate from college.

3.

She will have a baby.

4.

He will be fired from his job.

5.

He will become a citizen.

6.

He will buy a new car.

What is one change that will take place in your life in the next year or two?

C. Changes.

- In pairs, students discuss the changes that will occur in each person's life. Suggest that students spend no more than two minutes on each item. Every two minutes, announce the time and the item they should now be working on.
- Call on several pairs to tell the class their ideas about how life will change for each person shown. When correcting students, focus on the correct use and pronunciation of the future tense.

What is one change in your life that will take place in the next year or two?

- Brainstorm some possible ideas with the whole class. Then, ask students to take a few minutes to make a simple list of the changes that will take place in their own lives and the verbs they will use to describe them.
- Have them rehearse their statements with a partner. Then, call on different students to describe the changes that will take place in their lives to the class.

Active Grammar:
Future Time Clauses

A. Future plans.

• Have a student read aloud the two sentences with future time clauses in the box. Ask:

What is the difference in meaning between the two sentences? (There is no difference in meaning.) *How is the comma used in future time clauses?* (When the *if, when,* or *after* clause comes at the beginning of the sentence, it is followed by a comma. If the main clause comes first, no comma is used.

• Have students do this activity in pairs or in small groups. Check the answers with the whole class.

Now, use your imagination and continue to write about Sonia's future.

• Ask students to complete the sentences individually. Encourage them to come up with unusual ideas. For example: *Before Sonia gets married, she will sail around the world.*
• Review the answers orally with the whole class.

B. Pronunciation: *Stress.*
(CD1, Track 12)

• Explain that the syllables shown in capital letters are the syllables that get the strongest stress. Ask students to just follow along in their books as you play the audio the first time. Then, play the audio at least twice more as students listen and repeat each sentence.
• Call on individuals to say one sentence each. Point out any errors in stress and ask the student to say the sentence again. Have the class repeat.

Active Grammar: Future Time Clauses

A. Future plans. Sonia, a young college student, is dreaming about her future. Match these sentences that tell about her plans. *(Answers may vary.)*

Future Time Clauses

a. If I study hard, I'll graduate in two years. b. I'll graduate in two years if I study hard.
   (time clause)   (main clause)   (main clause)   (time clause)

The main clause and the time clause can be reversed. If the time clause is at the beginning of the sentence, use a comma **after** the time clause. No comma is necessary if the time clause is at the end of the sentence.

_b_ **1.** If she works hard, **a.** she'll buy a new car.

_d_ **2.** When she takes a vacation, **b.** she'll get a promotion.

_a_ **3.** After she saves some money, **c.** she'll accept the best offer.

_e_ **4.** If she meets the right person, **d.** she'll travel around Europe.

_c_ **5.** After she interviews for several jobs, **e.** she'll get married.

Now, use your imagination and continue to write about Sonia's future. Each sentence has a time clause. The main clause takes the future tense.
(Sample answers only. Answers will vary.)

1. Before Sonia gets married, _she'll finish college_ .

2. _She'll buy a house_ when she has children.

3. If she decides to become a full-time mother, _she'll leave her job_

4. _She'll travel with her husband_ after her children are grown.

5. If Sonia decides to change careers, _she'll study computers_

6. When Sonia has enough money, _she'll buy a larger house_ .

7. _She'll move to Arizona_ when she retires.

 B. Pronunciation: *Stress.* Listen and repeat these sentences.
1. I'm going to BUY a comPUTer when I GET a RAISE.
2. He's going to TAKE his vaCAtion when his SON gets MARried.
3. She's going to STUDy SPANish before she GOES to MEXico.
4. I'm going to REgister for SCHOOL after I reTURN from vaCAtion.

5. After he reTIRES, he's going to MOVE to FLOrida.
6. We're going to RENT a CAR when we LAND in ChiCAgo.

Practice these sentences with a partner.

C. Maybe tomorrow. Ask and answer these *When* questions with a sentence containing a future time clause. Use *before*, *after*, *if*, or *when*. (Answers will vary.)

> When are you going to get married?
> I'm going to get married when I find the perfect man/woman.

1. When are you going to get married?
2. When are you going to graduate?
3. When are you going to do your homework?
4. When are you going to call your parents?
5. When are you going to pay the telephone bill?
6. When are you going to travel out of the country?
7. When are you going to take a day off?
8. When are you going to give a party?
9. When are you going to open a savings account?
10. When are you going to get a credit card?

D. A happy life. George is 20 years old. Talk together and put these events in his life in order from 1 to 8. Make sentences about his life using *before*, *after*, or *when*.
(Answers will vary.)

> Before George finds a job, he's going to graduate from college.
> He's going to get married when he meets a wonderful woman.

find a job

buy a house

get married

graduate from college

have a daughter

have a son

meet a wonderful woman

save a lot of money

Family Matters **43**

Practice these sentences with a partner.

Students practice saying the sentences in pairs. Move around the room as they work offering corrective feedback as necessary.

C. Maybe tomorrow.

Students take turns asking and answering the questions in pairs. When they finish, invite several pairs to present one or two of their questions and answers to the class.

D. A happy life.

• Review the instructions and sample sentences in the box with the class. Then, have students sit in pairs and number the pictures in the order they think the events happen. (Students may come up with several different sequences of events that are reasonable.)
• Students work in pairs and describe the events in George's life. Encourage students to speak about the sequence using *before*, *after*, and *when*.

Suggestion

Play a game in which students make up events about a fictitious student at their school. You might choose a name such as Nilda. One student makes a future tense statement about something Nilda is going to do. (For example: *Nilda is going to get a new job next year.*) The next student makes a related statement containing a future time clause. (For example: *After Nilda gets a new job, she is going to move to a bigger apartment.*) Play continues until students run out of ideas.

☀ The Big Picture:
The Divorce Agreement

A. Before You Listen.

Have students read the passage to themselves. Then, discuss it with the whole class. Then, ask several students to try summarizing the second paragraph in a single sentence. (For example: *Mediators help divorcing couples make good decisions.*)

⊪ B. Listen for numbers.
(CD1, Track 13)

• Read the instructions and explain new vocabulary as necessary. Some students may not be familiar with these terms: *salary* (how much a person is paid every week or month); *mortgage* (your monthly payment to the bank when you are buying a house, not renting one); *retirement* (the period of time after you stop working when you are older).
• Play the audio and have students fill in the numbers. You may wish to pause the audio after each chunk of information to give students time to write their answers.
• Play the audio a second time so they can check their answers. Go over the answers orally and clear up any misunderstandings.

C. Tom's and Amy's assets.

Without replaying the audio, ask a different student to answer each question. Have other students listen carefully and raise their hands if they hear a wrong answer.

☀ The Big Picture: The Divorce Agreement

A. Before You Listen. Read and discuss.

Tom and Amy are working with a mediator. She is trying to help them come to an agreement about their divorce.

In mediation, a professional mediator works with a couple who is getting a divorce. The mediator does not represent the man or the woman. The mediator meets with the man and woman several times, both separately and as a couple. Together, the mediator helps the couple to develop an acceptable divorce agreement, including how to divide their possessions, child support, alimony, visitation rights, and any other matters related to the divorce. The agreement is a legal document and both people must follow it.

⊪ B. Listen for numbers. Listen as the mediator meets with Tom and Amy and reviews their assets. Complete the information below.

Tom's and Amy's Assets		
Tom's salary:	$ 42,000	a year
Overtime:	$ 500–1,000	a month
Savings account:	$ 10,000	
House:		
Original price:	$ 50,000	
Value today:	$ 120,000	
Mortgage and taxes:	$ 800	a month
Cars:		
Minivan:	paid off	
New car:	$ 300	a month for 1 more year(s)
Retirement account:	$ 40,000	
Other assets:	electronic equipment and dog	

C. Tom's and Amy's assets. Answer these questions.

1. Does Tom always earn overtime? No, he doesn't.
2. How much money does Amy earn? None.
3. When did they buy their house? Ten years ago.
4. Do they have any loans? No.
5. What other assets do they own? Electronic equipment and a dog.

Audio Script

B. Listen for numbers. Listen as the mediator meets with Tom and Amy and reviews their assets. (CD1, Track 13)

Mediator: I have met with you both about your assets. I'd like to review this information with the two of you today. I have a statement for each of you. Tom, your base salary is $42,000 a year.

Tom: Right.

Mediator: You work a lot of overtime, and so you earn between $500 and $1000 extra a month with overtime.

Tom: Yes, usually. But some months, when work is slow, I don't work any overtime.

Mediator: Amy, you have no income. You are a full-time homemaker.

Amy: Yes.

Mediator: You are savers. You have $10,000 in the bank, in a savings account.

Tom: Yes.

Mediator: And you have a house. You bought it for $50,000 ten years ago and today it's worth $120,000. Your monthly mortgage and taxes are $800.

(Audio Script continues on page 252.)

D. Listen as the mediator reviews the agreement between Tom and Amy. Complete the information about the agreement.

Divorce Agreement

House: _____Amy_____ will live in the house for _____10_____ more years.

Tom will pay $_____500_____ a month.

Amy will pay $_____300_____ a month and _____housing costs_____.

When they sell the house, _____half_____ the sale price will go to each person.

Savings: Tom: $_____5,000_____   Amy: $_____5,000_____

Retirement: Tom: $_____20,000_____   Amy: $_____20,000_____

Cars: New car: (Tom) Amy   Minivan: Tom (Amy)

Insurance on cars: _Each pay his or her own insurance._

Furniture: Tom (Amy)

Electronic equipment: (Tom) Amy

Children: During the week: Tom (Amy)

On weekends: (Tom) Amy

July: Tom (Amy)   August: (Tom) Amy

Child support: $_____600_____ a month

Alimony: $_____400_____ a month for _____3_____ years

Dog: (Tom) Amy

E. Discuss the answers to these questions.

1. How much will each person pay of the mortgage and taxes? Why do you think that Tom is going to continue to pay part of this expense?
Tom-$500/month Amy-$300/month -Tom has a job
2. Who will pay the insurance for Amy's car? Amy
3. When Tom works overtime, who will receive his overtime pay? Tom
4. Why does Amy need alimony? To help with expenses until Amy can get more education and more experience
5. Is this custody agreement good for the children?
(Answers will vary.)
6. Is this agreement fair for both Tom and Amy?
(Answers will vary.)
7. How is this agreement similar to or different from divorce agreements in your country?
(Answers will vary.)

Culture Note
Child support is a legal obligation. If a parent does not pay child support, the court will arrest him/her.

Family Matters   **45**

D. Listen as the mediator reviews the agreement between Tom and Amy.
(CD1, Track 14)

Play the tape and have students record their answers in their books. Tell them to skip an answer if they aren't sure and go on to the next one. Play the tape a second time so students can check their answers and fill in any missing answers. Ask individual students to give the correct answers, using the future tense.

E. Discuss the answers to these questions.

Discuss the answers with the whole class. Explain that there is no one correct answer for questions 4 to 7. Encourage students to express a variety of ideas and to disagree with each other in a friendly way.

Audio Script

D. Listen as the mediator reviews the agreement between Tom and Amy.
(CD1, Track 14)

Mediator: After meeting with you separately and together, it looks like we have a divorce agreement. Now, let's go through the agreement item by item. First, the house. Amy, you'll continue to live in the house. Tom will pay part of the mortgage and taxes— $500 a month. And Amy, you'll pay the other part of the mortgage, $300 a month, and you will take care of all housing costs, including insurance, heat, electricity, and cable. Amy, you can live in the house until the children graduate from high school. That's ten years from now. At the time you sell the house, half the sale will go to Tom and the other half of the sale will go to you, Amy.

Tom: What happens if Amy meets someone and remarries?

Mediator: At that time, she must sell the house and you will divide the sale price. Next, your savings. You'll divide your savings in half. Each of you will have $5,000. Now, let's look at the retirement money. Tom, you have $40,000 in your retirement plan at your company. At this point, we are going to divide this in half and you'll each have $20,000 for your retirement. Any new money in the account is just for Tom. Amy, when you find a job, you need to start your own account and begin to save for retirement. Any questions?

(Audio Script continues on page 252.)

A. Before You Read.

• Ask students to answer the questions at the top. Then, talk about the picture. Explain that the couple in the picture met on the Internet.

• Read and discuss the three questions at the top with the whole class. Then, ask students to do the reading on their own. When they finish, go back and divide the class into five groups and assign one paragraph to each. Their task is to come up with a statement that summarizes the content of their paragraph. For example, the paragraph 1 summary might be something like this: *Jim and his future wife liked each other immediately when they met on the Internet. They've been married for four years and have a small son.*

Suggestion

Invite students to take turns making up questions about the reading to ask their classmates. Invite volunteers to ask their questions and choose who they want to answer. They might ask questions such as:

Who had a good experience with Internet dating? (Jim E.)
What problems did Joanne W. have? (She met a married man.)

B. Choose the best title for this story.

Discuss the answer to this question with the class.

A. Before You Read. (Answers will vary.)

1. Are you married or do you have a boyfriend/girlfriend? How did you meet?

2. What do you know about Internet dating services?

3. Do you know anyone who has met this way?

Luisa and Jim

Working long hours and being tired in the evenings, Jim E. had little opportunity to meet someone special. One Friday night, he entered a computer chat room for Florida singles. He found himself **attracted to** one of the participants, so they left the public chat room and continued to a private computer chat room for the next three hours. Jim explained, "We were communicating so well, finding ourselves interested in the same things and sharing the same views, that we took a giant step and decided to share phone numbers that same night." They spoke on the phone the rest of the night. Two days later, they met in person at a nearby diner. "We **clicked** immediately." Jim and Luisa have been married for four years and their son, Jacob, is eight weeks old.

Joanne W., 30 years old, was not as lucky. After subscribing to an Internet dating service, she read the bios (information) of dozens of men and then wrote information about herself. Bob L. e-mailed her the next week. They chatted on the computer, then by phone, and met a few weeks later. After dating for two months, she discovered that Bob was married and the father of three children. She was upset, but she says, "The same thing can happen when you meet someone at a club."

Internet chat rooms and dating services are the new **matchmakers**. Chat rooms are the easiest places to meet someone on the computer. Some chat rooms are for singles only. Other chat rooms **target** specific interests, such as music, tennis, or French cooking. If two people take a special interest in one another, they can enter a private chat room.

Internet dating services provide a more detailed search for long-term relationships. Members send a photo and enter information about themselves and the person they would like to meet. Members usually describe their personalities and are sometimes asked to complete sentences, such as "I would love to take a vacation to _____" or "When I have free time, I like to _____." By providing this information, members hope to meet a **compatible** person.

Members pay for the service by the month. They enter the dating site and can **browse** for hours through the hundreds of photos, bios, and other information. No personal names are used. Each person has a username, or handle, such as *LuckyLady* or *Niceguy2*. If one member is interested in another member, he or she clicks on the e-mail button and sends a message. Will this member respond? Will they "click" online? Will they meet in person and continue their relationship?

B. Choose the best title for this story.

1. How to Meet Your True Love

②. Internet Dating

3. Beware of Internet Dating

C. Vocabulary in context. (Circle) a word or phrase that is similar in meaning.

1. He found himself **attracted** to one of the participants.
   a. close to   **b.** interested in   c. talking to

2. We **clicked** immediately.
   a. talked to   **b.** liked each other   c. met

3. Internet chat rooms and dating services are the new **matchmakers**.
   a. people who arrange marriages   b. people who like each other
   c. computer programmers

4. Other chat rooms **target** specific interests, such as music, tennis, or French cooking.
   a. present   b. contain pictures of   **c.** concentrate on

5. By providing this information, members hope to meet a **compatible** person.
   a. athletic   **b.** like-minded   c. beautiful

6. They enter the dating site and can **browse** for hours through the hundreds of photos, bios, and other information.
   a. look   b. sleep   c. talk

D. Sit in a group and discuss Internet dating. Check (✓) *do* or *don't* for each idea based on what you would or would not do. (Answers will vary.)

	Do	Don't
1. Send an up-to-date photo.	___	___
2. Give personal information, like your salary.	___	___
3. Get involved emotionally on the Internet.	___	___
4. Meet in a public place, like a restaurant or museum.	___	___
5. Describe yourself honestly.	___	___
6. Give out your address.	___	___
7. If you think you might like someone, try to meet them soon.	___	___
8. Believe everything you read in a chat room.	___	___

E. Give your opinion. (Answers will vary.)

1. Would you ever try Internet dating? Why or why not?

2. Do you think that people who use an Internet dating service might be better matched than people meeting at a party or a club?

3. What are some of the positive aspects of using an Internet dating service?

4. What are some problems that might occur when using an Internet dating service?

C. Vocabulary in context.

Ask students to complete this exercise individually and then check their answers with a partner.

Suggestion

To further clarify the meaning of the vocabulary items, and to provide practice using them in everyday situations, ask volunteers to make up original sentences using each. Correct errors and awkward usages by rewording student sentences. For example:

S: *I browsed her name in the phone book.*

T: *That's the right idea, but you need to say it this way: I browsed through the phone book looking for her name.*

Have students write particularly useful sentences in their notebooks.

D. Sit in a group and discuss Internet dating.

Set a time limit for the discussion, perhaps ten minutes. Check the answers by calling on one group to give its answers while other groups agree or disagree and give reasons for their opinions.

E. Give your opinion.

Do this activity with the whole class. Try to elicit a variety of opinions from students.

Writing Our Stories: More about Me

A. Read this information about an Internet dating service member.

Ask students to read the information on their own. Then, have them ask a partner for help understanding anything that isn't clear to them. Ask the pairs to tell you which words or phrases caused problems. Write them on the board and discuss them with the whole class.

B. Circle the adjectives that describe you.

• On their own, have students circle the adjectives that describe them. Discuss the meaning of any new words.

• Check students' comprehension of the adjectives by calling on different students to explain what each one means in his/her own words.

A. Read this information about an Internet dating service member.

My Bio

Age: 27
Location: Massachusetts, Boston area
Hair: Brown   Eyes: Brown
Height: 6' (182.88cm)
Body Type: Athletic
Language: English, Spanish
Ethnicity: Hispanic
Occupation: Electrician
Education: Some college
Income: I'll tell you later
Married: Never married   Children: None

More about me . . .

I never thought I would use an Internet dating service, but here I am. I'm a friendly, fun-loving person. My friends say that I'm easy to talk to, happy, and helpful. If a friend needs a ride or help with moving, I'm the one they call. I like to keep in shape, so I work out at the gym three or four times a week. When I have a free day, you can find me walking in the park, watching a baseball game, or lying on the beach. A perfect evening is a romantic dinner in a fine restaurant, talking about things we enjoy. I want to begin a relationship with an interesting, active woman. Let's start out as friends and see what develops.

B. Circle the adjectives that describe you. (Answers will vary.)

friendly	hardworking	athletic	intelligent
romantic	shy	outgoing	supportive
happy	helpful	competitive	dependable
funny	sensitive	serious	artistic
generous	energetic	fun-loving	honest

C. Verbs after *like*, *love*, *enjoy*, and *go*. Complete the sentences with the gerund or infinitive form of the verbs in parentheses.

> We often use a verb after **like**, **love**, **enjoy**, and **go**. After these verbs, use the gerund form (simple verb + *-ing*).
> I **enjoy** eating at ethnic restaurants.
> I **like** walking in the park.
> I **go** dancing on the weekends.
> After **like** and **love**, we can also use the infinitive (*to* + simple verb).
> I **like** to walk in the park.

1. I enjoy (listen) ____listening____ to music and (dance) ____dancing____.

2. I like (watch) __watching / to watch__ romantic movies.

3. On the weekends, I often go (camp) ____camping____.

4. When I have free time, I like (read) __reading / to read__ or (visit) __visting / to visit__ an interesting museum.

5. Family is very important to me. I enjoy (spend) ____spending____ time with them.

6. My passion is sports. I love (play) __playing / to play__ baseball, (practice) __practicing / to practice__ kung fu, or (ride) __riding / to ride__ my bicycle.

7. You'll find me serious and sensitive. I enjoy (talk) ____talking____ about politics and world events.

D. You have decided to use an Internet dating service to attract that special someone. Write a short paragraph describing your personality and the things you enjoy in life. *(Answers will vary.)*

> More about me . . .
>
>
>
>
>
>

 Looking at the Internet

The U.S. Census Web site is filled with interesting facts and statistics about life in the United States. Enter www.uscensus.gov and browse the site. Copy one interesting fact about life in the United States.

C. Verbs after *like*, *love*, *enjoy*, and *go*.

Read and discuss the explanation and the sample answer with the class. Then, have students complete the rest of the sentences on their own. Review the correct answers orally with the whole class.

D. You have decided to use an Internet dating service to attract that special someone.

• Suggest that students use the description on page 48 as a model for this assignment. Remind them that they can also use words from the list on page 48 in their writing.

• Have students complete their descriptions in class and share them with a partner. Invite several volunteers to read their work aloud to the class.

Suggestion

If some students feel awkward about pretending to use a dating service, have them write a profile for a single relative or friend.

Looking at the Internet

You might want to assign different areas of information to different groups of students so that you elicit a variety of information for presentation in class. For example, different groups could report on family income, state populations, and housing costs.

Practicing on Your Own

A. Complete these conversations with an offer to help or a promise.

Ask students to complete the conversations on their own and check their answers with a partner. Review some of the answers with the whole class.

B. Sentence combining.

Explain how sentence combining works and read the item 1 example to the class. Point out that usually only one of the verbs in a sentence with a future time clause is in the future tense.

Suggestion

You can extend the practice by having students try combining a sentence from one item with a sentence from another item. Emphasize that some of the results might be amusing, but that they must make sense. For example: *After we get married, my husband is going to cook dinner* makes sense. *When I get home from work, she will only stay for a week* doesn't work.

 Practicing on Your Own

(Sample answers only. Answers will vary.)

A. Complete these conversations with an offer to help or a promise. Use *will*.

1. **Child:** Dad, I'm sorry. I broke the window when I was playing baseball.
   Father: Don't worry. I'll fix it.

2. **Wife:** I'm tired tonight. I don't feel like making dinner.
   Husband: No problem. We'll eat out.

3. **Mother:** Your bedroom looks like a disaster area!
   Daughter: Don't worry. I'll clean it when I get home.

4. **Father:** You can use the car, but don't bring it back with an empty tank.
   Son: Don't worry. I'll fill it up.

5. **Daughter:** I have to be at school tomorrow morning at 7:00 for band practice.
   Mother: No problem. We'll leave the house at 6:40.

6. **Son:** Mom, my uniform is dirty and we have a baseball game tomorrow.
   Mother: Don't worry. I'll wash it tonight.

7. **Son:** Dad, my driving test is next week. Can you take me out to practice?
   Father: Sure. We'll practice every morning.

B. Sentence combining. The students in one ESL class gave these "hints" for a happy marriage. Combine their sentences using the words in parentheses and a future time clause.

1. I'm going to get married. I'm going to meet the right person. (when)
   I'm going to get married when I meet the right person.

2. We're going to get married. My husband and I are going to have separate bank accounts. (after) After we get married, my husband and I...

3. My husband is going to cook dinner. I'm going to feel tired. (when)
   My husband is going to cook dinner when I feel tired.

4. I'm going to be busy. My wife is going to cut the lawn. (when)
   When I'm busy, my wife is going to cut the lawn.

5. We are going to have an argument. The whole family isn't going to know about it. (when) When we have an argument, the whole family isn't going to know about it.

6. My mother will come for a visit. She will only stay for a week. (when)
   When my mother comes for a visit, she'll only stay for a week.

7. My husband is going to tell me something in confidence. I'm going to keep it to myself. (when) When my husband tells me something in confidence, I'm going to keep it to myself.

8. I'm still going to laugh. My husband is going to tell the same joke twice. (if)
   I'm still going to laugh if my husband tells the same joke twice.

9. We are going to go to bed each night. I'm going to tell my husband I love him. (before) Before we go to bed each night, I'm going to tell my husband I love him.

10. We are going to have a son. We are going to name him after my husband.
    (when) When we have a son, we are going to name him after my husband.

Grammar Summary

▶ 1. The future tense

We use the future tense to talk about actions in the future time, such as tomorrow, next week, next year, etc. There are two forms of the future: **be + going to** and **will**.

Both future forms talk about future actions and plans.

In addition, **will** expresses promises or predictions.

▶ 2. Present continuous tense: Future meaning

If a specific time in the future is stated or understood, the present continuous tense can show future meaning.

Tom is **leaving** this weekend.

He'**s taking** the children on vacation in July.

▶ 3. Future time expressions

tomorrow	next week	in a few minutes	soon
the day after tomorrow	next month	in an hour	later
	next year	in a little while	

▶ 4. Future

be + going to	will + verb
I'**m going to move** next month.	I **will move** next month.
She'**s going to get** a divorce.	She **will get** a divorce.
Are you **going to move**?	**Will** you **move**?
Is Tom **going to pay** alimony?	**Will** Tom **pay** alimony?
When **are** you **going to move**?	When **will** you **move**?
Where **is** Tom **going to live**?	Where **will** Tom **live**?

▶ 5. Future time clauses

A time clause begins with words such as *if, when, before, after,* and *as soon as*.

A time clause has a subject and a verb, but it is not a complete sentence by itself.

A time clause may come at the beginning or at the end of a sentence. With a future time clause, the verb in the main clause is in the **future tense**. The verb in the time clause is in the **present tense**.

I'll get married **when I meet the right person**.
 (main clause)   (time clause)

When I meet the right person, I'll get married.
   (time clause)   (main clause)

Note: When a time clause comes at the beginning of a sentence, use a comma to separate it from the main clause.

Grammar Summary

- Review the five grammar explanations and sample sentences with the class. Invite students to make up alternate sentences for each example in the chart. For example, in place of *I'm going to move next month*, a student might say, *We're going to go home soon.*
- Answer any questions students may have about the grammar items.
- See the Grammar Summary Expansion on page 260 for a more complete explanation of these grammar points.

Unit 4

Comparisons—

Discuss what the person in the unit title art is doing. Ask:

• *What do you see next to the number 4?* (A man balancing on one hand)
• *What is he doing?* (He's balancing on a globe of the world with one hand and holding a traffic signal in one hand.)
• *What does this have to do with the unit?* (The unit is about worldwide issues so that's why the globe is there. The unit is also about local issues. That's why the traffic signal is there.

A. Find the countries listed in the box and label them on the map.

Have students label as many of the countries as they can working independently. Then, have them share their work with a partner and add as many more names as they can. Review the correct answers with the whole class.

Suggestion

If students in your class come from countries not listed in the box at the bottom of the page, ask them to write the name of their country on the map along with the name and location of the city or town they come from. Using a large wall map, invite students to show the class where they come from and tell the rest of the class something about their hometowns.

4 Comparisons—

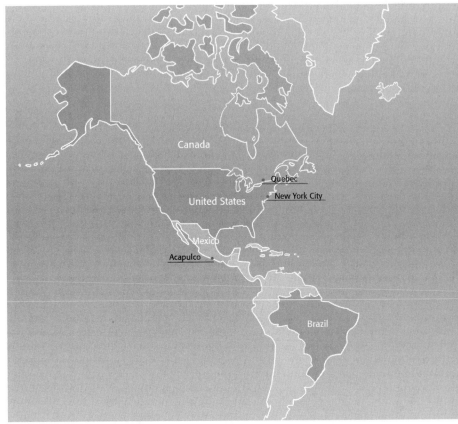

A. Find the countries listed in the box and label them on the map.

| Brazil | South Korea | Russia | United States | India | Egypt |
| Japan | Turkey | Canada | Mexico | Thailand | China |

Global and Local

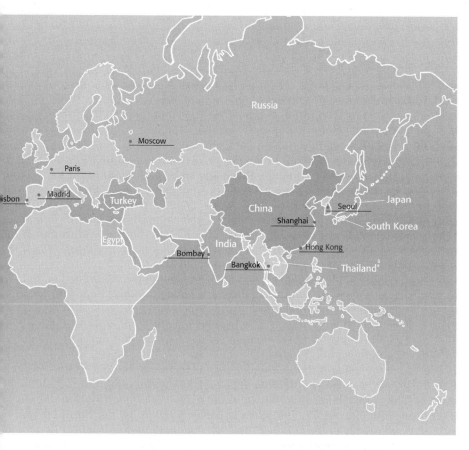

B. Locate each city listed in the box.

Have students use the same sequence of activities they used in Exercise A to place the cities on the map.

B. Locate each city listed in the box. Then, write the name of each city on the line on the map.

| Hong Kong | Madrid | Bombay | Lisbon | Shanghai | New York City |
| Paris | Seoul | Bangkok | Moscow | Quebec | Acapulco |

Active Grammar:
Comparative and Superlative Adjective Forms

A. Complete the sentences with the correct form of the adjectives in parentheses.

- Point out the three sections of the grammar chart and invite students to comment on and ask about what they see.
- Review the pronunciation of comparative adjectives ending in *-ier* and superlative adjectives ending in *-iest*. Explain that the letter *i* has the sound of long *e*, and the letter *e* has the short *e* sound (the sound of *e* in *let* or *met*).
- Review the three types of adjectives—one syllable, two syllables ending in *-y*, and two or more syllables not ending in *-y*. Ask students to give other examples of each type of adjective.
- Ask students to complete the fill-ins on their own and compare answers with a partner. Review the correct answers with the whole class.

In your notebook, write five sentences comparing your country or city to the countries and cities labeled on the map on pages 52–53.

- Ask students to complete this activity individually. Remind them that they can make use of the list of adjectives at the top of page 54 if they wish.
- Invite volunteers to read their sentences aloud to the class.

Active Grammar: Comparative and Superlative Adjective Forms

A. Complete the sentences with the correct form of the adjectives in parentheses.

	One-syllable adjectives	Two-syllable adjectives, ending with -y	Two or more syllables, not ending with -y
comparative forms	cleaner than	spicier than	more beautiful than less interesting than
superlative forms	the cleanest	the spiciest	the most beautiful the least interesting

When two people, items, or places are very different, add *much* to emphasize the difference. The summers in Seoul are ***much more humid than*** the summers in Quebec.

1. Egypt is _____ much warmer than _____ Russia. (warm)
2. Brazil's beaches are _____ the most beautiful _____ in the world. (beautiful)
3. Moscow's winters are _____ much colder than _____ Bangkok's. (cold)
4. South Korea is _____ much smaller than _____ the United States. (small)
5. Japan is _____ the most technological _____ of the Asian countries. (technological)
6. The United States is _____ less populated than _____ China. (populated)
7. Canada is _____ more modern than _____ Turkey. (modern)
8. Indian foods are _____ much spicier than _____ French foods. (spicy)
9. The subways in Japan are _____ much more crowded than _____ the subways in Canada. (crowded)
10. Which city is _____ the most interesting _____ city in the world? (interesting)

In your notebook, write five sentences comparing your country or city to the countries and cities labeled on the map on pages 52–53.

A. Look at the picture of an English class. Read the facts about the class. Write sentences comparing and contrasting the class. (Answer may vary. Sample answers below.)

More and fewer	Examples
more + noun + than	There are **more women than** men in this class. There are **many more students** with dark hair than with light hair.
fewer + noun + than	There are **fewer men than women** in this class.

Facts about the class

__4__ men	__1__ European	__6__ students over 5'4" tall
__11__ women	__10__ South Americans	__9__ students under 5'4" tall
__5__ single women	__2__ Carribeans	__6__ students with short hair
__3__ single men	__2__ Asians	__9__ students with long hair
__6__ married women		
__1__ married man		

1. There are _fewer men than women in this class._
2. _There are more single people than married people._
3. _There are many more South Americans than Caribbeans._
4. _There are fewer single men than single women._
5. _There are more students with long hair than with short hair._
6. _There are fewer students from Europe than Asia._
7. _There are fewer students over 5'4" tall than under 5'4" tall._

B. Now, with a group of students, make a list of facts about your class. Then, in your notebook, write eight sentences comparing the students in your class.

A. Look at the picture of an English class.

• Read and discuss the instructions. Then, call attention to the photograph and the list of facts about the class below it. Review the examples in the box and relate each one to specific students (or groups of students) in the photograph.

• Students write their sentences individually and compare answers with a partner. Have several students write one sentence each on the board. Review these sentences, pointing out any errors and inviting students to come to the board and make the necessary corrections. Then, explain the errors and make sure students understand why the changes are necessary.

B. Now, with a group of students, make a list of facts about your class.

• Tell students to model their eight sentences on the ones they wrote for exercise A. Encourage them to find other aspects of the class to compare such as age (*over 25 years old* vs. *under 25 years old*) and family status (*students who are parents* vs. *students who are grandparents.*)

• Ask volunteers to write one or two of their sentences on the board. Check the sentences for correctness. Invite students to copy any particularly useful or interesting sentences into their notebooks.

Suggestion

Have a contest to see who can come up with the most correct sentences using *more than* and *fewer than* to contrast the number of certain types of stores, restaurants, and other places of business in their hometown and in the place they live now. For example: *There are more bookstores in Boston than* in Cali. *There are fewer sidewalk cafés in Chicago than in Mexico City.* Set a time limit, perhaps five minutes. Then, poll the class to see which three students had the most sentences. Have them read their sentences aloud to the class. Correct grammatical errors as necessary. Have the class repeat some of the sentences.

 **Active Grammar:**

as . . . as

A. Read the information in the chart about tele-communications.

Answer any questions students have about the chart as they look at it.

🔊 **Listen and complete the comparisons. (CD1, Track 15)**

Have students just listen the first time you play the audio. The second time through, have them complete the sentences. List the correct answers on the board and play the tape a third time so students can check on any answers they missed.

 **Active Grammar:** *as . . . as*

> **As . . . as** shows that two items, people, or places are the same. The negative **not as . . . as** shows that two items, people, or places are not the same.
>
> France has **as many telephones as** it has televisions. Meaning: the number is the same.
>
> Brazil doesn't have **as many cell phones as** France does. Meaning: The numbers aren't the same.

A. Read the information in the chart about telecommunications.

Country	Telephones (million)	Cell phones (million)	Televisions (million)	Internet users (million)
Brazil	17	4.4	36.5	8.65
France	34.8	11	34.8	9
India	27.7	2.9	63	4.5
Japan	60.4	63.9	86.5	27
Russia	30	2.5	60.5	9.2
United States	194	69.2	219	148

Source: World Factbook 2001 at www.cia.gov

🔊 **Listen and complete the comparisons. Use *as many . . . as*.**

1. Brazil doesn't have _____as many telephones as_____ Russia does.
2. France has _____as many telephones as_____ it has televisions.
3. India doesn't have _____as many cell phones as_____ it has telephones.
4. Japan doesn't have _____as many televisions as_____ the United States does.
5. Russia doesn't have _____as many cell phones as_____ the other countries do.
6. Brazil has _____almost as many Internet users as_____ France does.
7. Russia has _____twice as many Internet users as_____ India does.

Audio Script

Listen and complete the comparisons. Use *as many . . . as*. (CD 1, Track 15)

1. Brazil doesn't have **as many telephones as** Russia does.
2. France has **as many telephones as** it has televisions.
3. India doesn't have **as many cell phones as** it has telephones.

4. Japan doesn't have **as many televisions as** the United States does.
5. Russia doesn't have **as many cell phones as** the other countries do.
6. Brazil has **almost as many Internet users as** France does.
7. Russia has **twice as many Internet users as** India does.

B. Pronunciation: *as . . . as* versus *not as . . . as.* Listen to each statement. Circle *same* if you hear *as . . . as.* Circle *different* if you hear *not as . . . as.*

1. (same) different
3. (same) different
5. same (different)
2. (same) different
4. same (different)
6. (same) different

 C. Practice reading the sentences to a partner. Circle the affirmative or the negative verb form. Your partner will listen and say "same" or "different." (Answers will vary.)

1. My city **is / isn't** as populated as this city.
2. The transportation here **is / isn't** as cheap as in my city.
3. The food here **is / isn't** as delicious as it is in my country.
4. The gasoline prices here **are / aren't** as expensive as those in my city.
5. My city **is / isn't** as diverse as this city.
6. The cars here **are / aren't** as small as those in my city.

D. Read the information in the bar graph. Then, circle *True* or *False*.

1. Bombay is more populated than Bangkok. (True) False
2. Seoul is less populated than Bangkok. True (False)
3. Shanghai is almost as populated as Bombay. (True) False
4. Tokyo is more populated than Seoul. True (False)
5. Bangkok is the least populated of the group. (True) False

E. Ask and answer these questions with a partner.

1. Is Bombay as populated as Bangkok? Yes. It is more populated than Bangkok.
2. Is Seoul more populated than Bangkok? Yes, it is.
3. Is Tokyo less populated than Seoul? Yes, it is.
4. Is Bangkok the least populated of the group? Yes, it is.
5. Is Tokyo as populated as Shanghai? No, it isn't.

Audio Script

B. Pronunciation: *as . . . as* versus *not as . . . as.* Listen to each statement. Circle *same* if you hear *as . . . as.* Circle *different* if you hear *not as . . . as.* **(CD1, Track 16)**

1. My city is as populated as this city.
2. The beaches in my city are as beautiful as this city's.
3. The traffic in this city is as heavy as the traffic in my city.
4. My country isn't as large as the United States.
5. Prices here aren't as cheap as those in my country.
6. The weather in this city is as humid as the weather in my city.

 B. Pronunciation: *as . . . as* versus *not as . . . as.* **(CD1, Track 16)**

Play the audio several times as students listen and circle *same* or *different.* Review the correct answers with the class and play the tape again to give students a chance to confirm the correct answers.

C. Practice reading the sentences to a partner.

Have students work individually as they circle the answers that apply to their cities. Then, have them find a partner and complete the activity.

Suggestion

If students are having difficulty making significant differences in their pronunciation of *is/isn't* or *are/aren't,* practice the contrasts in isolation. Suggest that they emphasize the final *t* sound in the negative verb forms.

D. Read the information in the bar graph.

• Point to the numbers at the left of the graph and explain that these are population numbers.
• Point out the legend under the graph and have students pick out which bar relates to each city.
• Make some statements about the information in the graph and ask students to repeat. For example: *Bombay has a population of 12,000,000 people.* Ask other students to make similar statements about other cities.
• Students read the five statements and circle their answers. Review the correct answers with the class.

E. Ask and answer these questions with a partner.

Have students complete the activity in pairs. Call on different students to give one answer each.

Active Grammar:
Superlative Adjectives

A. Compare modes of transportation.

- Review the meaning of the wording in the column heads in the chart. Ask questions such as:

  What makes a form of transportation convenient? (It is near your house. It operates many times a day.)
  What is kinds of transportation are not public transportation? (cars, bikes)

- Students discuss the information as they fill in the chart in groups of three or four students. Move around the room helping out as needed.

B. Ask and answer questions about your group's chart.

Students continue to work in the same groups as they ask and answer the list of questions about the chart. Review the correct answers by calling on an individual from each group to answer each question.

Active Grammar: Superlative Adjectives

A. Compare modes of transportation. With a group of three or four students, fill in the information in the chart. (Answers will vary.)

Student Name	Minutes to school	Miles/km to school	Daily cost of transportation	Convenient		Public Transportation		
				Yes	No	Bus	Train	Subway

B. Ask and answer questions about your group's chart. (Answers will vary.)

1. Who lives the closest to school? _____
2. Who lives the farthest from school? _____
3. Who takes the most time to come to school? _____
4. Who takes the least time to come to school? _____
5. Who lives in the most convenient neighborhood? _____
6. Who lives in the least convenient neighborhood? _____
7. Who spends the most money on transportation? _____
8. Who spends the least money on transportation? _____
9. Who spends the most time on public transportation? _____
10. Who spends the least time on public transportation? _____

C. Complete the sentences about your group's chart. Use the correct adjective form: comparative, superlative, or *as ... as.* (Answers will vary.)

1. _____ travels _____.
   (student name)   (adjective form)

2. _____'s neighborhood is _____.
   (student name)   (adjective form)

3. _____'s transportation is as _____ as _____'s.
   (student name)   (adjective form)   (student name)

4. _____'s neighborhood is as _____ as _____'s.
   (student name)   (adjective form)   (student name)

5. _____'s costs are _____ _____'s.
   (student name)   (adjective form)   (student name)

6. _____ has _____ transportation.
   (student name)   (adjective form)

D. Student to student dictation.

Student A: Turn to page 244.

Student B: Look at the pictures. Listen to Student A. In the chart below, (circle) the number of the family that matches the description. When you finish, change pages.

Family 1   **Family 2**   **Family 3**

1. Family ①A 2 ③B   4. Family 1 ②A ③B
2. Family 1 ②B ③A   5. Family ①B ②A 3
3. Family ①A 2 ③B   6. Family ①A ②B 3

Student B: Turn to page 244.

Student A: Look at the pictures. Listen to Student B. In the chart above, (circle) the number of the family that matches the description.

C. Complete the sentences about your group's chart.

- Read and discuss the instructions. Explain that each sentence in this exercise relates to information students discussed in Exercise B on page 58. If appropriate for your class, point out the correspondences between the two exercises. For example, Exercise C, Item 1, corresponds to *farthest*, Exercise B, Item 2.
- Have students complete the sentences individually. Then, ask group members to share their sentences with each other and correct each other's mistakes if possible. Call on individuals from each group to share a sentence or two with the class.

D. Student to student dictation.

- Read and discuss the instructions and be sure students understand how to proceed. Help students locate the sentences on page 244.
- Students work in pairs. First Student A reads the first set of statements on page 244 and Student B circles the correct number below the family pictures. Then, they reverse roles. Check the correct answers orally with the whole class.

Suggestion

Ask students to think of some more statements like those on page 244 that they could ask classmates. Set a time limit, perhaps three minutes. Then, have different students ask their original questions and call on classmates to answer.

☀ The Big Picture: What Happened to My Town?

☀ The Big Picture: What Happened to My Town?

A. Look at the picture and describe this town as it looked 25 years ago.

☀ The Big Picture: What Happened to My Town?

🔊 **A. Look at the picture and describe the town as it looked 25 years ago.**

• Ask students to describe the picture. You might use questions like these to get started:

Is this a big city or a small one?
What businesses do you see?
What other buildings can you name?

• Invite volunteers to describe the town in their own words. Supply vocabulary as necessary. Write any unfamiliar words on the board and have students repeat them.

🔊 **B. Listen and take notes about the changes in the town. (CD1, Track 17)**

• Play the audio once. Explain that students will be comparing what they hear on the audio with what they see in the picture. Point out the sample answers and ask students to point to the corresponding buildings or people in the picture.

• Explain each of the sample answers. For example:

T: *There are only two houses in the picture. What does the audio say about housing?*

S: *The audio says there's an entire development of houses in the town.*

• Play the audio once or twice more as students fill in their answers. Review the correct answers with the class and play the audio one final time so students can confirm their answers.

B. Listen and take notes about the changes in the town. What is different about the town today? (Answers may vary.)

1. _____ more housing _____
2. _____ new people _____
3. ___ 2 new elementary schools ___
4. ___ new middle school ___
5. ___ high school renovation ___
6. _____ no farms _____
7. _____ new factories _____
8. ___ large shopping mall ___
9. ___ traffic is heavier ___
10. ___ a computer manufacturer ___

Audio Script

B. Listen and take notes about the changes in the town. What is different about the town today? (CD1, Track 17)

My name's Kenny. I live in a big city now, but let me tell you about where I grew up. I grew up in a small farming community, with a population of only 703 people. There was one high school, and one combination elementary and middle school. There were only 175 students in my whole high school, so we all knew each other. I was in classes with almost the same kids from kindergarten all the way through high school.

I lived in a big house with my parents and five siblings—three younger sisters and two older brothers. I was in the middle. My family had a fruit-tree orchard. We grew apples and pears. My closest neighbors were a mile or two away, so I spent most of my time playing with my siblings or with my best friend. We used to go downtown to hang out. Downtown wasn't a big place. There was one traffic light in front of City Hall. Of course, the mayor was there, but the sheriff's office and the post office were also in the same building. There were only two places to eat downtown. My favorite was Millie's

(Audio Script continues on page 253.)

C. Read each statement about the town today. (Circle) the correct answers.

1. There are **more** / **fewer** residents.
2. Neighbors live **closer to** / **farther from** each other.
3. Traffic is **lighter than** / **heavier than** it used to be.
4. There are **fewer students** / **more students** than there used to be.
5. There are **fewer places** / **more places** to shop than there used to be.
6. The town has **many more jobs** / **fewer jobs** than it used to have.
7. The buildings are **as tall as** / **much taller than** they used to be.

D. Complete the sentences with the correct comparative or superlative form. Use the expressions from the box below and the words in parentheses.

(much) more . . . than	*as + adjective + as*	*as many + noun + as*
(much) adjective *+ er than*	*not as + adjective + as*	*not as many + noun + as*
fewer . . . than		

1. Twenty-five years ago, the town was ___not as populated as___ it is today. (populated)
2. Twenty-five years ago, there were ___not as many schools___ for children as there are today. (schools)
3. Twenty-five years ago, downtown was ___not as crowded as___ it is today. (crowded)
4. Today, traffic is ___more heavy than___ it used to be. (heavy)
5. Twenty-five years ago, the movie theater showed ___fewer movies than___ the new cineplex does today. (movies)
6. The waitresses at Millie's Luncheonette are ___as friendly as___ they were twenty-five years ago. (friendly)

E. **Which questions.** Ask and answer questions about the old town *and* the new town. Use the adjectives and nouns below.

Adjectives		Nouns
populated		parking
diverse		shopping
busy		farms
large		children
industrial		job opportunities

Which town is busier, the old town or the new town?
The new town is.

Which town has more parking, the old town or the new town?
The new town does.

C. Read each statement about the town today.

Students complete the activity individually. Check the answers orally with the whole class.

D. Complete the sentences with the correct comparative or superlative form.

Students can complete this exercise individually or in pairs. Review the answers orally with the class.

E. *Which* questions.

Review the information in the boxes at the right and left of the page to make sure students understand all the vocabulary. Then, call on students to compose original questions. Refine and correct students' questions and choose another student to answer each one.

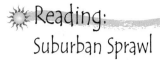

A. Before You Read.

• Discuss the answers to the questions at the top with the whole class. Then, have them complete the categorization activity individually. Check the answers orally.

• Have students look at the pictures that accompany the story and tell what they see. Point out the title, *Suburban Sprawl,* and have a student use the picture of the housing development on page 63 to explain something about the meaning of this term.

• Students read the passage on their own. Explain that they won't understand everything and should just aim to understand the main ideas.

Suggestion

Check for comprehension by reviewing the whole story and asking comprehension questions about each paragraph. (You might also ask about certain vocabulary items.) Possible questions for the first paragraph are:

What happens when people move from cities to suburban areas? (The suburban areas move further into the rural areas.)

What do you think a developer is? (A developer is someone who builds a lot of similar houses in a single area.)

Reading: Suburban Sprawl

A. Before You Read. (Answers will vary.)

1. What is the difference between rural, suburban, and urban areas?

2. In which type of area do you live? In which type of area would you like to live? Why?

3. Put the following words or phrases in the correct categories. Some words or phrases may fit into more than one category.

larger houses and yards	farms	high crime rates
traffic jams	many trees	tall apartment buildings
parking lots	pollution	wildlife
taxis	shopping malls	many open spaces

(Suggested answers only.)

Urban	Suburban	Rural
traffic jams	larger houses and yards	larger houses and yards
parking lots	parking lots	farms
taxis	taxis	many trees
pollution	farms	wildlife
shopping malls	many trees	many open spaces
high crime rates	shopping malls	
tall apartment buildings		

(Underlined sentences and numbers below are the AK for exercise C, page 63.)

As the population in the United States grows, many people move from the cities, and the services that they need, such as shopping centers and stores, move with them. The suburban areas outside of the cities become more crowded, and more housing is needed. Then, the suburbs begin to extend into the rural areas. The new residents need services; therefore, developers build more shopping centers, restaurants, and housing on the land in the rural areas. The rural areas begin to shrink. As a result, there is less open space in the rural areas. This effect is called suburban sprawl. According to the organization Sprawl City, by the year 2050, the United States will have 110 million fewer acres of rural countryside.

Why do people leave the urban areas? <u>They want large houses and yards, lower ①</u>
<u>crime rates, and better schools.</u> They are looking for a better quality of life.

Sprawl is becoming an increasing problem, and environmentalists are protesting the growth into the rural areas. Community organizations are also fighting the development. They say that sprawl contributes to the decline of natural habitats for wildlife. As cities spread, suburban development may damage the water quality when chemicals go into the water. Wildlife, such as birds, disappears from the area.

Besides environmental changes, sprawl also brings changes to rural communities. For example, a rural community might have one movie theater that shows two movies. It has one hardware store that has everything that a household needs. There is one grocery store, and the employees live in the community and know everyone who shops at the store. When the nearby suburb begins to expand, large chain store companies open stores closer to the expanding suburb, and gradually other stores, restaurants, and a large twelve-screen movie theater move into the area. The rural store owners become worried. They provide friendly, personal service to the town residents, but they cannot compete with the prices and services offered at the chain stores. When the rural residents begin to shop at the chain stores, and the residents go to movies at the new movie theater, the rural center begins to die.

People who support the chain stores say that there will be more tax revenues for the town, lower prices for residents, and new jobs. The people who are against the stores argue that there will be more traffic, only minimum-wage jobs, and the small town will have less of a small-town feeling. Is your area experiencing sprawl?

B. Reread the first paragraph. On the lines below, explain the process of sprawl.

(Wording of answers may differ.)

1. People leave the cities and move to the suburbs.

2. Services such as shopping centers and stores move with them.

3. More housing is needed and suburbs extend into rural areas.

4. Services move into the rural areas.

C. Listing paragraphs. The reading contains several listing paragraphs. These paragraphs describe more than one reason/cause/effect/characteristic, etc. Find and <u>underline</u> this information in the reading. (See answers set in A on page 62-63.)

1. Find three reasons that people leave urban areas.

2. Find three negative effects of sprawl.

3. Find two effects of sprawl on rural communities.

4. Find three positive effects of building chain stores in rural areas.

5. Find three negative effects of building chain stores in rural areas.

B. Reread the first paragraph.

Students complete the activity individually and check their answers with a partner. Review the answers orally with the whole class.

C. Listing paragraphs.

• Read and discuss the instructions. Explain the meaning of the terms *positive effect*, *negative effect*, and *characteristic* as necessary.

• Have students scan the story and underline the information asked for in the questions. Review the answers with the whole class.

☀ Writing Our Stories: Three Cities

A. Read.

- Point to the picture and explain that the student is talking about what life was like in three different cities where he has lived. Then, ask students to do the reading on their own.
- When they finish, invite different students to tell which of the three cities they would like to live in and why.

B. *Like, alike.*

- Read and discuss the sample sentences in the box. Have students make up similar sentences with *like* and *alike* using true information about their own lives. For example: *My father and I look alike. My hair is like my father's hair. My hair is not like my sister's hair.*
- Students then complete the sentences in the book on their own and check their answers with a partner.

☀ Writing Our Stories: Three Cities

A. Read.

I have lived in three cities: Seattle, Miami, and Boston. Boston is a much better city for college students; there are many more excellent colleges and universities there than in the other two cities. For weather, I prefer Miami because the winters are much warmer. I can go to the beach all year long. Seattle and Boston are much colder in the winter. Boston is a much older and more historical city, so it has the most museums and historical sites to visit. Miami is like Boston. Both cities have many fun places to go for entertainment, and there are many theaters, clubs, and shops. Seattle is the best place if you like the outdoors. You can visit beautiful Mount Rainier. It's the best place for hiking. I don't know which city is my favorite. I like all three.

Andres

B. *Like, alike.* Complete the sentences with *like*, *alike*, *not like*, or *not alike*. (Answers will vary.)

> The weather in Miami is **like** the weather in my country.
> Meaning: The weather is similar.
> The weather in Miami and the weather in my country are **alike**.
> Meaning: The weather is similar. Use *alike* at the end of a sentence.
>
> The weather in Miami is **not like** the weather in New York.
> The weather in Miami and the weather in my country are **not alike**.

1. The buses in this city and in my native city are _____.
2. The winters in this city and the winters in my native city are _____.
3. My home in this city is _____ my home in my native country.
4. This city is _____ my hometown.
5. The gasoline prices in this city are _____ the prices in my native city.
6. The cost for clothing in this country and the cost for clothing in my native country are _____.

C. Comparing cities. Choose three cities in your area to compare and contrast. Use the information in the chart to organize your composition.
(Answers will vary.)

Location	Transportation	Downtown	Entertainment
near school	bus	busy	excellent
near my job	train	crowded	good
near my relatives	subway	quiet	average
near downtown	near airport		poor

Job Opportunities	Population	
excellent average few	(City #1) _____	(Population) _____
	(City #2) _____	(Population) _____
	(City #3) _____	(Population) _____

In your notebook, write a composition comparing three cities.

D. Edit. There is one <u>underlined</u> mistake in each sentence. Correct the mistakes.

1. There are ~~less~~ *fewer* soccer players in the United States than basketball players.
2. Russia is one of the ~~large~~ *largest* countries in the world.
3. The subways in Paris are <u>as convenient</u> *as* the subways in Montreal.
4. The ~~most long~~ *longest* river in China is the Yangtze River.
5. Spanish is not ~~difficulter~~ *as difficult* as English.
6. Indian food is <u>much spicier ~~then~~</u> *than* Japanese food.
7. The United States is not <u>as bigger</u> as Canada.
8. China is *the* <u>most populated</u> country in the world.

 Looking at the Internet

There are many Web sites that can help you find facts about different countries and cities. Search the Internet for the U.S. Census to find facts about the United States. For international facts, search for an almanac or *The World Factbook*. Share one interesting fact about the United States and one interesting international fact that you found with the class.

C. Comparing cities.

- First have students fill in the names of the three cities on the chart and add the approximate population of each.
- Then, read through the other information on the chart and elicit examples of how students can use this data to compare and contrast the cities. For example:

Location: Oakfield is nearer to my school than Elmwood.
Transportation: There are more trains in Elmwood than in Oakfield.
Downtown: The Downtown in Benville is busier than the downtown in Oakfield.
Entertainment: The entertainment opportunities in Oakfield are better than in Benville.
Job Opportunities: There are fewer job opportunities in Benville than in Oakfield.

In your notebook, write a composition comparing three cities.

Students write their compositions individually and exchange them with a partner. Have them comment on each other's work and offer suggestions for corrections.

D. Edit.

Have students correct the sentences on their own. Review the correct answers with the whole class.

Looking at the Internet

You might want to divide the class into groups and have each group choose a different type of information to research. They can choose from headings from the chart in Exercise C (transportation, entertainment, job opportunities, population) and compare how various cities or countries measure up on these factors.

Practicing on Your Own

A. Complete each sentence with the correct adjective form.

Ask students to complete the sentences on their own and check their answers with a partner.

B. Complete the sentences with the correct comparative form.

• Point out that the graph in this exercise works the same way as the one in Exercise A on page 57.

• Students complete the sentences on their own and check their answers with a partner.

Suggestion

Divide the class into small groups and have them compete to see which group can write the greatest number of correct sentences in five minutes using these comparative forms: *more . . . than, as many . . . as,* and *fewer . . . than.* You can suggest a topic (such as football teams or popular singers), or you can let students choose their own topics.

Practicing on Your Own

A. Complete each sentence with the correct adjective form. (Answers may vary.)

1. Seoul is one of _____ the most humid _____ (humid) cities in the summer.
2. Shanghai's port is _____ the busiest _____ (busy) in Asia.
3. Paris is _____ more fashionable than _____ (fashionable) Moscow.
4. Istanbul is _____ less modern than _____ (modern) Quebec.
5. China is _____ the most populated _____ (populated) country.
6. Acapulco has some of _____ the most beautiful _____ (beautiful) beaches.
7. New York City is _____ more diverse than _____ (diverse) Madrid.
8. Summers in Shanghai are _____ hotter than _____ (hot) those in Seoul.
9. People in Madrid eat dinner _____ later than _____ (late) people in Tokyo.
10. Mexico is not _____ as rainy as _____ (rainy) France.

B. Complete the sentences with the correct adjective form. Use the information in the chart. You can use *more . . . than*, *as many . . . as*, or *fewer . . . than*.

FRANCE: 75,500,000
ITALY: 41,200,000
CHINA: 31,200,000
MEXICO: 20,600,000
CANADA: 20,400,000

Top Tourist Spots

Source: World Tourism Organization

1. France has _____ more than 75,500,000 _____ visitors per year.
2. China has _____ fewer visitors than _____ both Italy and France.
3. _____ Fewer _____ visitors go to Italy _____ than _____ to France.
4. _____ More _____ visitors go to France _____ than _____ to China.
5. Canada has almost _____ as many _____ visitors _____ as _____ Mexico.
6. Canada has _____ the fewest _____ visitors of the group.
7. France has _____ more _____ visitors _____ than _____ China.

66 UNIT 4

Grammar Summary

▶ **1. Comparative adjectives**

   a. Use the comparative form of an adjective to compare two people or things.

     New York City is **larger than** Boston.

     New York City is **more diverse than** Boston.

     Canada is **less populated than** China.

   b. When two items, people, or places are very different, add *much* to emphasize the difference.

     Canada is **much less populated than** China.

One-syllable adjectives	Two-syllable adjectives, ending with -*y*	Two or more syllables, not ending with -*y*
larger than	*busier than*	*more populated than*

▶ **2. Superlative adjectives**

   a. Use the superlative form of an adjective to compare three or more people, places, or things.

     Brazil is **the largest** country in South America.

   b. Use the superlative form of an adjective to compare one person, place, or thing to a larger group.

     China is **the most populated** country in the world.

One-syllable adjectives	Two-syllable adjectives, ending with -*y*	Two or more syllables, not ending with -*y*
the largest	*the busiest*	*the most populated*

▶ **3. Comparing nouns**

   a. Use *more* + **noun** + *than* or *fewer* + **noun** + *than* to compare count nouns.

     There are **more women than** men in our class.

     There are **fewer men than** women in our class.

   b. Use *more* + **noun** + *than* or *less* + **noun** + *than* to compare non-count nouns.

     There is **more traffic** in Mexico City **than** in Montreal.

     There is **less pollution** in my hometown **than** in this city.

▶ **4. *as* + adjective + *as* / *not as* + adjective + *as***

   a. Use *as* + **adjective** + *as* to show that two items, people, or places are the same.

     Moscow's winters are **as cold as** St. Petersburg's winters.

   b. Use *not as* + **adjective** + *as* to show that two items, people, or places are not the same.

     Japan is **not as large as** India.

▶ **5. *as many* + noun + *as* / *not as many* + noun + *as* / *as much* + non-count noun + *as***

   a. Use *as many* + **noun** + *as* to show that two people, places, or things are the same.

     France has **as many telephones as** it has televisions.

   b. Use *not as many* + **noun** + *as* to show that two people, places, or things are not the same.

     Brazil doesn't have **as many telephones as** it has televisions.

   c. Use *as much* + **noun** + *as* to compare non-count nouns.

     Rural areas don't have **as much traffic as** urban areas do.

Grammar Summary

• Review the five grammar explanations and sample sentences with the class. Invite students to make up alternate sentences for each example in the chart. For example, in place of *Brazil is the largest country in South America*, a student might say, *Rhode Island is the smallest state in the United States.*

• Answer any questions students may have about the grammar items.

• See the Grammar Summary Expansion on page 261 for a more complete explanation of these grammar points.

Unit 5
Leisure Activities

Discuss what the person in the unit title art is doing. Ask:

• *What do you see next to the number 5?* (A man balancing upside-down on one hand)
• *What is he doing?* (He's painting a picture with one hand and diving into the water with the other hand.)
• *What does this have to do with the unit?* (The picture shows two leisure activities—painting and swimming.)

A. Label the hobbies and leisure activities.

• Explain that hobbies and leisure activities are the same things. They are things that people do when they aren't working, things they enjoy, and things they find relaxing.
• Have students label as many of the pictures as they can individually. Then, ask them to compare answers with a partner and fill in any missing labels.
• Review the answers with the whole class. Encourage students to add comments about each hobby. For example:

I think fishing is boring, but many people find it relaxing. My brother plays cricket every Saturday.

Suggestion

Invite students to identify any other leisure activities they enjoy. Write these words on the board and encourage students to tell why they enjoy each activity and who they do it with.

5 Leisure Activities

Label the hobbies and leisure activities. Which do you like to do?

1. dominoes
2. cricket
3. mah-jongg
4. sewing
5. video games
6. dancing
7. fishing
8. cards
9. painting
10. cooking
11. word games
12. gardening
13. photography
14. surfing the Internet
15. skiing

Active Grammar: Yes/No Questions

A. Complete the questions in each category. If you need more help in writing the questions, look at the Grammar Summary on page 83.

(Answers will vary.)

1. Are you going to _____ go fishing _____ this weekend?
2. Will you _____ next month?
3. Are you going to _____ next month?
4. Will you _____ by 2010?

5. Were you _____ at a club _____ last weekend?
6. Were you _____ yesterday?
7. Were you _____ last month?

8. Do you _____ take photographs _____ ?
9. Do you _____ every day?
10. Do you _____ every weekend?

11. Did you _____ play a sport in your country _____ ?
12. Did you _____ yesterday?
13. Did you _____ back in your native country?

14. Are you _____ playing a card game _____ now?
15. Are you _____ right now?
16. Are you _____ right now?

B. Ask and answer the questions in Exercise A with a partner.

Yes, I am. No, I'm not.	Yes, I do. No, I don't.	Yes, I was. No, I wasn't.
	Yes, I did. No, I didn't.	Yes, I will. No, I won't.

Active Grammar: Yes/No Questions

A. Complete the questions in each category.

- Read the instructions and complete the last three items in the first part of the exercise with the whole class. Accept several possible answers for each sentence and choose one to write on the board.
- Have students complete the rest of the items on their own.

B. Ask and answer the questions in Exercise A with a partner.

- Review the short answers in the grammar box. Ask students to identify the verb tense associated with each short answer. For example:

  Yes, I am = present tense *be*.
  Yes, I do = present tense of most verbs.
  Yes, I was = past tense *be*.
  Yes, I did = past tense of most verbs.
  Yes, I will = future tense.

- Students take turns asking and answering the questions in pairs. One student reads all the questions he/she wrote and his/her partner gives the answers. Then, they switch roles.

A. *Who/Whom/Whose.*
(CD1, Track 18 through CD1, Track 20)

• Read the instructions and point out the three pictures. Remind students that when they take notes, they should just write one or two words to help them remember each idea. They should not write complete sentences.

• Play the audio and have students just listen the first time. Then, play it one or two more times as students make their notes about the three people's hobbies.

B. Circle the correct question word.

• Ask students to study the grammar chart and read the sample questions. Then, ask students to make up original questions using *whose, who,* and *whom.*

• Point out that two answers are required for each item in the exercise; they must circle the correct *wh-* word in the question, and then fill in the correct name in the answer. Do the first item with the whole class. Then, have students complete the rest of the items on their own and compare answers with a partner.

C. Sit with a small group of students.

• Students fill in the question words individually and check their answers with the group. Then, they take turns asking and answering the questions with other group members.

• Review the exercise with the whole class by calling on pairs of students from different groups to ask and answer each other's questions.

A. *Who/Whom/Whose.* Listen to these people talk about how they spend their free time. Take notes.

Gina   Roberto   Yelena

B. Circle the correct question word. Then, answer the questions with the name of the correct speaker.

Whose umbrella is under the chair?	*Whose* refers to possession.
Who likes sports?	*Who* refers to the subject.
Whom are you going to go to the movies with?	*Whom* and *who* can both refer to
Who did you call last night?	the object. *Whom* is more formal.

1. **Who** / Whom / Whose likes to go dancing?   ___Gina___ does.
2. Who / Whom / **Whose** father taught her chess?   ___Yelena___'s did.
3. **Who** / Whom / Whose has many books about his hobby?   ___Roberto___ does.
4. Who / **Whom** / Whose does Gina go dancing with?   __Her boyfriend__
5. Who / Whom / **Whose** friends often meet at dance clubs?   ___Gina___'s do.
6. Who / **Whom** / Whose does Roberto meet once a week?   __A few friends__
7. **Who** / Whom / Whose worries about water chemistry?   ___Roberto___ does.
8. **Who** / Whom / Whose has more free time now?   ___Yelena___ does.
9. Who / **Whom** / Whose is Yelena going to teach chess to?   __Her grandson__

C. Sit with a small group of students. Write the correct question word: *Who, Whom,* or *Whose.* Ask and answer the questions.

1. ___Who___ has a hobby?
2. ___Who___ often goes to a park?
3. ___Whose___ music do you like?
4. ___Who___ is planning a vacation?
5. ___Who___ works full time?
6. ___Who___ has a pet at home?
7. ___Whom___ do you spend time with?
8. ___Who___ lives close to school?

Audio Script

A. *Who/Whom/Whose.* Listen to these people talk about how they spend their free time. Take notes.
(CD1, Track 18)

Gina: How do I spend my free time? I like to go dancing. My boyfriend and I go dancing almost every weekend. Every Friday and Saturday night we go dancing at clubs in our area. We meet our friends and we make new friends when we go dancing. We like all kinds of music, but we usually go to clubs that play Latin music or hip-hop. Those are our favorite kinds of music.

Oh, and once a month, my boyfriend and I take a dance class together. Dancing is a really good way to keep in shape. I don't need to work out at a gym. Dancing keeps me fit.

(CD1, Track 19)
Roberto: I spend my time taking care of my tropical fish. I have a large aquarium in my living room, and I have many books about tropical fish and how to take care of them. I also have a few friends who like keeping fish, too. We get together once a week at a

(Audio Script continues on page 253.)

D. Look at the pictures. Then, read the questions and match each question with the appropriate answer. Finally, label the people in the pictures.

 Irina

 Kazuki

 Eric

 Ryan and April

_f_ **1.** Who is nervous about his match?		**a.** Kazuki does.
_e_ **2.** Who had a match a few minutes ago?		**b.** Eric does.
_b_ **3.** Who collects comic books?		**c.** Ryan and April do.
_g_ **4.** Who is planning a trip?		**d.** Eric will.
_h_ **5.** Who plays a sport well?		**e.** Irina did.
_d_ **6.** Who will probably add to a collection?		**f.** Kazuki is.
_a_ **7.** Who wants to win?		**g.** Ryan and April are.
_c_ **8.** Who likes to spend time outdoors?		**h.** Irina does.

E. Each student in your class should take a personal possession, such as a watch, notebook, keys, sunglasses, or pen, and put it on a desk in the middle of the classroom. Then, take turns asking *Whose* questions to find the owner of each item.

Whose book is that?

It's Jaime's.

D. Look at the pictures.

• Have students look at the four pictures for 60 seconds. Then, ask them to close their books and say what they can remember about each one. Repeat each statement and ask other students if they agree. For example:
The karate student has a gold medal.
One chess player looks nervous.
• Have students open their books again. Ask them to make other statements about the pictures now that they can see them again.
• Students complete the matching activity on their own. Check the answers orally with the class. Then, have students label the people in the pictures.

E. Each student in your class should take a personal possession, such as a watch, notebook, keys, sunglasses, or pen, and put it on a desk in the middle of the classroom.

• Ask students to read the instructions and look at the sample dialogue. Answer any questions they may have about how to do the activity.
• Give each student a chance to hold up a possession from the pile and ask another student who it belongs to.

Suggestion

If you have a very large class, you may wish to divide the class into two groups. On the other hand, if you have a very small class, you may want to have each student put several objects on the desk in order to provide more opportunity for practice.

F. *How* Questions.

- Ask students to close their books. Ask each question in the first column of the chart and call on different students to give possible answers. For example:

  T: *How often do you come to school?*

  S1: *Three days a week.*

  T: *How much money do you have?*

  S2: *Two dollars.*

- Have students open their books and study the questions and answers in the chart. Answer any questions they may have. Then, have them complete the activity on their own. Review the correct answers orally with the whole class.

G. Mixed questions.

- Point out the questions in the shaded box. Ask students to identify the question type and verb tense used in each question. Answers:

  Are you a pet owner? = *Yes/No* question, present tense of *be*

  What is your address? = *Wh-* question, present of *be*

  When does class begin? = *Wh-* question, present tense

  Where did you buy that CD? = *Wh-* question, past tense

  What kind of car do you have? = *Wh-* question, present tense

- Students make up the questions individually and check them with a partner. Then, they ask you the questions. Try to be as truthful as possible in your answers.

Write two more questions for your teacher.

Students write out two additional questions to ask you. Call on different students to ask you one or two questions each. Correct question formation as necessary. Answer the questions as truthfully as you can.

F. *How* questions. Complete these questions with the correct *How* expression. Then, ask and answer the questions.

How often do you come to school?	Once a week.	Every day.
How much money do you have?	Five dollars.	A little.
How many tickets do you have?	Six.	Just one.
How long did you wait?	Six months.	Thirty minutes.
How do you get to work?	By bus.	I drive.
How far is it to your home?	Five miles.	Twenty minutes.

1. __How often_____ do you visit your native country?
2. __How many_____ siblings do you have?
3. __How much_____ do you spend on transportation to school?
4. __How long_____ are you going to live in this country?
5. __How many_____ hours do you sleep a night?
6. __How far_____ do you live from your job?
7. __How_____ did you find out about this school?
8. __How often_____ do you go to the movies?
9. __How long_____ did it take you to get to class today?
10. __How far_____ is it from your home to school?

G. Mixed questions. Form questions with these cues. Then, take turns asking your teacher each question.

1. Where / you / grow up?
   Where did you grow up?
2. How many siblings / you / have?
   How many siblings did you have?
3. What / you / want to be / when you were a child?
   What did you want to be when you were a child?
4. you / speak / another language?
   Did you speak another language?
5. How many languages / you / speak?
   How many languages do you speak?
6. When / you / start to teach at this school?
   When did you start to teach at this school?
7. What kind of music / you / like?
   What kind of music do you like?
8. Who / your favorite musician?
   Who is your favorite musician?
9. you / take / a vacation / next summer?
   When will you take a vacation next summer?

Write two more questions for your teacher.

Are you a pet owner?
What is your address?
When does class begin?
Where did you buy that CD?
What kind of car do you have?

H. Student to student dictation: How Faye became interested in cooking.

Student A: Turn to page 245.

Student B: Listen to Student A and write the questions in the correct space. When you finish, change pages.

1. Who cooked when you were growing up ?

   My father did.

2. Who taught you how to cook ?

   My father did, and I taught myself from cookbooks.

3. Do you watch cooking programs on TV ?

   Yes, I regularly watch cooking shows on public television.

4. Is your kitchen big enough for you ?

   No, but we remodeled it a few years ago to make it better for cooking.

5. What kind of cooking classes did you take before now ?

   I took Indian cooking, candy-making, and afternoon tea, to name a few.

Student B: Turn to page 245 and read questions 6–10.

Student A: Listen to Student B and write the questions in the correct space.

6. Does your husband like to cook ?

   Sometimes. He took a couple of classes with me.

7. What classes did you take together ?

   We took a Valentine's Day class and a Mexican cooking class.

8. What was the first dish that you cooked ?

   I cooked oatmeal, but it was terrible!

9. How does your husband like your food ?

   He likes everything that I cook.

10. Why did you decide to go to cooking school ?

    Because my old job wasn't fun anymore, and I love to cook.

Practice asking and answering the questions above.

H. Student to student dictation: How Faye became interested in cooking.

• Read and discuss the instructions and be sure students understand how to proceed. Help students locate the sentences on page 245.

• Students work in pairs. First Student A reads the first set of statements on page 245 and Student B writes the questions at the top of the page. Then, they reverse roles and Student A writes the questions at the bottom of the page. Check the correct answers orally with the whole class.

Practice asking and answering the questions above.

Students take turns asking and answering the questions they have just completed.

I. Interview: A collector.
(CD1, Track 21)

• Ask students to look at the pictures and comment on what they see. Ask: *Do you know what this cartoon character is called? Do you know anyone who collects something unusual?* and invite them to describe any unusual collections they have heard of.

• Review the information in the note-taking box. Make sure students know what a *comic book* is and understand how the word *case* is used in this exercise. (Here, a *case* is a container with glass sides use to display things.)

• Ask students to just listen the first time you play the audio. Then, play it a second time and have students make notes as they listen. Review the notes with the whole class.

J. Complete these questions and answers about Laurence's collection.

Students will use the notes they took in Exercise I to help them answer these questions. Review the correct questions and answers by having different students read one question each and then call on a classmate to answer the question.

I. Interview: A collector. Laurence collects items of a popular cartoon character. Listen to the interview. As you listen, take notes.

> **Note Taking**
>
> _____ comic book
> _____ objects

J. Complete these questions and answers about Laurence's collection.

1. What _did his sister buy him_____?
   His sister bought him a _n old alarm clock_____.
2. Where _did she find it_____?
   She found it at a _yard sale_____.
3. How many objects _does he have in his collection___?
   He has _more than 2,000_ objects in his collection.
4. Where _does he keep_____ his collection?
   He keeps it in _the basement of his house_____
5. Where _does he find them all_____?
   He finds them at yard sales, _garage sales_____,
   and _toy sales_____.
6. What _is he looking for_____?
   He's looking for a _1950's cookie jar_____.

Audio Script

I. Interview: A collector. Laurence collects items of a popular cartoon character. Listen to the interview. As you listen, take notes. **(CD1, Track 21)**

W: So, Laurence, tell me about your collection. How did your collection get started?
L: Well, my sister bought me an old alarm clock for my birthday in 1985.
W: Really? Where did she find it?

L: She found it at a yard sale. I really liked it, and the next thing you know, I was looking for more objects.
W: What was the first thing that you bought for yourself?
L: I bought a 1943 comic book.
W: So, how many objects do you have in your collection now?
L: How many? It's hard to say, … I think I have more than two thousand objects.
W: More than two thousand? Where do you keep them all?
L: That's a problem. When we were living in our New York apartment, it was getting

crowded, but we moved to a house a few years ago. Now I keep most of my collection in the basement. I keep most things in glass cases so that my family, friends, and I can look at everything. Many things are hanging on the walls.
W: Does your family complain about all of the things that you collect?
L: Not often. Sometimes a closet opens and a lot of stuff falls out. Then, it's a problem.
W: So, where do you find these objects?

(Audio Script continues on page 253.)

A. **Pronunciation: Tag questions.** Listen and draw an arrow showing the correct intonation. <u>Underline</u> the main verbs.

> Example 1: They <u>are having</u> a nice time, **aren't they?** ↘
> (The speaker expects a "yes" answer.)
>
> Example 2: You <u>don't like</u> to fish, **do you?** ↗
> (The speaker isn't sure of the answer.)

1. They <u>like</u> to fish, don't they? ↘
2. Fishing <u>isn't</u> expensive, is it? ↗
3. There <u>aren't</u> a lot of boats in the lake, are there? ↘
4. They <u>don't fish</u> every day, do they? ↗
5. They're <u>fishing</u> in a lake, aren't they? ↗
6. It<u>'s not</u> a hot day, is it? ↘
7. Fishing <u>isn't tiring</u>, is it? ↗
8. They <u>hope</u> to catch a lot of fish, don't they? ↘

B. **Fill in the correct tag.**

1. You are studying English, ___aren't you___?
2. You will be in class tomorrow, ___won't you___?
3. Our teacher is from the United States, ___isn't he/she___?
4. This classroom isn't small, ___is it___?
5. You're thirsty, ___aren't you___?
6. We're not from Canada, ___are we___?
7. We don't have English class on weekends, ___do we___?
8. It wasn't snowing yesterday morning, ___was it___?
9. You didn't come to class late today, ___did you___?
10. I can't leave class early today, ___can I___?

C. **Ask and answer the questions in Exercise B with a partner. Use rising or falling intonation according to the answers you expect.**

Active Grammar: Tag Questions

A. **Pronunciation: Tag questions (CD1, Track 22)**

- Read the explanations and examples aloud, emphasizing the rising and falling intonation as indicated by the arrows. Reread the examples and ask students to repeat.
- Play the first two items on the audio and ask students to follow along in their books. Then, play the rest of the items and have them mark the rising and falling intonations with arrows. Review the correct answers by writing the item numbers on the board and having a student add the rising or falling arrows as you play the audio once more.

Suggestion

Using meaningless sounds instead of words may make it easier for students to identify the intonation patterns. You might try "singing" several different sentences with tag endings using syllables like "la, la, la" in place of the actual words. Ask students to say whether the tag has *rising* or *falling* intonation.

B. **Fill in the correct tag.**

Students fill in the answers individually. Check the correct answers orally with the whole class.

C. **Ask and answer the questions in Exercise B with a partner.**

- Have students take turns asking and answering the questions. Remind them that it's important for the second student to notice which intonation the first students uses, and to respond with the expected affirmative or negative answer.

Audio Script

A. **Pronunciation: Tag questions.** Listen and draw an arrow showing the correct intonation. <u>Underline</u> the main verbs. **(CD 1, Track 22)**

Example 1: They <u>are having</u> a nice time, aren't they? ↘

Example 2: You <u>don't like</u> to fish, do you? ↗

1. They like to fish, don't they? ↘
2. Fishing isn't expensive, is it? ↗
3. There aren't a lot of boats in the lake, are there? ↘
4. They don't fish every day, do they? ↗
5. They're fishing in a lake, aren't they? ↗
6. It's not a hot day, is it? ↘
7. Fishing isn't tiring, is it? ↗
8. They hope to catch a lot of fish, don't they? ↘

Suggestion

Check for accuracy by calling on different pairs of students to role-play the questions and answers for the class. Ask the rest of the students to listen for rising and falling intonation and note if the second person answers with the expected response.

The Big Picture: My Hobby

A. What is Robert's hobby?

- Read the instructions and ask students to look at the pictures and guess what Robert's hobby is. (He likes photography.)
- Ask students to work alone to label as many of the pictures as they can. Then, have them check the labels they were able to do and complete the labeling process with a partner. Answer any questions students may have about the terms in the box at the top of the page.

B. Listen and retell the story.
(CD1, Track 23)

- Play the audio and have students just listen the first time through. Then, play it one or two more times to help increase student comprehension of the details of the story.
- Invite a volunteer to retell the story to the class. When the student finishes, ask other students to add any key facts that were omitted.

The Big Picture: My Hobby

A. What is Robert's hobby? Look at the pictures below. Label the pictures.

one-time-use camera	photography club	portrait
scanning a photo	camera lenses	wedding photo
darkroom	an SLR camera	black-and-white photo

1. wedding photo

2. one-time-use camera

3. portrait

4. an SLR camera

5. camera lenses

6. darkroom

7. a black-and-white photo

8. photography club

9. scanning a photo

B. Listen and retell the story.

76   UNIT 5

Audio Script

B. Listen and retell the story.
(CD1, Track 23)

Robert: Hobby? Sure. I have a hobby. My hobby is photography. Six days a week, I work at my father's hardware store. It's the family business. It's a good business, and it's a good job. I like talking with customers, especially our regular customers, and I like to help people with their home improvement projects, but working in a hardware store isn't my dream. My dream is to work as a full-time photographer.

First, I started taking pictures of my friends at parties. I used those one-time use cameras because they were easy to use and pretty cheap. I took pictures on family vacations, too. Then, I decided to buy a real camera with a zoom lens. My pictures started looking more interesting, but I didn't know how to use all of the features of the camera. So, I took a course at the adult community center. The course really helped, and my photos improved. Then, I took another course on black-and-white photography and started taking black-and-white photos, too. I used my family members to experiment with the different film and camera features. I continued to take photography courses and joined a photography club.

Now, I'm learning how to develop my own film. I really like it. I'm thinking about putting a darkroom in one of my closets. A few of my friends have asked me to take their wedding photos, and this weekend I'm going to take photos at my cousin's wedding. I hope I do a good job. If my cousin is happy with the pictures, that will give me the courage to start working professionally. I'm taking a computer course now so that I can learn how to scan photos and put them on a Web site. I want to advertise on the Internet. I'll put some of my best photos on the Internet and maybe someone will hire me.

C. Listen and write the questions. Then, circle the answers.

1. Where does Robert work _____?
   a. At a film store.   **b.** At a hardware store.   c. In the morning.

2. How many days a week does he work _____?
   a. Every day.   **b.** Six days a week.   c. Weekends only.

3. What is his dream _____?
   a. To get married.   b. To open a hardware store.   **c.** To be a photographer.

4. What kind of camera did he first use _____?
   a. A Polaroid® camera.   b. An SLR camera.   **c.** A one-time-use camera.

5. Where did he learn to take better photos _____?
   a. From classes.   b. A few years ago.   c. From a friend.

6. Where is he going to take photos this weekend _____?
   a. At a birthday party.   **b.** At a family event.   c. Take photos.

7. What course is he taking now _____?
   a. A color photo course.   b. A career course.   **c.** A computer course.

D. Complete each question with the correct word from the list below. Then, ask and answer the questions with a partner.

Is	Was	Were	Does	Did

1. __Does__ Robert work for his father?
2. __Was__ working at the store his dream?
3. __Was__ his first camera expensive?
4. __Did__ his father teach him how to use the camera?
5. __Did__ he take pictures of his friends?
6. __Were__ his photos better after he took a course?
7. __Is__ he a member of a photography club?
8. __Does__ he know how to scan photos?
9. __Is__ he going to put a darkroom in his father's store?
10. __Does__ he want to become a professional photographer?

C. Listen and write the questions. (CD1, Track 24)

• Point out that this exercise has two parts. First students write the questions they hear on the tape in this exercise. Then, they answer each question based on the facts in the story they listened to in Exercise B.

• Review the correct answers by calling on one student to read aloud the question. Then, have a second student say the letter and the words of the correct answer.

D. Complete each question with the correct word from the list below.

• Have students complete the questions individually. Review the answers orally with the class.

• Students take turns asking and answering the questions with a partner. Correct the exercise by calling on one student to read aloud each question, while a second student gives the correct *Yes/No* answer.

Audio Script

C. Listen and write the questions.
Then, circle the answers. (CD1, Track 24)

1. Where does Robert work?
2. How many days a week does he work?
3. What is his dream?
4. What kind of camera did he first use?
5. Where did he learn to take better photos?
6. Where is he going to take photos this weekend?
7. What course is he taking now?

☀ Reading:
Stamp Collecting

A. Before You Read.

Ask students to answer the questions at the top. Then, talk about the pictures of stamps on this page. Ask questions such as:

What kinds of pictures are on these stamps? What country is each stamp from?

B. Vocabulary.

• Point out the list of five words and phrases students will be looking for as they scan the reading. Remind them that when they scan they should not try to read and understand every single word. They should keep the target word or phrase in mind and move their eyes down the page until they find it.

• Students scan the story and write the definitions. Have students write the definitions on the board. Review the definitions with the class.

• Students read the story at their own rates. When they finish ask some general comprehension questions. For example:

T: *What kinds of things do people collect?*
S1: *Coins, records, cars, dishes, furniture, and stamps.*
T: *What do the pictures on the stamps reflect?*
S2: *They tell us about a country's history, people, art, and culture. Some stamps are worth $15,000 to $20,000.*

A. Before You Read. (Answers will vary.)

1. Do you have a collection at home?
2. Do you notice the stamps on your letters?
3. Do you keep stamps that are particularly interesting or beautiful?
4. Look at the stamps in the reading. What countries do they come from?

B. Vocabulary. Scan the reading to find the definitions of the following vocabulary. Then, write the definitions. (Suggested answers below.)

1. greeting cards: <u>birthday and anniversary cards and others</u>
2. philatelic: <u>to do with stamp collecting</u>
3. auctions: <u>public sales</u>
4. a fresh stamp: <u>a new and not used stamp</u>
5. a cancellation mark: <u>a black circular mark on a stamp</u>

Collecting is one of many popular hobbies. Popular items to collect include dolls of all kinds, coins, records, cars, dishes, furniture, and more.

The United States Postal Service (U.S.P.S.) delivers more than two hundred billion pieces of mail a year, and 46 percent of the world's letters and **greeting cards,** such as birthday and anniversary cards, are delivered by the U.S.P.S. Each of those cards and letters cannot be delivered without a stamp. Stamp collecting has been a leisure activity for many years.

Every country's postal service sells stamps that reflect its history, people, arts, and culture. Stamp collectors can buy stamps of animals, flowers, historical events, and so forth. Most countries have clubs or societies that serious stamp collectors can join to share information. In addition, there are societies or clubs for collectors who specialize in particular categories of stamps. For example, collectors can join a Christmas **Philatelic** Club, whose members collect Christmas-related stamps.

One famous stamp collector was President Franklin D. Roosevelt. He was so interested in stamps that he designed several stamps. His stamp designs reflected what was happening in the country at the time. It was Roosevelt's design that was used for the first Mother's Day stamp. A woman wrote the President a letter giving him the idea. The stamp was first available on May 2, 1934.

Stamp collectors add to their collections by checking letter envelopes and postcards, and by attending stamp collecting societies and **auctions** – public sales where people compete to buy a valuable stamp. The Internet is another place where collectors can buy and sell valuable stamps and exchange information with others about hard-to-find stamps.

Many factors determine the value of a stamp. **A fresh stamp** is new and not used. The black circular mark that you usually see on a stamp on your mail is called a **cancellation mark.** This mark tells the date and place where the letter was mailed. If only part of the stamp is covered by the mark, the stamp is considered partially cancelled.

An example of how valuable a stamp can become is the story of the "Inverted Jenny" stamp. The "Inverted Jenny" is one of a group of stamps that have printing errors. This stamp was sold at the end of World War I in 1918. A "Jenny" was an old airplane and, by mistake, the post office printed the plane flying upside down. The exact story is not clear, but one story is that a stamp collector went to a post office and asked for one hundred airmail stamps. He noticed the mistake on the stamps, and later, he sold the stamps to another collector for $15,000, who sold them to another collector for $20,000. In 2002, one single "Inverted Jenny" sold at auction for $135,000.

There are also stamps that raise awareness of social or medical problems and may even earn money for an organization. On July 29, 1998, the U.S.P.S. issued the "Breast Cancer Awareness" stamp, which was the first U.S. stamp to earn money for a cause. Two hundred million stamps were originally printed, but the stamp was so popular that eighty million more stamps were printed. The stamp was valued at 33 cents, but it cost 40 cents to purchase. The profits from sales raised 27.2 million dollars for breast cancer research. The next time you receive a letter, pay attention to the stamp. Will it become part of a collection?

C. Reading for details. Read each statement. (Circle) *T* for *true* or *F* for *false.*

1. The U.S. Postal Service delivers more than half of the world's mail.   T   (F)

2. Each country has stamps that show its culture.   (T)   F

3. Some collectors collect particular types of stamps.   (T)   F

4. President Roosevelt's mother suggested the Mother's Day stamp.   T   (F)

5. Stamp collectors sometimes compete to buy a stamp.   (T)   F

6. A fresh stamp has a cancellation mark.   T   (F)

7. The "Inverted Jenny" was valuable because it was a new stamp.   T   (F)

8. Some stamps can raise money for social causes.   (T)   F

D. Look at your letters at home. Bring in letters that have interesting stamps. Look for examples of cancellation marks. Share them with your classmates.

C. Reading for details.

Students complete this exercise on their own and check their answers with a partner. Review the correct answers with the whole class. Ask the student giving the answer to also read aloud the sentence or sentences that support the answer.

D. Look at your letters at home.

After showing their envelopes to the class, invite students to display them on a bulletin board in the room.

Suggestion

Invite students who have other types of collections to bring some of these items to school and share them with the class. Encourage students to ask questions about each other's collections.

Writing Our Stories: How to Cut a Pineapple

A. Read.

Have students read the text straight though without stopping. Then, have them read it again, underlining anything they don't understand. Ask students to read the underlined portions aloud. Rephrase them in your own words and ask questions that will help students understand the meaning of these sentences.

B. A process.

• Read through the lettered list of procedures with students. Ask them to read aloud any words or phrases they don't understand. Explain their meaning using explanations, gestures, and simple diagrams on the board.
• Students number the list individually and check their answers with a partner. Have a student write the correct answers on the board and ask the rest of the class to check their work against it.

Writing Our Stories: How to Cut a Pineapple

A. Read.
(Circles are the answers for page 81, exercise C.)

Pineapple is a very popular fruit in my country and in other Carribean, South American, and Southest Asian countries. Some people do not know how to cut a pineapple properly, so they waste the fruit. (First,) put the pineapple upside down on a table for a few minutes so that the most delicious juice can drip into the rest of the pineapple. (Second,) twist the green top off. (Then) with a sharp knife, cut the pineapple in half lengthwise. (Then) cut the halves in half. Take one quarter of the pineapple, and slice off the tough inner core. Some people like to eat this part, so don't throw it away. (Finally,) slice the pineapple off the tough skin, and slice it into smaller pieces. It's ready to serve.

B. A process. Read the following sentences about how to prepare stamps for a collection. Put the steps in order from 1 to 10. Then, rewrite the sentences in paragraph form in your notebook. Use the transition words in Exercise A.

   9   **a.** Flatten the dry stamps in a heavy book for a few days.

   7   **b.** Rinse the stamps in the clean water.

   2   **c.** First, find a few envelopes with interesting stamps and cut them off the envelope.

   4   **d.** Put the stamps in the small bowl, picture side up.

   1   **e.** It is easy to start a stamp collection.

   6   **f.** Get a second bowl of clean water.

   5   **g.** Wet the stamps until they easily slide off the envelope paper.

   3   **h.** Fill a small bowl with lukewarm water.

  10   **i.** Finally, put the stamps in a stamp album.

   8   **j.** Place the stamps on dry newspaper and let them dry.

C. Transition words. You can use the following transition words to describe a process. Look at the reading on page 80 and (circle) the transition words.

(See page 80 for the Answer Key.)

- First,
- Second, Third,
- Next,
- After that,
- Then,
- Finally,

D. In your notebook, write directions on how to do something related to one of your hobbies or interests. Use transition words in your paragraph. Here are some examples of topics. *(Answers will vary.)*

- How to play dominoes
- How to take care of an aquarium
- How to take care of a pet
- How to buy a bicycle

E. Edit. Find and correct the mistakes.

1. What are you doing?
2. Why does she have so many pets?
3. Where did you find these stamps?
4. How long will they play this game?
5. Are you going to work in your garden?
6. Who played a sport last weekend?
7. Whom are they playing tennis with?

 Looking at the Internet

There are many Web sites that have information about hobbies and leisure activities. Click on **Search** and enter the name of a hobby or activity that you find interesting. For example, search "coin collecting," "bowling," or "salsa dancing."

C. Transition words.

After reviewing the answers, ask students which transition words are not found in the reading on page 80. Have them suggest appropriate places in the reading where those words could be used correctly.

D. In your notebook, write directions on how to do something related to one of your hobbies or interests.

Brainstorm with students a list of possible topics for this writing assignment. Help students choose topics. The writing can be done as homework.

Suggestion

If appropriate for your class, have students do the writing in class with partners to provide support. Remind students to use transition words from Exercise C. Move around the room offering help as needed.

E. Edit.

Have students correct the sentences on their own. Review the correct answers with the whole class.

Looking at the Internet

- Encourage students to write down three things about each useful Web site they find:
  1. The Web address
  2. The name of the Web site
  3. One interesting or unusual fact they learned
- During the next class, have students share their information orally and write on the board any Web addresses others may wish to visit.

A. Write questions with these cues.

Ask students to write out the questions and answers on their own. After reviewing the correct question forms with the class, ask different students to read aloud their answers to each question.

A. Write questions with these cues. Then, write the answers.
(Answers will vary.)

1. who / your teacher?
   Who is your teacher?

2. who / immigrate / to this country with you?
   Who immigrated to this country with you?

3. where / you / live /?
   Where do you live? / Where are you living? / Where will you live?

4. when / you / come / to this country?
   When did you come to this country?

5. how / you / feel / today?
   How are you feeling today?

6. what / you / do / right now?
   What are you doing right now?

7. what kind of books / you / like?
   What kind of books do you like?

8. whom / you / usually / speak English with?
   Who do you usually speak English with?

9. how many people / in your family?
   How many people are there in your family?

10. why / you / take / this class?
    Why did you take this class? Why are you taking this class?

Grammar Summary

> **1. Yes/No questions**

You are a student.	**Are you** a student?
She is jogging.	**Is she** jogging?
They were tired.	**Were they** tired?
We are going to watch TV.	**Are we** going to watch TV?
We study English.	**Do you study** English?
I had a test yesterday.	**Did you have** a test yesterday?
She will get married soon.	**Will she** get married soon?

> **2. Who questions** **Who** takes a singular verb form.

Who is a student?	I am.
Who is jogging?	They are.
Who is going to play soccer?	Those girls are.
Who studies every day?	We do.
Who had a test yesterday?	I did.

> **3. Whom/who** **Whom** and **who** can both refer to the object in a sentence. Both are used in speaking and in writing, but **whom** is considered more formal. **Whom** is often used with a preposition.

Jamie sends e-mails to **his cousins**.	**Whom** does he send e-mails to?
	To whom does he send e-mails?
	Who does he send e-mails to?

> **4. Whose questions** **Whose** refers to possession. A singular or plural noun can follow **whose.**

Whose photo is that?	That is my photo.
Whose CDs did you borrow?	I borrowed my cousin's CDs.

> **5. Wh-questions**

Where were you yesterday?	**Why** do you collect stamps?
What do you do in your free time?	**How much** is your collection worth?
When are you going to take a trip?	**How many** stamps do you have?
How did you learn how to do that?	**How long** does it take to get there?

> **6. Tag questions** Tag questions have rising or falling intonation. Falling intonation shows that the speaker expects a "yes" answer. Rising intonation shows that the speaker isn't sure of the answer. The tag depends on the main verb.

You like football, **don't you?**	It isn't expensive, **is it?**
Your favorite music is classical, **isn't it?**	You won't be free tomorrow, **will you?**
They didn't drive, **did they?**	We're having a good time, **aren't we?**

Grammar Summary

- Review the six grammar explanations and sample sentences with the class. Invite students to make up alternate sentences for each example in the chart. For example, in place of *Whose photo is that?* a student might say, *Whose book is this?*
- Answer any questions students may have about the grammar items.
- See the Grammar Summary Expansion on page 262 for a more complete explanation of these grammar points.

Unit 6
Driving

Discuss what the person in the unit title art is doing. Ask:

• *What do you see next to the number 6?* (A woman holding a steering wheel)

• *What does her hair look like?* (It's blowing in the wind.)

• *What does this picture have to do with the unit?* (The picture shows a woman driving a car. Her foot is on the accelerator. She must be going fast because of the way her hair is blowing around.)

A. Read each traffic sign.

• Point out the twelve lettered descriptions at the top of the page. Read each one aloud and call on different students to re-state the descriptions in their own words. For example:

  T: a. *You must not ride bikes here.*

  S1: *People aren't allowed to ride a bicycle in this place.*

  T: b. *Trucks must not use this road.*

  S2: *You can drive a car on this road, but not a truck.*

• Ask students to match the signs and rules individually and then check their answers with a partner. As you check the answers with the whole class, explain any signs that students still don't understand.

Driving

A. Read each traffic sign. Match each sign with the correct traffic rule.

a. You must not ride bikes here.

b. Trucks must not use this road.

c. You must not turn left.

d. You must stop for pedestrians.

e. You must not park here or you will be towed.

f. You must stay to the right.

g. You must look out for deer.

h. You must slow down. This is a school zone.

i. You must not park here.

j. You must slow down. The road is slippery when wet.

k. You must slow down and be prepared to stop. Construction ahead.

l. You must turn right. One-way street.

1. _f_   2. _g_   3. _k_

4. _i_   5. _d_   6. _h_

7. _a_   8. _e_   9. _b_

10. _l_   11. _c_   12. _j_

Active Grammar: Modals—Must/Must not

Must shows rules, obligation, or necessity.
You **must** stop at a stop sign.

Must not shows that an action is against the law or rules, or is not permitted.
Drivers **must not drive** through a red light.

I He Drivers	must	stop at a red light. drive at the speed limit.
	must not mustn't	drive without a license.

A. Use each sentence to state the traffic law. Use *must* or *must not*.

1. Stop at a stop sign. — *You **must stop** at a stop sign.*
2. Pass cars on the right. — *You **must not pass** on the right.*
3. Pay traffic fines. — You must pay traffic fines.
4. Drink and drive. — You must not drink and drive.
5. Register your car. — You must register your car.
6. Drive over the speed limit. — You must not drive over the speed limit.
7. Leave the scene of an accident. — You must not leave the scene of an accident.
8. Wear your seat belt. — You must wear your seat belt.
9. Stop for a school bus with flashing lights. You must stop for a school bus with flashing lights.
10. Drive without a license. — You must not drive without a license.

B. Rules at school. Read each rule. Check (✓) *Yes* or *No* about your school. (Answers will vary.)

Rules	Yes	No
1. We must arrive on time.		
2. We must pay for this class.		
3. We must call our teacher if we are absent.		
4. We must wear uniforms.		
5. We must speak English.		
6. We must buy our books.		

Write three more rules about your school. (Answers will vary.)

1. We must _____
2. We must _____
3. We must not _____

Driving **85**

Active Grammar:
Modals—Must/Must not

A. Use each sentence to state the traffic law.

- Review the grammar explanation and the sample sentences with the class. Ask students to give original examples of the correct use of *must* and *must not*.
- Do the exercise with the whole class. Answer any questions students may have.

Suggestion

If appropriate for your class, give students a quick oral review of *must* and *must not*. Have them close their books. In random order, read aloud the sentences in Exercise A and call on different students to state the traffic law using *must* or *must not*.

B. Rules at school.

Students complete the exercise and check their answers with a partner. Review the answers with the whole class.

Write three more rules about your school.

Students write the rules on their own. Review their responses orally with the whole class.

Suggestion

Write several of the student responses on the board and have students practice reading the list to a partner.

Teacher's Guide, Unit 6 **85**

☀ Have to/Doesn't have to/ Don't have to

A. Complete the sentences with *have to* or *has to.*

• Review the grammar explanation and the sample sentences with the class. Ask students to give original examples of the correct use of *have to* and *has to.*

• Do the exercise with the whole class. Point out the use of *has to* with *he* and *she.* Answer any questions students may have.

B. Restate each sentence.

Review the explanation and sample sentences at the beginning of the exercise. Have students take turns restating the sentences to a partner. Then, call on different students to restate one sentence each for the class.

☀ Have to/Doesn't have to/Don't have to

> **Have to** shows *obligation* or *necessity*. **Have to** can be used in most situations instead of **must.**
>
> I **have to** get car insurance.
> You **have to** do your homework.
> She **has to** babysit her niece.

I You We They	have to	stop at a red light. drive at the speed limit. drive with a license.
She He	has to	

A. Complete the sentences with *have to* or *has to.* Use the verbs in parentheses.

1. She __has to move__ her car to another area. (move)
2. She __has to pay__ for the ticket. (pay)
3. She __has to mail__ the fine to City Hall in a few days. (mail)
4. He __has to change__ the tires. (change)
5. He __has to call__ for help. (call)
6. He __has to buy__ new tires. (buy)

7. They __have to sell__ their sports car. (sell)
8. They __have to buy__ a bigger car. (buy)
9. They __have to get__ a car seat. (get)

B. Restate each sentence. Use *doesn't have to* or *don't have to.*

> **Doesn't have to / Don't have to** shows that something is *not* necessary.
> You **don't have to** own a car.

I You We They	do not have to don't have to	buy a new car. work today. go to school today.
She He	does not have to doesn't have to	

1. It's not necessary for a new driver to buy a new car.

   A new driver **doesn't have to** *buy a new car.*

2. It's not necessary for you to have a radio in your car.
   You don't have to have a radio in your car.
3. It's not necessary for new drivers to have jobs.
   New drivers don't have to have jobs.
4. It's not necessary for a new learner to go to a private driving school.
   A new learner doesn't have to go to a private driving school.
5. It's not necessary for drivers to have cell phones.
   Drivers don't have to have cell phones.
6. It's not necessary for a new driver to have a high school diploma.
   A new driver doesn't have to have a high school diploma.
7. It's not necessary for drivers to wash their cars every week.
   Drivers don't have to wash their cars every week.

C. Listen to Rebecca talk about her schedule. Check (✓) the tasks that she has completed.

Task	To Do (✓)
buy stamps	✓
mail her bills	
do the laundry	
go to the supermarket	
make a bank deposit	✓
visit her parents	✓
make a dentist appointment	
put gas in her car	

Ask and answer questions about Rebecca's to-do list. Use the information in her list in Exercise C.

Does Rebecca have to buy stamps?

No, she doesn't. She bought some yesterday.

D. Tell a partner the things that you had to do or didn't have to do before you came to this country and when you first arrived in this country.
(Answers will vary.)

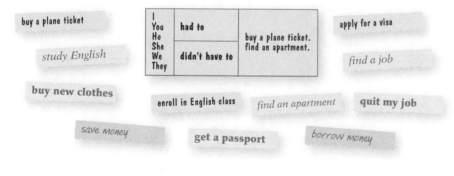

buy a plane ticket

study English

buy new clothes

save money

	had to	
I You He She We They	didn't have to	buy a plane ticket. find an apartment.

enroll in English class

find an apartment

get a passport

apply for a visa

find a job

quit my job

borrow money

Driving **87**

Audio Script

C. Listen to Rebecca talk about her schedule. (CD2, Track 1)

Uh, let's see, what do I have to do today? Do I need stamps? Hmm. I don't think so. I bought some yesterday. Here they are. OK, so I have to mail my gas bill and my phone bill. I can stop by the post office on the way to the Laundromat. I have to do some laundry or I won't have anything to wear. While my clothes are in the wash, I have to go to the supermarket to get some eggs, milk, and something to eat for dinner. Oh, did I deposit my check in my checking account? Yes, I did, and here's the deposit slip from last Saturday. I don't have to visit my parents today. I saw them yesterday morning. Oh, my tooth hurts. I have to make a dentist appointment right away. OK, I think I'm ready to go, but I have to remember to put some gas in the car. I think it's almost on empty.

C. Listen to Rebecca talk about her schedule.
(CD2, Track 1)

Students just listen the first time you play the audio. The second time, they can check the tasks Rebecca has completed. The third time through, they check their answers. Review the correct answers orally with the class.

Ask and answer questions about Rebecca's to-do list.

• Explain that the answers in this part of the activity are based on the audio they have just listened to. Play the audio again if students want an additional review before doing this part of the activity. Answer any questions about the audio they may have.
• Point out the sample question and answer. Then, have pairs practice asking and answering the questions. Review the answers with the class by having different pairs present one question and answer each.

D. Tell a partner the things that you had to do or didn't have to do before you came to this country and when you first arrived in this country.

Students complete the activity with a partner. Review the answers by calling on different students to say one sentence each. (Answers may vary.)

☀ Can/Can't

 A. Pronunciation:
Can versus *can't*.
(CD2, Track 2)

- Review the grammar explanation and the sample sentences with the class. Ask students to give original examples of the correct use of *can* and *can't*.
- Play the audio once as students just listen. Answer any questions they may have. Then, play the audio once or twice more and have students complete the sentences and check their answers with a partner. Review the correct answers with the whole class.

Suggestion

If appropriate for your class, explain the differences in the pronunciation of *can* and *can't*:

The word can *is usually shortened so that it sounds almost like* kən. *The word* can't *ends in the letter* t, *but you often cannot hear that* t *pronounced. When you hear the word* can't, *it may just sound like the letter* a *is held longer.*

Demonstrate by repeating pairs of *can/can't* phrases several times, emphasizing the differences: *can go* (kən go), *can't go* (kaah go).

B. Find someone who . . .

- Read the instructions and answer any questions about how to do the activity. Remind students to write only the student's name after each question, not a full-sentence answer.
- Set a time limit (perhaps ten minutes) for students to complete the activity.

 ☀ Can/Can't

> *Can* shows ability or possibility.
> I **can** drive a truck.
>
> *Can* also shows that an action is permitted.
> ***Can't/Cannot*** shows inability or an action that is *not* permitted.
> I **can** drive at night by myself.
> You **can't** drive through red lights.

I You She He We They	can / can't	drive. park in this area.

 A. Pronunciation: *Can* versus *can't*. Listen to Marcus talk about his driving experience. Complete the sentences with *can* or *can't*.

1. He ___can't___ drive very well.
2. He ___can___ drive only with a licensed driver in the car.
3. He ___can___ back up.
4. He ___can't___ parallel park.
5. He ___can___ drive on a busy highway.
6. He ___can't___ drive at night alone.
7. He ___can't___ drive with the radio on.

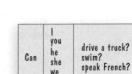

B. Find someone who . . . Walk around the room. Ask your classmates what they can do. If someone answers, "Yes, I can," write the name in the space. If someone answers, "No, I can't," ask another person. (Answers will vary.)

Can	I you he she we they	drive a truck? swim? speak French?

Question	Name
1. speak another language	
2. dance	
3. cook well	
4. bake a cake	
5. type	
6. drive	
7. swim	
8. use a computer	
9. play a musical instrument	

88 UNIT 6

Audio Script

A. Pronunciation: *Can* versus *can't*. Listen to Marcus talk about his driving experience. Complete the sentences with *can* or *can't*. **(CD2, Track 2)**

I'm a terrible driver. I finally got my driving permit three months ago, and it took me three tries to pass the written test. Now, I can only drive with a licensed driver in my car, so my mom or my dad has to drive in the car with me. I can back up, but I can't parallel park. I'm a terrible parker, so I sometimes drive around the corner a few times to find an easy space to park in. I can drive on a busy highway, but I feel nervous. I can't drive at night alone because I'm only 17. I can't drive with the radio on because I can't concentrate. Maybe I need to take the bus.

88 ENGLISH IN ACTION 4

C. Can you identify the car parts? Label the pictures.

I can identify **all / most / some / none** of the car parts.

accelerator	hood	stick shift
brake	horn	tires
bumper	signal	trunk
clutch	steering wheel	windshield
		windshield wipers

trunk

hood

bumper

bumper

tires

steering wheel

signal

horn

2 windshield wipers/windshield

shift stick

clutch/brake/accelerator

 D. Interview: An accident. Listen to Emily talk about her car accident.

1. When was the accident? *Yesterday.*
2. Was Emily hurt? *No.*
3. Where did the accident happen? *On a hill.*
4. Who were the drivers in the accident? *An elderly woman and Emily.*
5. Who caused the accident? *The elderly woman.*
6. What did Emily have to do after the accident happened? *Exchange insurance information with the woman.*
7. Did Emily have to call the police? *No.*
8. What does she have to do now? *File a police report.*

Driving **89**

C. Can you identify the car parts?

- Read the list of words aloud and ask students to repeat. Then, have them write as many of the words as they can in the correct places on the pictures.
- Review the list of words with the whole class and have students correct any mistakes and add any missing labels. Practice the pronunciation of words such as *accelerator, stickshift,* and so forth as necessary.

D. Interview: An accident. (CD2, Track 3)

- Have students just listen the first time you play the audio. Invite two students to describe the accident. Play the tape again and invite another student to describe the accident again.
- Play the audio again and have students listen carefully. Call on a different student to answer each question orally. Play the audio a third time to invite students to confirm or question the answers given by other students.

Audio Script

D. Interview: An accident. Listen to Emily talk about her car accident. (CD2, Track 3)

A: Hi, Emily. Wow! What happened to your car?

B: You won't believe it. I was in a car accident yesterday.

A: Are you OK?

B: Yeah, I'm fine, but look at my car! It's a mess!

A: It does look pretty bad. What happened?

B: Well, I was waiting for a light on a hill. There was one car in front of me. The driver was an elderly woman and her dog was sitting on her lap. The dog started barking at a kid on a bicycle and started jumping all over the car. The woman wasn't paying attention and her car started to roll back towards me.

A: Didn't you honk your horn?

B: Of course I did. I couldn't back up, I kept honking my horn. Her car started moving faster and then, it smashed into my car!

A: Unbelievable. What happened next?

B: Well, I had to get out of the car and exchange insurance information with the woman.

A: Did you call the police?

B: No, we didn't. No one was hurt and I was late for an appointment, but I had to call my insurance company right away. I just talked to the company and they told me that I had to file a police report. I'm on my way to the police station now.

A: Good luck with your car.

B: Thanks.

☀ Should/Shouldn't

A. Look at the grammar explanation.

• Review the grammar explanation and the sample sentences with the class. Ask students to give original examples of the correct use of *should* and *shouldn't*.

• Students complete the activity in small groups. Set a time limit, perhaps ten minutes, for this activity. For each item in the exercise, call on a different student to tell whether they agree or disagree and give reasons. After each presentation, invite a person who may feel differently to respond.

B. Give advice in each situation.

• Ask students to work in pairs and discuss the answers to each situation. Move around the room, offering language support as needed.

• Review the answers by asking two or three people to explain to the class their response to each question. Write any new words on the board and suggest that students copy into their notebooks any that they think will be useful to them.

☀ Should/Shouldn't

A. Look at the grammar explanation. Then, read each statement. Check (✓) your opinion. Then, discuss your reasons with a small group of classmates.
(Answers will vary.)

> *Should* expresses an opinion or advice.
> I **should buy** a smaller car.
> Reason: Small cars get good gas mileage.
> *Shouldn't/Should not* shows that something is *not* a good idea.
> You **shouldn't put** your packages in the back seat.
> Reason: Someone will see them.
> You **should put** them in your trunk.

I You She He We They	should / shouldn't	drive at night. buy that car.

Opinion	Agree	Disagree
1. Drivers should drive more carefully near elementary schools.		
2. Teenagers are too young to drive cars.		
3. Small children should always ride in the back seat of a car.		
4. People over 80 years old should not drive.		
5. Drivers should not eat and drive at the same time.		
6. The highway speed limit is too low.		
7. All drivers should have car insurance.		

B. Give advice in each situation. Use *should* or *shouldn't*. Discuss your answers with a classmate. (Answers are opinions and should vary.)

1. A family of five children is shopping for a new car. What kind of car should the family buy?

2. Chen wants to learn how to drive. Who should teach him—his grandfather, his mother, or a private teacher?

3. Valeria is 16 years old. In her state, teenagers can drive at 16 years of age. Should she try to get her driver's license now, or should she wait until she is out of high school?

4. Pierre is a new immigrant to the United States. Everyone at his job speaks his native language. He doesn't speak any English. What should he do?

5. Rafael and Marcello are classmates in English class. They are from different countries. They need conversation practice. What should they do?

6. Andrea is new in town. She's living with her aunt and uncle, but she doesn't know anyone her own age. How should she meet some people her own age?

90 UNIT 6

> **Had better** expresses a strong warning.
> **Had better** is stronger than **should.**
>
> You'd **better check** your tire.
> (Or you'll have a flat tire.)
>
> I'd **better not miss** another class.
> (Or I'll fail the class.)

I You She He We They	had better 'd better	wear your seat belt. use a car seat.
	had better not 'd better not	drive without a license. forget to fill the gas tank.

 A. Pronunciation: *'d better / 'd better not.* Listen and complete the sentences.

1. <u>I'd better stay</u> home. I don't feel well.
2. <u>You'd better put</u> the baby in the car seat.
3. <u>She'd better call</u> the police and report the accident.
4. <u>We'd better bring</u> the party inside. It's beginning to rain.
5. <u>He'd better eat</u> another piece of cake. He'll get sick.
6. <u>You'd better not get</u> a dog. Your landlord won't allow it.
7. <u>She'd better slow</u> down. The roads are icy.
8. <u>I'd better not buy</u> that. I can't afford it.

Listen again and repeat the sentences to a partner.

B. Give a warning in each situation. Use *'d better* or *'d better not.*
(Answers will vary. Sample answers below.)

You'd better wear a helmet.

You'd better put the baby in a carseat.

You'd better not put on makeup when you drive.

You'd better get out your license and registration.

You'd better turn on your fog lights.

You'd better turn down the music in the car.

Audio Script

A. Pronunciation: *'d better/'d better not.*
Listen and complete the sentences.
(CD2, Track 4)

1. **I'd better stay** home. I don't feel well.
2. **You'd better put** the baby in the car seat.
3. **She'd better call** the police and report the accident.
4. **We'd better bring** the party inside. It's beginning to rain.
5. **He'd better not eat** another piece of cake. He'll get sick.
6. **You'd better not get** a dog. Your landlord won't allow it.
7. **She'd better slow** down. The roads are icy.
8. **I'd better not buy** that. I can't afford it.

 *Had better/
Had better not*

 **A. Pronunciation: *'d better/
'd better not.* (CD2, Track 4)**

• Read and discuss the grammar explanation. Point out that *had better* is stronger than *should.* Review the sample sentences and answer any questions students may have.

• Have students just listen the first time you play the audio. Then, tell them they must listen carefully and fill in their answers as you play it the second time. Review the answers by playing the audio, pausing after each sentence and asking one student to repeat the full sentence. The other students check their answers.

Listen again and repeat the sentences to a partner.
(CD2, Track 4)

Play the audio one more time. Then, have students take turns repeating the sentences to each other in pairs.

Suggestion

Extend the practice with *'d better* and *'d better not* by reading aloud the second sentences that appear in some items and having students come up with a different warning. For example:

T: *I don't feel well.*
S1: *Yes, you'd better not go to work.*
T: *The roads are icy.*
S2: *We'd better not drive tonight.*

B. Give a warning in each situation.

• Do the exercise with the whole class. Repeat each warning given by a student, confirming or correcting the response. Then, call on another student to repeat the warning.

A. Jennifer is 17 years old and very excited. (CD2, Track 5)

- Ask students to read through the chart before you play the audio. Answer any questions they may have about vocabulary.
- Have students just listen the first time you play the audio. Then, play it again and ask them to fill in the missing information. Play the tape a third time so they can check their answers. Review the correct answers with the whole class.
- Looking at the chart, ask individual students to describe one thing Jennifer has to do in order to get her license.

☀ The Big Picture: Getting a Driver's License

A. Jennifer is 17 years old and very excited. Listen to Jennifer talk about getting her driver's license. Complete the chart. What does she have to do to get her license?

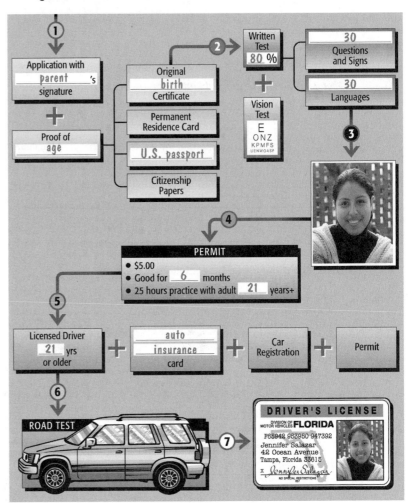

Audio Script

A. Jennifer is 17 years old and very excited. (CD2, Track 5)

I am so excited. Tomorrow, my mother's taking me to the Division of Motor Vehicles to get my learner's permit. I have to have my parent's signature on my application because I'm only 17. I have to show proof of my age, too. I grew up in Peru, but I was born here in the U.S., so I can show my U.S. passport. People can also use original birth certificates, permanent resident cards, or citizenship papers. I'm going to take the written test today. There are 30 questions and signs on the test. I have to get 80 percent correct to pass the test. I speak English well, but my reading is still a little weak. I don't have to take the test in English because the DMV gives the test in 30 languages, including mine—Spanish. I also have to take a vision test to check my eyesight. Then, they are going to take my picture.

After I pay five dollars, I can get my learner's permit. After I get the permit, I can use it for three to six months to practice. I'll need a lot of practice, about 25 hours or more. I was hoping that my older sister could teach me to drive, but in my state, I must have an adult 21 years or older in the car with me. That's the law for people under 18. My sister's only 19, so my mother's going to teach me.

I'm going to practice as much as I can before the road test. My mother will drive me to the road test because I must have a licensed driver 21 years of age or older in the car. My parents will get the auto insurance card, and we need to show the car's registration. Of course, I also have to show my permit. Then, I can take the road test. Wish me luck!

B. Getting the facts. Read each sentence about the process of getting a driver's license. Circle *T* for *true* or *F* for *false*. If the answer is false, tell the correct information.

1. Jennifer must take two tests before she gets her permit.   (T)   F
2. Jennifer has to show her birth certificate for proof of age.   T   (F)
3. Jennifer can take the written test in her native language.   (T)   F
4. Jennifer has to get 90 percent correct to pass the written test.   T   (F)
5. She can practice six months with her permit.   (T)   F
6. Jennifer's sister can teach her how to drive.   T   (F)
7. Eighteen-year-olds must drive with someone 21 or older.   T   (F)
8. Jennifer has to show an auto insurance card to take the road test.   (T)   F
9. Jennifer must go to the road test with a licensed driver.   (T)   F

Talk about getting a driver's license in your state. How is the process the same or different from Jennifer's state? Has anyone in the class gotten a license recently?

C. Ask and answer questions about getting a driver's license.

B. Getting the facts.

Students complete the exercise individually and check their answers with a partner. Review the correct answers with the whole class, having students give the correct information for each answer that they marked *false*.

Talk about getting a driver's license in your state.

Do this activity with the whole class. Help students pool their information to uncover as many facts as possible about the process.

C. Ask and answer questions about getting a driver's license.

Ask two students to read the sample dialogue. Then, have students ask and answer questions in pairs. Review the answers with the whole class by calling on different pairs to say one question and answer each.

☀ Reading:
The Written Test

A. Before You Read.

Ask the students to look at the license. Ask them:

What state is this license from? (Florida)
Where does the driver live?
(12 Bay Street in Tampa)

Then, discuss the answers to the questions at the top of the page.

B. Read each sample question of a driving test.

Ask students to read through the test questions and answers and raise their hands if there is anything they don't understand. Answer questions as necessary. Students complete the test on their own.

☀ Reading: The Written Test

A. Before You Read.
(Answers will vary.)

1. Do you have a driver's license?
2. If so, did you take the written test in English?
3. What was the minimum passing score?

B. Read each sample question of a driving test. Fill in the circle next to the correct answer.

● ⊗ ☑ ◑
Yes No No No

1. A driver approaching a flashing red traffic signal must . . .
   ○ **a.** drive carefully without stopping.
   ● **b.** stop first, and then, pass through the intersection.
   ○ **c.** go through the light slowly.
   ○ **d.** slow down at the intersection.

2. You must stop your vehicle . . .
   ○ **a.** at an intersection with a stop sign.
   ○ **b.** where there is a red light.
   ○ **c.** when a traffic officer orders you to stop.
   ● **d.** all of the above.

3. You must turn on your headlights . . .
   ○ **a.** when you turn on your wipers.
   ● **b.** in the evening.
   ○ **c.** one half hour before sunset.
   ○ **d.** all of the above.

4. If you are driving behind a school bus, and it shows a flashing red light, you must . . .
   ○ **a.** slow down.
   ○ **b.** slow down and pass on the left.
   ● **c.** stop at least 25 feet away.
   ○ **d.** all of the above.

5. You are driving on a highway with a 65 mph limit. Most of the other vehicles are driving 70 mph or faster. You may legally drive . . .
   ○ **a.** 70 mph or faster.
   ● **b.** no faster than 65 mph.
   ○ **c.** between 65 and 70.
   ○ **d.** as fast as you like.

6. You have a green light, but the traffic is blocking the intersection. You must . . .
   ○ **a.** pass the traffic on the left.
   ○ **b.** honk your horn.
   ● **c.** wait until the traffic clears. Then, go.
   ○ **d.** pass the traffic on the right.

7. You must obey instructions of school crossing guards . . .
   ● **a.** at all times.
   ○ **b.** when school is closed.
   ○ **c.** in the morning.
   ○ **d.** when it is raining.

8. If you pass your exit on a highway, you should . . .
   ● **a.** go to the next exit.
   ○ **b.** turn around on the highway and return to your exit.
   ○ **c.** cross to the other side of the highway and make a U-turn.
   ○ **d.** back up slowly to the exit that you want.

9. What does the sign mean?
   ○ **a.** Three-way intersection.
   ○ **b.** Stop.
   ● **c.** Railroad crossing ahead.
   ○ **d.** No turns.

10. What does the sign mean?
    ○ **a.** One-way street ahead.
    ○ **b.** Pass other cars on the right.
    ○ **c.** Left turn only.
    ● **d.** You cannot go straight ahead.

Check your answers below.

1. b 2. d 3. b 4. c 5. b 6. c 7. a 8. a 9. c 10. d

| 8 correct | **CONGRATULATIONS!** You pass! Get your driver's license. |
| Below 8 correct | **SORRY.** You're not ready to drive. Study for two more weeks. Then, come back and retake the test. |

Students use the answer key on page 95 to check their own work. Discuss any answers that several students got wrong.

Suggestion

If possible, obtain copies of your state's manual that tells how to go about getting a driver's license. Photocopy a sample test from the manual and have students take the test in class. Correct it together orally and discuss any new vocabulary as well as the different rules and regulations that appear on the test.

A. Look at the street map.

• Ask students to work alone as they read both sets of directions. Then, have them read the directions in Conversation 1 a second time, marking it on the map with a pencil as they read.

• Next, have students read and mark with a pen the directions in Conversation 2. Ask them to share their maps with a partner and help each other correct any mistakes in the routes they drew. Review the completed routes with the whole class.

☀ Writing Our Stories: Giving Directions

A. Look at the street map. Then, read the driving directions from the starting point.

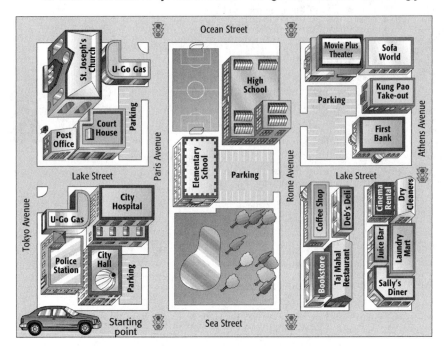

Conversation 1

A: My sofa is getting old. I need to buy a new sofa. How do I get to Sofa World? I heard that there's a great selection of sofas there.

B: That's right. Sofa World has a large selection of sofas. You're on Sea Street. Go to the first traffic light and turn left. That's Paris Avenue. Traffic is usually light. Take Paris straight to Ocean Street. There's a gas station on your left and a soccer field on your right. Turn right. Go through one traffic light. Sofa World is the second building on the right. It's on the corner of Ocean Street and Athens Avenue.

Conversation 2

A: I have to pick up sandwiches for a meeting at my office. How do I get to Deb's Deli? I heard that I can get a great sandwich there.

B: That's right. The sandwiches are delicious. It's easy. This is Sea Street. Go to the second light, turn left. That's Rome Avenue. Go to the next corner. That's Lake Street. It's difficult to park around there, so you should park in the municipal parking lot on the corner. Deb's Deli is across the street from the parking lot.

B. In your notebook, write directions from school to your home or workplace. Include the names of important streets and landmarks such as gas stations, banks, and stores.

C. Unnecessary sentences. When you write a story or composition, it is important to include details to help the reader understand. It is also important to stay on topic. Do not include unnecessary information that may confuse the reader. Read each paragraph. ~~Cross out~~ the unnecessary sentence(s). Why did you cross out each sentence? *(Answers may vary. Suggested answers below.)*

1. I think that all people should wear seat belts. Seat belts save lives. Three years ago, I was in an accident. I was on my way to work on a cold, snowy winter day. ~~I don't like winter because I am from a warm country, and it doesn't snow there.~~ The road was icy, but I was driving a little too fast. When I stepped on the brakes to stop at a stop sign, the car slid. I couldn't stop the car, and I slid through the stop sign into the intersection. I hit a truck. I had on my seat belt, so I wasn't hurt. The other driver didn't have on his seat belt. He had to go to the hospital for his injuries.

2. ~~I think that the new cell phone laws are ridiculous.~~ My parents gave me a cell phone when I got my driver's license. I have a part-time job, and I have to work in the evenings. ~~It was very difficult for me to find a job, so I want to keep this job until I finish high school.~~ I always call my mother from my car to tell her that I'm on my way home. ~~My cell phone is very cute. It's red, and it plays my favorite song when it rings.~~ A few months ago, I had a flat tire on the way home. I used my cell phone to call my father. He called our auto association to come and help me. Then, my father called me back and kept talking to me as he drove to my location to wait with me. I was very nervous and scared. I was very happy to have my cell phone.

D. Edit. Find and correct the mistakes.

1. She must puts money in the parking meter.
2. Can you ~~driving~~ a stick shift? *(drive)*
3. Drivers ~~has~~ to follow the traffic rules. *(have)*
4. I didn't have to ~~took~~ the test in English. *(take)*
5. The baby should ~~to~~ ride in the back seat.
6. He better not take another day off, or he'll lose his job. *(had)*
7. We ~~had not~~ buy a new car because we found a used one in good condition. *(didn't have to)*

Looking at the Internet

Many states have Web sites for the Department of Motor Vehicles. The Web sites give information to current drivers as well as potential drivers. Search the Internet to find your state's Department of Motor Vehicles. Here's an example: Search "Florida" and "Motor Vehicles." Share the information you find with your classmates.

B. In your notebook, write directions from school to your home or workplace.

• Before they begin the writing part of this assignment, suggest that students draw a simple map that includes the streets and landmarks they pass on their route from school to their home or workplace.

• Next, ask them to work with a partner, describing the route and tracing it on the map with a finger. Then, have them write out the directions and reread them to be sure they haven't made any mistakes.

• Students show their maps to new partners and read the directions aloud. The partner traces the directions on the map with his/her finger.

C. Unnecessary sentences.

• The first time through, have students read the story without crossing out anything. The second time through, have them cross out the unnecessary sentences.

• Review the correct answers by reading the story aloud one sentence at a time and having students raise their hands when you read a sentence that can be dropped. Invite students to tell why the sentence should be eliminated.

D. Edit.

Have students correct the sentences on their own. Review the correct answers with the whole class.

 Looking at the Internet

To help ensure that students will come up with a variety of useful information, you can assign specific topics to different groups of students. One group can research the Frequently Asked Questions on the Web site; another can look into driver testing; a third can find out how to obtain license plates.

Practicing on Your Own

A. Traffic regulations.

Ask students to complete the sentences on their own and check their answers with a partner.

B. Compare the driving rules in the state where you live now to the driving rules in your native country.

Students complete the sentences individually. Then, review the completed sentences with the class.

In your notebook, write two more rules about driving in your country.

When students have finished writing their rules, invite volunteers to read their work aloud to the class. If a rule doesn't make sense to another student, ask the person who wrote the statement to explain why the rule is necessary.

Suggestion

As a change of pace, ask students to make a list of actions called "Recipe for a Car Accident." In it, they can describe all the things a driver *can*, *must*, and *had better do* to cause a big accident. For example:

You must talk on a cell phone and drive at the same time.
You had better not drive slowly in the rain.

Students can take turns reading their recipes to the class.

Practicing on Your Own

A. Traffic regulations. Fill in the blank in each sentence with the correct modal. There's more than one correct answer. (Sample answers below. Answers will vary.)

must must not	has to doesn't have to	have to don't have to	should shouldn't	had better had better not

1. You _____don't have to_____ take the written test in English.
2. You _____shouldn't_____ drive over the speed limit.
3. Learners _____must_____ get permits before they can drive.
4. Children under seven _____have to_____ ride in car seats.
5. You _____had better not_____ drive and talk on a cellular phone.
6. You _____had better_____ use a hands-free cellular phone.
7. Drivers _____shouldn't_____ drink and drive, or they will lose their licenses.
8. You _____don't have to_____ wash your car.
9. You _____should_____ change your car's oil every 3,000 miles.
10. Bicycle riders _____must_____ ride in the same direction as cars.

B. Compare the driving rules in the state where you live now to the driving rules in your native country. Add an appropriate verb. (Answers may vary. Sample answers below.)

can	can't	must	must not	have to	don't have to

1. In this state, I _____must wear_____ a seat belt.
2. In my country, I _____have to wear_____ a seat belt.
3. In this state, children _____have to sit_____ in car seats.
4. In my country, children _____don't have to sit_____ in car seats.
5. In this state, drivers _____have to have_____ auto insurance.
6. In my country, drivers _____don't have to have_____ auto insurance.
7. In this state, you _____can_____ obtain a license when you are __16__ years old.
8. In my country, you _____can't_____ obtain a license when you are 16 years old.

In your notebook, write two more rules about driving in your country.

98 UNIT 6

Grammar Summary

Modals are a special group of verbs. Each modal carries its own meaning. For example, *Emilio goes to school* is a fact. *Emilio has to go to school* shows that it is necessary for Emilio to go to school. The meaning changes when you use a modal verb.

▶ **1. *Have to* and *must***   Use *have to* and *must* to express rules, obligation, or necessity.

I **have to wear** a seat belt.

I **must stop** at a red light.

He **had to pay** his traffic fine.

▶ **2. *Don't have to/Doesn't have to/Didn't have to***   The negative form of *have to* shows that an action is not necessary.

You **don't have to be** 21 years old to drive.

She **doesn't have to get** 100% correct on the written test.

I **didn't have to get** a visa before I came here.

▶ **3. *Must not* and *cannot***   *Must not* and *cannot* show that an action is against the law or rules.

You **cannot go** through a red light.

Students **cannot copy** from other students.

You **must not go** through a red light.

Students **must not copy** from other students.

▶ **4. *Can***

a. *Can* shows ability or possibility.

I **can drive** a truck.

I **can meet** you after class.

Cannot shows inability or no possibility.

He **cannot drive** a stick shift.

They **cannot take** more than four classes.

b. *Can* also shows that an action is permitted.

I **can park** here.

He **can use** his father's car.

▶ **5. *Should***   *Should* expresses an opinion or advice. *Shouldn't/Should not* shows that something is <u>not</u> a good idea.

I **should buy** a smaller car.

He **should study** English.

You **shouldn't buy** a larger car.

She **shouldn't study** in the cafeteria.

▶ **6. *Had better/Had better not***   *Had better/had better not* expresses a strong warning. *Had better* is stronger than *should*, and it expresses the idea that something bad might happen.

I **had better renew** my license this week.

(Meaning: My license will expire this week.)

You **had better not** park here.

(Meaning: Your car will be towed away.)

Grammar Summary

• Review the six grammar explanations and sample sentences with the class. Invite students to make up alternate sentences for each example in the chart. For example, in place of *I didn't have to get a visa before I came here*, a student might say, *I didn't have to wear a coat today.*

• Answer any questions students may have about the grammar items.

• See the Grammar Summary Expansion on page 263 for a more complete explanation of these grammar points.

Unit 7
Sports

Discuss what the person in the unit title art is doing. Ask:

• *Who is standing next to the number 7?* (A man)
• *What is he doing?* (He's balancing a soccer ball on his knee.)
• *What does this have to do with the unit?* (The unit is about sports, and soccer is one of the most popular sports in the world.)

A. Match.

Ask students to match each word with the correct picture. Review the answers with the whole class.

Suggestion

Conduct a class poll to find out which sports students enjoy playing and which ones they enjoy watching. Draw a two-column chart on the board. List the sports along the left-hand side of the chart and write the word *Play* over the first column and *Watch* over the second column. Ask students to raise their hands in response to questions such as *Who likes to play basketball?* Record the numbers on the chart and discuss the results with the class.

B. Discuss.

• Ask students to read through the questions and underline any they don't understand. Clarify the meaning of these items by restating the question using different words.
• Call on a student to answer all nine questions. Paraphrase each response to confirm that you understand, and correct the student's language as necessary.

Suggestion

Have students work in pairs, taking turns asking and answering the questions.

Sports

A. Match. Write each word from the box under the correct picture.

football	bowling ball	golf ball
tennis ball	soccer ball	volleyball
basketball	baseball	ping pong ball

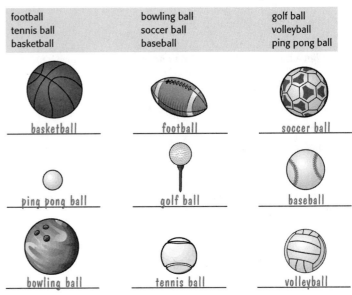

basketball   football   soccer ball

ping pong ball   golf ball   baseball

bowling ball   tennis ball   volleyball

B. Discuss.   (Answers will vary.)

1. What sport do you play?
2. Are you on a team?
3. How long have you been playing _____?
4. How often do you play _____?
5. Did you play a sport in high school?
6. Did you ever win a competition?
7. What sport do you enjoy watching?
8. What is your favorite team?
9. Who is your favorite player?

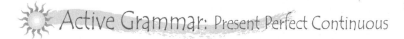

The **present continuous** describes what a person is doing now.
The **present perfect continuous** tells *how long* a person has been performing that action.
He's **playing** soccer now.
He's **been playing** soccer for an hour.

I You We They	have	been	**playing** tennis **watching** the game	for an hour. for two hours. since 2:00.
He She	has			

Contractions
I have—I've
you have—you've
he has—he's
she has—she's
we have—we've
they have—they've

A. Read and complete.

It's 5:00.

Carl <u>is playing</u> basketball.

Carl <u>began</u> to play basketball at 4:00.

He <u>has been playing</u> basketball for an hour.

He's <u>been playing</u> basketball since 4:00.

It's 3:00.

The men <u>are playing</u> soccer.

They <u>began</u> to play soccer at 1:00.

They <u>have been playing</u> soccer for two hours.

They<u>'ve been playing</u> soccer since 1:00.

It's 12:00.

The women <u>are playing</u> tennis.

They <u>began</u> to play tennis at 10:00.

They <u>have been playing</u> tennis for two hours.

They <u>'ve been playing</u> tennis since 10:00.

It's 5:00.

I <u>am playing</u> golf.

I <u>began</u> to play golf at 2:00.

I <u>have been playing</u> golf for three hours.

I <u>'ve been playing</u> golf since 2:00.

Sports **101**

Active Grammar: Present Perfect Continuous

A. Read and complete.

- Ask a different student to read aloud each of the sentences that can be formed using the words in the grammar chart. Discuss the meaning of each sentence. Lead students to understand that the activities described are continuous. They began at a specific time and are still taking place.
- Read aloud the list of contractions and have students repeat.
- Point to the first picture and have a student read aloud each of the sentences. After each sentence, have another student explain the time period of the action. For example:

  "Is playing" means that Carl is taking part in a game of basketball right now or at this moment.
  "Began to play" means that Carl started a game of basketball at some time in the past.
  "Has been playing" means that Carl started playing a game of basketball at some time in the past and is still playing.

- Repeat this activity for the sentences about the men playing soccer. Then, have students complete the activity on their own.

☀ Active Grammar:
For and *Since*

A. Write each word or phrase under the correct column.

Read and discuss with students the descriptions of the use of *for* and *since*. Then, have them write the phrases in the correct columns. Review the correct answers with the class.

B. Complete the sentences using *for* or *since*.

Ask students to complete the sentences and check their answers with a partner. Review the correct answers orally with the class.

Suggestion

Divide the class into two teams. (If you have a large class, you may wish to have several sets of teams.) Have a competition in which a member of one team makes a statement using *since* or *for,* and a member of the other team responds using the other word. The second team's response must communicate exactly the same fact. For example:

S1: *I have been sitting here since 9:00.*

S2: *You have been sitting there for two hours.*

Each team gets one point for each correct response it gives.

A. Write each word or phrase under the correct column.

For
For shows an amount of time:
for a few minutes
for three days

Since
Since tells when an action started:
since 2000
since Monday
since she moved to the city

✓ she began to play tennis	he joined the team	several days
✓ three hours	a long time	I was a child
a few minutes	about two weeks	many years
2:00	he broke his arm	Saturday

For	Since
three hours	she began to play tennis
a few minutes	2:00
a long time	he joined the team
about two weeks	he broke his arm
several days	I was a child
many years	Saturday

B. Complete the sentences using *for* or *since*.

1. She's been playing professionally ___*for*___ five years.
2. You've been hitting better ___*since*___ you took lessons.
3. He's been working out ___*since*___ 8:00 this morning.
4. The team has been practicing ___*for*___ about three hours.
5. She's been riding her bicycle ___*for*___ two hours.
6. He's been speaking with the coach ___*since*___ he got on the field.
7. The players have been listening to the coach ___*for*___ 30 minutes.
8. He hasn't been running well ___*since*___ he hurt his leg.
9. The fans have been watching the game ___*since*___ 4:00.
10. He's been playing golf ___*since*___ he was a child.

☀ What have you been up to?

 A. Pronunciation. Listen and repeat. (Circled answers are for the following exercise.)

1. **a.** She's taking tennis lessons. **b.** She's been taking tennis lessons.
2. **a.** She's learning how to drive. **b.** She's been learning how to drive.
3. **a.** He's playing baseball. **b.** He's been playing baseball.
4. **a.** I'm looking for a new apartment. **b.** I've been looking for a new apartment.
5. **a.** She's recovering from her accident. **b.** She's been recovering from her accident.
6. **a.** He's studying Chinese. **b.** He's been studying Chinese.
7. **a.** He's working hard. **b.** He's been working hard.
8. **a.** I'm training for a new job. **b.** I've been training for a new job.

 Listen again. Circle the sentence you hear.

Practice these sentences with a partner.

 B. Listen to the conversation. Then, practice the conversation with a partner.

A: Hi, Juan. What've you been up to?

B: I've been painting the house.

A: And how about the family?

B: We're all fine. Maribel is 16 now, so she's been learning how to drive.

A: I've been through that! And your parents? How have they been enjoying their retirement?

B: They've been traveling. They're in China now.

A: Say "Hi!" to them for me!

B: I will.

C. Form sentences with these cues. Use the present perfect continuous tense. Then, develop a conversation similar to the one in Exercise B.

1. put in a lot of overtime
2. look for a job
3. coach my son's baseball team
4. travel
5. put in a new bathroom
   (Answers will vary.)
6. take dance lessons
7. practice for my driving test
8. go out with someone new
9. study for my final exams
10. play a lot of golf

Sports **103**

 ☀ What have you been up to?

 A. Pronunciation. **(CD2, Track 6)**

Play the audio and have students listen and repeat.

Listen again. **(CD2, Track 7)**

• Have students look at the pairs of sentences in Exercise A. Explain that they will hear only one sentence and they should circle the one they hear.

• Play the audio once as students circle the sentences they hear. Play it a second time so they can check their answers. Review the correct answers with the whole class.

Practice these sentences with a partner.

Students take turns saying the sentences to a partner. Encourage students to provide helpful feedback about each other's pronunciation if they can.

B. Listen to the conversation. **(CD2, Track 8)**

• Ask students to follow along in their books as you play the audio. Answer any questions students may have. Then, have them listen again.

• Students practice the conversation in pairs. Move around the room listening and providing feedback on the pronunciation of the present perfect continuous verb phrases.

Audio Script

A. Pronunciation. Listen again. Circle the sentence you hear. **(CD2, Track 6)**

1. She's been taking tennis lessons.
2. She's learning how to drive.
3. He's been playing baseball.
4. I've been looking for a new apartment.
5. She's recovering from her accident.
6. He's studying Chinese.
7. He's been working hard.
8. I've been training for a new job.

C. Form sentences with these cues.

• Do the first part of the activity with the whole class. Write some of the sentences on the board. For example: *I've been putting in a lot of overtime. She's been looking for a job.*

• Make up a sample conversation with the class before

asking pairs to do it on their own. They can use the first line of the conversation in Exercise B as their opening line. They can also adapt other lines for their conversations using the vocabulary in Exercise C.

D. Student to student dictation.

• Read and discuss the instructions and be sure students understand how to proceed. Ask different students to describe the situation shown in each picture. Then, help students locate the sentences on page 246.

• Students work in pairs. First, Student A reads his/her statements on page 246 and Student B writes each statement next to the correct picture on page 104. Then, they reverse roles and Student B reads his/her statements on page 246 and Student A writers each one in the correct place on page 104. Check the correct answers orally with the whole class.

Suggestion

Provide oral practice of this structure by inviting students to make up additional questions to ask about the people in the pictures. Have the student make up a sentence using the present perfect continuous and call on another student to tell which picture it applies to. For example: *It hasn't been starting on cold mornings* goes with the picture of the driver talking to the mechanic.

D. Student to student dictation.

Student A: Turn to page 246. Read the sentences to Student B.
Student B: Look at the pictures below. Listen to Student A and write each sentence next to the correct picture. When you finish, change pages. Student B will read eight new sentences.

"Roger is in the lead!"

1. B: They've been running for two hours.
   A: The fans have been cheering.
2. B: They've been drinking a lot of water.
   A: Roger has been in the lead for 20 minutes.

"I'm not sure what's wrong."

1. B: I haven't been feeling well.
   A: I've been having trouble sleeping.
2. B: I've been having pains in my stomach.
   A: I haven't been eating right.

"You've always been an outstanding worker. Is anything wrong?"

1. B: You haven't been coming to work on time.
   A: You've been making a lot of mistakes in your paperwork.
2. B: We've been receiving complaints about your work.
   A: You haven't been getting along well with your coworkers.

"Could you take a look at it?"

1. B: It's been making strange noises.
   A: It's been overheating in traffic.
2. B: It's been leaking.
   A: It hasn't been running smoothly.

Have you been watching the game?	Yes, I have.	No, I haven't.
Have they been watching the game?	Yes, they have.	No, they haven't.
Has she been watching the game?	Yes, she has.	No, she hasn't.
Has he been watching the game?	Yes, he has.	No, he hasn't.

| How long | have | you they | been watching | the game? |
| | has | he she | | |

A. Listen to this interview between Robert and a reporter. Then, answer the questions.

1. How old is Robert? *Seven.*
2. What did he just win? *The tennis state championships.*
3. How long has he been playing tennis? *Four years.*
4. Who taught him how to play? *His father.*
5. Does he take private lessons? *Yes.*
6. How long has he been taking private lessons? *Two years.*
7. How often do his parents want him to practice? *Three or four days a week.*
8. What is his dream? *To be a professional tennis player.*

B. Listen to this interview between Anna and a reporter. Then, use the cues to ask and answer questions.

choreographer— a person who coordinates music and dance

1. About how old / Anna? *About how old is Anna? (Answers will vary.)*
2. What / she / just win? *What did she just win? A skating competition.*
3. she / have / good coach? *Does she have a good coach? Yes, she does.*
4. How long / she / work with her coach? *How long has she been working with her coach? / 5 years.*
5. she / work with a new choreographer? *Has she been working with a new choreographer? / Yes, she has.*
6. she / do the same routine? *Does she do the same routine? / No, she doesn't.*
7. she / practice / triple jump? *Has she been practicing a triple jump? / Yes, she has.*
8. When / try the triple jump in competition? *When will she try the triple jump in competition? Maybe next season.*

Sports **105**

A. Listen to this interview between Robert and a reporter. (CD2, Track 9)

• Review the questions and answers in the grammar chart at the top of the page. Answer any questions students may have.

• Point out the picture and ask a student to tell what has happened to the boy. Read through the list of questions with the class and explain what *private lessons* are if necessary.

• Play the audio as students think about their answers. Play the audio a second time. Then, ask students to answer the questions.

B. Listen to this interview between Anna and a reporter. (CD2, Track 10)

• Review the vocabulary in the list of questions, and answer any questions students may have.

• Point out the illustration and ask a student what sport he/she participates in.

• Play the audio as students only listen. Then, play the audio a second time. Call on a student to form the question. Repeat correct questions, or correct the wording if necessary and have the student repeat. Then, choose a second student to give the answer.

(Audio Script for Exercise B appears on page 254.)

Audio Script

A. Listen to this interview between Robert and a reporter. (CD2, Track 9)

Reporter: Congratulations! You just won the state championship.
Robert: Thank you.
Reporter: Robert, how old are you?
Robert: Seven.
Reporter: Seven! And how long have you been playing tennis?
Robert: Since I was three.
Reporter: Who taught you how to play?
Robert: My father. And I take private lessons, too.

Reporter: Here at the tennis club?
Robert: Yes, I've been taking lessons for two years.
Reporter: How many days a week do you play?
Robert: About three or four. I want to practice every day, but my parents say three or four days is enough. I like to play video games with my friends, too.

(Audio Script continues on page 254.)

C. Ask your teacher these questions.

Discuss the instructions and role-play the dialogue at the top of the page with a student. Then, invite students to ask you the questions and form the *How long* questions where appropriate. Give truthful answers whenever possible.

D. Sit in a group of four or five students.

• Read the instructions and explain how to use the chart to record answers. Then, help students form groups of five and have them complete the activity. Set a time limit, perhaps ten minutes, to help keep them on task.

• When the time is up, review a few of the questions and answers with the whole class.

Use the information in your chart to complete these sentences.

• Have each group work together to complete the sentences based on the information in the chart.

• Have a volunteer from each group read two or three sentences aloud to the class.

C. Ask your teacher these questions. If your teacher answers **Yes,** ask a question with **How long.** (All answers on this page will vary.)

> **Student:** Are you reading anything good now?
> **Teacher:** Yes, I'm reading *River Town* by Peter Hessler.
> **Student:** How long have you been reading that book?
> **Teacher:** Well, I got it out of the library two weeks ago and I've been reading it for about a week.

1. Do you play a musical instrument?
2. Do you wear contacts?
3. Do you play a particular sport?
4. Do you live in this city?
5. Do you drive?
6. Do you take vitamins?
7. Do you have a hobby?
8. Do you work at this school full time?
9. Are you studying a foreign language now?
10. Are you reading anything good now?

D. Sit in a group of four or five students. Write each person's name in the first column of the chart. Answer these five questions. Use the chart to record each person's answers.

1. How long have you been living in the United States?
2. How long have you been driving?
3. How long have you been studying English?
4. How long have you been attending this school?
5. How long have you been working in the United States?

Students' Names	Question 1	Question 2	Question 3	Question 4	Question 5
1.					
2.					
3.					
4.					
5.					

Use the information in your chart to complete these sentences.

1. _____ has been living in the United States the longest.
2. _____ has been driving longer than _____.
3. _____ doesn't drive.
4. _____ has been studying English for _____.
5. _____ has been studying English since _____.
6. _____ has been attending this school the longest.
7. _____ doesn't work.
8. _____ has been working longer than _____.

A. Read the information about these athletes. Ask and answer questions using the information in the boxes.

Possible questions
Who's this?
What sport does he/she play?
How old is he/she?
How long has he/she been playing _____?
What country is he/she from?

Tiger Woods
Born: 12/30/1975—USA
Started to play when he
was one year old

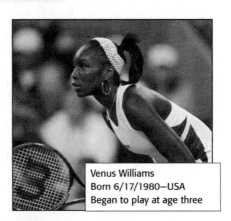

Venus Williams
Born 6/17/1980—USA
Began to play at age three

Ronaldo
Born: 9/22/1976—Brazil
Began to play professionally
in 1990

Pyrros Dimas
Born: 1972 in Albania of
ethnic Greek parents
Three Olympic gold medals
for Greece
Began to lift weights in 1991

Well-Known Athletes

A. Read the information about these athletes.

• Point out the four pictures and ask students to read the information about each person. Answer any questions they may have and invite them to provide additional facts they may know about any of the athletes.

• Model a question and answer exchange with students using the first picture. Ask each question in the box at the top and have the class repeat. Then, call on a different student to answer the question.

• Go on to the other three pictures, having students take turns asking the questions and calling on a classmate to answer. For example:

S1: *Who's this? Carmel.*
S2: *It's Venus Williams.*
S3: *What sport does she play? Antonio.*
S4: *She plays tennis.*

Suggestion

Invite students to cut out newspaper or magazine pictures of famous athletes and bring them to class. They can work in pairs, asking and answering the questions in the box on this page. This can be done in pairs or with the whole class if the picture is large enough for all to see or can be placed on an overhead projector.

☀ The Big Picture:
The Soccer Game

A. Label these people in the picture.

Do this activity as a class. As students suggest labels for each person, discuss that person's contribution to the game. For example:

T: *What is a "fan"?*

S1: *Somebody who likes a team.*

S1: *That's right. It's a person who likes a team or a player a lot. A fan goes to a lot of games to see the team or the player.*

⊪ B. Listen to a description of this scene. (CD2, Track 11)

• Read the instructions. Discuss the meaning of each question. Be sure students understand the meaning of the terms *in the lead* (having the most points) and *minutes . . . left in the game* (number of minutes before the end of the game).

• Play the audio twice as students just listen. Then, read the questions aloud and call on a different student to answer each one. If students are unsure of an answer, replay the related portion of the tape once or twice and give them another chance to answer.

☀ The Big Picture: The Soccer Game

A. Label these people in the picture.

players
fans
announcer
coach
referee
concession workers

concession worker

announcer

players

STARS 2
KINGS 1
10 Minutes

⊪ B. Listen to a description of this scene. Then, answer the questions.

1. Who's playing? **The Kings and the Stars**
2. Which team is in the lead? What's the score? **The Stars**
3. How long have they been playing? **They have been playing since 2:00.**
4. How many minutes are left in the game? **10 minutes**
5. How many fans are watching the game? **More than 20,000**
6. What have the concession workers been doing? **Walking up and down the stands, selling soda, and water**
7. What have people been buying? **Soda, water, and food**
8. Has there been any fighting on the field? **No**
9. What have the coaches been doing? **Shouting instructions and putting in new players**
10. Which player has everyone been watching? **The forward for the Stars, Number 7**

Audio Script

B. Listen to a description of this scene. Then, answer the questions. (CD2, Track 11)

Today is the championship soccer game between two teams, the Kings and the Stars. The game started at 2:00. It's the second half of the game, with only 10 minutes left to play, and the Stars are in the lead. They're winning 2-1. TV and radio are covering the game and the announcers have been calling the game and describing every play.

The stadium is full, with more than twenty thousand excited fans watching their team in the championship. The fans have been cheering and shouting for their favorite teams. Some of the fans are waving banners and holding up signs.

It's a hot summer day, so the fans have been buying lots of drinks. The concession workers have been walking up and down the stands for an hour, selling soda and water. People have been waiting in line for 10 minutes or more to buy food. The players are hot because they've been running since the game started. They've been drinking a lot of water

and energy drinks. The referees have been watching the players carefully to prevent any illegal play. A few of the players have been calling one another names and pushing hard during the game. But so far, all of the players are still in the game. The coach has been shouting instructions and putting in new players. Both of the goalies are strong and have been stopping goal shots all game, but the players are fast and accurate today. Everyone has been watching the forward for the Stars, Number 7. He's their top player and he now has the ball.

C. Complete the sentences using the correct verb in the present perfect continuous tense.

buy	run	wait	shout
watch	describe	call	make
	be	cheer	

1. The fans _____ have been making _____ a lot of noise.
2. The fans _____ have been buying _____ a lot of soda and water.
3. People _____ have been waiting _____ in line to buy food.
4. An announcer _____ has been describing _____ the game.
5. The players _____ have been running _____ up and down the field.
6. A few of the players _____ have been calling _____ each other names.
7. The coach _____ has been shouting _____ instructions.
8. Everyone _____ has been watching _____ player number 7.
9. The players _____ have been making _____ fast and accurate moves.
10. The fans _____ have been cheering _____ for their favorite teams.

D. Match the short answers with the questions.

1. Is the stadium full? _____ d   a. Yes, there are.
2. Did the game start at 2:00? _____ e   b. Yes, he has.
3. Are there more than twenty thousand fans? _____ a   c. Yes, he does.
4. Have the fans been cheering? _____ i   d. Yes, it is.
5. Are the fans hot? _____ f   e. Yes, it did.
6. Has the coach been giving instructions? _____ b   f. Yes, they are.
7. Do the Stars have four goals? _____ j   g. No, it isn't.
8. Does player number 7 have the ball? _____ c   h. No, they haven't.
9. Is the score 4-1? _____ g   i. Yes, they have.
10. Have the refs been calling many illegal plays? _____ h   j. No, they don't.

C. Complete the sentences using the correct verb in the present perfect continuous tense.

Have students write their answers individually and check them with a partner. Check the correct answers by having different students write one answer each on the board. Review the answers with the whole class, correcting them as necessary.

D. Match the short answers with the questions.

Ask students to complete the matching exercise individually and check their answers with a partner. Review the correct answers orally with the whole class.

Reading: Lance Armstrong

A. Before You Read.

- Read and discuss the prereading questions at the top with the class.
- Then, ask students to read the entire story without stopping. Explain that they won't understand everything. Suggest that they just try to understand the main ideas the first time through.
- Discuss the paragraphs one at a time. Ask one or two simple comprehension questions about each one. For example, for paragraph 1: *What is special about Armstrong's athletic career?* (He became the number one biker in the world. He had a lot of difficulties doing this.)
- Point out the bold words. Ask a student to read aloud each sentence containing a bold word. Call on other students to paraphrase the sentence.

Reading: Lance Armstrong

A. Before You Read. (Answers will vary.)

1. Look at the picture of Lance Armstrong. What is his sport? Have you ever heard of this athlete?

2. The Tour de France is one of the most difficult cycling races in the world. What do you know about this event?

Soccer, baseball, basketball . . . millions of people follow these sports and watch their favorite teams on TV. Cycling doesn't have the media coverage of some other sports, but most people can name the number one cyclist in the world—Lance Armstrong. His story is amazing for both his athletic **accomplishments** and his difficult road to **achieving** them.

Lance Armstrong was born on September 18, 1971, in Plano, Texas, and raised by a single mother. He began riding at an early age and was entering triathalons (running, swimming, and cycling competitions) before he was a teenager. By the age of 20, Armstrong was the U.S. National Amateur Cycling Champion.

From 1991 to 1996, Lance Armstrong continued to enter and win races. In 1993, he became the U.S. Pro Champion, and he won one million dollars in the Thrift Drug Triple Crown. In 1995, he won the Classico San Sebastion in Italy—the first American ever to win that race. By 1996, Armstrong was the number one cyclist in the world.

However, in October 1996, Armstrong began to lose energy and feel sick. A visit to the doctor brought terrible news. Armstrong had cancer, and it had spread to his lungs, brain, and abdomen. Armstrong **feared** he might never race again or that he might not even **survive**. He was **facing** the most difficult **challenge** of his life. In the months after his diagnosis, Armstrong had three major operations and then months of strong chemotherapy. In 1997, the doctors declared that Armstrong was cancer free.

Armstrong states that the cancer was a "wake-up call." Cancer gave him the strength to fight, to get back on his bicycle and win. He says, "Anybody who lives with cancer is a hero." Armstrong **founded** the *Lance Armstrong Foundation*, a nonprofit organization that raises money for cancer research, awareness, and early **detection**.

As Armstrong grew stronger, he entered the world of bicycling competition again, winning more titles and races. He returned to the U.S. Postal Service team, this time with a strong belief in himself and a **determination** to win. In 1999, Armstrong won the Tour de France, a three-week event, which takes riders more than two thousand miles through the valleys and high mountains of France. He won the event again in 2000, 2001, and 2002. On the Internet, it is possible to follow Armstrong's career since 2002 and to learn about the work of the *Lance Armstrong Foundation*.

B. Vocabulary. Look at the words in bold print in the reading. Write each word from the reading next to its definition.

1. strong will ___determination___
2. looking at ___facing___
3. live ___survive___
4. was afraid of ___feared___
5. the discovery of a problem ___detection___
6. started an organization ___founded___
7. difficult problem ___challenge___
8. reaching a goal ___achieving___
9. successes ___accomplishments___

C. Sentence sense. It is possible to understand the meaning of a sentence even when you do not understand every word. Read the sentences from the story and circle the sentence with a similar meaning.

1. Cycling doesn't have the media coverage of some other sports.
   a. You don't see a lot of bicycle racing events on TV.
   b. Bicycling, like other sports, is popular with TV viewers.

2. His story is amazing for both his athletic accomplishments and his difficult road to achieving them.
   a. In bicycling, the roads are often high and difficult.
   b. Armstrong had some difficult times on his way to becoming a top athlete.

3. In 1995, he won the Classico San Sebastion, the first American ever to win that race.
   a. Americans always come in first in the Classico San Sebastion.
   b. This was the first time that an American won the Classico San Sebastion.

4. Armstrong feared he might never race again or that he might not even survive.
   a. Armstrong was afraid that he was going to die.
   b. Armstrong was afraid to get back on his bicycle and race again.

5. Armstrong was facing the most difficult challenge of his life.
   a. It was very difficult to win bicycling competitions
   b. Facing cancer was more difficult than competing in a bicycle race.

6. Armstrong states that the cancer was a "wake-up call."
   a. Cancer helped Armstrong to become a more serious bicyclist.
   b. Armstrong could finally forget about having cancer.

7. He returned to the U.S. Postal Service team, this time with a strong belief in himself and a determination to win.
   a. Armstrong believed that he could win competitions again.
   b. Armstrong believed he would be strong enough to race again.

Sports **111**

B. Vocabulary.

Ask students to complete the exercise individually and check their answers with a partner. Review the correct answers with the whole class.

C. Sentence sense.

Have students complete this activity individually. Review the correct answers with the whole class. Invite students to make up additional alternate sentences that mean the same as each numbered sentence.

Suggestion

Locate a short news article or interview with Lance Armstrong on the Internet or in a newspaper or magazine. Make copies for each student. Ask them to read through it and see how much they can understand. Set a time limit, perhaps ten minutes, and then discuss the article with the class. You can then have students underline any words or phrases they still don't understand and work in groups using dictionaries and group discussion to clarify what they mean. Review the results with the whole class.

☀ Writing Our Stories: A Friendly Letter

A. Read this letter from Maria to her friend in Ecuador.

Ask students to read the letter on their own. When they finish, answer any questions they have.

B. Compound sentences.

• Read and discuss the instructions and sample sentences. Point out the use of the comma before the words *and, but, so,* and *or.*

• Ask students to locate sentences with *and, but, so,* and *or.* Have a student read each of these sentences aloud and discuss the function of these connecting words. (*And* adds information, *but* provides contradictory information, *so* shows that the second statement is the result of the first statement, and *or* indicates that two choices are involved.)

☀ Writing Our Stories: A Friendly Letter

A. Read this letter from Maria to her friend in Ecuador.

November 12

Hi Paula,

Sorry I haven't written for so long. I have been very busy and I have lots of news for you.

This year, school is much better. It was very difficult last year because my English wasn't too good. Now, I feel much more comfortable here.

I'm studying business and hotel management. My courses are really interesting and I've been doing well. My roommate is American, so I've been speaking English every day, all day. She's really nice.

I met someone really special! My roommate lifts weights and she talked me into going over to the gym with her. You know me, I never exercise! The second day I was there, the guy on the treadmill next to me started to talk to me. I went back at the same time the next day, and we just continued talking, so I began to use the gym every day! I've never been so healthy! Ron and I have been going out for three months. Ron is on the tennis team at college, so I've been going to lots of tennis matches. He's been trying to teach me how to play tennis, but I'm not very good!

Thanksgiving is a big American holiday and I have two invitations for dinner. I might visit my roommate's family in Boston or I might meet my boyfriend's family in New York. I'm not sure yet.

What have you been doing? How is school this year? Please write and tell me about everyone! I miss you!

Love,

Maria

B. Compound sentences. We can combine two short sentences with words like *and, but,* and *so,* and *or.* Each part of the new sentence has a subject and a verb. Remember to use a comma.

> Some friends are coming from Brazil, **and** they are going to visit me next week.
> I've been trying to learn Japanese, **but** I don't have anyone to speak to.
> I've been taking tennis lessons, **so** my game is improving.
> My parents are going to fly to the U.S., **or** I'm going to fly to Brazil.

In your notebook, combine these sentences.

1. My sister and brother are going to arrive tomorrow. They are going to stay with me for a week. *..., and they are ...*

2. I might major in art. I might study graphic design. *... art, but I might ...*

3. I've been calling Jack for a week. He hasn't returned my calls. *... week, but he ...*

4. Bill hasn't been attending soccer practice. The coach is going to suspend him from the team. *... practice, so the coach ...*

5. Julie hasn't been feeling well. She made a doctor's appointment. *... well, so she ...*

6. Ben wanted to attend private college. He couldn't afford the tuition. *... college, but he ...*

7. I bought a digital camera. My roommate is going to show me how to use it. *... camera, and my roommate ...*

8. My boyfriend is going to make dinner tonight. We're going to order take-out food tonight. *... tonight, or we're ...*

C. Write an informal letter to a friend. Tell him/her what you have been doing.

D. Edit. Find and correct the mistakes in these sentences.

1. I ^have^ been playing a lot of soccer.
2. He has been show~ing~ me how to play golf.
3. She ^has^ been very busy lately.
4. We have been going out ~~for~~ ^since^ the first day of school.
5. He ^has^ ~~have~~ been doing well in class.
6. She ~~is~~ ^has been^ going out with him since September.
7. They have been living in Tampa ~~since~~ ^for^ six months.
8. She has been work~ing~ at a restaurant for two months.
9. What ~~you have~~ ^have you^ been doing?
10. Have you ~~see~~ ^seen^ any of our old friends?

 Looking at the Internet

What athlete do you admire? Click on *Search* and enter the name of the athlete. Find a photo of the athlete and print it. Tell your classmates the name of the athlete, the sport he or she plays, the team he or she plays for, and two or three interesting facts about the athlete.

In your notebook, combine these sentences.

Ask students to complete the assignment individually. Review the correct sentences with the class, writing on the board any that students had difficulty with.

C. Write an informal letter to a friend.

• Students can use Exercise A as a model as they complete this activity.

• Ask some students to read their letters aloud to the class. Invite other students to give positive feedback.

D. Edit.

Have students correct the sentences on their own. Review the correct answers with the whole class.

Looking at the Internet

To assure variety, you may wish to assign names of athletes for students to research, or brainstorm a list of choices for students to choose from. You should probably allow no more than three students to sign up for the same person.

☀ Practicing on Your Own

A. Circle the sentence that shows the same meaning.

Students complete the exercise individually and check their answers with a partner. Discuss with the class any answers that several students miss.

B. Complete these questions and answers.

Students complete the exercise individually. Have different students write one question and answer each on the board. Review the correct answers with the class.

Suggestion

For additional practice, have some or all students write out additional pairs of questions and answers using the present perfect continuous tense. You might give them cues that they can apply to their lives and the lives of their families and friends. For example:

1. you – live – your present apartment
2. Carl – work – the cafeteria

☀ Practicing on Your Own

A. Circle the sentence that shows the same meaning.

1. Tara began to play volleyball at 1:00. It's 3:00 and she is still playing volleyball.
   a. Tara has been playing volleyball for two hours.
   b. Tara played volleyball for two hours.

2. Tom played tennis in the park from 4:00 to 5:00. Then, he went home.
   a. Tom has been playing tennis for an hour.
   b. Tom played tennis for an hour.

3. Yesterday Martin rode his bicycle from 8 A.M. to 1 P.M.
   a. Martin has been riding his bicycle for five hours.
   b. Martin rode his bicycle for five hours.

4. The soccer stadium is full. The fans took their seats an hour ago and they are watching the game.
   a. The fans watched the game for an hour.
   b. The fans have been watching the game for an hour.

5. Juan lifts weights at the gym every day from 7:00 to 8:00. It's 7:30 now.
   a. Juan lifted weights for 30 minutes.
   b. Juan has been lifting weights for 30 minutes.

6. That was a very long basketball game. I got to the arena at 4:00 and the game ended at 7:00.
   a. I've been sitting in the arena for three hours.
   b. I sat in the arena for three hours.

B. Complete these questions and answers.

1. **A:** How long ___has he been playing___ golf? (play)
   B: He ___has been playing___ golf for seven years.

2. **A:** How long ___have you been living___ in Chicago? (live)
   B: I ___have been living___ here for five years.

3. **A:** How long ___have they been listening___ to the news? (listen)
   B: They ___have been listening___ to the news for an hour.

4. **A:** How long ___have you been having___ these pains in your back? (have)
   B: I ___have been having___ these pains for two weeks.

5. **A:** How long ___has she been waiting___ to hear about the job? (wait)
   B: She ___has been waiting___ for a week.

6. **A:** How long ___have you been studying___ for the test? (study)
   B: I ___have been studying___ for three hours.

Grammar Summary

▶ 1. Present perfect continuous

The present perfect continuous talks about an action that started in the past and continues in the present. The action is not yet complete.

He **has been watching** the game since 8:00.

They **have been playing** tennis for an hour.

I You We They	have			since 8:00.
		been	playing	
He She It	has			for two hours.

▶ 2. *For* and *since*

For shows an amount of time.

for an hour

for three days

Since tells when an action started.

since 12:00

since the game started

▶ 3. *Yes/No* questions

Have you **been practicing** all afternoon?	**Yes**, I **have**.	**No**, I **haven't**.
Has she **been playing** tennis since 2000?	**Yes**, she **has**.	**No**, she **hasn't**.
Have they **been running** for two hours?	**Yes**, they **have**.	**No**, they **haven't**.

▶ 4. *How long* questions

How long **has** she **been playing** basketball?

How long **have** they **been running**?

Grammar Summary

- Review the four grammar explanations and sample sentences with the class. Invite students to make up alternate sentences for each example in the chart. For example, in place of *Have you been practicing all afternoon*, a student might say, *Has she been living here since September?*
- Answer any questions students may have about the grammar items.
- See the Grammar Summary Expansion on page 264 for a more complete explanation of these grammar points.

Unit 8
Changes

Discuss what the person in the unit title art is doing. Ask:
- *What do you see next to the number 8?* (A woman with suitcases in both hands)
- *What is she doing?* (She's swinging the suitcases around in the air.)
- *What does this have to do with the unit?* (The unit title is "Changes." The woman is visiting or moving to a new place. Travel and relocation are important kinds of change.)

A. Family reunions.

Point out the photo of a family reunion and ask students to describe what they see. Review the meaning of the phrases in the box. Then, ask different students to answer the questions. Call on more than one student to answer each question. Point out the different ways families stay or don't stay in touch.

B. A phone call. (CD2, Track 12)

- Have students just listen the first time you play the audio. Then, read the statements, and answer any questions students have.
- Play the audio once or twice more as students circle their answers. Review the correct answers with the whole class.

8 Changes

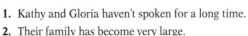

A. Family reunions. Discuss these questions. (Answers will vary.)

1. How large is your family?
2. How do you keep up-to-date on what is happening in your extended family?
3. When do you see your whole family?
4. What is a family reunion? Did you ever have a family reunion? If so, give some details.

> **Immediate family:** The family you live with.
>
> **Extended family:** The whole family! Count your parents, grandparents, brothers and sisters, children, aunts and uncles, and cousins.

 B. A phone call. Listen to Kathy and Gloria talk about the plans for a family reunion. Then, read each sentence and circle *T* for *true* or *F* for *false*.

1. Kathy and Gloria haven't spoken for a long time.   (T) F
2. Their family has become very large.   (T) F
3. The family has just had a reunion.   T (F)
4. Angela has sent out the invitations already.   T (F)
5. Gloria has just become a grandmother.   T (F)
6. Michael has just retired.   T (F)
7. Michael has opened a small business.   (T) F

116   UNIT 8

Audio Script

B. A phone call. (CD2, Track 12)

Gloria: Hi, Kathy. This is Gloria.

Kathy: Gloria! How are you? We haven't spoken for ages!

Gloria: I know. We all get so busy. Have you heard? Angela's planning a family reunion.

Kathy: A family reunion? That's great! We haven't gotten together, all of us, for about five years. What's the date?

Gloria: August. I think she said August 15.

Kathy: August 15. That's two months from now. And where's it going to be?

Gloria: At Angela's. She's going to send out the invitations soon. And we'll all help and bring food.

Kathy: Of course. How many of us are there?

Gloria: About 75. Plus two more. My sister, Jenny, just had twins. Two little girls. Identical twins.

Kathy: Beautiful. You're an aunt now. How's Jenny doing?

Gloria: She's tired, but doing well. I help her out a few days a week.

Kathy: Did you hear that Michael has changed jobs?

Gloria: No? What's he doing?

Kathy: He's opened a small business. He's installing big-screen TVs and sound systems in people's homes.

Gloria: Wish him my best.

Kathy: I will. It'll be great to see everyone and hear what's happening.

Gloria: See you in August.

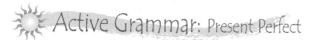

Active Grammar: Present Perfect

A. <u>Underline</u> the present perfect tense in the sentences below. (Circle) *for* or *since*.

> The **present perfect** tells about an action that began in the past and continues into the present.
> They **have lived** in this country for five years.
> She **has worked** at that company since she graduated from college.
>
> The present perfect can also talk about the recent past. These sentences often use *just*, *recently*, or *lately*.
> I **have** *just* **quit** my job.
> He **hasn't felt** well *lately*.
>
> Use the past participle form of the verb with *have / has*.

I You We They	have haven't	been friends with him gone out with him	for two years.
He She	has hasn't	worked with him	since January.

1. Kathy and Gloria <u>haven't spoken</u> (**for**) / **since** several months.
2. Michael <u>has managed</u> a small business (**for**) / **since** three years.
3. Tuan and Lana <u>have been married</u> **for** / (**since**) 1989.
4. Henry <u>has belonged</u> to the volunteer fire department **for** / (**since**) 2000.
5. Joanna <u>has sold</u> life insurance (**for**) / **since** ten years.
6. Rita <u>has been divorced</u> (**for**) / **since** six months.
7. Richard <u>has owned</u> his own business **for** / (**since**) he moved to Ohio.
8. Tom <u>has been</u> in college (**for**) / **since** six years.
9. Anna <u>has walked</u> two miles a day **for** / (**since**) she had her heart attack.
10. Brian <u>hasn't found</u> a job **for** / (**since**) he graduated from college.

B. *Since*. Make sentences with the information on the left and the *since* clauses on the right. Many combinations are possible. (Answers will vary.)

1. I haven't had a good night's sleep
2. I have had several complaints from my neighbors
3. I have lost 10 pounds
4. I've made several new friends
5. I haven't been able to concentrate on my job

since I fell in love.

since I had the baby.

since I joined the health club.

since I bought a dog.

Active Grammar: Present Perfect

A. Underline the present perfect tense in the sentences below.

- Review with students the information in the grammar box about the uses and forms of the present perfect tense. Have students use the words in the various column to make up a variety of different sentences.
- Students complete the circling activity individually and check their answers with a partner. Review the correct answers orally and answer any questions students may have.

B. Since.

Review the sentences and clauses to be sure students understand what each one means. Then, call on different students to match up a sentence and a clause that make sense together. There are many acceptable combinations.

Suggestion

Play a game in which a student on Team A makes a true present perfect statement using *for* or *since*, and a student on Team B responds by restating the sentence using whichever word Team A student didn't use. For example:

Team A: *We've been in the library for two hours.*

Team B: *We've been in the library since 3:00.*

The team with the most correct responses wins.

C. Listen and repeat.
(CD2, Track 13)

• Play the audio. There is time after each verb to allow students a chance to repeat. Give extra practice on any set of forms that students have difficulty pronouncing. Point out the difficulty, and model the correct pronunciation. For example:

T: *Listen to the word* gone. Gone. Gone. *The* o *in* gone *is not pronounced like the* o *in the word* go. *The* o *in* gone *is pronounced* /aw/, *like the words* saw *or* thought. Gone. *Repeat.* Gone

SS: *Gone*

D. Complete the sentences with the correct form of the verbs in the present perfect.

• Students complete the sentences on their own and check their answers with a partner. Point out that they should use the list in Exercise A if they need help with the past participles.

• List the item numbers on the board and have different students write the correct past perfect form after each. Review the correct answers with the class.

C. Listen and repeat.

Simple form	Simple past	Past participle	Simple form	Simple past	Past participle
be	was/were	been	leave	left	left
bear	bore	born	lose	lost	lost
become	became	become	make	made	made
begin	began	begun	meet	met	met
break	broke	broken	pay	paid	paid
bring	brought	brought	put	put	put
buy	bought	bought	quit	quit	quit
come	came	come	read	read	read
do	did	done	say	said	said
drink	drank	drunk	see	saw	seen
drive	drove	driven	sell	sold	sold
eat	ate	eaten	send	sent	sent
fall	fell	fallen	sit	sat	sat
feel	felt	felt	sleep	slept	slept
find	found	found	speak	spoke	spoken
forget	forgot	forgotten	spend	spent	spent
get	got	got/gotten	take	took	taken
give	gave	given	teach	taught	taught
go	went	gone	tell	told	told
grow	grew	grown	think	thought	thought
have	had	had	understand	understood	understood
hear	heard	heard	win	won	won
know	knew	known	write	wrote	written

D. Complete the sentences with the correct form of the verbs in the present perfect.

1. I (know) _____ have known _____ Juan for ten years.
2. She (fall) _____ has fallen _____ in love.
3. He (make) _____ has made _____ the soccer team at high school.
4. Stanley (get) _____ has _____ just _____ gotten _____ his driver's license.
5. Silvia (find) _____ has found _____ a new job recently.
6. Henry (become) _____ has become _____ a model.
7. My sister (come) _____ has _____ just _____ come _____ from Japan.
8. They (sell) _____ have sold _____ their house recently.
9. My uncle (buy) _____ has bought _____ an airplane!
10. My mother (be) _____ has been _____ a teacher since 1990.

E. Pronunciation. Listen to the stress as each speaker <u>clarifies</u> the information. <u>Underline</u> the word that is stressed.

1. **A:** I hear that David has bought a sailboat.
   B: Not exactly. He's bought a <u>motorboat.</u>

2. **A:** I hear that Amy has moved to North Carolina.
   B: Close. She's moved to <u>South</u> Carolina.

3. **A:** I hear that Nora has gotten her driver's license.
   B: No, just the opposite. She's <u>lost</u> her driver's license.

4. **A:** I hear that Joe and Tom have opened an Italian restaurant.
   B: Not Italian. They've opened a <u>Mexican</u> restaurant.

Practice the sentences above with a partner. Then, complete these conversations and practice them with a partner. (Answers will vary.)

5. **A:** I hear that Paul has made the baseball team.
   B: No, he's made the _____ team.

6. **A:** I hear that Alex and Kathy have gotten a cat.
   B: Not exactly. They've gotten a _____ .

F. Changes. Describe five changes in these people's lives. (Sample answers given.)

1.

Allen ten years ago

Allen today

Allen has cut his hair.
Allen has gotten a new job.
Allen has bought a sports car.
Allen has bought expensive clothes.
Allen has gotten married.

2.

Mary and Tom five years ago

Mary and Tom today

Mary and Tom have had two more children.
They have bought an SUV.
They have bought a house.
Mary has gained weight.
Tom has lost some hair.

Changes **119**

E. Pronunciation. (CD2, Track 14)

• Read the instructions and demonstrate the stress pattern in the first example by reading it aloud. Then, play the audio as students listen carefully. Play it a second time and have students underline the stressed words.

• Review the answers by playing the audio again, pausing after each pair of sentences, and asking students which word received the strong stress.

Practice the sentences above with a partner.

Students practice reading the sentences with a partner. Then, they work together to fill in the blanks in items 5 and 6 and practice role-playing the dialogues with each other. Invite some pairs to present their completed dialogues to the class.

F. Changes.

• Conduct a brief discussion of each picture. Ask leading questions to help students discover the differences between the "before" and "after" pictures. For example: *What is Allen wearing? What kind of transportation does he use?*

• Ask students to work with a partner to describe changes they notice. Remind them to stress the key words that describe the change. For example, *Allen used to ride a <u>motorcycle</u>. Now he drives a <u>car</u>.*

G. Find someone who . . .

- Read the instructions and answer any questions about how to do the activity. Point out the sample language at the top and ask a pair of students to read the dialogues aloud. Remind students to write only the student's name after each question, not a full-sentence answer.
- Set a time limit (perhaps ten minutes) for students to complete the activity. When they finish, ask students to share some of the interesting things they learned about each other.

H. Conversation.

- Point out the sample conversation and have students read it and ask any questions they may have about how to do the activity. Then, have students write their conversations with a partner.
- Invite several pairs to read their conversations to the class.

I. Contrast.

Review the differences between the use of the present perfect and the past. Ask students to make up pairs of original sentences that demonstrate this difference. For example: *My cousin, Anna, has just had her third baby. She had two other children before she came to this country.*

G. Find someone who . . . Stand up, walk around the classroom, and ask your classmates about their activities this month. Try to find someone who answers *Yes* to each item. Write that student's name on the line. (Answers will vary.)

| Have you changed jobs? | No, I haven't. | (Continue to ask other students!) |
| Have you changed jobs? | Yes, I have. | (Write that student's name.) |

1. buy / any new clothes? _____
2. see / a good movie? _____
3. go / to a party? _____
4. move? _____
5. have / a haircut? _____
6. take / a test? _____
7. be / late for class? _____

H. Conversation. Write a conversation with one student who answered *Yes* to one of the questions above. Then, read your conversation to the class. (Answers will vary.)

A: Have you bought any new clothes?	B: Yes, I have.
A: What did you buy?	B: I bought a pair of jeans.
A: Where did you get them?	B: At Shoppers' World.

A: Have you _____ ?

B: _____ .

A: _____ ?

B: _____ .

A: _____ ?

B: _____ .

I. Contrast—present perfect and simple past.

The **present perfect tense** tells about actions that began in the past and continue into the present.
I *have lived* in this country for three years.
She *has lived* in that apartment since she graduated from college.

The **present perfect tense** describes events in the recent past.
He *has found* a new job.
They *have* just *won* the lottery.

The **past tense** describes an action completed in the past. The time is stated or known.
She *graduated* from college in 2001.
They *moved* to New Mexico two years ago.

Complete the sentences using the correct form of the verbs in the past or the present perfect.

1. Dave moved into his apartment one year ago.

   He (live) _____ has lived _____ in his apartment for a year.

   The landlord (just / increase) _____ has just increased _____ his rent by $200!

2. My mother and father (be married) _____ have been married _____ for a long time.

   They (get) _____ got _____ married in 1950.

3. I (join) _____ joined _____ the Democratic Party ten years ago.

   I _____ have belonged _____ to the Democratic Party for ten years.

4. She _____ began _____ to work at the nursing home three years ago.

   She (work) _____ has worked _____ at the nursing home for three years.

5. I (take) _____ took _____ my examination two weeks ago.

   I (just / receive) _____ just received _____ my grade.

6. Carol (look) _____ has looked _____ for a new job for several months.

   She (quit) _____ quit _____ her job four months ago.

7. Richard (start) _____ started _____ his diet two months ago.

   He (lose) _____ has lost _____ fifteen pounds since he started his diet.

8. George (drive) _____ has driven _____ his convertible for over 25 years!

   He (buy) _____ bought _____ it in 1975.

9. I (take) _____ took _____ my first art class five years ago.

   Since that time, I (paint) _____ have painted _____ over one hundred pictures.

10. Sofia (have) _____ had _____ a heart attack last month.

    She (negative - eat) _____ hasn't eaten _____ any fried foods since then.

11. They (move) _____ moved _____ to California in 2001.

    They (live) _____ have lived _____ in Los Angeles since they arrived.

12. Sherry and Kathy (be) _____ have been _____ best friends for a long time.

    They (meet) _____ met _____ for the first time when they were in high school.

Complete the sentences using the correct form of the verbs in the past or the present perfect.

Have students complete the sentences and check their answers with a partner. Review the correct answers with the whole class.

Suggestion

Hand out newspapers or magazines and have students look through articles and circle examples of the present perfect tense. (You can also do the activity using an intermediate ESL reader.) Set a time limit of five minutes. Have students write different present perfect sentences they find on the board. Discuss each one, explaining (or asking a student to explain) why the writer chose to use the present perfect tense.

Active Grammar: Already and Yet

A. Reunion plans.

(CD2, Track 15)

• Read and discuss with students the descriptions of the sample sentences showing how to use *already* and *yet* at the top of the page. Then, review the list of things to do for the reunion.

• Play the audio and have students mark their answers. Play it a second time so they can check their answers. Review the correct answers with the whole class.

B. The to-do list.

Call on different students to explain about each item on Angela's list using *already* or *yet*.

C. My goals.

Before they write anything, have students discuss what their goals were before they came to the United States with a partner. Then, have them each write out their own lists of three goals.

Read each goal to your group.

Ask one or two students to share one of their goals with the class and then tell whether or not they have accomplished it yet. Then, have students discuss all their goals this way in their groups.

Active Grammar: Already and Yet

> **Already** shows that an action is completed. Use **already** in affirmative sentences. You can use the present perfect tense or the past tense.
> She *has* **already** *bought* the invitations.   She **already** *bought* the invitations.
> She *has bought* the invitations **already**.   She *bought* the invitations **already**.
>
> **Yet** shows the action has not been completed. Use **yet** in negative sentences and in questions. You can use the present perfect tense or the past tense.
> Has she *sent* the invitations **yet**?   Did she *send* the invitations **yet**?

A. Reunion plans. Listen to the conversation between Angela and Gloria. Check the things that Angela has already completed.

Completed	Not completed	Things to do for the reunion
✓		form a committee to help plan the reunion
✓		set a date
✓		make the invitations on the computer
✓		find the addresses of relatives who have moved
	✓	send the invitations
	✓	plan the activities and games
	✓	order the cake
✓		plan the menu
✓		buy the decorations
✓		hire two people to help cook, serve, and clean up

B. The to-do list. Discuss each item on Angela's list using *already* or *yet*.

> She has **already** formed a committee to plan the reunion.
> They haven't sent the invitations **yet**.

C. My goals. Before you came to the United States, what were three of your goals? Did you want to learn English? Did you want to buy a car? Write three of your goals below.
1. (Answers will vary.) _____
2. _____
3. _____

Read each goal to your group. Explain whether you have accomplished that goal since you came to this country. Use *already* or *yet* in your answer.

122 UNIT 8

Audio Script

A. Reunion plans. (CD2, Track 15)

Gloria: How are the reunion plans coming?

Angela: Very well. Everyone wants to help. I asked a few people to help out with the plans, just a small committee, but it's made things much easier.

Gloria: And the date is the fifteenth, right? August 15?

Angela: Yes. We've already made the invitations. Tony's son made the invitations on the computer. We're going to send them out next week.

Gloria: Were you able to find everyone's address?

Angela: I think we have them all.

Gloria: Have you done anything else yet?

Angela: Well, we haven't planned the games or the activities, but we've already planned the menu. We're having chicken on the grill and everyone is going to bring a salad

(Audio Script continues on page 254.)

👥 **D. After the party.** George and Monica had a party and almost all of the guests have left. They have just begun to clean their home. Use the cues below to talk about their progress. What have they done? What haven't they done? (Answers will vary.)

put away the food	collect the cans and bottles
clear off the table	blow out the candles
take down the decorations	eat the last piece of cake
sweep the floor	close the windows
wash the dishes	get Monica's brother to leave
empty the garbage can	turn off the stereo

👥 **E. What have you done today?** Ask one another about your day so far. (Answers will vary.)

> Have you gotten your mail yet?
> Yes, I have. I got it at 10:00. *or*
> No, I haven't. I don't get my mail until 4:00.

go to work

get your mail

eat a piece of fruit

buy anything

do your homework

exercise

make a phone call

take a shower

make your bed

speak in class

watch TV

read the newspaper

👥 D. **After the party.**

• Read and discuss the instructions. Then, have students cover the list of cues below the picture. Invite them to comment on what they see. Accept any reasonable comment, repeating correct comments and phrasing any incomplete or incorrect statements in full sentence form. For example:

S: *Everyone didn't leave.*
T: *That's right. Not everyone has left yet.*

• Then, have students look at the list of cues and work with a partner talking about the progress George and Monica have made. Walk around the classroom, listening and assisting students with their sentences.

👥 E. **What have you done today?**

• Read the instructions and review the sample dialogue with the class. Then, working in pairs, have students take turns using the cues to ask and answers questions about their own lives.

• Review the answers by calling on several different pairs to present one or two of their dialogues to the class.

Suggestion

Have students form a single line and play a game of "What have you done?" You might start them off with cues such as *pay my taxes, have a medical checkup,* and *go to the dentist.* The first student makes a statement such as, *I haven't paid my taxes yet.* The second student tells whether or not he/she has paid the taxes and adds a second item: *I have already paid my taxes. I haven't had a medical checkup.* Each new student reports on whether or not he/she has done each of the previous activities mentioned, and adds a new one to the list.

☼ The Big Picture:
Gossip

A. Discuss this vocabulary.

Ask students the meaning of the new vocabulary. To help with the meaning of some of the words, refer students to the pictures in Exercise B. For example:
The teenage girl is grounded. When a child is "grounded," the parents won't let the child leave the house except to go to school.

B. Gossip.
(CD2, Track 16 through 21)

Play the audio and ask students to label the pictures with the correct names. Play it a second time, pausing after each conversation. Ask students what the gossip is about each person.

C. Answer these questions about the gossip you heard.

Have students answer each question by writing the correct name at the end of the sentence. Then, ask different students to read a question aloud and choose another student to answer.

☼ The Big Picture: Gossip

A. Discuss this vocabulary.

gossip	clinic	grounded
broken off	face-lift	date / go out with

B. Gossip. Listen to these people talk about their friends, family, and coworkers. Label each person in the pictures.

| Rosa | Paul | Grandpa | Diana | Mary | Amy |

1. _____Rosa_____ 2. _____Paul_____ 3. _____Grandpa_____

4. _____Diana_____ 5. _____Mary_____ 6. _____Amy_____

C. Answer these questions about the gossip you heard.

1. Who has had a face-lift? Rosa
2. Who has just been promoted? Paul
3. Who has begun to date a much older man? Mary
4. Who has broken off her engagement? Diana
5. Who has bought a red convertible? Grandpa

Audio Script

B. Gossip.

Conversation 1 (CD2, Track 16)
A: Have you heard about Diana?
B: No. What happened?
A: Well, remember her engagement party?
B: Sure.
A: She's not engaged anymore.
B: No! I really liked Chris.
A: She's broken off the engagement. She met this new guy who moved into her apartment building and she's fallen in love with him.
B: And what about Chris?

A: She's given him back his ring.
B: Really? Do you have Chris's phone number?

Conversation 2 (CD2, Track 17)
A: Have you seen Rosa lately?
B: Hmm-mm. I spoke to her yesterday.
A: She looks great, doesn't she?
B: Yes, she said her vacation was really relaxing.
A: She didn't take a vacation. She went to a clinic.
B: A clinic?
A: Yes, she had a face-lift. That's why she looks so good.
B: Let me know the name of that clinic! I'm going to make an appointment myself.

Conversation 3 (CD2, Track 18)
A: Have you heard about Amy? She's in big trouble.
B: What happened this time?
A: She took her mom's car without her permission. And she had an accident on the way to the mall.
B: Oh, no! Was she hurt?
A: No, she hit a mailbox. But, she's been grounded for a month. I've tried to call her three times, but her parents won't let me talk to her. They've taken away her cell phone.

(Audio Script continues on page 254.)

6. Who has just been in an accident? **Amy**

7. Who has just been at a clinic? **Rosa**

8. Who has been grounded? **Amy**

9. Who has fallen in love with a neighbor? **Diana**

10. Who has left to travel across the country? **Grandpa**

11. Who has taken away their daughter's cell phone? **Amy's parents**

D. Read these statements. (Circle) T for *true* and F for *false*.

1. Diana still has Chris's ring. — T **(F)**
2. Rosa looks wonderful! — **(T)** F
3. Rosa told all her friends that she had a face-lift. — T **(F)**
4. Amy's parents have taken away her cell phone. — **(T)** F
5. This is the first time that Amy has gotten in trouble. — T **(F)**
6. Paul has been promoted. — **(T)** F
7. Paul has the best sales record in the company. — T **(F)**
8. Mary is dating a man who is much older than she is. — **(T)** F
9. Grandpa has bought a new car. — **(T)** F
10. Grandpa now has gray hair. — T **(F)**

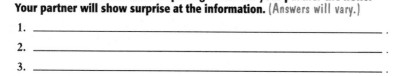

E. Surprise intonation. To show surprise and interest, a listener often repeats a few words of a speaker's conversation with question intonation. Listen and repeat the surprise intonation.

1. **A:** He bought a new convertible. **B:** A new convertible?
2. **A:** He left yesterday. **B:** He left?
3. **A:** He's just been promoted. **B:** Promoted?
4. **A:** She's run off with a man twice her age. **B:** Twice her age?

Listen and show surprise at statements 5–10.

F. Write three statements with surprising news. Tell your partner the news. Your partner will show surprise at the information. (Answers will vary.)

1. _____ .
2. _____ .
3. _____ .

D. Read these statements.

Ask students to answer the questions individually. Then, ask individual students to read each statement and tell if it is true or false. If it is false, the student should supply the correct information.

E. Surprise intonation.
(CD2, Track 22)

• Read the explanation and play the audio. Ask students to listen carefully for the surprise intonation. Then, play the audio again and have them repeat each question with surprise intonation.

• Ask pairs of students to role-play the sample dialogues. Encourage them to emphasize or exaggerate the surprise intonation in each.

Listen and show surprise at statements 5–10.
(CD2, Track 23)

Continue with Exercise E, playing items 5 through 10. Pause after each one and call on a student to give a response that shows surprise.

F. Write three statements with surprising news.

• Ask students to think of original ideas for their surprising news. Encourage them to be a little outlandish, if they wish. For example:

S1: *I want to have ten children.*
S2: *Ten children?*

• Students practice their dialogues with a partner. Invite several different pairs to present their best dialogues to the class.

Audio Script

E. Surprise intonation. (CD2, Track 22)

1. **A:** He bought a new convertible.
   B: A new convertible?
2. **A:** He left yesterday.
   B: He left?
3. **A:** He's just been promoted.
   B: Promoted?
4. **A:** She's run off with a man twice her age.
   B: Twice her age?

Listen and show surprise at statements 5–10. (CD2, Track 23)

5. They've moved to Alaska.
6. She bought a horse.
7. He's just won $50,000.
8. He's been fired.
9. She's expecting triplets.
10. She has 50 pairs of shoes.

Reading: A Family Newsletter

A. Skimming for the main idea.

- Point out the photos in the newsletter and ask students to briefly describe each person.
- Introduce the idea of skimming and then have students do the activity on their own. Review the answers with the whole class.

Teacher Note

You may wish to conduct a short lesson in how to skim a reading passage. You can suggest the following:

1. Move your eyes quickly through the reading. Don't try to read every word.
2. Try running your finger down the middle of the page and following it with your eye to help you remember to continue reading without stopping on individual words or sentences.
3. Pause after each paragraph and summarize in your own words what you just read.

B. Scanning for details.

- Explain scanning for details: *This is like skimming for the main idea, except that you have a certain fact in mind that you're looking for. For item one, the fact you're looking for is the date of the reunion. Keep this in mind as you scan through the reading. When you find the information, underline it.*
- Have students locate the details individually and check their answers with a partner. Discuss with the whole class any items that students had trouble with.

C. Vocabulary.

Have students match the words with their meanings and fill in the sentences on their own. Then, have them check their answers with a partner.

A. Skimming for the main idea. The first four sections of this family newsletter on page 127 talk about a specific event. Look quickly at the four sections and write the events they describe.

Section 1: __Plans for the family reunion__   Section 3: __Grandma Mayra turned 99.__

Section 2: __Debbie Nelson is graduating__   Section 4: __Ann and Fred are retired.__
__and has a job.__

B. Scanning for details. Look quickly through the information in the newsletter. Answer these questions.

1. What are the dates for the family reunion? August 14th and 15th
2. Where is the barbecue on Saturday? Essex Park
3. Where is the family going on Sunday? The beach
4. What did Debbie major in? Does she have a job yet? Social work. Yes, she does.
5. How old is Grandma Nelson? 99
6. Where did Fred and Ann move? What did Fred buy?
They moved to Florida. Fred bought a fishing boat.
7. Where are they volunteering?
They are volunteering at the local community center.
8. What kind of an operation did Laura have? She had a knee replacement.
9. What kind of information is Karen looking for? She is looking for job leads.

C. Vocabulary. Match these words from the newsletter with their meanings. Then, complete the sentences below with the words in their correct form.

_d_ **1.** adjust to	**a.**	contribute money or time
_f_ **2.** hassle-free	**b.**	became
_g_ **3.** elderly	**c.**	job possibilities
_b_ **4.** turned	**d.**	meet or handle changes in your life
_a_ **5.** chip in	**e.**	in the future
_e_ **6.** ahead	**f.**	easy
_c_ **7.** leads	**g.**	people who are very old.

1. Sunday is the only _____hassle-free_____ day of the week.
2. All the children _____chipped in_____ to buy their parents a trip to Bermuda.
3. My sister, who just had twins, has many sleepless nights _____ahead_____.
4. I'm 19. I'll _____turn_____ 20 on March 5.
5. Greg has just graduated with a degree in physical therapy. He is looking into several _____leads_____.

126 Unit 8

The Nelsons in the News

Circle August 14th and 15th on your calendars! This year's reunion committee includes Doris, Frank, Lynn, and Roberto. For Saturday, we've already reserved ten tables in Essex Park, close to the children's playground and across from the pond. We'll all **chip in** for the chicken and burgers and each family will bring a salad and dessert. Most people have asked us to plan Sunday as a day at the beach. People have requested a relaxing, **hassle-free** day. We're talking to different delis in the area and are planning to order a large picnic lunch. Look at the next issue for more details! We'd love your suggestions and comments. Call Angela at 555-8739.

Congratulations to Debbie Nelson. After eight years at college, sometimes full-time, sometimes part-time, Debbie has just completed all her course work in social work. She will graduate in May. Debbie has accepted a position at Atlantic Community Services, where she will be working with troubled teens.

 Grandma Mayra Nelson **turned** 99 on January 2nd. She lives with her daughter, Eva, and son-in-law, Brad. Mayra enjoys TV, her flower garden, and visits from her four children, 12 grandchildren, and 30 great-grandchildren. She will become a great, great-grandmother in March! Mayra says that she is looking forward to her 100th birthday. She tells her children, "I expect a big party to celebrate my wonderful family."

Hi everyone!
Our new home in Florida is only five blocks from the beach. After working for 40 years, Ann and I were wondering how we would **adjust to** retirement. It wasn't hard! Ann has joined a tennis group and she plays three mornings a week. I've bought a little fishing boat and you'll find me on the water two or three mornings a week. I haven't caught "the big one" yet, but I'm planning to! Ann and I are also volunteering at the local community center. We deliver Meals on Wheels to the **elderly** one day a week. Two days a week, we read with children in an after-school program for kids who need extra help with their schoolwork. Don't worry—we haven't forgotten about all of you. We'll be coming up for the family reunion. If you are planning a trip to Florida, we'd love to see you. Our number is 555-3494.
Fred

Send your get-well cards to Laura. Her knee replacement went well, but she has several months of physical therapy **ahead**. Her address: 346 Windsor Avenue.

Karen is looking for job **leads**. Her company closed its doors last month, leaving 75 accountants looking for work. If you have any suggestions, please call her at 555-9087.

Congratulations to Todd! He has been accepted to Duke University, his first-choice college.

Suggestion

Some students may be interested in writing a class newsletter modeled after the Nelson newsletter. Give the students a few minutes of class time to meet to plan the topics each will write about as homework. Ask them to bring their work to the next class. Students exchange their paragraphs and correct each other's work. Ask a volunteer to combine the stories and word-process the newsletter so it can be distributed to the whole class.

Writing Our Stories: A News Article

A. Newsletters include information about family events, both large and small.

Ask students to check off all the events from this list that have occurred in their families recently. Encourage them to add special events not mentioned in the blank after the word *other*.

Tell the class about one of these events.

Give students a few minutes to prepare before asking them to tell about their event. They may wish to make a few notes on a piece of paper to help them remember what they want to say. Ask two or three students to share an event.

B. Read this news article from a family newsletter.

Ask students to read the letter on their own.

C. Getting the facts.

Read and discuss the examples of specific details. Then, have students expand each simple statement by adding details. Invite several students to read their expanded statements to the class.

Writing Our Stories: A News Article

A. Newsletters include information about family events, both large and small. Did anyone in your extended family recently . . . *(Answers will vary.)*

☐ graduate	☐ celebrate a birthday	☐ lose a job
☐ get married	☐ celebrate an anniversary	☐ accept a new job
☐ get engaged	☐ take a vacation	☐ have an accident
☐ get divorced	☐ move	☐ have an operation
☐ have a baby	☐ retire	☐ pass away (die)

Other: ☐ _____

Tell the class about one of these events.

B. Read this news article from a family newsletter.

Henry has just accepted a position as distribution manager at Davis and Bates. Davis and Bates is a growing furniture manufacturer in the West. Henry will coordinate all the company's deliveries. Currently, the company employs 25 people in its distribution center. They are planning to expand this to 50 employees. Henry is selling his house, and he will leave for California next month. His wife, Paula, and their two children will move to California after they sell their house.

C. Getting the facts. When reporting facts, it is important to get all the details. Specific facts provide interesting and clear information. Read the examples. Then, use your imagination to write specific facts about each statement.

1. Thomas graduated from college.

   Thomas graduated from the University of Maryland in May with a degree in biology.

   _____

2. Tuan and Lana had a baby.

   Tuan and Lana had an eight-pound baby girl on September 18th. They have named the baby Kathy, after Lana's mother.

3. Linda celebrated her birthday.
(Answers will vary.)

_____

4. Tom was in a bad car accident.

_____

_____

5. Ken and Susan celebrated their wedding anniversary.

_____

_____

6. Karin and Juan have just returned from a wonderful vacation.

_____

_____

D. A news article. Write a short factual article about an event in your family, your class, or your school. (Answers will vary.)

E. Edit. Find and correct the mistakes in these sentences.

1. She ~~have~~ has just found a new job.
2. They haven't gotten married ~~already~~ yet.
3. They will get married on October 10.
4. They ~~has~~ have just celebrated their tenth wedding anniversary.
5. Jason has come already home from the hospital.
6. They have lived in the same house ~~for~~ since 1990.
7. Olga ~~has~~ graduated from Duke University last month.
8. Ron has taken a job in Arizona.
9. Grandma Barnes passed away on June 15.
10. The whole family ~~have~~ has just enjoyed a wonderful family reunion.

 Looking at the Internet

Click on **Search** and enter the words "family reunion." What kinds of services can you find at a family reunion Web site? What can you buy to make the reunion more fun or more memorable? Tell your classmates what you found.

D. A news article.

• Suggest that students outline what they are going to write about using single words or partial sentences to record each idea. Then, have them look at their outlines and think of ways to add specific details. They can jot down these additional ideas on their original lists.

• Collect the articles. As you correct the articles, focus on details. Point out to students what additional information would be interesting. Ask students to word-process their corrected articles so you can display them on the classroom wall for others to read.

E. Edit.

Students correct the mistakes and check their work with a partner.

Looking at the Internet

After students report back to the class about what they learned about giving a family reunion, ask them to tell what they think the single most important thing about planning a reunion is.

Practicing on Your Own

A. A changed city.

Students complete the sentences on their own and check their answers with a partner.

B. A changed student.

Remind students to use the present perfect tense to describe what Tommy has accomplished so far this semester. Have them check their answers with a partner or in small groups.

Suggestion

Invite some or all students to write stories called "A Changed Friend" or "A Changed Relative." Have them describe a personal transformation using the present perfect tense to describe changes that have begun to take place in the person's life.

Practicing on Your Own

A. A changed city. Last year, Tamara returned to her native country for the first time in ten years. Complete these sentences about the changes in her hometown. Use the present perfect tense.

1. Ten years ago, there were two doctors. Now there is a small clinic with six doctors. The health care system (improve) _____ has improved _____.

2. The population (increase) _____ has increased _____ from 25,000 to 50,000.

3. Many new restaurants (open) _____ have opened _____.

4. The unemployment rate (decrease) _____ has decreased _____ from 15 percent to 9 percent.

5. Tourism (become) _____ has become _____ a major industry.

6. The city (hire) _____ has hired _____ fifteen new police officers.

7. The crime rate (drop) _____ has dropped _____ substantially.

8. Many new businesses (move) _____ have moved _____ into the area because of the strong economy.

9. Her quiet village (change) _____ has changed _____ into a busy, noisy town.

B. A changed student. Tommy had a difficult first semester at college and is now on academic probation. He's changed and become a serious student. Compare his first and second semesters at school using the present perfect tense.
(Answers may vary.)

First Semester: The "old" Tommy	Second Semester: The "new" Tommy
1. He missed ten days of school.	1. He has missed only one day of school.
2. He was late for his classes.	2. He hasn't been late for his classes.
3. He failed every test.	3. He has passed every test.
4. He didn't ask for extra help.	4. He has asked for extra help
5. He didn't do his homework.	5. He has done his homework
6. He failed two courses.	6. He has passed two courses
7. He didn't study for tests.	7. He has studied for tests
8. He didn't write any papers.	8. He has written all of his papers

130 UNIT 8

Grammar Summary

▶ **1. Present perfect**

  a. The present perfect tense tells about an action that started in the past and continues into the present. The action is not completed.

    They **have lived** in Miami for six years.

    He **has owned** that company since he moved to Wisconsin.

  b. The present perfect describes actions in the recent past. It is often used with *just, lately,* and *recently.* If the sentence gives a specific time or date, use the past tense.

    She **has just found** a new job.

    She **found** a new job last week. (This sentence gives a specific past time.)

    I**'ve spoken** to him recently.

    I **spoke** to him yesterday. (This sentence gives a specific past time.)

  c. The present perfect is used with *already* and *yet.*

    She **has already bought** her plane ticket.

    I **haven't registered** for my classes **yet**.

▶ **2. Statements**

  Use *have* or *has* and the past participle to form the present perfect.

I You We They	have haven't	**worked** here **known** him	for two years.
He She	has hasn't	**been** married	since 2001.

▶ **3. *Yes/No* questions**

Have	I you we they	**worked** here **known** him	for two years?
Has	he she	**been** married	since 2001?

Grammar Summary

• Review the three grammar explanations and sample sentences with the class. Invite students to make up alternate sentences for each example in the chart. For example, in place of *I have known him for two years,* a student might say, *I have worked as a waiter since I was 18 years old.*

• Answer any questions students may have about the grammar items.

• See the Grammar Summary Expansion on page 265 for a more complete explanation of these grammar points.

Unit 9
Job Performance

Discuss what the person in the unit title art is doing. Ask:
- *Who is standing next to the number 9?* (A woman)
- *What is she doing?* (She's standing in front of a chart with a plus sign, a minus sign, and an OK sign on it.)
- *What does this have to do with the unit?* (The unit is about job performance, and those three signs indicate that a person's performance is not so good, average, or very good.)

A. Discuss the different jobs in the pictures.

- Read the list of questions aloud. Explain any terms that students don't understand. For example:

Production work involves making something, usually in a factory. Service work involves doing something for people. Service jobs are found in stores, banks, and other offices.

- Point to the pictures one by one and ask the questions again. Accept all reasonable answers. Encourage several students to contribute to answering each question.

B. Sit in a group of two or three students.

- Set a time limit for the discussions. Move from group to group answering questions and offering language support as needed.
- Invite volunteer pairs from one group to present the questions and answers to the class. Encourage other students to ask for additional information if they wish.

---

9 Job Performance

A. Discuss the different jobs in the pictures. (Answers will vary.)

1. What is the job title for each person?
2. Does this person work in production or service?
3. What skills does this person need for the job?
4. Would you like this kind of work? Why or why not?

B. Sit in a group of two or three students. Talk about your jobs. (Answers will vary.)

1. What company do you work for?
2. What product does this company make or what service does it provide?
3. How many employees work for your company?
4. What kinds of positions does your company have?
5. Is there a human resources or personnel office?
6. How long have you worked there?
7. What do you do? What are your job responsibilities?
8. What benefits do you receive?
9. How often do you receive a performance evaluation?

Suggestion

Ask students to take turns making quick sketches on the board showing themselves at work. Have other students guess what the person's job is and ask the questions in Exercise A as well as any other questions that come to mind. Help with student responses as necessary.

> **How long** asks about an amount of time.
> How long **has** she **been repairing** TVs?   She's **been repairing** TVs for two hours.
>
> **How many** asks about a specific number.
> How many TVs **has** she **repaired**?   She **has repaired** four TVs.
>
> When we use the **present perfect**, it shows that the action is <u>not yet completed.</u>
> The person is still working or performing the action.
>
> **Note:** When we use the **past**, it shows that the action is <u>completed.</u>
>
> How many TVs **did** she **repair**?   She **repaired** 25 TVs. (Her work is finished.)

A. Read this conversation.

> **A:** What is Harry doing?
> **B:** He's registering students for classes.
> **A:** How long has he been sitting at the registration counter?
> **B:** He's been sitting there for two hours.
> **A:** How many students has he registered so far?
> **B:** He's registered 18 students so far today.

B. Ask and answer questions about each picture. Use Exercise A as an example.

(Answers will vary.)

What is he/she doing?
How long has he/she been _____?
How many _____ has he/she _____?

1.  2.  3.

4.  5.  6.

☀ **Active Grammar:**
How long and
How many

A. Read this conversation.

- Review the *How long* questions and answers in the grammar charts at the top of the page. Answer any questions students may have.
- Ask a pair of students to read the conversation to the class.

B. Ask and answer questions about each picture.

- The partners take turns asking and answering questions about the pictures, using the conversation in Exercise A as a model. Explain that students will have to make up some of the information. For example, they won't know exactly how long the woman making pizzas has been working or how many pizzas she has made.
- Review the exercise by having different pairs present one of their dialogues to the class. Have other students suggest corrections if necessary.

Active Grammar:
Repeated Past Actions

A. Ask your teacher about his/her job and interests.

• Ask students to study the grammar explanations at the top of the page. Read the sentences of explanation aloud and ask different students to restate them in their own words. For example:

T: *These actions have occurred several times and may occur again.*

S: *These actions didn't happen just one time. They happened more than once. They also may happen again in the future.*

• Discuss the adverbs of frequency and ask students to assign rough percentages to each. For example: *Always = 100%, Sometimes = 50%, Never = 0 %, and so forth.*

• Invite students to ask you the questions. Use the present perfect and present perfect continuous and make your answers as truthful as possible.

B. Ask and answer these questions about work.

Students should work with a partner and take turns asking and answering questions about actual work experiences. Invite several pairs to role-play some exchanges for the class.

Ask your partner two more questions about work.

The partners ask and answer some original questions about each other's jobs.

Indefinite time expressions and adverbs of frequency

We use the **present perfect** to talk about *repeated past actions*. These actions have occurred several times and may occur again. In these sentences, we are interested in the action, and not in the time of the action. We often use indefinite time expressions and adverbs of frequency in these sentences.

1. Place most indefinite time expressions at the end of a sentence.

from time to time	a few times	once
two times so far this month	so far	twice

I have missed work **from time to time.**   I have missed work **two times this month.**

2. Place adverbs of frequency before the main verb.

always	often	seldom
frequently	sometimes	never

I have **never** been late for work.   I have **seldom** missed work.

A. Ask your teacher about his/her job and interests. (Answers will vary.)

1. How long have you been teaching at this school?
2. Have you ever worked at a different school?
3. Have you ever taught any other subjects?
4. Have you ever studied another language?
5. Have you ever had a different kind of a job?
6. Have you ever gotten stuck in traffic on your way to work?
7. Have you ever visited _____?
8. Have you ever eaten _____ food?
9. Have you ever acted in a play?
10. Have you ever played on a sports team?

B. Ask and answer these questions about work. (Answers will vary.)

A: Have you ever taken a personal day?
B: Yes, I've taken one personal day this year.

1. call in sick?
2. have an accident at work?
3. quit a job?
4. receive a raise?
5. get a promotion?
6. receive a performance evaluation?
7. complain to your boss?
8. complain about your boss?
9. work a double shift?
10. attend a training program?
11. have a problem with a coworker?
12. (be) laid off?

Ask your partner two more questions about work.

☀ Active Grammar: Time Expressions—Review

> **Time expressions are usually placed at the end of a sentence.**
> I began to work here **in 2000.**   I have worked here **for two years.**
> **Pay attention to the placement of adverbs of frequency and indefinite time expressions in the present perfect tense.**
> 1. Place adverbs of frequency before the main verb.
>   Laura has **never** received a warning at work.
> 2. Place **just**, **already**, and **finally** before the main verb. **Already** can also be placed at the end of the sentence.
>   Henry has **just** gotten a raise.   I've **already** had dinner. OR
>   I've had dinner **already.**
> 3. Place **yet**, **recently**, and **at last** at the end of the sentence.
>   I've spoken to him **recently.**   Bill hasn't finished the report **yet.**
> 4. Place indefinite time expressions at the end of a sentence.
>   I have changed jobs **twice.**   She's taken four breaks today **so far!**

👥 A. Make four sentences about each picture using the cues. Place the adverbs and time expressions in the correct place in the sentences. Use the simple past or the present perfect. (Answers will vary.)

go on a job interview

1.

| twice | just |
| yesterday | last week |

take a vacation

2.

| never | last summer |
| two years ago | recently |

get a promotion

3.

| last year | yet |
| twice | in 2002 |

complete the order

4.

| yesterday | finally |
| an hour ago | already |

☀ Active Grammar:
Time Expression — Review

👥 A. Make four sentences about each picture using the cues.

- Ask students to study the list of time expressions and grammar explanations at the top of the page. Point out the placement of time expressions in the simple past and in the present perfect.
- Students practice making sentences about the pictures. Call on different students to say one sentence each. If a student makes an error, ask another student to correct the sentence and read aloud the related rule from the grammar box at the top of the page.

Suggestion

Write on the board some time expression like those at the top of page 135. For example: *a week ago, yet, finally, last year.* Then, point to an expression and ask students to make up true sentences about themselves using that expression.

B. Pronunciation. (CD2, Track 24)

- Play the audio once as students follow along in their books. Next write 've on the board and say the 've sound in isolation several times. Have students repeat.
- Play the audio again. This time have students listen and repeat the sentences.

Listen again and circle the sentence you hear.
(CD2, Track 25)

Have students circle the sentences as you play the audio. Play it again so students can check their work.

Practice these sentences with a partner.

Students take turns reading sets of *a* and *b* sentences to their partners. (They should first read all the *a* sentences and then read all the *b* sentences. It's important for them to read the similar sentences one after the other so they can contrast the verb endings.)

C. Listen to each sentence.
(CD2, Track 26)

Review the instructions and play the audio as students circle their answers. Play it a second time so they can check their work. Review the correct answers with the class.

B. Pronunciation: Simple past tense versus present perfect tense. Listen and repeat.

> **Note:** Sometimes it's difficult to hear if a person is using the past or present perfect. It's important to know which one is being used because it can change the meaning.

1. a. I sold five cars.   (b.) I've sold five cars.
2. a. She worked five hours.   (b.) She's worked five hours.
3. (a.) They made 500 donuts.   b. They've made 500 donuts.
4. a. She walked five miles.   (b.) She's walked five miles.
5. (a.) I helped 10 customers.   b. I've helped 10 customers.
6. (a.) He planted five trees.   b. He's planted five trees.
7. a. She read 20 pages.   (b.) She's read 20 pages.
8. a. I cleaned seven rooms.   (b.) I've cleaned seven rooms.
9. (a.) He typed four reports.   b. He's typed four reports.
10. a. I checked in 50 passengers.   (b.) I've checked in 50 passengers.

Listen again and circle the sentence you hear.

Practice these sentences with a partner.

C. Listen to each sentence. Circle the letter of the sentence that shows the correct meaning.

1. a. The doctor is still seeing patients.
   (b.) The doctor is finished seeing patients for the day.
2. (a.) Benji is still ironing shirts.
   b. Benji is finished ironing shirts for the day.
3. (a.) The men are still planting trees.
   b. The men are finished planting the trees.
4. (a.) The teacher has more papers to correct.
   b. The teacher finished all the papers.
5. a. Carlos is finished for the day.
   (b.) Carlos is still in his truck, delivering packages.
6. (a.) Mary is not going to call any more people today.
   b. Mary will call 100 more people.
7. (a.) She retired from the hospital.
   b. She's still working at the hospital.
8. (a.) He will drive farther today.
   b. He's going to stop for the day.
9. a. There are still customers in line.
   (b.) She is going home because the bank is now closed.

Audio Script

B. Listen again and circle the sentence you hear. (CD2, Track 25)

1. I've sold five cars.
2. She's worked five hours.
3. They made 500 donuts.
4. She's walked five miles.
5. I helped 10 customers.
6. He planted five trees.
7. She's read 20 pages.
8. I've cleaned seven rooms.
9. He typed four reports.
10. I've checked in 50 passengers.

C. Listen to each sentence. (CD2, Track 26)

1. The doctor saw all his patients for the day.
2. Benji has been ironing shirts for five hours.
3. The men have planted five trees so far.
4. The teacher has checked 30 papers.
5. Carlos has delivered 40 packages.
6. Mary called 100 people today.
7. Kathy worked at the hospital for 50 years.
8. Josh drives a truck between New York and Florida. He's driven 300 miles today so far.
9. Debbie was busy at the bank today. She handled over two hundred transactions.

We use the **past tense** to describe an action that occurred at a <u>specific</u> time or event.
  I **ate** lunch at La Salsa last Friday. The food was delicious.
We can use the **present perfect** to describe an action that occurred at an <u>unspecified</u> time in the past. The sentence does not talk about a specific event or time. The action is more important than the exact time.
  I've **eaten** at La Salsa. The food is delicious.

A. Complete the sentences with the past or the present perfect of the verbs in parentheses.

1. Bob _____received_____ (receive) a raise last year.
2. Bob ___has received___ (receive) two raises this year and it's only July.
3. Laura ___has had___ (have) six job interviews so far this year.
4. Laura ___had___ (have) a job interview in Dallas yesterday.
5. I ___have heard___ (hear) that song a hundred times.
6. I ___heard___ (hear) that song a few minutes ago.
7. Sarah ___took___ (take) two sick days when she had the flu.
8. Sarah ___has taken___ (take) two sick days this year.
9. We ___have hired___ (hire) three new workers, and we need one more.
10. We ___hired___ (hire) the four new workers that we needed.

B. Ask and answer the questions. Be careful of the tense! (Answers will vary.)

1. Have you missed any days of school this year?
2. How many days have you been absent so far?
3. Why did you miss class last week?
4. How many different jobs have you had in your life?
5. Where do you work now? How long have you been working there?
6. Where did you work before this?
7. Why did you leave that job?
8. How many different countries have you lived in?
9. Have you ever traveled to _____?
10. Where did you go on your last vacation?

Active Grammar:
Simple Past versus Present Perfect

A. Complete the sentences with the past or the present perfect of the verbs in parentheses.

• Discuss the grammar explanations and sample sentences. Answer any questions students may have. Then, have students complete the sentences on their own.

• Review the answers with the class. Call on different students to give the reason for their choice of verb. For example:

T: *In sentence 2, why did you use "has received" instead of "received?"*

S: *We don't know when he got the raises. The time is not specified. Also, the idea that he got the raises is more important than when he got them.*

B. Ask and answer the questions.

Ask students to work in pairs to ask and answer questions. Circulate around the room, helping students to formulate their answers.

☀ Job Performance

A. Read George's job description. (CD2, Track 27)

- Read the job description, clarifying any new vocabulary such as *obey, discharge,* and *designated.* Help students use the sentence context to figure out the meaning of these words.
- Go over the list of questions with the class, and answer any questions they may have. Play the audio and have students listen to find the answers to the five questions. Play the audio a second time. Ask students to describe any other details they remember about George's job.

B. Complete this information about George and his job.

Have students complete the sentences on their own and check their answers with a partner. Review the correct answers with the whole class.

Suggestion

Invite students to bring their own job descriptions to class. Duplicate copies of one description and discuss it with the class. You can point out useful vocabulary items in the descriptions.

☀ Job Performance

A. Read George's job description. Then, listen as he describes his job. Answer the questions.

> **Job Description for Metro Transit Drivers**
>
> 1. Report to work on time and in full uniform.
> 2. Drive carefully and obey all traffic and safety laws.
> 3. Pick up and discharge passengers at designated bus stops.
> 4. Collect correct fares.
> 5. Greet and treat passengers with courtesy.
>
> Company policy: Employee pay starts at $9.00 an hour. All employees with good evaluations receive a pay increase of $0.50 a year. If the employee has no accidents in five years, pay will increase to $13.00.
>
> George's Salary (1998–2003)
>
> | 1998 | 1999 | 2000 | 2001 | 2002 | 2003 |
> |------|------|------|------|------|------|
> | $9.00 | $9.50 | $10.00 | $10.50 | $11.00 | $13.00 |

1. How long has George been working for Metro Transit? **5 years**
2. What year did he begin to work there? **He began in 1998.**
3. How much was his starting salary? **His starting salary was $9.00 an hour.**
4. Has his salary increased each year? **Yes, it has.**
5. Has he ever had an accident? **No, he hasn't.**
6. What year is it? **2003**
7. How many pay increases has George received since 1998? **Five pay increases.**
8. What is his salary now? **$13.00**

B. Complete this information about George and his job. Use the past or present perfect form of the verbs in parentheses.

1. Before he started at Metro Transit, George _____ **worked** _____ (work) as a school bus driver.
2. He _____ **didn't like** _____ (negative—like) the noise on the school bus.
3. He _____ **saw** _____ (see) an ad in the newspaper for Metro Transit.
4. He _____ **applied** _____ (apply) for the job and _____ **received** _____ (receive) a job offer the next week.
5. When George began at Metro Transit, he _____ **earned** _____ (earn) $9.00 an hour.

Audio Script

A. Read George's job description. (CD2, Track 27)

My name is George Pappas and I am a bus driver for Metro Transit. I started here in 1998. Before that, I was a school bus driver. In the morning, the kids were tired and they were quiet, but on the way home, they were really excited and noisy. One day, I saw an ad in the newspaper for a city bus driver. I applied and was really lucky—I got a job offer the next week. I started here at $9.00 an hour. The company has a very clear salary policy. If a driver receives a good evaluation, he or she receives a fifty-cent pay raise a year. I've always received good evaluations, so I've always received my raise. If an employee has no accidents in five years, the pay will increase to $13.00. There is a top limit, so no one at this company makes more than $18.00 an hour. There's lots of opportunity for overtime, too. Most of us here work about ten hours a week overtime. Overtime pay is time and a half. And another thing . . . speeding tickets. The company is very strict about tickets. If you get a ticket, you have to pay for it. Also, the company fines you another $250. If you receive two or more speeding tickets in a year, you're fired. I've only received one ticket and I don't plan to get another one! I like this job and I want to keep it.

6. He _____has received_____ (receive) a pay raise every year since then.

7. His performance evaluations _____have_____ always _____been_____ (be) very good.

8. He _____has had_____ (have) two or three passenger complaints, which is less than the company average.

9. George _____has_____ only _____had_____ one serious problem at work. (have)

10. Two years ago, he _____got_____ (get) a ticket for speeding.

11. He _____paid_____ (pay) a fine of $200 and the company _____charged_____ (charge) him another $250.

12. George _____has_____ always _____been_____ polite and courteous to the passengers. (be)

C. Employee performance. These four insurance agents have been working for CarCo for one year or more. Look at the chart and answer the questions about their job performance.

Employee	Years at CarCo	Policies Last Year	Policies This Year to Date	Customer Complaints This Year
Jeff	3	125	43	2
Katie	1	67	40	5
George	4	55	22	0
Ellen	2	88	35	10

1. Who has worked at CarCo the longest? George

2. How long has George worked there? 4 years

3. Is George the best agent at CarCo? Why or why not? No, he has written the least amount of policies.

4. Who wrote the most policies last year? Who wrote the fewest? Jeff wrote the most and George wrote the fewest.

5. Who has written the most policies so far this year? Jeff has written the most policies this year.

6. Which agent has received the fewest complaints? George has received the fewest complaints.

7. Ellen has sold many policies so far this year. Why is the boss dissatisfied with her performance? Ellen has the most customer complaints this year.

8. George has never received a customer complaint. Why is the boss dissatisfied with his performance? George sells the fewest policies each year.

9. Katie has worked at CarCo for only one year. How would you evaluate her performance? (Answers will vary.)

10. Who is the best agent at CarCo? Jeff

C. Employee performance.

• Do this activity with the whole class. Have students study the statistics for a few minutes. Answer any questions they may have.

• Call on a different student to answer each question. Ask the rest of the students to raise their hands if they think an answer is incorrect. Have the students who raised their hands explain their choice of answers.

A. Evaluation forms.

• Invite students to comment on and ask questions about the picture. You may also wish to have students answer each other's questions. For example:

S1: *How does Katie look?*
S2: *I think she's scared.*
S3: *I think she's worried about her job evaluation.*

• Read and discuss the instructions. Explain new vocabulary as necessary.

◦◑ B. Katie's evaluation.
(CD2, Track 28)

• Read and discuss the instructions. Then, have students study the performance evaluation form. Answer questions about any terms students don't understand. For example, words such as *initiative, maintain,* and *transaction* may be unfamiliar.
• Play the audio twice as students mark and check their answers. Review the correct answers with the whole class.
• Then, have students answer the questions at the top of page 141. Call on a different student to answer each question orally.

☼ The Big Picture: Performance Evaluations

A. Evaluation forms. Mr. Davis owns a large jewelry store. Every six months he evaluates his employees. Today he is talking to two employees, Katie and Amy. Read the job description and look at the evaluation forms. Discuss any new words or phrases.

Davis Jewelry: Sales Assistant

Assist customers in making jewelry selections
Maintain and restock displays
Perform sales transactions accurately
Follow all store procedures and policies

 B. Katie's evaluation. Listen as Mr. Davis evaluates Katie and check the appropriate boxes. He will focus on Katie's strengths and areas that need improvement. If Mr. Davis does not mention an area, you can check that she meets expectations. Then, answer the questions about her evaluation.

	Exceeds Expectations	Meets Expectations	Requires Improvement	Unsatisfactory
General				
Reports to work as scheduled			✓	
Appearance is neat and appropriate		✓		
Shows initiative			✓	
Maintains displays on a daily basis				✓
Customer service				
Assists customers in a professional manner	✓			
Uses effective sales techniques	✓			
Transactions and procedures				
Performs sales transactions accurately			✓	
Reports messages and information effectively		✓		

Audio Script

B. Katie's evaluation. Listen as Mr. Davis evaluates Katie and check the appropriate boxes. (CD2, Track 28)

Mr. Davis: Katie, have you looked at your evaluation yet?
Katie: Yes, I have.
Mr. Davis: Let's go over some of these areas. You are always available to work, but you've arrived late several times. Since I've spoken to you about this, you have improved.
Katie: I've been trying. I was only late once last month.

Mr. Davis: You see that you also require improvement on showing initiative. Katie, when you don't have a customer, you stand and daydream. If I ask you to do something, you're always willing. But when you don't have customers, I expect you to polish the jewelry and the mirrors, put new paper in the cash register, restock the boxes, and do other things without being asked.
Katie: OK.

(Audio Script continues on page 255.)

1. Is Mr. Davis pleased with Katie's work? No
2. Has she always arrived on time? Has her on-time arrival improved? No. Yes.
3. Does she show initiative at work? Explain your answer. No. When she doesn't have a customer, she stands and daydreams.
4. How are Katie's sales? Great.
5. Has she used effective sales techniques? How do you know? Yes, this is her number one strength.

6. What has happened when she has overcharged the customers? What has happened when she has undercharged the customers? The customer complained. The store lost money.
7. When does Katie make mistakes in her sales transactions? When the store is busy.
8. What has Mr. Davis decided to do? He has decided to have Ms. Nickerson retrain Katie.
9. Does Katie like her job? Yes.

 C. Amy's evaluation. Listen as Mr. Davis evaluates Amy and check the appropriate boxes. He will focus on Amy's strengths and areas that need improvement. If Mr. Davis does not mention an area, you can check that she meets expectations. Then, answer the questions about her evaluation.

	Exceeds Expectations	Meets Expectations	Requires Improvement	Unsatisfactory
General				
Reports to work as scheduled		✓		
Appearance is neat and appropriate			✓	
Shows initiative	✓			
Maintains displays on a daily basis	✓			
Customer service				
Assists customers in a professional manner		✓		
Uses effective sales techniques			✓	
Transactions and procedures				
Performs sales transactions accurately		✓		
Reports messages and information effectively				✓

1. Is Mr. Davis pleased with Amy's appearance? No
2. Why doesn't Mr. Davis like Amy's nails? They distract the customers.
3. How has Amy shown initiative? With her creative idea for the jewelry display.
4. Has Amy ever thought of studying art or design? Yes.
5. How are Amy's sales? Average
6. Has she always used effective sales techniques? No, she could use more effective techniques.

7. In what other area does Amy need improvement? Taking messages.
8. What kind of mistakes has Amy made on the phone? She has taken the wrong information.
9. Why has this caused a problem? Mr. Davis hasn't been able to return calls.
10. What does Mr. Davis want Amy to do? He wants Amy to repeat everything back to the caller.
11. Does Amy like her job? Yes

 C. Amy's evaluation.
(CD2, Track 29)

• Review the instructions and the items in the evaluation form as you did for Exercise B. Play the audio twice and have students record their answers on the chart. Review the correct answers. Replay the audio as necessary to clarify any answers that several students got wrong.
• Read aloud the questions below the chart and call on a different student to answer each one. Replay sections of the audio as necessary to clarify any information several students misunderstood.

Suggestion

If appropriate for your class, create a student self-evaluation form. The column headings can be the same as the ones in the book. The row heads at the left could include: *Comes to class on time, Hands in assignments on time, Writes neatly, Participates orally in class,* and so forth. Have students rate themselves and discuss their ratings with a partner.

Audio Script

C. Amy's evaluation. (CD2, Track 29)

Mr. Davis: Amy, have you looked over your performance evaluation?

Amy: Yes, I have.

Mr. Davis: Let's talk about several of these areas. Please notice that I checked *Requires Improvement* under *Personal Appearance.* Do you know what that's about?

Amy: Yes, my nails.

Mr. Davis: You promised at your job interview that you would keep them shorter and paint them only one color.

Amy: I forgot. I really like them long.

Mr. Davis: Amy, people are looking at your nails, not our jewelry. It's distracting when your nails are striped or black with gold stars or whatever color or design you come in with each week. I'd like you to keep them shorter and one color.

Amy: OK.

Mr. Davis: Amy, you have an eye for color and design. You showed some real initiative on our displays. You had some creative ideas for our jewelry

displays and our counters have never looked so attractive. And you've done a wonderful job in our front window. Many of the customers have commented on how nice it looks. Have you ever thought of studying art or design?

Amy: Sometimes. It's my favorite part of the job.

(Audio Script continues on page 255.)

Reading: The Changing Workforce

A. Before You Read.

• Ask students to match the vocabulary words and definitions and check their answers with a partner. Review the correct answers and ask different students to form original sentences using each word.

• Ask students to look at the picture and describe the different types of people they see. You may wish to write some cues on the board to help them get started. For example: *male, female, older, younger, Hispanic, Caucasian, Asian,* and so forth. Students may give responses such as:

> *There are fewer Asians than Caucasians.*
> *About half of the workers are female.*

• Students read the passage individually in class. Point out the vocabulary words in bold and ask students to pay special attention to the sentences where they appear. As students read, move around the room answering questions as necessary.

Note: Spend some time discussing terminology, such as "white" and "Caucasian" or "black" and "African-American."

A. Before You Read. Match each vocabulary word with its meaning.

_b_ 1. to outnumber		a. to grow larger	
_d_ 2. to age		b. to have a greater amount or number	
_a_ 3. to increase		c. equal	
_f_ 4. to be in demand		d. to get older	
_c_ 5. to account for		e. to stay	
_e_ 6. to remain		f. to be needed or required	

The workforce of the United States includes everyone who is now working and everyone who is looking for a job. The Bureau of Labor Statistics evaluates the current workforce and employment opportunities, and it makes predictions about the future.

Between 2000 and 2010, approximately 17 million new workers will enter the workforce, bringing the total number of workers in the United States to 168 million. What will this workforce look like? The number of women in the workforce has **increased** steadily from 1945 to the present. Because of this, almost half of all workers will be women (48%). The workforce is **aging**, too. Baby boomers—people born between 1946 and 1964—make up almost half the workforce. As this group ages, more workers will be in their 50s and 60s. The social security retirement age is gradually rising, influencing how long workers **remain** on the job. The workforce will become more ethnically diverse, also. In 2000, 73.1 percent of the workforce was classified as White, non-Hispanic. By 2010, this will fall to 69.2 percent. The Hispanic workforce will soon **outnumber** all other ethnic groups, accounting for 13.3 percent of the total workers. Blacks will make up 12.7 percent and Asians 6.1 percent.

The labor department defines two types of jobs—goods-producing jobs and service-providing jobs. Goods-producing jobs include manufacturing, agriculture, mining, and fishing. There will be almost no growth in goods-producing jobs because of the increasing use of machinery and because most goods are now produced in other countries. Any growth in this area will be for replacement workers, taking the jobs of workers who are retiring or moving to other employment.

Service providers, in industries such as education, health services, finance, transportation, and communications, will **account for** 20.2 million new jobs between 2000 and 2010. Many of these new jobs will require a college degree. Occupations such as computer programmers, educators, professional health-care workers, and librarians are four-year college degree programs. Businesses will be looking for accountants, public-relations managers, and computer information systems managers. There will be at least five million new service jobs such as food preparers, health-care support workers, transportation workers, and security guards. Most of these will require only high school graduation and possibly a short training program. Salespersons and cashiers will also **be in demand**.

Every two years, the United States government publishes the *Occupational Outlook Handbook*, which presents specific information about the job market and the job outlook. Each job is described in detail with job descriptions, training required, salary information, and future prospects. The reference section of every library has this book to help students and workers plan for their future careers.

Source: Bureau of Labor Statistics; *Occupational Outlook Handbook*

B. Understanding numbers. Check the reading again and decide if these statements are true or false.

1. By 2010, there will be about 168 million workers in the U.S.   (T)   F

2. Soon there will be more women than men in the workforce.   T   (F)

3. The workforce is growing older.   (T)   F

4. As the age for social security retirement rises, people will work longer.   (T)   F

5. The white, non-Hispanic workforce is now 73.1 percent of the labor force.   (T)   F

6. By 2010, there will be more Hispanic workers than black workers.   (T)   F

7. There are more Asians than blacks in the workforce.   T   (F)

8. The number of goods-producing jobs will continue to increase.   T   (F)

9. There will be 20.2 million new jobs in education and health services.   T   (F)

10. All new service jobs will require a college degree.   T   (F)

C. Read the second paragraph again. List three general characteristics of the labor force in 2010. (Answers may vary.)

1. The workforce will be more ethnically diverse.

2. The workforce will be older.

3. The workforce will be larger.

Job Performance   **143**

B. Understanding numbers.

Ask students to complete the exercise individually. Review the answers with the whole class. After each answer is given, ask a student to read aloud the sentence that contains the information needed to answer that question correctly.

C. Read the second paragraph again.

Ask students to complete the activity individually and check their answers with a partner. Review the correct answers with the whole class.

Writing Our Stories: Looking at Careers

A. Read.

- Have students close their books. Write the words *dental hygienist* on the board and ask students to tell what they think this job involves. Confirm correct answers and explain why any incorrect answers are wrong.
- Ask students to read the passage once to themselves without stopping to try to figure out anything they don't understand. Ask a few simple questions to check general comprehension. For example: *Do dental hygienists take X-rays?* (Yes) and *Is there a need for a lot of dental hygienists today?*(Yes)

B. Thinking about jobs.

Students check their job skills individually.

Suggestion

Extend the discussion of careers by having students number their five favorite tasks in Exercise B. They can write 1 after the job skill they like best, 2 after their second choice, and so forth. Invite different students to name their favorite types of work from the list and tell why they like doing each thing.

Writing Our Stories: Looking at Careers

A. Read.

I am considering a career as a dental hygienist. A dental hygienist usually works in a dentist's office. A dental hygienist removes plaque and deposits from teeth, takes dental X-rays, and explains to patients how to clean and floss their teeth. In some offices, dental hygienists administer anesthetics, fill cavities, and assist the dentist.

All dental hygienists must be licensed by their state. It is necessary to attend an accredited dental hygiene program and to pass a written and a clinical examination. Many community colleges offer dental hygienist programs and most dental hygienists have their associate degree. At school, students study in classrooms, in clinical settings, and in laboratories. They take many science courses, such as anatomy, physiology, chemistry, and radiography. There is a strong job outlook for dental hygienists. In this field, many people work part-time and the hours can be flexible. The average salary is about $25.00 an hour.

I'm interested in this career because I like working with people and helping people. The working conditions are clean and pleasant. My favorite subject in high school was biology and I did very well. I'm a little concerned about chemistry, because I didn't do well in that subject. I don't have the time to attend college for four years. An occupation that only requires a two-year program and has a good salary and job prospects is appealing to me.

B. Thinking about jobs. What are you good at? Check your job skills. (Answers will vary.)

☐ selling	☐ designing	☐ repairing things
☐ planning	☐ calculating	☐ inspecting
☐ managing money	☐ researching	☐ teaching
☐ writing reports	☐ supervising people	☐ public speaking
☐ organizing	☐ managing people	☐ helping people
☐ operating equipment	☐ programming	☐ using software

Check the job values that are the most important to you:

- ☐ salary
- ☐ job status
- ☐ promotion possibilities
- ☐ benefits
- ☐ job security
- ☐ job training

C. Researching a job. Choose a career that sounds interesting to you. Look in the *Occupational Outlook Handbook* in the library or online (www.bls.gov). Or, use America's Career InfoNet online (acincet.org). Find out the following information about a career. Take short notes. *(Answers will vary.)*

Career title:	
Nature of the work (job description):	
Working conditions:	
Education or training required:	
Earnings:	
Job outlook:	

D. Writing: Looking at careers. Write a paragraph or two describing the job you researched. Then, explain why this career is or is not a good job choice for you.

E. Edit. Find and correct the mistakes in these sentences.

1. I have never ~~take~~ *taken* a sick day.
2. She has gotten along with her coworkers ~~always.~~ *always* ^
3. He ~~has spoken~~ *spoke* to the boss a few minutes ago.
4. She has ~~receive~~ *received* an award as the top salesperson twice this year.
5. Have you ~~never~~ *ever* attended a sales meeting?
6. They have never ~~went~~ *gone* on a job interview.
7. She ~~have~~ *has* not always followed company policies.

Looking at the Internet

Many Web sites contain helpful information about jobs, requirements, training, salaries, and job outlooks. Check one of these sites. What jobs have the best job outlook for the future?

Occupational Outlook Handbook   www.bls.gov
American's Career InfoNet   www.acinet.org

Check the job values that are most important for you.

Discuss what a *job value* is and use the vocabulary items to clarify the concept. Invite some students to name their most important job value and tell why they feel this way.

C. Researching a job.

- Encourage students to investigate a job in which they are truly interested. You might ask some guiding questions to assist their research. Suggest that they set realistic goals which may require them to undertake additional study, but which they stand a good chance of being able to achieve.
- Remind students not to copy long passages, or even whole sentences, but to write just a few words after each heading in the chart.

D. Writing: Looking at careers.

Students use the notes they took in Exercise C to write their descriptions. Suggest that they make use of the lists of the *job skills* and *job values* they just discussed as they begin to explain why this career is or is not a good choice for them.

E. Edit.

Have students correct the sentences on their own. Review the correct answers with the whole class.

 Looking at the Internet

When students complete their research, conduct a summary discussion in class in which students help you compile a list of the ten jobs with the best outlook for the near future.

Practicing on Your Own

A. An evaluation.

Ask students to do the activity individually and check their answers with a partner.

B. Evaluation reports.

Students complete the evaluation reports on their own. Explain that there are several different correct answers to each question. For example, other correct answers to question 1 include: *David hasn't been on time one day this week* and *David has gotten to work after 10:00 twice this week.*

Practicing on Your Own

A. An evaluation. Rewrite the sentences. Put the adverb or time expression in the correct place in the sentence.

1. Susan has worked overtime. (several times this month)
   <u>Susan has worked overtime several times this month</u>.

2. She has followed company policies. (always)
   <u>She has always followed company policies</u>.

3. She has spoken to the human resources department about a promotion. (already)
   <u>She has already spoken to the human resources department about a promotion</u>.

4. We have received a complaint about her work. (rarely)
   <u>We have rarely received a complaint about her work</u>.

5. She has taken an advanced software course. (recently)
   <u>She has taken an advanced software course recently</u>.

6. She has been able to solve problems. (usually)
   <u>Usually she has been able to solve problems</u>.

7. She has completed a sales management course. (just)
   <u>She has just completed a sales management course</u>.

B. Evaluation reports. The owner of Excel Electronics is writing her monthly evaluation reports on two of her employees. Karl is going to receive a promotion. David is going to lose his job. Using the present perfect, compare the two workers. (Answers may vary.)

Karl	David
1. He has always arrived on time.	1. <u>David has been late ten times.</u>
2. He has taken one sick day.	2. <u>David has taken many sick days</u>.
3. He has sold 150 televisions.	3. <u>David hasn't sold any televisions</u>.
4. <u>He hasn't made any mistakes on bills of sale</u>.	4. He has made mistakes on seven bills of sale.
5. He has always written the correct address on delivery notices.	5. <u>He has never written the correct address and delivery notices</u>
6. He has often worked overtime.	6. <u>He has never worked overtime</u>.

Grammar Summary

▶ 1. *How many* questions

We often use the present perfect with *How many* questions. In these sentences, the person is still working or performing the action.

What is Stella doing?   She is repairing TVs.

How many TVs **has** she **repaired**?   She **has repaired** seven TVs.

Note: When we use the past tense, it shows that the action is completed.

How many TVs did she repair yesterday?   She repaired ten TVs.

▶ 2. Repeated past actions

We use the present perfect to talk about repeated past actions. These actions may have occurred several times in the past and may occur again. We are more interested in the action than the time of the action. We often use indefinite time expressions or adverbs of frequency in these sentences.

Have you ever visited Vietnam? No, I haven't.

Have you ever gotten a promotion? Yes, I've gotten two promotions.

I **have** seldom **taken** a sick day.

I **have taken** three sick days this year.

I **have taken** a sick day from time to time.

▶ 3. Past actions

We can use the present perfect to talk about actions that happened in the past. In these sentences, we are interested in the action, not the specific time that the action occurred.

She **has spoken** to the boss.

He **has gotten** the job.

Note: Use the past tense to talk about actions that occurred at a specific time in the past. We often use past time expressions in these sentences, or the speakers know the time that the action occurred.

She **spoke** to the boss yesterday.

He **got** a new job last month.

▶ 4. Present perfect with adverbs

We often use the present perfect with the following adverbs:

already	I **have** *already* **filled** that order.
	I **have filled** that order *already*.
yet	She **hasn't completed** the report *yet*.
finally	The company **has** *finally* **given** the workers a raise.
at last	The new computers **have arrived** *at last*.
just	He **has** *just* **received** a large order.
recently	I **have changed** jobs *recently*.
	I **have** *recently* **changed** jobs.

Grammar Summary

- Review the four grammar explanations and sample sentences with the class. Invite students to make up alternate sentences for each example in the chart. For example, in place of *She has spoken to the boss,* a student might say, *We have finished nine units in this book.*
- Answer any questions students may have about the grammar items.
- See the Grammar Summary Expansion on page 266 for a more complete explanation of these grammar points.

Unit 10
Regrets and Possibilities

Discuss what the person in the unit title art is doing. Ask:

• *Who is standing next to the number 10?* (A woman with a vacuum cleaner and a graduation gown)

• *What is she doing?* (She's using the vacuum cleaner, but she's thinking about the graduation gown.)

• *What does the picture have to do with this unit?* (The unit is about regrets and possibilities. She may be regretting that she didn't go to college, or she may be thinking that college may be a possibility for her in the future.)

A. Read the thoughts and discuss each picture.

• Review each picture, reading each thought bubble aloud and discussing how it relates to the picture.

• Help students summarize the situations all the people in the pictures find themselves in: *They all made decisions that are causing a problem now.*

A. Read the thoughts and discuss each picture.

Active Grammar: Past Modals—*Should have*

A. Review the past participle forms. Write the correct past participle form of each verb.

Simple Form	Past participle	Simple form	Past participle
buy	bought	leave	left
try	tried	meet	met
drive	driven	see	seen
forget	forgotten	lose	lost
fill	filled	pay	paid
send	sent	sleep	slept
eat	eaten	spend	spent
break	broken	tell	told
feel	felt	write	written

B. Listen and complete.

1. I _____ should have bought _____ a new one.
2. I _____ shouldn't have bought _____ a used one.
3. She _____ should have studied _____ harder.
4. I _____ shouldn't have registered _____ for so many courses.
5. I _____ should have left _____ earlier.
6. I _____ should have remembered _____ to bring it.
7. They _____ should have filled _____ the tank.
8. He _____ shouldn't have driven _____ without a license.
9. We _____ should have sent _____ the check on time.
10. She _____ shouldn't have forgotten _____ it.

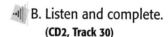
Active Grammar: Past Modals— *Should have*

A. Review the past participle forms.

- Ask students to fill in as many of the forms as they can individually and then check their answers with a partner.
- Review the correct answers with the class.

B. Listen and complete.
(CD2, Track 30)

Explain that these sentences describe situations in which people made mistakes. Read the instructions and tell students that they will be writing about the mistakes people wish they hadn't made. Play the audio and have them write their answers. You may wish to pause the audio after each statement to give students time to write their answers. Play it a second time so they can check their work. Review the correct answers with the whole class.

Suggestion

For additional oral practice, ask students to take turns restating each sentence in Exercise B replacing affirmative statements with negative ones and negative statements with affirmative ones. For example, if the answer was affirmative (*They should have filled the tank*), the student would say: *They shouldn't have run out of gas*. If the answer was negative (*I shouldn't have taken so many courses*), the student would say: *I should have taken fewer courses*.

Audio Script

B. Listen and complete. (CD2, Track 30)

1. I bought a used car. I should have bought a new one.
2. I didn't buy a new car. I shouldn't have bought a used one.
3. She didn't study for the test. She should have studied harder.
4. I registered for six courses. I shouldn't have registered for so many courses.
5. I left too late for the airport. I should have left earlier.
6. I didn't have a photo ID. I should have remembered to bring it.
7. Their car ran out of gas. They should have filled the tank.
8. He got a ticket for driving without a license. He shouldn't have driven without a license.
9. The electric company charged us a late fee. We should have sent the check on time.
10. She forgot to bring her homework. She shouldn't have forgotten it.

C. Complete each sentence.

• Review the use of *should have* and *shouldn't have* with the class. Then, have students complete the sentences individually.

• Review the correct answers orally.

👥 D. What should they have done?

• Before having students work in pairs, ask them to look at the person in each picture and describe the problem they are having. Review all six pictures this way. For example, in the first picture a student might say: *The family has too much luggage.*

• Point out the six verbs in the box and remind students to use each one in one of their sentences. Then, have students work with partners. They take turns making statements about the pictures. Review the answers orally with the whole class.

C. Complete each sentence. Use *should have* and the correct form of the verb.

> **Past Modal: *Should have***
> ***Should have*** expresses a regret about a **past action**.
> ***should + (not) have*** + past participle
> I **should have studied** more. (Meaning: I didn't study enough.)
> We **should have brought** warm clothes. (Meaning: We didn't bring warm clothes.)
> They **shouldn't have left** their umbrellas at home. (Meaning: They didn't bring their umbrellas.)

1. I took too many courses and now my grades are falling.
   I _____ shouldn't have taken _____ (take) so many courses.

2. Akiko forgot to bring her book, and she needs it for the exam.
   She _____ shouldn't have forgotten _____ (forget) her book.

3. Sandra's cellular phone rang during the exam.
   She _____ should have turned off _____ (turn off) her phone before the exam.

4. Jim stayed up very late. The next morning, he overslept and was late.
   He _____ shouldn't have stayed up _____ (stay up) so late.

5. Marie wanted to take a psychology course, but she registered too late.
   She _____ should have registered _____ (register) earlier.

6. Paul didn't type his paper and received a low grade.
   He _____ should have typed _____ (type) his paper.

👥 **D. What should they have done?** Look at each picture. Make a statement about each picture. Use *should have* and your imagination. (Answers will vary.)

bring	put	remember	take	wear	eat

☀ May have, might have, and could have

Past modals of possibility

May have, might have, could have all express possibility about a past event. They have similar meanings. **Could have** also expresses a choice.

I You He She We They	may have might have could have	gone to the movies. forgotten to bring it. been busy. lost her key.

A. Match each statement with the correct statement of possibility.

_e_ **1.** Frank didn't come to work yesterday.

_b_ **2.** I wonder where the neighbors went.

_g_ **3.** I saw Tariq with a strange woman. Who was she?

_a_ **4.** Marco was wearing a suit yesterday. He usually wears jeans.

_c_ **5.** Madeline was in a toy store yesterday. What did she buy for her niece?

_f_ **6.** Anna isn't happy with her new job.

_d_ **7.** I can't find my keys.

a. He might have had a job interview.

b. They may have gone to Florida.

c. She might have bought her a teddy bear.

d. You could have left them in the restaurant.

e. He may have been sick.

f. She could have taken that other job.

g. That might have been his sister. I hear that she's in town.

B. Read each sentence. With a partner, write two possibilities in your notebook. Use *might have*, *may have*, or *could have* and an appropriate verb.
(Answers will vary.)

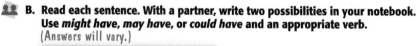
The teacher was late to class.
The teacher might have gotten stuck in traffic.

1. A classmate missed an important exam.
2. A classmate looked ill yesterday. Today, she didn't come to class.
3. A friend was at a travel agency last Saturday.
4. A strange woman was talking to your friend's husband.
5. A friend called you to pick her up at a hospital emergency room.
6. A very large package was delivered to your neighbors.

☀ May have, might have, and could have

A. Match each statement with the correct statement of possibility.

• Discuss the explanation and examples with the class. Then, have students take turns making up possible sentences using the words in the three columns. Accept any reasonable statements. For example: *I may have forgotten to bring it. She might have been busy. They could have gone to the movies.*

• Have students complete the matching exercise on their own. Review the correct answers by having one student read a statement from column 1 and another student read the correct statement of possibility from column 2.

B. Read each sentence.

Students complete this exercise in pairs. Write the numbers 1 through 6 on the board and have different students fill in the two sentences they wrote for that item. Review these answers with the class, making corrections as necessary.

☀ Must have —
Deduction

A. Listen to a man calling 911 to report a problem in his apartment. (CD2, Track 31)

• Briefly discuss the meaning of the explanation at the top of the grammar box. You may wish to paraphrase it in simpler terms. For example: *When you are talking about something that probably happened in the past, but you aren't completely sure, you use "must have."*

• Have students take turns making up possible sentences using the words in the three columns. Accept any reasonable statements. For example: *You must have been sick. She must have lost her keys. He must have broken his leg.*

• Read the instructions and explain that a house has been robbed. Point to the pictures and ask students to describe what they see in each one. For the first picture they might say: *The lock on the door is broken.* Review all eight pictures this way.

• Ask students to read deductions *a* to *h*. Review the instructions for the exercise and play the audio. Students record their answers in the blank above each picture. Review the answers with the whole class.

Suggestion

If appropriate for your class, ask students to role-play phone calls to a 911 line. Have them prepare their scripts in pairs. List the following items on the board as a guide.
Be prepared to:

• give your name
• tell your location (address)
• describe the emergency
• say what kind of help you need

☀ Must have—Deduction

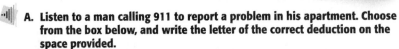

Must have expresses a probability or deduction based on a past event.

I You He She We They	must have must (not) have	been sick. lost (her) keys. broken (his) leg. had an appointment.

Culture Note
Call 911 to report an emergency to the police, fire department, or rescue squad.

A. Listen to a man calling 911 to report a problem in his apartment. Choose from the box below, and write the letter of the correct deduction on the space provided.

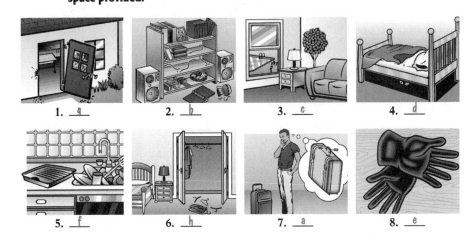

1. __g__   2. __b__   3. __c__   4. __d__

5. __f__   6. __h__   7. __a__   8. __e__

a. The burglar must have used it to hide the other clothes.
b. The burglar must have taken it.
c. The burglar must have gotten scared and left through the window.
d. The burglar must have scared the cat.
e. The burglar must have dropped the gloves when he left.
f. The burglar must have been hungry.
g. Someone must have broken in.
h. The burglar must have put on one of your suits.

Audio Script

A. Listen to a man calling 911 to report a problem in his apartment. (CD2, Track 31)

1. I came home and found my lock broken and my door open.
2. My stereo is missing.
3. The window's open, but I'm sure I locked it when I left.

4. My cat has been hiding under the bed, and he won't come out.
5. A steak is missing, and there are dirty dishes in the sink.
6. My favorite suit is missing.
7. My large suitcase is missing and so are some of my shirts.
8. I found a pair of gloves on the floor.

B. Pronunciation: Past modals. Listen and repeat.

1. You must've left your book at home.
2. She might've studied French.
3. I should've made an appointment.
4. We could've gone on a vacation.
5. He must've had to work.
6. She couldn't have walked that far.
7. We shouldn't have spoken to her.
8. They shouldn't have arrived late.
9. He may not have had an opportunity.
10. I must not have heard you.

 Practice saying the sentences with a partner.

 C. Pronunciation: Word stress. Listen to the conversation and <u>underline</u> the stressed words.

A: <u>Hi</u>, Julia. <u>Why</u> didn't you <u>come</u> to my <u>party</u>? Everyone <u>missed</u> you.

B: <u>What</u> party?

A: I had a <u>party</u> last <u>Saturday</u>.

B: You should've <u>called</u> me.

A: I <u>did</u>. I left a <u>message</u> on your <u>machine</u>.

B: I <u>changed</u> my <u>number</u>. You could've <u>sent</u> an <u>invitation</u>.

A: I <u>did</u>. I <u>mailed</u> it <u>two weeks</u> ago.

B: You must've <u>sent</u> it to the <u>wrong address</u>. I <u>moved three weeks</u> ago.

A: You should've <u>told</u> me.

B: <u>Sorry</u>. Anyway, how was the <u>party</u>?

A: It was <u>fun</u>. You should've <u>been</u> there.

 D. Practice saying the conversation with a partner. Use the correct stress. Substitute your partner's name.

Audio Script

C. Pronunciation: Word Stress.
(Note: Apart from the examples in the first A and B, stressed words are underlined in Teacher's Guide only.) **(CD2, Track 33)**

A: <u>Hi</u>, Julia. <u>Why</u> didn't you <u>come</u> to my <u>party</u>? Everyone <u>missed</u> you.

B: <u>What</u> party?

A: I had a <u>party</u> last <u>Saturday</u>.

B: You should've <u>called</u> me.

A: I <u>did</u>. I left a <u>message</u> on your <u>machine</u>.

B: I <u>changed</u> my <u>number</u>. You could've <u>sent</u> an <u>invitation</u>.

A: I <u>did</u>. I <u>mailed</u> it <u>two weeks</u> ago.

B: You must've <u>sent</u> it to the <u>wrong address</u>. I <u>moved three weeks</u> ago.

A: You should've <u>told</u> me.

B: <u>Sorry</u>. Anyway, how was the <u>party</u>?

A: It was <u>fun</u>. You should've <u>been</u> there.

 B. Pronunciation: Past modals. (CD2, Track 32)

- Play the audio and ask students to focus on the pronunciation of the affirmative and negative modals + *'ve*. You may wish to say just these parts of each sentence and have students repeat each one.
- Play the audio again pausing after each sentence and asking students to repeat.

Practice saying the sentences with a partner.

As students practice saying the sentences in pairs, move around the room offering pronunciation support as needed.

 C. Pronunciation: Word stress. (CD2, Track 33)

- Read aloud the instructions and the first two lines of the dialogue as students follow along in their books. Emphasize the stress on the underlined syllables.
- Play the audio as students follow along in their books. Pause after the first two lines of dialogue and ask if students have any questions. Finish playing the audio as students underline the stressed words. Play it again so they can check their answers. Review the correct answers with the whole class.

 D. Practice saying the conversation with a partner.

Students complete the activity in pairs.

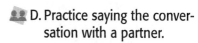

-ing versus -ed Adjectives

A. Read and look at the pictures.

• Discuss the pictures and the sentences using -ed and -ing adjectives. Remind students that we use -ing to talk about things and -ed to talk about feelings.

• Answer any questions students may have about the pictures and sentences.

B. Listen and repeat.

(CD2, Track 34)

Have students listen the first time through. Discuss the meaning of any word pairs students don't understand. Then, play the audio again pausing after each pair, and have students repeat the words.

C. Make sentences about each picture.

• Discuss what is happening in each picture. Have students make a simple statement about each. For example: *This student looks really confused.*

• Call on different students to make statements about each picture using the words in the box in Exercise B. Encourage students to use other -ed or -ing adjectives that fit the situations in the pictures. Explain to the students that -ing adjectives usually modify a noun that does something. For example, the noun "woman" does something, she bores the man, thus the woman is boring. The -ed adjective has a passive meaning. The man is bored by someone.

☀ Active Grammar: -ing versus -ed Adjectives

A. Read and look at the pictures.

1. The students are interested.

The professor is interesting.

2. The man is bored.

The woman is boring.

> Many adjectives end in either **-ing** or **-ed**.
> This is a very **exciting** city, and I am **excited** to be here.
> The museum was **fascinating**. I've never been so **fascinated** by a museum before.

B. Listen and repeat. Discuss any new vocabulary.

annoyed	annoying	exhausted	exhausting	interested	interesting
confused	confusing	disgusted	disgusting	surprised	surprising
excited	exciting	embarrassed	embarrassing	frustrated	frustrating
depressed	depressing	frightened	frightening	challenged	challenging

C. Make sentences about each picture. Use adjectives from the list. (Answers will vary.)

The student is confused by the math problem.
The math problem is confusing.

1.

the student / the math problem

2.

the music / the neighbors

3.

the children / the costume

4.

the mother / the triplets

5.

the climber / the mountain

6.

his cooking / his wife

D. Student to student dictation: Good News/Bad News

Student A: Turn to page 247.

Student B: Use the cues in numbers 1–5 to tell Student A what happened last weekend. Student A will be a good listener and give an appropriate response.

Last weekend, I had a car accident.

You must have been scared.

1. I / have to work overtime / all weekend
   B: I had to work overtime all weekend.
   A: You must have been exhausted.
2. I / not find / keys / for two hours
   B: I couldn't find my keys for two hours.
   A: You must have been frustrated.
3. not get / the new job
   B: I didn't get the new job.
   A: You must have been disappointed.
4. my son / win / football championship
   B: My son won the football championship.
   A: You must have been proud.
5. get / promotion
   B: I got the promotion.
   A: You must have been thrilled.

Student B: Turn to page 247.

Student A: Use the cues in numbers 6–10 to tell Student B what happened last weekend. Student B will be a good listener and respond with an appropriate response.

6. my daughter / get engaged
   A: Last weekend my daughter got engaged.
   B: You must have been pleased.
7. I / get lost in a strange neighborhood / for an hour
   A: I got lost in a strange neighborhood for an hour. B: You must have been worried.
8. at the bank / I / cannot express myself in English
   A: At the bank, I couldn't express myself in English. B: You must have been frustrated.
9. I / receive a bonus
   A: I received a bonus. B: You must have been excited.
10. my friends / have a birthday party / for me
    A: My friends had a birthday party for me. B: You must have been surprised.

E. Read each statement. Give a response with *That must have been* or *You must have been* and an appropriate adjective from the box.

bored	boring	embarrassed	embarrassing	challenged	challenging
frightened	frightening	interested	interesting	disgusted	disgusting

1. We spent ten hours at the museum. (You) You must have been interested.
2. My family and I were fishing when our boat sank. (That)
   That must have been frightening.
3. I started a new job, and I had to learn many new things. (That)
   That must have been challenging.
4. I ordered soup at a restaurant, and there was a cockroach in it. (You)
   You must have been disgusted.
5. I was talking about my boss when she walked into the room. (You)
   You must have been embarrassed.
6. We were taking a test when my cell phone rang. (That)
   That must have been embarrassing.
7. I was home alone when I heard someone break a window. (You)
   You must have been frightened.
8. I am afraid of heights, and my friends took me to the 45th floor. (That)
   That must have been frightening.

D. Student to student dictation: Good News/ Bad News

• Read and discuss the instructions. Point out the two sets of cues on this page, one for Student A to use and one for Student B. Then, have students look at the sample dialogue and the list of *-ed* and *-ing* adjectives on page 247. Explain that they will use these adjectives as they reply to their partner's statements. Have a pair of students read the sample dialogue aloud.

• Students work in pairs, taking turns reading the statements and giving appropriate responses. Have the pairs correct each other's work as they go along.

• Review the correct answers by calling on different pairs to role play each exchange.

E. Read each statement.

Students complete the activity in pairs. Review the correct answers by calling on different pairs to role play each exchange.

Suggestion

Have students write out two original situations like those in Exercise E, preferably taken from their own lives. Then, have individuals read their sentences aloud and call on one or two different classmates to give appropriate answers using *must have been* plus one of the adjectives from the box in Exercise E.

The Big Picture:
In the Counselor's
Office

A. Mr. Dellaventura is the school counselor at Plains High School.
(CD2, Tracks 35 and 36)

• Ask students to describe what is happening in the pictures. You might use questions like these to get started:

Who are these people?
Where are they?
What are they doing?
What do you think they are saying?

• Point out the places where students can take notes. Play the audio and ask students to take notes about what the counselor says to each student. Pause the audio after each conversation to give students a chance to finish their notes.

B. Match each student with the correct problems and concerns.

Students complete the matching exercise on their own. Review the correct answers orally with the class.

The Big Picture: In the Counselor's Office

A. Mr. Dellaventura is the school counselor at Plains High School. Students come to see him when they have academic or personal problems. Sometimes the teachers send students to see him. Other times, the students come to see him on their own. Listen to Mr. Dellaventura counsel two students. Take notes in the spaces provided.

Notes: Amber
-Editor of school paper
-Lost her job
-VP punishing Amber
-Wrote story about football team—untrue
-Boyfriend broke up with her

Notes: Miguel
-Doing poorly in school
-Doing better in Math—met with teacher
-Can speak English, has trouble with writing
-Went to writing center once -Didn't like tutor
-Works at bookstore—2 nights a week all day Saturday

B. Match each student with the correct problems and concerns.

Student	Problems
Amber (a,c,e)	**a.** relationship
	b. problems with a class
	c. college plans
Miguel (b,d,f)	**d.** poor grades
	e. lost a job
	f. needed a job

156 UNIT 10

Audio Script

A. Mr. Dellaventura is the school counselor at Plains High School.

Conversation 1 (CD2, Track 35)

Mr. D.: Come in, Amber. Have a seat. You look upset.

Amber: Well, you know I am the editor of the school newspaper.

Mr. D.: I know. The paper's been very good this year.

Amber: Thank you. I work very hard on it.

Mr. D.: Why did you come see me today?

Amber: The vice principal took away my job! I'm not the editor anymore! I need that job for my college applications! How am I going to get into college now?

Mr. D.: Hold on, hold on. Do you know why he did that?

Amber: I don't know. I'm the best writer on the staff!

Mr. D.: You must have some idea why he did that.

Amber: I guess he's punishing me.

Mr. D.: Punishing you? Why would he do that?

Amber: I think he's upset because I wrote a story that wasn't true about the football team.

Mr. D.: Now, Amber, why did you do that?

Amber: I was upset at my boyfriend. He's the captain of the football team. He had just broken up with me.

Mr. D.: You must have been very upset.

Amber: Yes, I was.

Mr. D.: So, do you think the vice principal should've punished you for printing incorrect information? The team must've been very upset, too.

Amber: I know. Yeah, I guess I shouldn't have done that. I shouldn't have used the paper to get back at him.

Mr. D.: It sounds like you're sorry. I'll talk to the vice principal. Maybe he'll just suspend you for one issue.

Amber: Thanks, Mr. D.

(Audio Script continues on page 255.)

156 ENGLISH IN ACTION 4

C. Listen again to Amber's conversation. Then, answer the questions.

1. What job does Amber have at school?
   She is the editor of the school newspaper.
2. What does the counselor think about Amber's work on the school paper?
   He thinks that her work is very good.
3. Why is Amber upset?
   The vice principal took away her job.
4. Is she good at her job?
   Yes, she is.
5. Why is the job important to her? *She needs her job for her college applications.*
6. What did Amber do? Why? *She wrote a story about the football team that wasn't true. Because her boyfriend broke up with her.*
7. Is she sorry?
   Yes, she is.
8. What is the counselor going to do to help her? *He will talk to the vice principal.*

D. Amber's regrets. Complete the sentences. Use *shouldn't have* or *should have* and the verb in parentheses to express the facts and your opinion.

1. Amber ___*shouldn't have written*___ (write) incorrect information.
2. Amber ___*should have spoken*___ (speak) to her boyfriend about her feelings.
3. Amber ___*should have thought*___ (think) more carefully before she wrote the article.
4. In my opinion, the vice principal ___*should have taken/shouldn't have taken*___ (take) away her job.

 E. Listen again to Miguel's conversation. Then, answer the questions.

1. Is Miguel a good student? Has he improved? *No, but he has improved.*
2. Did Miguel do the things that the counselor suggested? *No.*
3. What could Miguel have done to improve his math grades?
   He could have gone to a tutor.
4. Which is harder for Miguel—speaking English or writing English?
   Writing English.
5. Why didn't Miguel get help from a tutor? *Because he didn't like the tutor.*
6. Where is Miguel working now? *He is working at a bookstore.*
7. What's his schedule? *He works two nights a week and all day Saturday.*

F. Complete the sentences about Miguel. Use *should have, must have, could have,* or *couldn't have* and the verb in parentheses.

1. Miguel ___*could have found*___ (find) a math tutor, but he didn't need to.
2. Miguel's math instructor ___*must have been*___ (be) pleased at his progress.
3. Miguel ___*must have made*___ (make) a good impression at his job interview.
4. Miguel ___*should have found*___ (find) a different writing tutor.
5. Miguel ___*couldn't have gotten*___ (get) the job without his counselor's help.

Regrets and Possibilities **157**

 C. Listen again to Amber's conversation.

(CD2, Track 35)

Ask students to read through the list of questions. Answer any questions they may have. Then, play the first conversation on the audio again. Call on different students to answer each question.

D. Amber's regrets.

Give students two or three minutes to read the sentences and prepare their answers. Then, call on different students to complete each sentence.

 E. Listen again to Miguel's conversation.

(CD2, Track 36)

Have students read through the list of questions. Answer any questions they may have. Then, play the second conversation. Call on different students to answer each question.

F. Complete the sentences about Miguel.

Give students a few minutes to prepare their answers. Then, call on different students to complete each sentence.

Reading: Weekend and After-School Language and Culture Programs

A. Before You Read.

• Point to the pictures and invite students to comment. Ask:

Who do you think these people are? What are they doing?

• Invite several different students to answer the questions at the top of the page. Encourage them to add details if they wish. For example, *I have two nieces. They live in Colombia but they're coming here next year.*

• Ask students to read the story to themselves. Explain that it isn't important for them to understand every single word, but that they should try to understand the main ideas.

• When they finish, invite them to ask about anything they don't understand and to make any comments they wish about the reading.

Reading: Weekend and After-School Language and Culture Programs

A. Before You Read. (Answers will vary.)

1. Do you have children, grandchildren, or nieces and nephews?

2. Can the children speak, read, and write your native language?

3. Do you want the children to learn your native language and culture?

Family 1

I'm from Argentina. My family and I are living in the United States. We've been living here for almost three years now. My children can speak English fluently now, and they are in regular classes. I'm disappointed that they don't speak Spanish anymore. They've forgotten our language. I should've done something to help them maintain our language and learn about our Argentinean culture, but it's too late now.

Family 2

My daughter is very excited. This summer, we're going to visit my parents in Korea for the first time. I've been sending her to Korean school every weekend for the past year. Some friends told me that I should've concentrated on her English, but my husband and I decided that we wanted her to learn Korean, too. She's been writing letters to their grandparents, and the grandparents are thrilled to receive a letter that they can read. We made the right decision.

What can immigrant parents do to help their children learn or **maintain** their native language and culture? Children who grow up speaking one language outside the home and a different language inside the home learn to speak two languages. However, it is much harder for them to learn to read and write the language at an advanced level. Therefore, many parents send their children to weekend or after-school language and culture programs for an average of three to five hours a week. The **mission** of most programs is to help children of immigrant parents and/or grandparents learn their native language and culture. There are Polish schools, Chinese schools, Japanese schools, Greek schools, and Korean schools to name a few.

One Korean school in New York City offers six hours of instruction every Saturday. The school teaches reading and conversation, Korean history, Korean **fine arts**, including art, music, and calligraphy. Korean children who were adopted by American couples, Korean-Americans, Koreans, and non-Koreans are among the students who attend the classes.

A Greek school in Chicago teaches Greek language to children in their Greek Orthodox Church community. Most Greek schools are run by a Greek Orthodox Church. The school day lasts two and a half hours every Saturday. The students can learn to read, write, and speak Greek. One school has been in existence since 1922. One parent explained why she sent her daughter to Greek school. She said, "I studied Greek in an after-school program when I was a child, and I wanted my daughter to learn Greek, too. **Besides** learning the culture of my parents, she was also learning another language. The more languages she learns, the better off she'll be in the future." She added, "Sometimes it was a **struggle** to get her to classes, in terms of convenience and other school activities, but I kept her in the classes." When the daughter was older, she even took a trip to Greece with her classmates at the school.

B. Vocabulary. Guessing meaning from context.

1. What can immigrant parents do to help their children learn or **maintain** their native language and culture? *Maintain* means . . .

   a. to repair. (**b.**) to continue. **c.** to take care of. **d.** to speak.

2. The **mission** of most programs is to help children of immigrant parents and/or grandparents to learn the native language and culture. A *mission* is . . .

   (**a.**) a goal. **b.** a map. **c.** a lesson. **d.** a fight.

3. The school teaches reading and conversation, Korean history, Korean **fine arts**, including art, music, and calligraphy. Which of the following is not a *fine art*?

   a. drawing **b.** painting (**c.**) chemistry **d.** photography

4. **Besides** learning the culture of my parents, she was also learning another language. *Besides* means . . .

   a. but. (**b.**) in addition to. **c.** next to. **d.** if.

5. Sometimes it was a **struggle** to get her to classes. A *struggle* means . . .

   a. it was easy. **b.** it was confusing. (**c.**) it was challenging. **d.** it was exciting.

C. Read and discuss the questions. (Answers will vary.)

1. Are you similar to Family 1 or Family 2? Explain your answer.

2. Is it important for you if your children or future children learn to speak, read, and write your native language? Why or why not?

3. How many hours a week do most schools offer lessons?

4. Can American students attend Korean school?

5. What do you think about weekend language and culture schools for children?

B. Vocabulary.

• Briefly remind students that using context to find meaning involves reading the whole sentence and figuring out what the key word means based on the rest of the words in the sentence.

• Read the instructions and do the first answer with the whole class. Then, have students complete the exercise individually and check their answers with a partner. Review the correct answers with the whole class.

C. Read and discuss the questions.

Students discuss the questions in pairs. Then, have a class discussion comparing different viewpoints among various students. Encourage students to give reasons for their opinions. For example:

T: *Why is it important for your children to speak your native language when they grow up?*

S: *I want them to know where they came from. Also it could help them in their careers. Knowing more than one language is a big help.*

☀ Writing Our Stories: My Regrets

☀ Writing Our Stories: My Regrets

A. Read.

Ask students to read the story on their own. What were the writer's three regrets? What regrets did you have after you arrrived here? Ask volunteers to share their regrets with the class.

B. Use the following questions to organize your composition.

Read through the questions with students and answer any questions they may have. You may wish to have a student give a sample answer for each question. Write any new vocabulary words that come up in the question or the answers on the board and discuss them with the class.

In your notebook, write your composition.

Students complete the writing on their own.

Suggestion

If time allows, you may wish to have students write the first drafts of their compositions in class. If possible, review each student's draft and make suggestions for corrections and expansions.

A. Read.

It's difficult to move to a new city, especially to a new country. Looking back, there are many things that I should have done to prepare.

First of all, there's the language. I studied English in school, but I didn't take it seriously. I should've taken it more seriously. Also, I could've taken a class before I came here. Of course, now I'm taking English classes. Second, good jobs are hard to find. I finished my degree back in my country, but I didn't bring my transcripts. I should've brought my transcripts with me. I've ordered my transcripts from the university, but it's taking a long time for them to arrive. When they arrive, I may be able to find a job in my field. Finally, I didn't know how to drive when I arrived. In my country, pubic transportaition was very convenient and cheap, but in my state, many jobs are located outside the city. One of my friends is teaching me how to drive so that I will have more job opportunities.

B. Use the following questions to organize your composition. (Answers will vary.)

1. What did you forget to bring with you that you needed?
2. What did you bring with you that you didn't need?
3. What should you have done before you came here?
4. Could you have studied English before you came to this country?
5. Did you forget any important documents that you needed?
6. Did you contact relatives in this country when you were planning your trip?
7. In what city did you live when you first came to this country? Were you happy with your neighborhood?
8. Did you have information about job opportunities before you came to this country? Were you happy with your first job?

In your notebook, write your composition.

C. Using quotation marks. Read each sentence. Add a verb from the list below and add correct punctuation and quotation marks.

> **Use quotation marks when you want to repeat or write a conversation or someone's exact words.** Report conversation or exact words with a verb such as *said, shouted, yelled, cried, asked,* or *complained.* Punctuation of the conversation should be <u>inside</u> the quotation marks.
>
> She said, "I studied Greek in an after-school program when I was a child, and I wanted my daughter to learn Greek, too."
>
> The customer complained, "This doesn't work. I want a refund!"

asked	shouted	explained	said	complained

1. Sylvia _____ *shouted* _____, "Stop slamming the door!"
2. Ivan _____ *asked* _____ "When can I take the test?"
3. Marlene _____ *said* _____ "We should've called the police."
4. Juliette _____ *asked* _____ "Do you have any job openings?"
5. Karen _____ *explained* _____ "I must have overslept. I'm sorry I'm late."
6. Gustavo _____ *complained* _____ "I've been living here for two years and you've never come to visit me."
7. José _____ *said* _____ "You should have invited her to the party."

D. Edit. Find and correct the mistakes.

1. I could've ~~study~~ *studied* to be a doctor, but I chose computers instead.
2. We should have ~~not~~ eaten so much. I think I've gained five pounds. [*not* inserted after *have*]
3. You must ~~had~~ *have* enjoyed the party.
4. Peter might ~~has~~ *have* called after 10:00.
5. Edward should *have* enjoyed his surprise party, but he didn't.
6. That TV must have ~~be~~ *been* expensive. It's the newest model.
7. The performance was very ~~excited~~ *exciting*.
8. My job can be very ~~frustrated~~ *frustrating*.

 Looking at the Internet

Search the Internet for weekend language and culture schools. Use quotation marks to limit your search. For example, try "weekend schools" and "Polish." Find out if there is a school near you. Tell your classmates where it is.

Regrets and Possibilities **161**

C. Using quotation marks.

• Read and discuss with the class the explanations and examples concerning the use of quotation marks. Answer any questions they may have.

• Have students complete the sentences individually. Ask a different student to write each completed sentence on the board. Review the placement of each set of quotation marks with the whole class.

D. Edit.

Students correct the mistakes and check their work with a partner.

Looking at the Internet

You may wish to further limit the search by having students also type in the name of the city or town where students are living in quotes.

Suggestion

You might ask groups of students to go beyond the Internet research and use local phone books and other resources to assemble a comprehensive list of language and culture programs available in the area. Suggest that they prepare the information in chart form, listing the national or ethnic group in the first column, the location and hours of the program in the second column, and any other important details in the third column. Post the completed charts in the classroom.

 Practicing on Your Own

A. Modals—Review.

Ask students to complete the sentences on their own and check their answers with a partner.

Suggestion

For an extended review, have students write ten true sentences about their friends and family using the modals from the box. For example:

My friend Casey had to leave class early.
My sister must have studied hard for the test.

Have students share their sentences with a partner and answer any questions their partner has.

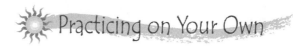 Practicing on Your Own

A. Modals—Review. Complete each conversation with the verb in parentheses and an appropriate modal chosen from the list. Use the present or past modal form. **(Answers may vary.)**

have to had to must (not)	doesn't / don't have to didn't have to	should (not) had better (not)	may (not) might (not) could (not)

1. **A:** Are you free this weekend?
   B: No, I'm not. I ___have to work___ (work) overtime.

2. **Driver:** What's the problem, Officer?
   Officer: You ___may not make___ (not make) a turn at that corner.
   Now, I ___must give___ (give) you a ticket.

3. **A:** How's the weather?
   B: It's very cloudy. It ___might rain___ (rain). You ___should take___ (take) your umbrella.

4. **A:** Why are you so late?
   B: It's a nice day, so I decided to walk. I ___should have taken___ (take) the bus instead.

5. **A:** Did you hear? Connie's husband was laid off last week.
   B: She ___must be___ (be) very upset.

6. **A:** Why does Steven wear blue shirts every day?
   B: I don't know. He ___must like___ (like) the color.

7. **Teacher:** This is your last chance. You ___may not miss___ (not / miss) another class.
   Student: I promise I won't be absent again.

8. **A:** Why didn't Peter take his driving test last Friday?
   B: I'm not sure. He ___must not have been___ (be) ready.

162 UNIT 10

162 ENGLISH IN ACTION 4

Grammar Summary

Past modals are formed by using a modal + *(not) have* + the past participle of the main verb.

▶ **1. Should have** Use *should have* to express a regret about a past action.

I **should have worn** a suit.

(Meaning: I didn't wear a suit. It was a bad idea. I wasn't dressed appropriately.)

She **shouldn't have worn** jeans.

(Meaning: She wore jeans. It was a bad idea. She wasn't dressed appropriately.)

▶ **2. Might have/May have/Could have** *Might have, may have,* and *could have* express past possibilities. *Could have* also expresses a past choice. *Couldn't have* means impossibility.

He **might have gone** to the movies.

(Meaning: I don't know where he went. Maybe he went to the movies.)

They **may not have taken** the exam yesterday.

(Meaning: Maybe they didn't take the exam yesterday. I don't know.)

I **could have studied** English in my country.

(Meaning: I didn't study English in my country. Classes were available, but I didn't enroll.)

▶ **3. Must have**—Probability and deduction *Must have* expresses a probability or deduction based on a past event.

We **must have been** out when you called.

(Meaning: We probably weren't at home when you called.)

You **must not have heard** the telephone.

(Meaning: You were at home when I called, but you didn't answer the telephone. You probably didn't hear the telephone ring.)

▶ **4. Must have**—Expressing sympathy or empathy *Must have* is also used to express sympathy or empathy when participating in a conversation.

A: I had a terrible car accident.   **A:** I went on a tour of the country last summer.

B: You **must have been** frightened.   **B:** That **must have been** interesting.

▶ **5. -ing versus -ed adjectives** Many adjectives end in either *-ing* or *-ed*. A general rule: Use *-ing* to talk about things; use *-ed* to talk about your feelings.

The Museum of Natural History is **interesting**. (Meaning: People like to visit there.)

I'm **bored** when I visit art museums. (Meaning: I don't like to visit art museums.)

Grammar Summary

- Review the four grammar explanations and sample sentences with the class. Invite students to make up alternate sentences for each example in the chart. For example, in place of *He might have gone to the movies,* a student might say, *She might have decided to go home.*
- Answer any questions students may have about the grammar items.
- See the Grammar Summary Expansion on page 267 for a more complete explanation of these grammar points.

Unit 11
Let's Get Organized

Discuss what the person in the unit title art is doing. Ask:

• *Who is standing next to the number 11?* (A woman)

• *What is she doing?* (She's holding up a large calendar.)

• *What does this have to do with the unit?* (The woman may be using the calendar to organize her time so that she doesn't forget anything and so that she gets things done on time.)

A. Comment on the desk in the picture.

Discuss the picture with the whole class. Then, ask several different students to answer each question at the top.

B. Are you organized?

• Have students take the quiz individually. Discuss student scores with the whole class.

• Point out "Miss Organization" next to the information about students' scores on the quiz. Explain that she will reappear from time to time to give students clues about how to organize their lives.

11 Let's Get Organized

A. Comment on the desk in the picture. Answer the questions.

1. Does an organized desk indicate an organized person? Yes.

2. What can you infer about the person who works at this desk? This person is not organ[ized]

3. Is your desk (or room) organized or disorganized? (Answers will vary.)

B. Are you organized? Take this short quiz. Do you know the exact location of each of these items in your house? Circle Yes or No for each item. (Answers will vary.)

1.	postage stamps	Yes	No	8.	rental agreement or deed	Yes	No
2.	scissors	Yes	No	9.	address book	Yes	No
3.	tape	Yes	No	10.	calculator	Yes	No
4.	aspirin	Yes	No	11.	birth certificate	Yes	No
5.	pencil sharpener	Yes	No	12.	last test paper	Yes	No
6.	car title	Yes	No				
7.	checkbook	Yes	No				

If you circled all twelve items, congratulations! You are a very organized person. If you circled ten or more items, you are doing well. If you circled fewer than ten items, it's not too late!! This unit and the suggestions of your classmates will have you organized in no time!

Active Grammar: Verb + infinitive

A. Read.

Are you a procrastinator?

    Everyone has plans and goals. Some plans are short-term and can be accomplished in a few hours or a weekend: I'm going to wash the car. I plan to organize my closet. I want to gather all my photos from the past five years and put them in a photo album. I need to study for the test next week. I plan to start an exercise program. Some goals are far in the future and will take years to accomplish: I expect to get my nursing degree. I want to start my own business. Do you find yourself making plans but not accomplishing them? Is it difficult to take the first step? Is it impossible to find the time? Could you be a procrastinator? A procrastinator waits for the last minute. A procrastinator believes, "There is always tomorrow."

Verb + infinitives

Use an **infinitive** (*to* + verb) after the following verbs.

agree	forget	manage	remember
ask	hate	need	seem
(be) able to	hope	offer	try
can afford	intend	plan	volunteer
choose	know how	prefer	wait
decide	like	prepare	want
expect	learn (how)	promise	wish
fail	love	refuse	would like

I plan *to attend* the school concert.

He promised *to baby-sit* for his cousin.

B. Use these cues to describe your weekend plans. (Answers will vary.)

1. would like / visit
2. plan / buy
3. expect / do
4. need / study
5. will try / finish
6. intend / call
7. hope / see
8. promised / help
9. will try / read
10. want / organize

C. Complete these sentences with some of your future goals. (Answers will vary.)

1. I intend _____.
2. I expect _____.
3. I have decided _____.
4. By next year, I will be able _____.
5. I would like _____.

Active Grammar: Verb + infinitive

A. Read

- Write the word *procrastinator* on the board and discuss what it means. (It's someone who always puts off work until later and is therefore sometimes late with assignments.)
- Ask students to read the passage individually. Answer any vocabulary questions they may have. Then, ask different students to describe various things that they do and don't procrastinate about. For example:

S: *I always do my homework on time, but I sometimes go weeks without cleaning the house.*

- Review the list of verb + infinitive combinations and elicit sentences using them from various students.

B. Use these cues to describe your weekend plans.

Give students two or three minutes to read the sentences and prepare their answers. Then, call on different students to say the sentences.

C. Complete these sentences with some of your future goals.

Have students complete the activity on their own and share their answers with a partner. Then, review some of the answers with the whole class. Write some sample answers on the board, underlining the verb + infinitive combination.

D. My teacher.

Do this activity with the whole class. Answer all questions as truthfully as possible. Write on the board any sample answers using new vocabulary items.

 Distractions and Excuses

A. Read

Point out Miss Organization and ask students to read her advice. Call on one or two students to summarize what she says in their own words.

B. My distractions.

Students fill in their own answers. Review the answers with the whole class.

C. Student to student dictation.

• Read and discuss the instructions. Point out the set of answer lines on this page and explain that both Student A and Student B will use these lines but they will be writing different information based on the sentences their partner reads to them.

• Have students locate the sentences on page 248 and complete the activity in pairs. When they finish, the pairs exchange books and correct each other's work.

Suggestion

Ask students to write down three things they would like to accomplish in the next two weeks and sign the paper. Place the slips of paper in an envelope and tell students you will open it and give them back their lists two weeks from today. Suggest that they try to accomplish the three things during the next two weeks.

D. My teacher. Ask your teacher these questions. (Answers will vary.)

1. What are your plans for this weekend?
2. Why did you decide to become a teacher?
3. Do you know how to speak another language?
4. Would you like to learn my language?
5. Do you want to live in another country for a few years?
6. Where would you like to travel?
7. Do you plan to teach at this school next year?
8. Do you expect to teach ESL for the next ten years?
9. In addition to teaching, what else do you like to do?
10. Do you plan to stay in this state or to move to another state sometime?
11. Do you know how to cook any ethnic foods?
12. Will you remember to pass me at the end of this class?
13. Would you agree to end class early today?

☀ Distractions and Excuses

A. Read.

It's hard to get started on your plans. It's easy to make excuses! And once you start on a goal, there are always distractions. You sit down to work at the computer, check your e-mail, and then start to chat with friends. A friend calls and wants you to go to the mall. It's time for your favorite TV show.

B. My distractions. Write your top two distractions. (Answers will vary.)

Example: <u>the telephone</u>

1. _____   2. _____

C. Student to student dictation.
Student A: Turn to page 248. Read the excuses. Your partners will copy them.
Student B: Listen and copy the excuses you hear. When you finish, change pages.

1. B: Every time I start to study, my kids interrupt me.
   A: I'd like to save $100 a month, but I like to shop at the mall.
2. B: I wanted to get up early, but I forgot to set my alarm clock.
   A: I'd love to travel, but I can't afford to.
3. B: I want to walk a mile after work, but I'm too tired when I get home.
   A: I need to study more, but the boss often asks me to work overtime.
4. B: I need to get a cavity filled, but I hate to go to the dentist.
   A: I decided to clean the basement, but there was a great movie on TV.
5. B: I decided to buy a computer, but I don't know which one to choose.
   A: I know we need to make a will, but I don't understand legal matters.

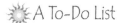 A To-Do List

A. Read.

You have commitments and appointments. There is homework, a big test, and a composition to write for school. You have many responsibilities at home.

Controlling your time is the key to success. Each day, sit down and write a list of the things you need to do that day. This is your to-do list. Then, number your list in order of importance. What needs to get done first? Do it! Check it off your list, and start number two.

B. Listen to Sergio talk about the things he wants to accomplish today. As you listen, write a to-do list for Sergio.

To Do
• Get an extra key for the house
• Finish homework
• Install the new DVD player
• Wax the car
• Drive son to the library
• Watch daughter's soccer game at 2:00
• Shop for wife's birthday present

C. Talk about the things that Sergio wants to do today. Put his list in order from 1 to 7. Is Sergio realistic? Can he accomplish all of these things today?

D. Write a to-do list for yourself for today or for tomorrow. What is the most important item on your list? Number your items in order of importance.

To Do
(Answers will vary.)

Audio Script

B. Listen to Sergio talk about the things he wants to accomplish today.
(CD3, Track 1)

It's Saturday, and I don't work on Saturdays. I work Sundays, so I need to get a lot accomplished today. Let's see, I'm supposed to get an extra key for the house. My son lost his key and he needs to have one. I go to school and I have homework. I have about an hour's homework. And I promised to install the new DVD player. We bought the DVD player last week, but I haven't had time to connect it to the TV. My wife said she would take the kids to the video store and

they would rent a movie for tonight. It's a nice day today, not too hot, a good day to wax the car. I haven't waxed it for about six months and it needs it. And let's see . . . My son—he's in fifth grade—needs to go to the library, so I'm going to drive him over there. He needs to find a few books about the planets for a class report. My daughter is on a soccer team. She's playing in the park today, so all of us are going to watch her at 2:00. And my wife's birthday is next week. I'd like a little time to shop for her. What should I buy her? Maybe a new watch?

A To-Do List

A. Read.

Point out Miss Organization and ask students to read her advice on their own. Call on one or two students to summarize what she says in their own words.

B. Listen to Sergio talk about the things he wants to accomplish today.
(CD3, Track 1)

Play the audio once as students just listen. Then point out the blank list and ask students to fill in what he plans to do as they listen the second time. You may wish to pause the audio periodically to give students a chance to make notes. Remind students to write words and phrases only, not complete sentences.

C. Talk about the things that Sergio wants to do today.

• Ask students to number Sergio's list from 1 to 7, with 1 being the most important thing on the list. Invite various students to tell what they put for number 1 and 7 and discuss differences among students' attitudes about what is really important.
• Conduct a class discussion using the questions given in the instructions.

D. Write a to-do list for yourself for today or for tomorrow.

Students can brainstorm their lists in no particular order and then number them after they finish.

Active Grammar: Verb + object + infinitive

A. Read.

• Have students read Miss Organization's suggestions. Ask students how they organize at night for the next day. What other suggestions can they add to the list?

• Discuss the Verb + object + infinitive sentences and review the list of verbs. Invite students to make up original sentences using each of the verbs. If students are unfamiliar with any of the verbs, write sentences using them on the board and suggest that they copy them into their notebooks for later study.

B. Advice for Paul.

Go over the sample restatements with the class. Then, call on individuals to restate each sentence.

Active Grammar: Verb + object + infinitive

A. Read.

Mornings are difficult for most people. It's helpful to organize the night before. These suggestions might help:

1. Check your calendar.
2. Lay out your clothes for the next day.
3. Make your lunch.
4. Put all your books and supplies in your bag or backpack.
5. Write your to-do list for tomorrow.

> **Verb + object + infinitive**
> Use an **object + an infinitive** after the following verbs:
>
> | advise | encourage | hire | remind | urge |
> |--------|-----------|------|--------|------|
> | allow | expect | invite | require | want |
> | ask | forbid | permit | teach | warn |
> | convince | help | persuade | tell | |
>
> My mother **asked** *me to clean* my room.
> My teacher **expected** *us to budget* our time.
> My brother **persuaded** *me not to quit* school.

B. Advice for Paul. Restate each comment using an infinitive.

1. His teacher said, "Turn in your report on time." (expect)
   His teacher expected him to turn in his report on time.

2. His teacher said, "Don't hand in your report late." (tell)
   His teacher told him not to hand in his report late.

3. His teacher said, "Buy a notebook and organize your papers." (advise)
   His teacher advised him to buy a notebook and organize his papers.

4. His mother said, "Lay out your clothes the night before." (convince)
   His mother convinced him to lay out his clothes the night before.

5. His sister said, "Buy a wall calendar for your bedroom." (tell)
   His sister told him to buy a a wall calendar for his bedroom.

6. His girlfriend said, "Get everything together before you go to sleep." (urge)
   His girlfriend urged him to get everything together before he went to sleep.

7. His boss said, "Don't be late for work." (warn)
   His boss warned him not to be late for work.

8. His father said, "Turn off your cell phone when you study." (remind)
   His father reminded him to turn off his cell phone when he studies.

9. His grandmother said, "Let's clean up your room." (help)
   His grandmother helped him to clean up his room.

10. His mother said, "Get up earlier." (urge)
    His mother urged him to get up earlier.

C. Problems. Complete these sentences. What advice did each person give? (Answers will vary.)

1. Gloria got a speeding ticket in another state. She doesn't want to pay the fine. She believes that you only need to pay a ticket for the state you live in.

   Her brother convinced <u>her to sign the ticket and send in the fine.</u>

2. Your brother lost his credit card.

   You advised _____.

3. Lisa is 24 years old; she's an only child and lives at home. Her company offered her a great job promotion, but she needs to move out of state.

   Her parents expect _____

   Her boss is encouraging _____

4. John has begun to hang around with a group of troublemakers. Two of them have dropped out of school and two of them have been in trouble with the law.

   His parents have forbidden _____.

   The baseball coach has invited _____.

   His brother is urging him _____.

5. Your friends are coming to this country for a month. You want to see them, but you don't want them to stay with you because you live in a studio apartment.

   You are going to tell _____.

   You are not going to invite _____.

6. Your sister was accepted to college, but she doesn't have enough money for tuition.

   Your parents have persuaded _____.

   Her teacher advised _____.

D. Answer these questions about growing up. (Answers will vary.)

1. When you were a child, what did your parents forbid you to do?
2. How many hours did they expect you to study?
3. Did your parents help you to do your homework?
4. Did they expect you to come right home after school?
5. When you were a teenager, how did they expect you to help at home?
6. Who taught you how to drive?
7. Did they allow you to go out on Saturday night?
8. Did they encourage you to play a sport?
9. Did you expect your parents to give you an allowance?
10. What did they advise you not to do?

C. Problems.

Review the sample answer. Then, give students ten minutes to write their answers individually. Call on different students to complete each sentence orally. Write any problematic sentences on the board.

D. Answer these questions about growing up.

• Point out that students can use the verb given in the question as they formulate their answers. For example, the question …*what did your parents forbid you to do?* can be answered, *They forbade me to stay out after 10:00 at night.*

• Students complete the activity in pairs. Review different students' answers with the whole class.

Suggestion

If appropriate for your class, have students change each of the past situations in Exercise D into a present or future situation, keeping the same situation and verb. For example, item 1 might become:

S1: *Now that you have children, what do you forbid them to do?*
S2: *I forbid them to ride their bikes in the street.*

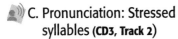

Active Grammar:

Be + adjective + infinitive

A. Read.

Read and discuss Miss Organization's advice with the class. Review the meaning of the words in the list of adjectives. Invite students to make up some original sentences using *be* + adjective + infinitive.

B. Make sentences about the busy pace of daily life in the United States.

Students match the phrases in the two columns to make up reasonable sentences. When they have used all the phrases in column 3, invite them to think of new column 3 items and make up some original sentences.

C. Pronunciation: Stressed syllables (CD3, Track 2)

- Discuss the instructions and go over the sample answers. Have students just listen the first time you play the audio. Then, play it a second time and have them mark the stressed syllables.
- Play the audio again so they can check their answers. Review the correct answers with the whole class.

D. In your notebook, write sentences with the adjectives from Exercise C.

- Read and discuss the sample answers. Then, have students write sentences in their notebooks. Circulate and help students as needed.
- Invite individual students to share a favorite sentence or two with the whole class.

Active Grammar: *Be + adjective + infinitive*

A. Read.

Make a schedule of your day or of your study time. It's easy to say, "I'll get it done sometime today." It's more helpful to make an appointment with yourself. If possible, find a time that is the most productive for you. Maybe that is right after class or as soon as you get home. What is your most productive time?

Be + adjective + infinitive
Use the infinitive form after these adjectives:

dangerous	good	important	polite	selfish
difficult	hard	impossible	possible	stressful
easy	healthy	interesting	reasonable	terrible
expensive	helpful	lonely	realistic	thoughtful
foolish	idealistic	necessary	romantic	wonderful

B. Make sentences about the busy pace of daily life in the United States.

It's difficult It's impossible It's hard	to	get started on a project. work and go to school. find time to exercise. stick to a schedule. accomplish everything I need to do. keep my papers in order. get enough sleep. have time for myself.

C. Pronunciation: Stressed syllables. Listen and mark the stressed syllable.

1. dán · ger · ous
2. i · de · a · lís · tic
3. im · pós · si · ble
4. in · ter · est · ing
5. po · líte

6. réa · son · a · ble
7. re · a · lís · tic
8. ro · mán · tic
9. stréss · ful
10. thought · ful

D. In your notebook, write sentences with the adjectives from Exercise C.

It's dangerous to drive when you are very tired.
It's idealistic to believe the promises of that politician.

E. **Use the adjectives to give suggestions for organizing your day.** (Answers will vary.)

| helpful | important | smart | necessary |

1. file your important papers   *It's helpful to file your important papers.*
2. check your appointment calendar daily
3. make a to-do list
4. hang a calendar in your kitchen or bedroom
5. plan your day
6. lay out your clothes for the next day
7. schedule your study time
8. organize your desk
9. take a break every two hours
10. post notes on your desk to help you remember things
11. have a pencil sharpener on your desk
12. keep a dictionary on your desk

Give two more suggestions for organizing your day.

F. **A study schedule.** Ali has a lot of homework this weekend. He likes to study in the morning. Look at his assignments and schedule his study time for Saturday and Sunday. Write the assignments in the chart below. Does he have enough time to complete all his work? (Answers will vary.)

Assignments
Grammar workbook—pages 153 to 156
Read article about Elvis (two pages)
Go to library and research a popular musician
Write a composition about a popular musician
Study infinitives for test on Monday

Saturday	Sunday
9:00	9:00
10:00	10:00
11:00	11:00

E. Use the adjectives to give suggestions for organizing your day.

• Give pairs of students a time limit for completing this activity, perhaps five minutes.
• Ask other students who want to check that a certain sentence is correct to read it to the class. Invite the rest of the class to confirm that it is correct or offer suggestions for correction, if necessary.

Give two more suggestions for organizing your day.

Give students one minute to jot down their answers. Ask several different students to share their suggestions with the class.

F. A study schedule.

• Ask students how many hours Ali will have for studying. (Six) Then, have students work in pairs to complete a suggested study schedule for Ali.
• Discuss the completed schedules with the whole class. Have students explain how many hours they think each task will take and tell why Ali will or won't have enough time if he studies only six hours this weekend.

☀ The Big Picture: The First Test

☀ The Big Picture: The First Test

⊪ A. Diana started college last month. (CD3, Track 3)

• Ask students to comment on the picture. Ask questions such as:

What is Diana supposed to be doing?
Who do you think these people are?
Do you ever end up talking when you should be studying?

• Play the audio once as students just listen. Play it a second time, pausing after Diana speaks with each person. Ask individual students to describe the conversation, using their own words.

B. Listen to the conversation again.

Ask students to mark their answers individually. Then, play the audio again and ask them to check their answers. Review the correct answers with the whole class.

🔊 A. Diana started college last month. Her first math test is tomorrow. Diana is supposed to be studying for her test now. Listen to her telephone conversations.

B. Listen to the conversation again. As you listen, (circle) *True* or *False*.

1.	Susan was able to stop and talk with Diana.	True	**(False)**
2.	Susan has to study for the math test.	True	**(False)**
3.	Diana's father expects her to do well in school.	**(True)**	False
4.	Diana called Jacob at his job.	**(True)**	False
5.	Jacob needs to write his lab report.	**(True)**	False
6.	He plans to see Diana later tonight.	True	**(False)**
7.	Alex is at school now.	**(True)**	False
8.	Alex asked her to join a study group.	**(True)**	False
9.	Katie invited Diana to go to the mall.	**(True)**	False
10.	Diana decided to stay home and study.	True	**(False)**

Audio Script

A. Diana started college last month. (CD3, Track 3)

Diana: Hi, Susan.
Susan: Hi, Diana. What are you doing?
Diana: I'm supposed to be studying for my math test.
Susan: That's tomorrow, right?
Diana: Right. I'm not really worried. I understood everything in class.
Susan: Well, good luck. I can't talk now. I'm writing this English paper.
Diana: The one about cities and pollution?

Susan: Yeah. I'm in the middle of it. I'll call you tomorrow.
Diana: OK.

Diana: Hi, Dad.
Dad: Hi, Diana. Studying for that math test?
Diana: I'm going to start in a few minutes.
Dad: You're great at math. You'll do well.
Diana: I hope so.
Dad: Remember to clean this room. How can you find anything in here?
Diana: Don't worry, Dad.

Diana: Jacob? You at work?
Jacob: Uh-huh. I'm getting off in an hour. I can't come over tonight.

Diana: I won't see you?!
Jacob: No, I've got this science homework to finish. You know, that lab report. How's it going with your math?
Diana: I'm going to start to study in a few minutes.
Jacob: Why don't you go over to the math center at school? It's quieter there.
Diana: Maybe.
Jacob: Well, I'll see you tomorrow night. How about 8:00? After I get out of work?
Diana: That's good. Ciao.
Jacob: Bye.

(Audio Script continues on page 256.)

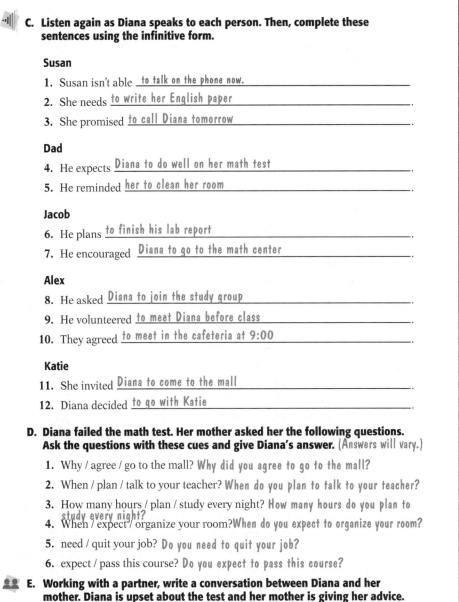

C. Listen again as Diana speaks to each person. Then, complete these sentences using the infinitive form.

Susan

1. Susan isn't able <u>to talk on the phone now.</u>
2. She needs <u>to write her English paper</u>
3. She promised <u>to call Diana tomorrow</u>

Dad

4. He expects <u>Diana to do well on her math test</u>
5. He reminded <u>her to clean her room</u>

Jacob

6. He plans <u>to finish his lab report</u>
7. He encouraged <u>Diana to go to the math center</u>

Alex

8. He asked <u>Diana to join the study group</u>
9. He volunteered <u>to meet Diana before class</u>
10. They agreed <u>to meet in the cafeteria at 9:00</u>

Katie

11. She invited <u>Diana to come to the mall</u>
12. Diana decided <u>to go with Katie</u>

D. Diana failed the math test. Her mother asked her the following questions. Ask the questions with these cues and give Diana's answer. (Answers will vary.)

1. Why / agree / go to the mall? <u>Why did you agree to go to the mall?</u>
2. When / plan / talk to your teacher? <u>When do you plan to talk to your teacher?</u>
3. How many hours / plan / study every night? <u>How many hours do you plan to study every night?</u>
4. When / expect / organize your room? <u>When do you expect to organize your room?</u>
5. need / quit your job? <u>Do you need to quit your job?</u>
6. expect / pass this course? <u>Do you expect to pass this course?</u>

E. Working with a partner, write a conversation between Diana and her mother. Diana is upset about the test and her mother is giving her advice.

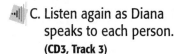

C. Listen again as Diana speaks to each person. (CD3, Track 3)

- Play the audio one section at a time. Pause long enough after each section for students to complete the related statements in their books.
- Review the correct answers with the whole class. Replay segments of the audio as necessary to clarify any questions students may have.

D. Diana failed the math test.

Role-play the first answer with a student. Then, have students prepare questions and answers to fit all six items. Review the answers orally with the whole class.

E. Working with a partner, write a conversation between Diana and her mother.

Have students write their conversations in pairs. Remind them that they can use many of the questions and answers from Exercise D in their conversations. Invite one or two pairs to present their conversations to the class.

Suggestion

Ask students to use the conversation in Exercise E as a model to write original conversations they might actually have in their own lives. They can work individually or in pairs. Remind them to use the verb + infinitive form. Invite volunteers to role-play their conversations for the class with a partner.

Reading: Active Learning

Active Learning

A. Active learners.

- Ask students to complete the checklist on their own. Then, lead a class discussion about which techniques people like and why. Also talk about which techniques people dislike or never use and find out the reasons.

- Ask students to read the passage on their own. Then, have students raise their hands if there is something they don't understand and read that passage aloud to the class. Help students use sentence and paragraph context to figure out the meaning of new words and phrases.

Reading: Active Learning

A. Active learners. (Circle) the study techniques you use when studying English. Add two more. (Answers will vary.)

1. I make lists and charts.
2. I write examples of the work we are doing in class.
3. I sit and look at the book.
4. I use an English study site on the Internet.
5. I study with a partner.
6. I try to read the newspaper.
7. I listen to a tape or CD. Sometimes I try to copy the sentences.
8. I repeat the sentences in the book aloud.
9. _____
10. _____

Once you have scheduled your study time, shut out distractions, sit down, and begin your assignments. How can you make the most of your study time? It is helpful to become an active student, both at home and outside of class. These students are all "active learners." How do they approach learning?

Because I'm really **pressed for time**, I have to plan carefully to find study time. One of the only places I have **downtime** is in my car. I made a tape with the verb forms and I play this over and over again. After we study a unit, I record ten or fifteen sentences as examples of the grammar. I **pop** the tape in the car stereo, listen to the sentences, and memorize them as I sit in traffic. I'm sure that drivers in other cars think I'm a crazy guy talking to myself.

For me, it's important to have a study partner. When I'm taking a new class, I look for a person who is serious about studying. After class, we meet in the library and review the material we studied in class. For example, I ask my partner the same questions we practiced in class, and she gives me the answers. Then, we switch roles. Our favorite activity is dictations of the sentences or paragraphs we studied. When we learned the past participles, we gave each other quizzes. I think this is the best way to study because we are using our grammar.

I enjoy **breaking** news stories so I'll choose one or two major stories. First, I'll watch the news on TV and look at the action to get the idea of the story. Then, I will read newspaper articles about the story. Finally, I'll look on the Internet. There are several great sites on news where I can look at the story and see photographs or video clips. Some of the sites even have audio. I've been able to **improve** my vocabulary and to learn some interesting information.

Country music is my ticket to English. Country music is easy to understand because the songs tell a story. I have CDs by Faith Hill, Reba McEntire, Garth Brooks, Tim McGraw, and lots of other popular country singers. I listen to their music, copy the words, and sing along with the **lyrics**. Many of the CDs have **inserts** with the words so that I can follow along. At other times, I'll ask an American student if she can help me figure out the words.

B. Vocabulary. Match each boldface word or phrase with the word or phrase that has the same meaning.

_e_ 1. I'm **pressed for time**.

_f_ 2. I have **downtime** in my car.

_g_ 3. I **pop** the tape into the car stereo.

_c_ 4. I sing along with the **lyrics**.

_b_ 5. Many of the CDs have **inserts**.

_a_ 6. I enjoy **breaking** news stories.

_d_ 7. I've been able to **improve** my vocabulary.

a. current
b. papers with the words
c. words
d. make better
e. I'm very busy.
f. free time
g. put

C. Discuss the meaning of each verbal phrase in the box . Then, write only the correct preposition in each sentence.

> look at   look in   look on   look for

1. He's looking __at__ the map of Africa to find the capital of Kenya.
2. He looked __in__ the dictionary to find the meaning of the word.
3. She is looking __for__ a study partner to practice her English with.
4. After I look __at__ the computer screen for a long time, my eyes get tired.
5. They look __on__ the Web to find movie times.
6. I need to look __for__ information about the election.
7. You can look __in__ the newspaper to find the movie times.
8. You can look __on__ the Internet to find the best prices for airline tickets.

D. Discuss your learning strategies. How would you approach each assignment?

(Answers will vary.)

1. You are going to have a test on infinitives.
2. You need to write a composition about the pros and cons of living in a large city.
3. You failed your last test on the present perfect.
4. You would like to improve your vocabulary.

Let's Get Organized   **175**

B. Vocabulary.

Students complete the matching exercise on their own and check their answers with a partner. Answer any questions they may have.

C. Discuss the meaning of each verbal phrase in the box.

• Review the general meanings of the four expressions: *look at* (turn your eyes toward something), *look in* (search for something in a written document), *look on* (search for something on a visual format such as a map or the Internet, and *look for* (try to find an object).

• Have students complete the sentences on their own. Review the correct answers with the whole class.

D. Discuss your learning strategies.

Have pairs discuss how they approach each learning situation. Then, lead a class discussion. Elicit several different approaches to successfully accomplishing each of the four tasks.

Writing Our Stories: Study Time

A. Read.

- Invite students to talk about the desk in the picture. Ask:
  What do they like about how things are organized?
  How would you set up this desk?
- Then, have students read the passage on their own. Answer any questions they may have.

B. Writing.

Discuss the assignment with the whole class and answer any questions they may have. Have students do the writing for homework and be prepared to read their descriptions to their classmates at the next class.

Suggestion

Some students may benefit from doing Exercise B in three steps. First they can brainstorm and list all the ideas that come to mind. Next, they can make a rough outline using words and phrases to indicate the order in which they will present the facts and how they will divide their writing into paragraphs. Finally, they can write the description using the outline as a guide.

Writing Our Stories: Study Time

A. Read.

My study area is a large table <u>in the corner of my bedroom</u>. There's a large desk lamp <u>in the corner</u>. <u>On the left side of my desk</u> is my high school graduation present—a laptop computer. My printer is <u>in back of the computer</u>. <u>Above the desk</u>, attached <u>to the wall</u>, is a long, narrow shelf, <u>about 6 inches wide.</u> It holds envelopes, a pencil sharpener, a small clock, a jar with pens and pencils— everything I need—all <u>in easy reach.</u> <u>To the right of my desk</u> is a small bookcase <u>for my books and notebooks and papers.</u> I keep a large calendar <u>over my desk</u> <u>for my work schedule and appointments.</u>

I like to study in the evening <u>from 7:00 to 9:30.</u> I check my assignments, open my books, and begin. I always do my writing first because it's my least favorite assignment. When that is finished, I relax a little and start my reading assignments. I leave my grammar and vocabulary <u>for last</u> because that is the easiest homework <u>for me.</u>

It's difficult to study <u>after 9:30</u> because I share my bedroom <u>with my older sister.</u> When she gets home <u>from work</u> <u>at 9:30,</u> she likes to watch TV <u>in the bedroom</u> or talk <u>on the phone</u> <u>with her boyfriend.</u> That's the time that I get <u>on the Internet,</u> e-mail my friends, and try to ignore her!

Note to Instructor: Prepositional phrases underlined above are the answers to Exercise C on page 177.

B. Writing. Describe your study area and your study time. (Answers will vary.)

1. Draw a picture of your study area. It could be your kitchen table, a desk in your bedroom, or the school library.
2. Look at the picture. Does it include everything you use? Where are your books, your pencils, your dictionary, your backpack? What other unusual items are in the picture?
3. Carefully describe your study area. Details add interest. Give locations.

4. Describe how you organize your study time. If you are completely disorganized, it is still important to describe your study area and time. Understanding what you do is the first step to making changes.

C. Preposition review. First, underline the prepositional phrases in the description on page 176. Then, describe the locations in this picture. In some of the sentences, the location is at the beginning of the sentence. In other sentences, the location is at the end. (Answers may vary.)

1. My stereo is _in the back righthand corner of my desk_.
2. My telephone is _to the left of my computer_.
3. There's a small clock _in front of my stereo_.
4. _To the left of the lamp_ is a photo of my girlfriend.
5. My laptop computer sits _in the middle of my desk_.
6. I'm always hungry when I study, so there's always a bag of potato chips _on my desk_.
7. The wastebasket that is _to the left of my desk_ often overflows with paper.

D. Edit. Find and correct the mistakes in these sentences.

1. I like ^to^ study on the kitchen table.
2. It's difficult ^to^ find time to study.
3. My mother told ^me^ to be home by 12:00.
4. ~~Is~~ ^It is^ impossible to complete all this homework.
5. She promised to ~~helped~~ ^help^ me.
6. My father encouraged my sister to do ~~his~~ ^her^ best.
7. The teacher urged to us ~~to~~ use the computer lab.
8. My grandfather offered ^to^ pay my tuition.

Looking at the Internet

Many Web sites help students organize their busy lives. Other sites help students with time management and study skills. Find an idea to help you better organize your time by entering one of these phrases in the *Search* box:

time management and study skills

time management and college

C. Preposition review.

• Ask students to underline the prepositional phrases in the description on page 176. Check the answers with the whole class by having students follow along in their books as you slowly read the passage aloud, one sentence at a time. Have students raise their hands when they hear a prepositional phrase. Call on a student to read the phrase aloud.

• Then, have students look at the picture and fill in the missing prepositional phrases on their own. Ask them to check their answers with a partner.

D. Edit.

Have students correct the errors and check their answers with a partner. Have the first people who finish the activity write the corrected sentences on the board. Go over them with the whole class.

Looking at the Internet

As students report back to the class about what they learned about making the most of their study time, have a student take notes. A student can then turn these notes into a poster for the classroom wall listing ten of the most useful ideas they discovered.

A. Use the cues.

Students complete the sentences on their own. Review the answers with the class, discussing the different ways some of the questions were answered.

B. Rewrite each sentence, using the verb in parentheses.

Students complete the sentences on their own and check their answers with a partner.

A. Use the cues. Write the question and give an answer about your weekend plans.

1. How many hours / need to study?
   A: _How many hours do you need to study this weekend?_
   B: _I need to study for three hours this weekend._

2. Where / plan / go?
   A: _Where do you plan to go this weekend_ ?
   B: _(Answers will vary.)_ .

3. Who / expect / visit?
   A: _Who do you expect to visit this weekend_ ?
   B: _(Answers will vary.)_ .

4. What movie / would like / see?
   A: _What movie would you like to see this weekend_ ?
   B: _(Answers will vary.)_ .

5. What / hope / do?
   A: _What do you hope to do this weekend_ ?
   B: _(Answers will vary.)_ .

B. Rewrite each sentence, using the verb in parentheses. You will need to change the wording in some of the sentences.

1. Luis's parents said, "We know you will do well in college." (expect)
   Luis's parents expect him to do well in college.

2. Laura's father said, "Take art lessons." (encourage)
   Laura's father encouraged her to take art lessons

3. My brother said, "You should become an engineer." (tell)
   My brother told me I should become an engineer

4. My high school counselor said, "Apply for a scholarship." (advise)
   My high school counselor advised me to apply for a scholarship

5. My friend said, "Don't turn in your paper late." (warn)
   My friend warned me not to turn in my paper late

Grammar Summary

▶ 1. Verb + infinitive

Use an infinitive (*to* + verb) after the following verbs:

agree	forget	manage	remember
ask	hate	need	seem
(be) able to	hope	offer	try
can afford	intend	plan	volunteer
choose	know how	prefer	wait
decide	like	prepare	want
expect	learn (how)	promise	wish
fail	love	refuse	would like

I **hope to finish** this report by 5:00.

He **forgot to do** his homework.

I **know how to organize** my time.

▶ 2. Verb + object + infinitive

Use an object + infinitive after the following verbs:

advise	encourage	hire	remind	urge
allow	expect	invite	require	want
ask	forbid	permit	teach	warn
convince	help	persuade	tell	

My parents **didn't permit me to go** out during the week.

The school **required all students to wear** uniforms.

My classmate **helped me to understand** the math problems.

▶ 3. *Be* + adjective + infinitive

Use the infinitive form after these adjectives:

dangerous	good	important	polite	selfish
difficult	hard	impossible	possible	stressful
easy	healthy	interesting	reasonable	terrible
expensive	helpful	lonely	realistic	thoughtful
foolish	idealistic	necessary	romantic	wonderful

It**'s important to have** clear plans and goals.

It **was difficult to accomplish** my goals.

Grammar Summary

• Review the three grammar explanations and sample sentences with the class. Invite students to make up alternate sentences for each one in the chart. For example, in place of *My classmate helped me to understand the math problems*, a student might say, *My parents taught me to be polite at all times*.

• Answer any questions students may have about the grammar items.

• See the Grammar Summary Expansion on page 268 for a more complete explanation of these grammar points.

Unit 12
Becoming a Citizen

Discuss what the person in the unit title art is doing. Ask:

- *Who is standing next to the number 12?* (A man)
- *What is he doing?* (He's holding a U.S. flag in one hand and some papers in the other.)
- *How does this relate to the unit?* (The man probably just became a citizen. The papers are probably the man's citizenship documents.)

 A. New citizens. (CD3, Track 4)

- Ask students to look over the pictures and explain what they think is happening in each one. Supply vocabulary as necessary. Repeat correct student statements and refine vague statements in more detail, using key vocabulary. For example:

  S: *She's talking with someone.*
  T: *Right. She's having an interview. An INS worker is interviewing her.*

- Have students just listen as you play the audio the first time. Then, play it again. Ask students to use the picture and retell Marco and Luciana's story in their own words.
- Point out the five steps in the citizenship process and ask students to read them to themselves. Explain terms such as *immigration, naturalization,* and *certified mail* as needed.

B. Discuss these questions about citizenship.

Discuss the questions with the whole class. Encourage any students who have completed the process to share their experiences.

Becoming a Citizen

A. New citizens. Listen to Marco and Luciana's story about becoming citizens of the United States.

1.

2.

3.

4.

INS Office

5.

6.

Citizenship Process
1. Fill out the application for citizenship.
2. Send application, three photographs, copies of requested documents, and check(s) to your regional Immigration and Naturalization Service (INS) office. Send your letter via certified mail.
3. Have your fingerprints taken.
4. Go for your citizenship interview and English test.
5. Take the Oath of Allegiance to the United States at your swearing in ceremony.

B. Discuss these questions about citizenship. (Answers will vary.)

1. Are you a citizen? Is anyone in your family a citizen?
2. What are the benefits of becoming a citizen?
3. What are the responsibilities of being a citizen?

Audio Script

A. New citizens. (CD3, Track 4)

Marco came to the United States in 1990 when he was 24. Ten years passed and during those 10 years, Marco learned English, changed jobs four times, met Luciana, and got married. In 2000, life was still busy, but Marco and his wife began to think about becoming citizens. Their children had been born in the United States and were citizens already. Marco knew he had a good life and a good job. He was going to visit his native country from time to time, but he was not going to return there to live.

Marco and his wife obtained their naturalization papers from the INS (Immigration and Naturalization Service) and carefully completed the paperwork. They sent all the required documents and check(s) to their local INS Regional Service Center. They knew they would have to wait six months to a year to hear from the INS.

While waiting for their appointments, Marco and Luciana studied for their citizenship test. Ten months later, they received an appointment for their citizenship interview and English test. The immigration officer

(Audio Script continues on page 256.)

Active Grammar: Verb + Gerund

Verb + gerund			
Use a **gerund** (simple verb form + *ing*) after the following verbs:			
admit	consider	imagine	recommend
anticipate	delay	like	regret
appreciate	discuss	love	resent
avoid	dislike	miss	start
begin	doesn't / don't mind	postpone	stop
can't help	enjoy	practice	suggest
can't stand	finish	quit	understand
continue	hate	recall	

They missed *seeing* their family for holidays and celebrations.

A. Listen to these sentences about Marco and Luciana. Fill in the gerund you hear.

1. Marco and Luciana discussed ____becoming____ citizens.

2. They delayed ____starting____ the process because Luciana's English was not strong.

3. Luciana regretted ____not beginning____ English classes earlier.

4. She began ____studying____ English at a local adult school.

5. A friend recommended ____enrolling____ in a citizenship class.

6. They didn't mind ____taking____ class one night a week.

7. Marco and Luciana enjoyed ____learning____ about U.S. history.

8. They practiced ____asking____ one another questions.

9. Luciana couldn't help ____feeling____ nervous before the test.

B. Restate these sentences. Use gerunds.

1. People discuss (leave) their countries for many years before making a final decision. People discuss leaving...

2. They anticipate (have) a better life for their children.
   They anticipate having...

3. New immigrants can't help (worry) about money and work.
   New immigrants can't help worrying...

4. Some immigrants begin (study) English soon after they arrive.
   Some immigrants begin studying...

5. Other students postpone (enroll) in English classes.
   Other students postpone enrolling...

6. Many new immigrants start (work) in low-paying jobs.
   Many new immigrants start working...

7. They imagine (find) better jobs.
   They imagine finding...

8. In the first year, many new immigrants consider (return) to their countries.
   In the first year, many new immigrants consider returning...

9. They miss (see) their families.
   They miss seeing...

10. They can't stand (hear) English all day!
    They can't stand hearing...

11. Older immigrants recommend (find) friends and activities in the United States.
    Older immigrants recommend finding...

12. They suggest (start) English classes.
    They suggest starting...

Becoming a Citizen **181**

Active Grammar: Verb + Gerund

A. Listen to these sentences about Marco and Luciana. (CD3, Track 5)

- Review the Verb + Gerund chart with the class. Ask different students to make up original sentences using each verb in the chart. Discuss the meaning of any verbs that are new to the class and write on the board sample sentences using these verbs in the verb + gerund format.
- Have students listen and complete the sentences with the gerunds they hear.

B. Restate these sentences.

Students take turns restating the sentences. Review the correct answers with the whole class.

Suggestion

Extend the Exercise B practice by calling on individuals to restate the sentences a second time. This time they keep the verb and gerund shown in each sentence, but change the sentence so it makes a true statement about their own lives. For example:

Original: *They anticipate having a better life for their children.*

Revised: *I anticipate having a good time at the party tonight.*

Audio Script

A. Listen to these sentences about Marco and Luciana. (CD3, Track 5)

1. Marco and Luciana discussed becoming citizens.

2. They delayed starting the process because Luciana's English was not strong.

3. Luciana regretted not beginning English classes earlier.

4. She began studying English at a local adult school.

5. A friend recommended enrolling in a citizenship class.

6. They didn't mind taking class one night a week.

7. Marco and Luciana enjoyed learning about U.S. history.

8. They practiced asking one another questions.

9. Luciana couldn't help feeling nervous before the test.

C. Before coming to the United States.

• Review the meaning of the verbs in the two charts. Use in a sentence any verbs that students aren't familiar with. Write a sample sentence for each of these new verbs on the board so that students can copy it into their notebooks if they wish.

• Have students work in small groups. Ask a pair to role-play the sample dialogue. Students then take turns describing their experiences using the verbs in the two charts.

D. After coming to the United States.

Have students spend a few minutes writing things they like and don't like in the chart. Invite different students to share some of their likes and dislikes with the class.

Sit in a small group of three or four students.

Students read the sample dialogue and then create their own similar dialogues. Invite volunteer pairs to present their conversations to the class.

C. Before coming to the United States. Sit in a small group. Use the verbs in the box to talk about your preparations to come to America. All these verbs are followed by gerunds. You might want to use some of the cues below to help recall your plans.

anticipate	discuss	recall	start
begin	finish	regret	stop
continue	quit	remember	

apply	work	learn (English)
save (money)	contact (relatives)	say good-bye
live	fill out	shop
take	buy	call
find out	write	pack

A: I began learning English. How about you?

B: No, I didn't study English. I regret not taking classes.

A: I continued working until the week before I left.

B: Me, too. I couldn't stop working.

D. After coming to the United States. What do you like about the United States? What don't you like? Write two or three items in each column. (Answers will vary.)

like/enjoy	don't mind	dislike/don't like	can't stand

Sit in a small group of three or four students. Compare your information and discuss the similarities and differences.

A: I can't stand wearing a heavy winter coat and hat and gloves.

B: Why?

A: I come from a tropical country. I don't like heavy clothing.

Active Grammar: Preposition + Gerund

> **Preposition + gerund**
> Use a gerund (simple verb form + *ing*) after the following prepositions:
> after   besides   in addition to   while
> before   by   instead of   without
>
> **After** *studying* the citizenship book, she easily passed the test.

A. Citizenship. Restate these sentences about citizenship. Use a gerund.

1. Before I applied for citizenship, I lived here for ten years.

   Before applying for citizenship, I lived here for ten years.

2. After I obtained the application for naturalization, I had my fingerprints taken.
   After obtaining the application for naturalization, I had my fingerprints taken.
3. After I filled out the application, I wrote the check.
   After filling out the application, I wrote the check.
4. Before I sent in the paperwork, I had the required photographs taken.
   Before sending in the paperwork, I had the required photographs taken.
5. After I sent in the papers, I waited a long time.
   After sending in the papers, I waited a long time.
6. While I waited, I studied for the citizenship test.
   While waiting, I studied for the citizenship test.
7. Before I took the Oath of Allegiance, I took and passed the citizenship test.
   Before taking the Oath of Allegiance, I took and passed the citizenship test.
8. After I took the Oath of Allegiance, I was a citizen.
   After taking the Oath of Allegiance, I was a citizen.

B. Time line. The time line shows Jarek's activities from 1990 to 2002. Use the information to complete the sentences.

> 1990—applied for a visa
> 1993—received his visa
> 1994—arrived in the United States
> 1995—began to study English; worked as a taxi driver
> 1997—began to work at an auto body repair shop
> 1999—applied for citizenship
> 2000—became a citizen
> 2001—met Dorota
> 2002—married Dorota; opened his own auto body repair shop

1. After _____ waiting _____ for three years, Jarek received a visa.
2. After _____ arriving _____ in the United States, Jarek found a job as a taxi driver.
3. Instead of _____ studying _____ English in Poland, Jarek waited until he came to the United States.
4. While _____ working _____ as a taxi driver, Jarek studied English.
5. After _____ driving _____ a taxi for two years, Jarek got a job in an auto body repair shop.
6. Before _____ meeting _____ Dorota, Jarek became a citizen.
7. After _____ marrying _____ Dorota, Jarek opened his own auto body shop.

Active Grammar: Preposition + Gerund

A. Citizenship.

- Read and discuss the explanation at the top of the grammar box. Have students take turns making up possible sentences using the prepositions in the chart followed by a gerund. Accept any reasonable statements. For example: *We went home after leaving school. I studied a lot before taking the test.*
- Read aloud the instructions and the pair of sample sentences. Then, call on different students to restate each of the rest of the sentences.

B. Time line.

Briefly discuss the time line with the class. Ask students to point out the verb in each time line item. Then, call on different students to complete each sentence with the missing gerund.

☀ Active Grammar:
Verb + Preposition + Gerund; *Be* + Adjective Phrase + Gerund

A. Complete these sentences about your experiences and feelings before and after coming to the United States.

• Review the contents of the two charts with the class. Point out that the items in the first chart consist of a verb + preposition and the items in the second chart consist of an adjective + preposition. Ask a student to make a master list on the board of all the prepositions mentioned in the charts. Then, have students check the charts to see that the students found them all.

• Ask different students to make up original sentences using items from both charts. Then, have pairs of students complete the sentences in the exercise. Review the exercise with the whole class by calling on two or three students to read their completions of each item.

Suggestion

Extend the practice with these two forms by asking students to make up pairs of sentences that mean the same thing. One sentence of each pair uses the verb + preposition + gerund form and the other uses the *be* + adjective phrase + gerund. For example:

1. I *don't approve of allowing* young children to stay up late.

2. I *am opposed to allowing* young children to stay up late.

☀ Active Grammar: Verb + Preposition + Gerund;
Be + Adjective Phrase + Gerund

Verb + preposition + gerund			
Use a **gerund** (simple verb form + *ing*) after the following verbs and prepositions:			
adjust to	complain about	give up	succeed in
approve of	concentrate on	insist on	suspect of
argue about	count on	keep on	talk about
believe in	depend on	look forward to	think about
blame for	dream about	plan on	warn about
care about	forget about	prevent from	worry about

New immigrants **plan on *working*** hard.

Be + adjective phrase + gerund			
Use a **gerund** (simple verb form + *ing*) after the following: *be* + adjective phrase:			
afraid of	good at	interested in	tired of
capable of	guilty of	opposed to	upset about
famous for	in favor of	proud of	

Antonio was **in favor of *coming*** to America, but his wife wasn't.

A. Complete these sentences about your experiences and feelings before and after coming to the United States. Use a gerund in each sentence. Then, read your sentences to a partner. (Answers will vary.)

Before coming to the United States . . .

1. I dreamed about _____.
2. I planned on _____.
3. I looked forward to _____.
4. I worried about _____.
5. I was interested in _____.

After coming to the United States . . .

6. I am proud of _____.
7. I have adjusted to _____.
8. I often complain about _____.
9. I think about _____.
10. I'm tired of _____.

B. Pronunciation: Linking. When a word begins with a vowel, link it with the word before. Listen to this conversation. Then, practice the conversation with a partner.

A: I thought life here was going to be_easy. I just can't_adjust to living here. I'm upset_about leaving my family.

B: You'll_always miss them. I plan_on visiting my family once_a year.

A: And I'm afraid_of losing my job.

B: Yesterday you were complaining_about working so much_overtime!

A: I gave_up working_at my family's business to come here.

B: You weren't interested_in working there. And you plan_on_opening your_own business someday.

A: I'm tired_of listening to English_all day! I'm thinking_of going back to Korea.

B: You've_only been here for nine months. Forget_about going back. Concentrate_on learning English_and making_a few friends.

C. I agree/I disagree. Eight commonly discussed issues are listed below. Use the phrases in the box, all requiring gerunds, and state your opinion. Give your reasons. (Answers will vary.)

I agree with	I disagree with
I am in favor of	I don't agree with
I approve of	I'm opposed to
	I'm against
	I object to

1. Limit new immigration
2. Mandate English only in government offices
3. Issue national identity cards
4. Prohibit the sale of automatic weapons
5. Increase the tax on cigarettes
6. Allow prayer in public school
7. Institute national health insurance
8. Raise the retirement age

Name two more controversial issues in your city, state, or in the nation. Give your opinion of the issue.

 B. Pronunciation: Linking.
(CD3, Track 6)

• Read and discuss the explanation. Point out specific examples of prepositions beginning with a vowel in the sample sentences. Then, play the audio and ask students to focus only on the links between the words that are marked in each sentence. You may wish to say just these parts of each sentence and have students repeat each linking transition.

• Students practice the conversation in pairs. Call on different pairs to say one sentence each for the class, remembering to make the links between words that are marked in the book.

C. I Agree/I Disagree.

Complete this exercise with the whole class. If students give different opinions about the same issue, note the differences and have students give a reason for their feelings. However, try not to spend too much time discussing an individual issue.

Name two more controversial issues in your city, state, or in the nation.

Call on different students to give their opinions on any issues they come up with.

Active Grammar:
Contrast—Infinitives and Gerunds

A. Contrast—Gerund or infinitive?

• Explain that the items in this exercise review the grammar taught in Unit 11 as well as the new grammar in Unit 12. You may wish to review the *be* + adjective + infinitive explanation on page 179 in Unit 11.

• Have students complete the exercise on their own and check their answers with a partner. Review the correct answers with the whole class.

B. Ask and answer the questions with a partner or a small group.

Set a time limit for the group work. Then, ask a person from each of the groups to tell their response to each of the questions.

A. Contrast—Gerund or infinitive? Do you use a gerund or an infinitive after these verbs? Read each sentence and use the correct form of the word in parentheses.

1. It was impossible (find) a job in my country.
It was impossible to find a job in my country.
2. I miss (see) my family and friends.
I miss seeing my family and friends.
3. I intend (visit) my native country next year.
I intend to visit my native country next year.
4. I expect my cousin (arrive) soon.
I expect my cousin to arrive soon.
5. Have you ever considered (become) a citizen?
Have you ever considered becoming a citizen?
6. How long do you plan (stay) in this country?
How long do you plan to stay in this country?
7. How long do you plan on (work) at your current job?
How long do you plan on working at your current job?
8. My parents appreciate (receive) a check from me each month.
My parents appreciate receiving a check from me each month.
9. She's proud of (start) her own import business.
She's proud of starting her own import business.
10. I promised (write) my grandparents often.
I promised to write my grandparents often.
11. Besides (have) difficulty finding a job when I first arrived, I didn't like (live) with my uncle.
Besides having difficulty finding a job when I first arrived, I didn't like living with my uncle.
12. Carlos enjoys (read) books about American history.
Carlos enjoys reading books about American history.
13. My uncle refused (change) his long name when he came here.
My uncle refused to change his long name when he came here.
14. Sometimes I regret (come) to this country.
Sometimes I regret coming to this country.
15. I sometimes complain about (come) here, but then I remember the reasons that I came.
I sometimes complain about coming here, but then I remember the reasons that I came.
16. In addition to (sponsor) his sister, Andres is supporting his parents.
In addition to sponsoring his sister, Andres is supporting his parents.
17. I have invited my cousins (live) with me their first month in the United States.
I have invited my cousins to live with me their first month in the United States.

B. Ask and answer the questions with a partner or a small group. (Answers will vary.)

1. When do you anticipate finishing your English studies?
2. When do you intend to visit your country?
3. Have you ever considered becoming a citizen?
4. What do you sometimes worry about?
5. What do you miss doing since you came here?
6. What do you enjoy doing in this country?
7. What do you dream about doing?
8. What do you advise new immigrants to bring with them?
9. Why did you decide to come to the United States?
10. Would you encourage your brother or sister to come to live here?

C. Listen: Citizenship decisions. Listen to each of these immigrants speak about citizenship. Then, answer the questions. Many include a gerund or an infinitive.

1. Why did they decide to come to the United States?
   Because of the opportunities
2. What was he concerned about?
   Finding a job
3. Where was he able to find a good job?
   A service station
4. What does he appreciate having?
   A nice apartment and a cat
5. What can he afford to do?
   Send his daughter to piano lessons
6. Why is he thinking about becoming a citizen?
   Because his life is here and he is not going back to his country
7. Who does he want to sponsor?
   His brother

8. How long has she been living in the United States?
   20 years
9. What country is she from?
   India
10. What does she enjoy doing?
    Traveling back to visit her brother, sister, and their families
11. Where has she been dreaming about retiring?
    India
12. Where do her children want to live?
    United States
13. What is her situation?
    Part of her life is in the U.S., part of her life is in India
14. What do you think she should do?
    (Answers will vary.)

D. Listen to Martin talk about becoming a citizen. Then, complete the questions.

1. How old _____was_____ he when _____he came to the United States_____?
2. _____Was_____ it easy for him _____to learn_____ English?
3. What _____was_____ he able_____to do_____?
4. Where _____does he_____ work?
5. What _____do_____ the people in his office enjoy_____doing_____?
6. Who _____encouraged_____ him _____to become_____ a citizen?
7. _____Was it_____ difficult _____to apply_____ for citizenship?
8. What _____Was he_____ able _____to do_____ in November?

Now answer the questions.

C. Listen: Citizenship deci-sions. (CD3, Tracks 7 and 8)

• Read and discuss the instructions. Play the audio once as students just listen. Ask students to point out examples of some sentences in the exercise that will be answered with a gerund and some that will be answered with an infinitive.

• Play the audio a second time. Then, have students take turns answering the questions using an infinitive or a gerund. Repeat correct responses and restate incorrect responses using the correct form.

D. Listen to Martin talk about becoming a citizen.
(CD3, Track 9)

Read and discuss the instructions. Play the audio and have students complete the questions individually. Review the correct answers with the class.

Now answer the questions.
(CD3, Track 9)

Have students ask and answer the questions about Martin in pairs. Invite volunteers to role-play the exchanges for the class.

Audio Script

C. Listen: Citizenship decisions.
(CD3, Tracks 7 and 8)

A: My wife and I decided to come to the United States because of the opportunities here. Before coming, I was concerned about finding a job. I was lucky. I'm good at fixing things and I was able to find a job as a mechanic at a service station. My life is good here. I appreciate having a nice apartment and a car. I can afford to send my daughter to piano lessons. And we're able to take a vacation to the beach every summer. I'm thinking about becoming a citizen. My life is here, my family is here, my work is here. I'm not going back to my country. As a matter of fact, I want to sponsor my brother. I'm encouraging him to come here and work with me.

B: I've been living in the United States for 20 years. I'm from India and I love my country. I enjoy traveling back to visit my brothers and sisters and their families. It's comfortable to walk around my hometown, speak my language, and see my old friends. I've been dreaming about retiring back in India. But now I'm not sure. My children are in the United States, and they plan on staying here. Part of my life is here, and part of my life is in India. I'm sure you know how I feel.

D. Listen to Martin talk about becoming a citizen. (CD 3, Track 9)

I came to the United States when I was only 20 years old. For me, it was easy to learn English and make friends. I was able to go to college and now I work in an accounting firm. At my office, people enjoy talking about politics and everything that is happening in the world. One of my friends encouraged me to become a citizen. He said I always had strong opinions about everything here. As a citizen, I'd be able to vote. It wasn't difficult to apply for citizenship. I became a citizen last summer, and I was able to vote for the first time in the November elections.

A. Look at the pictures.

- Ask students to describe what is happening in the pictures. In addition to the questions in the instruction line, you might use questions like these:

  Where does this man work? What do you think these people are talking about?

- Lead students to understand what the people in the pictures are doing in relation to the political campaign. (The people in the third picture are discussing the signs they will make and the mail they will send out. In the fourth picture, the woman is getting people to register to vote. In the fifth picture, the people are doing a mailing promoting a candidate. In the last picture, a candidate is practicing his speech.)

☶ B. Listen and retell the story about the local political campaign. (CD3, Track 10)

Have the students just listen the first time you play the audio. Then, remind them that their task is to retell the story on the audio in their own words. Play the audio again. Call on different students to retell part of the story on the audio.

Suggestion

Students may be interested in researching information on a local political campaign that is in progress. Encourage them to use newspapers, flyers, and other print materials. They can present their findings in the form of a chart listing the main points made by the candidate, or they can give short oral reports.

A. Look at the pictures. Who is running for office? What are the people doing?

① ② ③ ④ ⑤ ⑥

☶ B. Listen and retell the story about the local political campaign.

Audio Script

B. Listen and retell the story about the local political campaign. (CD3, Track 10)

Manuel: Hi. My name's Manuel. I've been a citizen for a few years now, but I never thought that I would get involved in politics. In fact, I've always avoided getting involved. I vote in the major elections, but sometimes I forget to vote in the city elections. Let me tell you what happened. A few years ago, a new neighbor moved in. His name is John. He's a nice guy and a great neighbor. He's married, and he has three children—a boy and two girls— and so do I. My family and his have become very friendly. We barbecue together in the summer. Our children play together, our wives enjoy spending time together, and our families like taking vacations together. John is an entrepreneur. He has a very successful bookstore and community computer center. He hires high school and college students for the computer center. He also has senior citizen volunteers to read to young children three times a week at the bookstore. He has a good business and he provides a wonderful service for our community.

(Audio Script continues on page 256.)

C. Listen again and (circle) True or False.

1. Manuel is a citizen.   (True)   False
2. Manuel has always been involved in politics.   True   (False)
3. Manuel votes in every election.   True   (False)
4. Manuel and John are good friends.   (True)   False
5. Manuel's and John's families enjoy spending time together.   (True)   False
6. John owns a computer company with Manuel.   True   (False)
7. John hires senior citizens for his bookstore.   True   (False)
8. John is running for mayor.   True   (False)

D. Complete the sentences.

donate	give	have
organize	set	shake
spend	work	

1. John complained about _____shaking_____ hands.
2. John is looking forward to _____giving_____ interviews.
3. Andrea is good at _____organizing_____ people.
4. Their friends have been talking about _____having_____ a voter registration drive.
5. They're thinking about _____setting_____ up tables at the supermarkets.
6. They are not worried about _____spending_____ too much money.
7. John's friends have insisted on _____donating_____ services.
8. Kathy quit _____working_____ to help with her husband's campaign.

E. Ask and answer questions about the story. Use the cues provided and the names in the box. You will need to use different verb tenses.

Who enjoys spending time together?   The families do.

1. who / enjoy / spend time together Who enjoys spending time together? The families.
2. who / interested in / work on the campaign Who is interested in working on the campaign? Manuel and Andrea.
3. who / quit / work Who quit working? Kathy.
4. who / interested in / make signs Who is interested in making signs? The children.
5. who / insist on / donate services Who insists on donating services? Friends and volunteers.
6. who / like / help John practice for the debate Who likes to help John practice for the debate? / Manuel.
7. who / enjoy / stuff envelopes Who enjoys stuffing envelopes? The children.

Manuel
Andrea
Kathy
friends
volunteers
the children
the families

C. Listen again and circle *True* or *False*. **(CD3, Track 10)**

Ask students to read through the list of questions. Answer any questions they may have. Then, play the audio and have students circle their answers. Review the correct answers with the whole class.

D. Complete the sentences.

Students complete the sentences on their own and compare answers with a partner. Review the correct answers with the whole class.

E. Ask and answer questions about the story.

• Review the names of people listed in the box. Then, have pairs of students take turns asking and answering questions based on the cues given. Move around the room as they work helping out as needed.

• Review the correct answers by calling on different pairs to present one question and answer each to the class.

Reading: The Citizenship Test

A. Before You Read.

- Point to the picture and invite students to comment. Ask:
  Who do you think these people are?
  What are they doing?
- Discuss the three questions at the top. Invite students who have already taken the test to tell a little about their experiences.

B. The U.S. Citizenship Test.

Read and discuss the paragraph with the class. Answer any questions students may have.

Read each sample question of the Citizenship Test.

Go over the sample question and how to correctly fill in the answer with the whole class. Then, have students take the test individually.

Reading: The Citizenship Test

A. Before You Read. (Answers will vary.)

1. What is the U.S. Citizenship Test?
2. Do you know anyone who has taken the test?
3. What is the best way to prepare for the test?

B. The U.S. Citizenship Test. This test is required for anyone who wants to become a U.S. citizen. An INS examiner asks a citizenship applicant a group of questions from a list of 100 questions. The questions are about U.S. history and government.

Read each sample question of the Citizenship Test. Fill in the circle next to the correct answer.

1. What are the colors of the United States flag?
   - ○ **a.** red and white
   - ● **b.** red, white, and blue
   - ○ **c.** red and blue.
   - ○ **d.** red, white, blue, and black

2. What do the stars on the flag mean?
   - ○ **a.** There is one star for each one hundred citizens.
   - ○ **b.** There is one star for each citizen.
   - ● **c.** There is one star for each state of the union.
   - ○ **d.** There is one star for each president.

3. How many states are there in the United States?
   - ○ **a.** 48
   - ○ **b.** 49
   - ● **c.** 50
   - ○ **d.** 51

4. What is the 4th of July?
   - ○ **a.** Memorial Day
   - ○ **b.** President's Day
   - ○ **c.** Flag Day
   - ● **d.** Independence Day

5. From whom did the United States win independence?
   - ○ **a.** Ireland
   - ● **b.** Great Britain
   - ○ **c.** France
   - ○ **d.** Germany

6. Who was the first president of the United States?
   - ○ **a.** Abraham Lincoln
   - ○ **b.** John Adams
   - ● **c.** George Washington
   - ○ **d.** Benjamin Franklin

7. Who becomes the president of the United States if the president should die?
   - ○ **a.** the secretary of state
   - ○ **b.** the defense secretary
   - ○ **c.** the first lady
   - ● **d.** the vice president

8. Who makes the laws in the United States?

   ○ **a.** judges   ○ **c.** the president

   ● **b.** congress   ○ **d.** the governors

9. Who was president during the Civil War?

   ● **a.** Abraham Lincoln   ○ **c.** Richard Nixon

   ○ **b.** George Washington   ○ **d.** Franklin D. Roosevelt

10. What is the 50th state of the union?

   ○ **a.** Alaska   ○ **c.** Puerto Rico

   ● **b.** Hawaii   ○ **d.** Florida

11. Who is the commander-in-chief of the U.S. military?

   ○ **a.** congress   ● **c.** the president

   ○ **b.** the secretary of defense   ○ **d.** the U.S. citizens

12. In what month do we vote for the president?

   ○ **a.** January   ○ **c.** July

   ○ **b.** April   ● **d.** November

Check your answers below.

1. b 2. c 3. d 4. d 5. b 6. c 7. d 8. b 9. a 10. b 11. c 12. d

C. Written English testing. In order to become a citizen, you must be able to speak, read, and write basic English. These are a few examples of the types of sentences that an INS officer may ask you to read or write. The sentences may be about history and government or about everyday life. Practice reading and dictating the sentences to a partner.

1. All United States citizens have the right to vote.

2. Martha Washington was the first first lady.

3. Our government is divided into three branches.

4. People vote for the president in November.

5. The president lives in the White House.

6. I am too busy to talk today.

7. My car does not work.

8. She can speak English very well.

9. The man wanted to get a job.

10. You drink too much coffee.

Check your answers below.

Have students use the answer key to correct their papers. After they have finished, answer any questions they may have about words or ideas they don't understand.

Suggestion

Write the words *Rights* and *Responsibilities* on the board. Then, brainstorm with students some of the rights and responsibilities that citizens of the U.S. have. Some rights: *freedom of religion, freedom of speech, trial by jury.* Some responsibilities: *obey the laws, vote in elections, pay taxes.*

C. Written English testing.

Students take turns reading the sentences to each other and writing what they hear. They can use the sentences in the book to check each other's work.

Writing Our Stories: A Political Platform

A. Read the two different political platforms.

- Ask students to read the two platforms, underlining any words or sentences they don't understand. Discuss each platform with the class, answering questions about the meaning of words and phrases as needed.
- Call on individuals to tell who they would vote for and why. Ask a second student to summarize each person's opinion. For example:

Ali: *I like Ms. Velez because she's in favor of improving education.*

Rita: *Ali would vote for Ms. Velez because she wants to improve the schools in the community.*

Suggestion

Make two columns on the board with the names of the candidates on top. Using phrases, help students compare the platforms (ideas) of the two candidates.

Writing Our Stories: A Political Platform

A. Read the two different political platforms. Which person would you vote for?

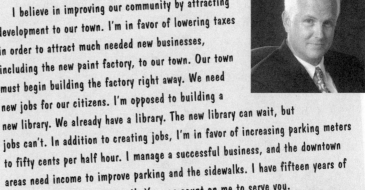

I believe in improving our community by attracting development to our town. I'm in favor of lowering taxes in order to attract much needed new businesses, including the new paint factory, to our town. Our town must begin building the factory right away. We need new jobs for our citizens. I'm opposed to building a new library. We already have a library. The new library can wait, but jobs can't. In addition to creating jobs, I'm in favor of increasing parking meters to fifty cents per half hour. I manage a successful business, and the downtown areas need income to improve parking and the sidewalks. I have fifteen years of experience on the town council. You can count on me to serve you.

Douglas McMurphy

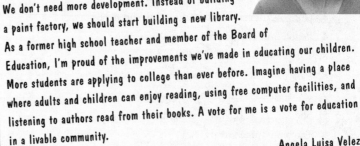

It's time for a change. The citizens of this town are used to hearing the same promises. They're tired of seeing heavy traffic and breathing factory pollution. They miss having peace and quiet in their community. We don't need more development. Instead of building a paint factory, we should start building a new library. As a former high school teacher and member of the Board of Education, I'm proud of the improvements we've made in educating our children. More students are applying to college than ever before. Imagine having a place where adults and children can enjoy reading, using free computer facilities, and listening to authors read from their books. A vote for me is a vote for education in a livable community.

Angela Luisa Velez

B. Pretend that you are a political candidate and you are running for a town council seat. In your notebook, write a paragraph describing your political platform. What is your opinion on (1) the new paint factory, (2) building a new library, and (3) raising parking meter prices to fifty cents per half hour? Choose one other issue that you want to discuss. Use the vocabulary below in your platform.

be opposed to	be in favor of	believe in

C. Sentence fragments. Read each sentence. Circle *Fragment* or *Correct*.

> *A **sentence fragment** is an incomplete sentence. Here are two examples:*
>
> Because traffic will increase.   **incorrect; incomplete idea**
> I'm opposed to building the mall
>   because traffic will increase.   **correct**
> Will be good for the town.   **incorrect; missing subject**
> A new library will be good for the town.   **correct**

1. After the airplane landed.   (Fragment) Correct
2. He regrets not studying English before.   Fragment (Correct)
3. When I considered leaving my country.   (Fragment) Correct
4. Because I needed to learn English.   (Fragment) Correct
5. I dislike taking the bus instead of driving myself.   Fragment (Correct)
6. I recall filling out an application when I arrived.   Fragment (Correct)
7. Is easy to learn English.   (Fragment) Correct

D. Edit. Find and correct the mistakes.

1. The mayor isn't interested in ~~run~~ *running* for another term.
2. The students have finished ~~to read~~ *reading* two novels.
3. ~~Because~~ I haven't registered to vote yet.
4. I'm tired of ~~walk~~ *walking* in the snow.
5. I've missed ~~see~~ *seeing* my family.
6. The council is opposed ⌄*to* building a new parking garage.
7. ~~When~~ I arrived in this country.
8. My daughter can't stand ~~wears~~ *wearing* heavy winter clothes.

 Looking at the Internet

Search the Internet for information on the citizenship process. Try to find a practice test that you can do online. Enter "citizenship test," or "how to become a citizen." Take the test and see how you do.

B. Pretend that you are a political candidate and you are running for a town council seat.

Read and discuss the instructions. Point out the vocabulary items they should include in their paragraphs. Suggest that students make a rough outline of what they are going to say before they begin writing the paragraph itself.

C. Sentence fragments.

• Review the explanation and examples of sentence fragments. Explain that we often use them in speaking, but that they are not usually used in writing.
• Have students circle their answers. Then, review the correct answers with the class.

D. Edit.

Students correct the mistakes and check their work with a partner.

Looking at the Internet

Invite students to complete the tests at home and bring them to the next class. Correct them together in class. Discuss any incorrect answers, explaining why they are wrong.

☀ Practicing on Your Own

A. Complete each sentence with the gerund form of the verb in parentheses.

Ask students to complete the sentences on their own and check their answers with a partner.

B. Contrast.

Students fill in the correct infinitive or gerund form. You can suggest that they review the Unit 11 material on the verb + infinitive form before completing this exercise.

Suggestion

Some students may enjoy making up original exercises similar to the ones on this page. Have them word process their exercises and give them to you to check. Make any necessary corrections and make class copies. Have students complete the test questions in class or as homework. Go over the answers together.

☀ Practicing on Your Own

A. Complete each sentence with the gerund form of the verb in parentheses.

1. Before _____registering_____ (register) for classes, she had to complete an application.
2. She couldn't stand _____waiting_____ (wait) in the long lines to register.
3. She postponed _____looking_____ (look) for a job until she knew her schedule.
4. She bought her textbooks after _____attending_____ (attend) her first class.
5. After she began _____studying_____ (study), she had more confidence.
6. She liked _____going_____ (go) to class and _____meeting_____ (meet) new people.
7. She missed _____seeing_____ (see) her family, so she started _____sending_____ (send) them e-mails every other day.
8. In class, she practiced _____speaking_____ (speak), _____reading_____ (read), and _____writing_____ (write).
9. She believed in _____working_____ (work) as hard as possible to achieve her goals.
10. After _____studying_____ (study) for a year, she was ready to enroll in an accounting degree program.

B. Contrast. Complete each sentence with the correct form of the verbs in parentheses. Use the gerund or the infinitive form.

1. After _____arriving_____ (arrive) in this country, he lived with his brother's family.
2. He didn't mind _____taking_____ (take) care of his nieces and nephews.
3. He didn't know how _____to speak_____ (speak) much English, but he could read.
4. His brother persuaded him _____to enroll_____ (enroll) in English classes.
5. Instead of _____working_____ (work) full-time, he decided _____to take_____ (take) a part-time job at his brother's company.
6. He has enjoyed _____studying_____ (study) and is a good student.
7. He has been trying _____to speak_____ (speak) as much English as possible.
8. He anticipates _____finishing_____ (finish) his English classes in a year.

Grammar Summary

► 1. Verb + gerund

Use a gerund (simple verb form + *ing*) after certain verbs. A list of some of the verbs is on page 181.

They **discussed coming** to the United States.

I **miss seeing** my family.

My friends **suggested starting** English classes.

► 2. Preposition + gerund

Use a gerund (simple verb form + *ing*) after most prepositions. A list of common prepositions that are followed by gerunds is on page 183.

Before coming to this country, I was a full-time student.

After arriving at the airport, my relatives took care of everything for me.

► 3. Verb + preposition + gerund

Use a gerund (simple verb form + *ing*) after most verb phrases with a verb and a preposition. A list of verbs + prepositions is on page 184.

I **look forward to visiting** my family.

I **dream about opening** my own business.

I **plan on voting** in the next election.

► 4. *Be* + adjective phrase + gerund

Use a gerund (simple verb form + *ing*) after the verb *be* + adjective phrase. A list of the adjective phrases is on page 184.

I **am good at following** directions.

The politician **is in favor of lowering** taxes.

We **are opposed to building** the new factory.

Grammar Summary

• Review the four grammar explanations and sample sentences with the class. Invite students to make up alternate sentences for each example in the chart. For example, in place of *I miss seeing my family,* a student might say, *She suggested calling my sister every Sunday night.*

• Answer any questions students may have about the grammar items.

• See the Grammar Summary Expansion on page 269 for a more complete explanation of these grammar points.

Unit 13
Business and Industry

Discuss what the person in the unit title art is doing. Ask:

• *Who is standing next to the number 13?* (A man)
• *What is he doing?* (He's standing on a globe of the world. Below him are an office building, some wheat, and some dollar bills.)
• *What does this have to do with the unit?* (The unit is about business and industry. The factory represents industry. The wheat and dollars are symbols of the buying and selling that all businesses do.)

A. Map study.

• Before asking students to answer the questions, have them point to any state or city that they know something about and tell what they know. For example:

S1: *My sister lives in Oklahoma City. They have bad winters there.*

S2: *Hollywood is in California. They make a lot of movies there.*

• Ask students to respond to the questions in complete sentences. For example: *Oregon is located north of California.*

Talk about the map and the products of each state.

• Invite different students to point out a particular product and say something about it. For example:

A lot of cheese is made in Wisconsin. I like cheddar cheese the best.

• Guide the discussion so that students talk about many of the products shown on the map. Encourage them to tell about any other products they know of that come from these states.

Business and Industry
A Product Map

A. Map study. Look at the map of the western half of the United States and answer the questions.

1. Find California. Which state is located north of California? Oregon
2. Find Kansas. Which state is located west of Kansas? Colorado
3. Find South Dakota. Which state is located north of South Dakota? North Dakota
4. Find Wyoming. Which state is located west of Wyoming? Idaho
5. Find Montana. Which state is located south of Montana? Wyoming
6. Find Minnesota. Which state is located south of Minnesota? Iowa
7. Find Oklahoma. Which state is located south of Oklahoma? Texas
8. Find Arkansas. Which state is located south of Arkansas? Louisiana

Talk about the map and the products of each state.

Active Grammar: Passive Voice

A. Product map vocabulary. Review the vocabulary with your teacher.

| mine | catch | grow | manufacture | produce | raise |

B. Write each product from the box next to the correct verb.

✓uranium	apples	shrimp
computers	farm equipment	rubber tires
lettuce	turkeys	natural gas
movies	✓copper	sheep
salmon	potatoes	cattle

mine	uranium, copper
catch	salmon, shrimp
grow	lettuce, apples, potatoes
manufacture	computers, farm equipment, rubber tires
produce	movies, natural gas
raise	turkeys, sheep, cattle

C. Look at the product map. Read and ⟨circle⟩ *True* or *False*.

> **Passive Voice: *Be* + Past Participle**
> The **active voice** emphasizes the **subject** that **performs** the action.
> The **passive voice** emphasizes the **subject** that **receives** the action.
>
> | **Active** | **Passive** |
> | Fishermen **catch** salmon in Oregon. | Salmon **are caught** in Oregon. |
> | | (*Fishermen* is understood.) |
> | Miners **mine** copper in Utah. | Copper **is mined** in Utah. |
> | | (*Miners* is understood.) |

1. Grapes are grown in California.   (True) False
2. Silver is mined in Montana.   (True) False
3. Potatoes are grown in New Mexico.   True (False)
4. Peanuts are grown in Oklahoma.   (True) False
5. Turkeys are raised in Utah.   True (False)
6. Gold is mined in Iowa.   True (False)
7. Cattle are raised in Nebraska.   (True) False
8. Rice is grown in Louisiana.   (True) False
9. Grapes are grown in Minnesota.   True (False)
10. Movies are produced in California.   (True) False

Active Grammar: Passive Voice

A. Product map vocabulary.

• Write the six vocabulary words on the board and help students think of products that are obtained through each process. For example:

Mine: coal, iron, copper
Catch: fish
Grow: corn, wheat, rice
Manufacture: cars, furniture, farm equipment
Produce: movies
Raise: sheep, cattle

• Then, have different students make up several sentences using each process word. For example: *Sheep are raised in Ohio. Fish are caught in Washington state.*

B. Write each product from the box next to the correct verb.

Review the meaning of the words in the list of products. Then, have students complete the exercise and check their answers with a partner. Review the correct answers with the class.

C. Look at the product map.

• Discuss the explanation of the passive voice and the sample sentences with the class. Then, review how the passive voice is used in the ten sentences. For each sentence ask:

T: *What is the object of sentence 1? What receives the action?*
S1: Grapes *receives the action.*
T: *Right. And who performs the action?*
S1: *We don't know. Probably farm workers.*
T: *That's correct. Farm workers probably grow the grapes. That part is understood.*

• Have students check their answers with a partner. Review the answers with the class.

D. Active or passive?

Review the use of active and passive at the top of the page and discuss the sample sentences. Then, have students complete the exercise on their own. Review the correct answers with the whole class.

E. Ask and answer questions about each of the products.

• Review the sample sentences with the class. Then, have students ask and answer the questions in pairs. Review the correct answers by calling on different pairs to say one question and answer each.

• Write on the board any questions that students have difficulty with and review how to form the passive.

Suggestion

Extend the practice by displaying pictures of various vegetable, animal, and manufactured products such as bananas, chickens, and cars. Hold up each picture and ask students to make statements about it using the passive voice. For example: *Corn is grown in Iowa. Popcorn is sold at the movies. Fresh corn is sold only in the summer.*

D. Active or passive? Circle the correct form of the verb.

> Farmers grow corn in Iowa.
> Corn is grown in Iowa.
>
> **Active**—the subject performs the action.
> **Passive**—the subject receives the action.

1. Farmers (grow) / are grown corn in Texas.
2. Gold **mines** / (is mined) in South Dakota.
3. Ranchers (raise) / are raised cattle in Nebraska.
4. Workers (mine) / are mined uranium in Nebraska.
5. Turkeys **raise** / (are raised) in Minnesota.
6. Farmers (grow) / are grown lettuce in Arizona.
7. Iron ore **mines** / (is mined) in Wyoming.
8. Ranchers (raise) / are raised hogs in Missouri.
9. Farmers (grow) / are grown apples in Washington.
10. Computers **manufacture** / (are manufactured) in Minnesota.

E. Ask and answer questions about each of the products.

> *Is* milk *produced* in Wisconsin?
> Yes, it is.
>
> *Are* tires *manufactured* in Wisconsin?
> No, they aren't.

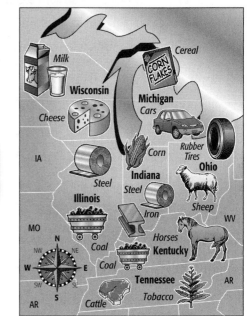

A. Work together in a group of three or four students. Choose a state to research. Go to your school library or use the Internet to find out the answers to the questions. Draw an outline of the state in the space below. Then, mark the places and location of products on your map. *(Answers will vary.)*

1. What is the state capital? Where is it located? Put a star next to the location of the state capital.

2. Mark the bordering states. Then, mark three major cities in your state on your map. Where are they located?

3. What is the largest airport in the state? Mark its location on the map.

4. Draw in one or two major rivers or bodies of water. Label them.

5. What farm products are grown in the state? What major industries are located there?

B. Tell your classmates about your state. Use verbs from the box.

border	locate	grow	manufacture	produce

_____ *is located* in the east / west / north / south.
_____ *is bordered by* (name of bordering states).

Choose a State:
A Research Assignment

A. Work together in a group of three or four students.

• Read the instructions and go over the five guiding questions with the class. Then, have a student come to the front of the room and name a state they want to research. Invite two or three other students interested in the same state to join that student. Form as many groups as necessary to include all students. Have them sit in groups as they begin work.

• Suggest that students divide up the work they will be doing outside of class. For example, one person could research the geographical material, another the products, and so forth. Allow class time for them to put their reports together, or arrange for them to meet outside of class.

B. Tell your classmates about your state.

Point out the verbs in the box and ask a student to complete the sample sentences. Review how these verbs are used to form new sentences. Then, have students present their finished reports to the class using the passive form of the verbs in the box as often as possible.

C. Well-known companies.

- Do the first part of the exercise with the whole class. First review how the verbs in the box are used in the passive voice. Then, write on the board the company names that students come up with.
- Students work in pairs to talk about the products. Review the answers with the whole class. Whenever possible, elicit sentences using several different company names associated with a certain product.

D. Write the names of four products that you or you and your family use in your home.

Students complete the exercise individually and then read their sentences to a partner. The partners help them check for correct use of the passive voice. Encourage them to move into a conversation about the different products they use at home.

C. Well-known companies. Read the list of products. Can you name a major company that each item is produced by? Use the verbs in the box to talk about the products with your partner.

design	refine
deliver	manufacture
make	produce

Copy machines *are manufactured by* _____.
                                        (name of company)

1.
copy machines

2.
razors

3.
stereos

4.
cell phones

5.
jeans

6.
baby food

7.
disposable diapers

8.
cosmetics

9.
gasoline

10.
soda

11.
packages

12.
cameras

D. Write the names of four products that you or you and your family use in your home. Then, complete the sentences. Use one of the verbs from Exercise C and the name of the company. Read the sentences to a partner. (Answers will vary.)

1. I / We use _____ .
                 (product)
   It / They _____ by _____ .
                 (passive verb)

2. I / We use _____ .
                 (product)
   It / They _____ by _____ .
                 (passive verb)

3. I / We use _____ .
                 (product)
   It / They _____ by _____ .
                 (passive verb)

4. I / We use _____ .
                 (product)
   It / They _____ by _____ .
                 (passive verb)

Active Grammar: Passive and *Wh-* Questions

A. Listen and write the questions. Then, look at the product map of a few Asian countries and write the answers to the questions.

(Answers may vary.)

1. Where are electronics manufactured?
   They are manufactured in South Korea.
2. Where is rice grown ?
   Rice is grown in China .
3. Which country is known for manufacturing automobiles ?
   South Korea is known for manufacturing automobiles .
4. What food products are grown in Thailand ?
   Rice and coconuts are grown in Thailand .
5. Where is clothing manufactured ?
   Clothing is manufactured in South Korea and Thailand .
6. Where are coconuts exported from ?
   They are exported from Thailand .
7. Where are financial services offered ?
   They are offered in Singapore .
8. What minerals are found in China ?
   Iron and coal are found in China .

Active Grammar: Passive and *Wh-* Questions

A. Listen and write the questions. (CD3, Track 11)

- Play the audio once and have students just listen. Then, play it again, pausing after each sentence to give students time to write the questions they hear in their books. Check their work by asking different students to read one question each to the class.
- Students look at the map to find the answers to the questions they just wrote. Have them write the answers individually and then check them with a partner.

Suggestion

Invite students to suggest any other products that come from the Asian countries shown on the map. Then, have them make statements about these products using the passive voice. For example: *Silk is made in Thailand. Kung Fu movies are produced in Singapore.*

Audio Script

A. Listen and write the questions.
(CD3, Track 11)

1. Where are electronics manufactured?
2. Where is rice grown?
3. Which country is known for manufacturing automobiles?
4. What food products are grown in Thailand?
5. Where is clothing manufactured?
6. Where are coconuts exported from?
7. Where are financial services offered?
8. What minerals are found in China?

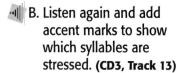

Describing Processes

 A. Pronunciation: Verb, noun, and adjective forms and syllable stress. (CD3, Track 12)

The first time through, have students just follow along in their books as you play the audio. The second time through, pause the audio after each word and ask students to repeat. Point out that the syllable that receives the stress changes across each set of three words.

 B. Listen again and add accent marks to show which syllables are stressed. (CD3, Track 13)

• This time pause the audio after each set of three words. If it seems necessary, replay each set of three words more than once as students mark the stressed syllable in each word.

• Review the correct answers by having a different student write each set of three words on the board, adding an accent mark on the stressed syllable of each word.

• Students may notice that there are two stresses in these words. Ask them to mark the strongest or primary stress with a mark above the stressed syllable and the lesser or secondary stress with a mark below that syllable. Demonstrate.

C. Gathering chocolate beans.

• Point out the eight pictures on page 203. Explain that students will be writing one sentence under each picture using the cues on page 202.

• Because there is quite a bit of specialized vocabulary in this exercise, you may want to do it with the whole

class, pausing to explain new terms such as *ripe, pods,* and *split open* as you go along. Refer to the pictures as you define each term. Review the correct answers with the whole class.

 Describing Processes

 A. Pronunciation: Verb, noun, and adjective forms and syllable stress.
Listen and repeat.

Verb	Noun	Adjective
1. ˈpasteurize	ˌpasteuriˈzation	ˈpasteurized
2. ˈsterilize	ˌsteriliˈzation	ˈsterilized
3. ˈstabilize	ˌstabiliˈzation	ˈstabilized
4. ˈimmunize	ˌimmuniˈzation	ˈimmunized
5. ˈconcentrate	ˌconcenˈtration	ˈconcentrated
6. ˈseparate	ˌsepaˈration	ˈseparated
7. reˈfrigerate	reˌfrigeˈration	reˈfrigerated

 B. Listen again and add accent marks to show which syllables are stressed.

C. Gathering chocolate beans. Look at the pictures on the next page. Use the cues from the box and write each sentence under the correct picture.

1. ripe pods / gather / every few weeks during the season
2. pods / cut down / from the cacao trees
3. pods / split open / and / seeds / remove
4. seeds / put in large wooden boxes for fermentation
5. the seed pulp / drain / for six to eight days
6. seeds / dry / by machine or the sun
7. seeds / put / into large sacks
8. beans / export / to chocolate makers all over the world

pasteurize—to partially sterilize a liquid, such as milk, to kill bacteria; milk is pasteurized

1. The ripe pods are gathered every few weeks during the season.

2. The pods are cut down from the cacao trees.

3. The pods are split open and the seeds are removed.

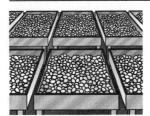

4. The seeds are put into large wooden boxes for fermentation.

5. The seed pulp is drained for six to eight hours.

6. The seeds are dried by machine or the sun.

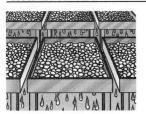

7. The seeds are put into large sacks.

8. The beans are exported to chocolate makers all over the world.

Provide further practice with the vocabulary and verb forms in Exercise C by having interested students write sentences using these terms in new contexts. For example:

Pods: I enjoy eating pea pods when I have Chinese food.

Cut down: Bananas are usually cut down before they are completely ripe.

A. Talk about the pictures.
(CD3, Track 14)

- Ask students to comment on the pictures. Ask questions such as:

  What are these people doing?
  What kind of place is this?
  What is happening to the T-shirts now?

- Play the audio twice as students just listen. Answer any questions they may have. Then, play it again and have students make a note under each picture. You may wish to pause the audio after each section to give students time to take notes. Explain that they will be using the notes to answer questions on the next page.
- Ask individual students to explain each step of the process in their own words.

☀ The Big Picture: T-shirts—From the Field
to Your Closet

A. Talk about the pictures. Then, listen and take notes on the pictures.
(See sample notes below pictures.)

1.  2.  3.

4.  5.  6.

7.  8. (image) 9.

1. Top 3 cotton producers: China, U.S., India
2. China: picked by hand, cleaned in ginner, put in bales, quality decided
3. Bales sold to spinners, cotton on spools, spools on knit machines, cotton made into fabric
4. To dye house: 20% dyed, 80% white
5. To sewing plant, patterns cut, sewn by piece: sleeve, neck, shoulders, bottom
6. Fold and package to printers, logo or embroidered, price $3
7. To warehouse, shipping, space, inventory—all increase price
8. Dept. store buys at $14 (200%↑), store doubles to $28; costs: help, insurance, advertising
9. 2–3 weeks → sale 15–25%; 6 weeks → discount $14

204 UNIT 13

Audio Script

A. Talk about the pictures. (CD3, Track 14)

1. The top three cotton producers in the world are China, the United States, and India. China is the top cotton producer of the three.
2. In China, the cotton is picked by hand. Then, it is sent to a ginner where it is cleaned. The cleaned cotton is put into bales and the quality is decided.
3. The bales are sold to large plants or factories called spinners. At the spinners, the cotton is put on spools. The spools are put on knitting machines and the cotton is made into cotton fabric.

4. The cotton fabric is sent to a dye house. At the dye house, only 20 percent is dyed different colors. The remaining 80 percent is processed white.
5. The fabric is sent to a sewing plant. At the plant, patterns are cut. Then, the pieces are sewn by workers on a line. One worker sews the sleeves, another sews the neck, another does the shoulders, and the last one hems the bottom.
6. The T-shirts are folded and packaged. The T-shirts are sent to printers, where a logo is transferred or embroidered onto the T-shirt. At this stage, the T-shirt only costs about $3.
7. The finished T-shirts are shipped to warehouses. Because of many costs, including

shipping, warehouse space, and inventory, the T-shirt price is increased.
8. The T-shirts are sold to a department store at an over 200 percent increase to $14. The store immediately doubles the price to $28. The store also has many costs, such as paying for sales help, insurance, and advertising. The T-shirt is marked and offered for sale for $28.
9. After two to three weeks, store customers have bought many of the shirts. Now, not all colors and sizes are available. The store advertises a 15 percent to 25 percent sale. After two more weeks, the price will be decreased again. Finally, after six weeks, any leftover T-shirts will be sent to discount stores. The price may be reduced to $14 or less.

B. Listen again and answer the questions about how a T-shirt is made.

1. What are the three top cotton-producing nations in the world?
   China, India, and the United States
2. How is the cotton picked in China—by hand or by machine?
   By hand
3. What happens at the ginner?
   The cotton is cleared.
4. Where are the bales of cotton sent?
   They are sent to the spinners.
5. What percent of the cotton fabric is dyed different colors?
   20 percent
6. Does one person complete an entire T-shirt? Explain your answer.
   No, the pieces are sewn together by workers on a line.
7. What is the original cost for a T-shirt?
   $3
8. Why is the T-shirt price increased at the warehouse?
   Because of many costs, including shipping, warehouse space, and inventory.
9. How much is the price increased at the department store?
   The price is doubled.
10. How long does it take before a T-shirt is sent to a discount store?
    6 weeks

C. Fill in the verbs. Some of the verbs are passive; others are active. Then, put the sentences in chronological order from 1–9.

- _6_ **a.** The fabric __is sent__ (send) to a sewing plant.
- _9_ **b.** The T-shirts __are shipped__ (ship) to a warehouse.
- _4_ **c.** The spinners __knit__ (knit) the yarn into fabric.
- _1_ **d.** The cotton __is picked__ (pick) by the workers.
- _5_ **e.** The dye houses __dye__ (dye) the shirts different colors.
- _2_ **f.** The ginners __clear__ (clean) the cotton.
- _7_ **g.** The T-shirts __are sewn__ (sew) together on a line.
- _8_ **h.** The printers __embroider__ (embroider) designs on the shirts.
- _3_ **i.** The bales of cotton __are sold__ (sell) to spinners.

D. Sentence completion. Complete the sentences according to the story.

1. Before the cotton is put into bales, it __is cleared__.
2. When the fabric is sent to a dye house, it __is dyed different colors__.
3. After the T-shirts are sewn, they __are folded and packaged__.
4. After the patterns are cut, the workers __sew the pieces on a line__.
5. When the T-shirts are sent to the warehouse, the price __is increased__ over 200 percent.
6. Before a T-shirt is discounted, the store __sells__ it for the full price.
7. The T-shirts are discounted after they __have been on sale for two to three weeks__.
8. The unsold T-shirts are discounted for $14 or less when __they have been on sale for six weeks__.

B. Listen again and answer the questions about how a T-shirt is made.
(CD3, Track 14)

• Ask students to read through the questions. Explain any vocabulary items that students don't understand. Play the audio again and have students listen carefully.

• Call on a different student to answer each question. Remind them that they can refer back to the notes they took on page 204 as they formulate their answers.

C. Fill in the verbs.

Students work alone to fill in the verbs and number the sentences in chronological order. Remind them to refer back to page 204 as necessary. Review the correct answers with the class.

D. Sentence completion.

Have students complete the sentences and check their answers with a partner. Review the correct answers with the whole class.

Reading: An Alternative Energy Source

A. Before You Read.

- Point to the pictures and help students figure out what they show. Ask:

  What is the name of this machine?
  Have you ever seen a windmill?
  What does a windmill do?
  How well do you think it works?

- Invite several different students to answer the questions at the top of the page. On the board, write any new vocabulary words that come up—especially any that appear in the reading passage or that might be useful in later discussions. Define and discuss each one.

- Ask students to read the article to themselves. Explain that it isn't important to understand every single word, but that they should look for the main ideas.

- When they finish, invite them to ask about anything they don't understand and to make any comments they wish about the reading.

Suggestion

Have some students research where the electrical power they use comes from. Is it atomic power, water power, or does the utility burn fuel to make electricity? As they present their findings to the class, discuss the advantages and disadvantages of each type of energy source based on what students found in the reading passage in Exercise A.

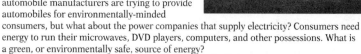

Reading: An Alternative Energy Source

A. Before You Read. (Answers will vary.)

1. What do you do to save energy in your home?
2. Can you list two sources of energy?
3. How can today's cars save energy?

Automobile companies have already begun to manufacture "hybrid" cars—cars that use two sources of power. These cars use typical fuel, such as gasoline, but the cars also have batteries to supply power to an electric motor. Hybrid cars send fewer pollutants into the air. A few automobile manufacturers are trying to provide automobiles for environmentally-minded consumers, but what about the power companies that supply electricity? Consumers need energy to run their microwaves, DVD players, computers, and other possessions. What is a green, or environmentally safe, source of energy?

A significant source of green energy is wind. Windmills have been around for hundreds of years. Traditionally, windmills have been used to pump water for farmers. Today, millions of windmills and wind turbines are found throughout the United States and the world. In California, there are more than fifteen thousand wind turbines to generate power for its increasing population. One percent of California's power is generated by wind turbines. In West Texas, wind energy turbines have become a source of income for people who own groups of wind turbines, or wind farms.

Wind is different from other energy sources, such as coal and gas, which cause pollution and use up the world's natural resources. Wind has an advantage—it does not generate harmful emissions like coal and gas do. The average household consumes approximately 10,000 kwh (kilowatt-hours) of electricity. A 10-kw wind turbine generates enough power to serve a typical household for a year. Wind energy is also included as one of the options in "green power" plans in some of today's electric companies. Customers can choose to use a certain amount of wind energy every month instead of conventional energy. California, Colorado, and Texas are some of the states that offer "green power" options to their customers. The top three users of wind energy in 2002 were Europe, the United States, and India. In fact, ten percent of Denmark's energy is powered by the wind.

Although wind energy is a clean source of energy, not everyone is in favor of wind turbine generators. First of all, opponents of wind energy say that large birds may fly into the moving blades and be killed. Advocates of wind energy say that more birds are killed by automobiles than by wind turbines. Second, opponents say that wind turbine generators are noisy and disturb residents. Advocates say that there are no studies that prove that residents suffer any problems because of wind turbine farms. A wind turbine is no louder than a refrigerator. Third, residents complain that the wind turbine farms are ugly and reduce housing prices. In fact, one wind advocacy group says that the oldest wind farm in Cornwall, England, has attracted over 350,000 visitors. In addition, there has been no evidence that housing prices have been affected by wind turbine farms.

B. Sentence sense. (Circle) the sentence with the closest meaning to the original.

1. A significant source of green energy is wind.

   a. Wind energy is a clean source of energy.

   b. Wind energy is not popular.

   c. Wind energy is not an environmental source of energy.

   d. Wind energy is not good for the environment.

2. Wind energy is included as one of the options in "green power" plans.

   a. Energy consumers can choose wind energy to power their homes.

   b. Consumers must use wind energy.

   c. Consumers must paint their houses green.

   d. Wind energy is more expensive than other plans.

3. Wind energy has an advantage—it does not generate harmful emissions like coal and gas do.

   a. Wind energy sends pollution into the air.

   b. Wind energy is like coal and gas; all three pollute the air.

   c. Wind energy pollutes as much as coal and gas do.

   d. Unlike coal and gas, wind energy does not pollute the environment.

C. Pro or con. Read each statement. Write *pro* if the statement is positive about wind energy, and write *con* if the statement is negative about wind energy.

1. These windmills send no pollutants into the air. ___pro___

2. Coal and gas cause pollution and use up the world's natural resources. ___pro___

3. Wind energy does not generate harmful emissions. ___pro___

4. Wind energy is a clean source of energy. ___pro___

5. Wind turbine generators are noisy and disturb neighborhoods. ___con___

6. A wind turbine is no louder than a refrigerator. ___pro___

7. Wind turbine farms are ugly and reduce housing prices. ___con___

B. Sentence sense.

Have students complete the exercise individually. Then, discuss the answers with the class. Ask students to explain why each wrong answer is wrong, as well as why the correct answer is the right one.

C. Pro or con.

Students complete the exercise on their own and discuss their answers with a partner. Go over the correct answers with the whole class. Ask students to point out the word or words that lead to the label *pro* or *con*.

Writing Our Stories: Business and Industry in My Country

A. Read.

- Ask students to look at the map and take turns describing what they see. They might mention the cities and geographical features such as mountains and bodies of water. Invite them to add any other information they know about Japan. For example: *Japan has a large population contained in a small amount of space.*

- Then, have students read the story on their own. Ask some simple comprehension questions such as: *Is rice an important crop in Japan?* (Yes, it is grown in many parts of Japan.) *What are the best known Japanese manufactured products?* (Cars and electronics)

B. Draw a map of your country.

Discuss the instructions and the guiding questions with the class. Suggest that they model their paragraphs after the one in Exercise A.

Writing Our Stories: Business and Industry in My Country

A. Read.

I am from Tokyo, Japan. Tokyo is located in the eastern part of Japan on Honshu, the largest of the four islands in Japan. Tokyo is also the capital city. Japan is an island. It is bordered by the Pacific Ocean to the east, the Sea of Japan to the west, and the China Sea to the southwest. Because much of Japan is mountainous, the Japanese people live in a small area of the country. Japan has a very large population of 126,974,628 (2000), and we need to import many products, such as wood and natural gas, for our people.

Rice is an important product for the Japanese people. Rice is grown in many parts of Japan. Many vegetables, including sugar beets and radishes, and fruit, such as apples, are grown on Japanese farms. Fishing is also a large industry. In fact, Japan is known to supply about 15 percent of the world's fish. Many resources are imported because our country has very few natural resources. Oil, wood, and iron ore are some of the products that are imported.

Japan is best known for its automobiles and electronics. In fact, three of the largest automobile companies in the world are Japanese. Japan is also known for its consumer electronics. For example, DVD players, portable stereos, and televisions are manufactured by Japanese companies. Look in your home. How many Japanese-made electronics can you find?

B. Draw a map of your country. Show the bordering countries. Then, add products and natural resources. Use the following questions to guide you in writing a paragraph about your country's industry and products. (Answers will vary.)

1. What city are you from, and where is it located?
2. What are three major products that are produced in your country?
3. What are the major industries in your country?
4. What natural resources are found in your country?

C. *For example, such as, and* *including.*

> *For example, such as,* and *including* introduce examples.
> Many minerals, *such as* copper and iron ore, can be found in my country.
> Many industries are in trouble right now. *For example,* two steel plants have laid off workers.
> Tourists can visit a number of famous places in Japan, *including* Kyoto and Mt. Fuji.
>
> **Note:** *Including* and *such as* are not used at the beginning of a sentence.

Complete the sentences with examples. (Answers will vary.)

1. Dye houses dye the T-shirts a variety of colors, such as _____ and _____.

2. T-shirts are sold at discounted prices at many stores, including _____, _____, and _____.

3. There are many countries represented in my class. For example, there are students from _____, _____, and _____.

4. The United States has many natural resources, such as _____, _____, and _____.

5. Agricultural products, including _____ and _____, are grown in my state.

D. Edit. Find and correct the mistakes.

1. Coffee is ~~grow~~ grown in South and Central America.
2. Italy is ~~bordering~~ bordered by Switzerland, Germany, Austria, and Slovenia.
3. The cacao pods are carefully picked, and then they are opened.
4. After the cotton is picked, it is sent to the ginner.
5. Computer software ~~develops~~ is developed in Washington.
6. Dairy cows are raised by farmers.
7. France and Italy ~~is~~ are known for their fashions.
8. Wind energy turbines are ~~locate~~ located in many parts of Europe.

Looking at the Internet

Search for a process on the Internet. Type a phrase in quotation marks such as "How candy is made," or "How orange juice is made." How many steps are involved in the process? Share the information with your classmates.

C. *For example, such as, and* *including.*

Ask students to read the explanation at the top of the page and answer any questions they may have. Help them create additional sentences relating to their own lives that make use of the three terms. For example:

I love many different kinds of food <u>such as</u> *pizza, Chinese food, and hamburgers.*

Complete the sentences with examples.

Students complete the sentences with the appropriate term and check their answers with a partner. Check the answers by having different students read one sentence each to the class.

D. Edit.

Students correct the mistakes and check their work with a partner.

Looking at the Internet

As students prepare to report back to the class about what they have learned, suggest that they refer back to the exercises on pages 202–205 for guidance on how to describe the process they have researched.

A. Complete the sentences about the product map of European countries.

Students complete the sentences on their own. Review the answers with the class, pointing out alternate answers whenever possible. For example: *Footwear is designed in Italy. Footwear is manufactured in Italy.*

B. Complete the questions and answers about the product map of Europe.

Students complete the sentences on their own and check their answers with a partner.

※ Practicing on Your Own

A. Complete the sentences about the product map of European countries.

design
raise
produce
grow
assemble
manufacture
build

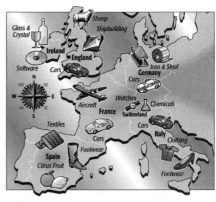

1. Watches _____are designed_____ in Switzerland.
2. Automobiles ____are assembled____ in _England, Germany, France, and Italy_ .
3. Glass and crystal _are produced in Ireland_ .
4. Ships _are built in England_ .
5. Footwear _is designed in Spain_ .
6. Iron and steel _are produced in Germany_ .
7. Sheep _is raised in England_ .
8. Citrus fruit _is grown in Spain_ .
9. Chemicals, such as pharmaceuticals, _are produced in Switzerland_ .
10. Clothing _is designed in Italy_ .

B. Complete the questions and answers about the product map of Europe.

1. (watches) _Where are watches designed and manufactured?_
   Watches are designed and manufactured in Switzerland.

2. (software) _Where is software manufactured_ ?
   It is manufactured in Ireland.

3. (citrus fruit) _Where is citrus fruit grown_ ?
   It is grown in Spain.

4. (aircraft) _Where is aircraft built_ ?
   It is built in France.

5. (automobiles) _Where are automobiles assembled_ ?
   They are manufactured in England, France, Italy, and Germany.

6. (footwear) _Where is footwear designed_ ?
   It is designed in Spain and Italy.

7. (textiles) _Where are textiles produced_ ?
   They are produced in Spain.

8. (glass and crystal) _Where are glass and crystal produced_ ?
   They are produced in Ireland

Grammar Summary

> **1. Active and passive voice**

Active: **Farmers grow** grapes in California.

The active voice emphasizes the **subject** that **performs** the action.

Passive voice: **be** + past participle

Grapes are grown (by farmers) in California.

The passive voice emphasizes the **subject** that **receives** the action.

> **2. Uses of the passive voice**

a. Use the passive voice to emphasize the product, the action, or the process.

   Oranges **are transported** to processing plants.

b. Use the passive voice when the person who performed the action is unknown or understood.

   Coffee beans **are roasted** before they are processed into powder or bars. (understood)

   The milk **was spilled** all over the floor. (unknown)

c. Use the passive voice for general statements of fact.

   Windmills **are found** throughout the United States and the world.

> **3. Passive and _by_**

Use **_by_** to introduce a known person, company, or performer of the action.

Movies **are produced by** both small and large movie studios.

> **4. Questions**

Cattle **are raised** in Texas.	**Are** cattle **raised** in Texas?	Yes, they are.
Grapes **are grown** in California.	Where **are** grapes **grown**?	In California.
Lettuce **is grown** in Arizona.	What **is grown** in Arizona?	Lettuce.

Grammar Summary

- Review the four grammar explanations and sample sentences with the class. Invite students to make up alternate sentences for each example in the chart. For example, in place of _Oranges are transported to processing plants_, a student might say, _Pineapples are grown in my country._

- Answer any questions students may have about the grammar items.

- See the Grammar Summary Expansion on page 270 for a more complete explanation of these grammar points.

Unit 14
Technology Today

Discuss what the person in the unit title art is doing. Ask:

• *Who is standing next to the number 14?* (A man)
• *What do you see above the man?* (It's a giant light bulb.)
• *What does this have to do with the unit?* (The light bulb is a symbol for a new idea. New technology comes from new ideas, and the man probably has an idea for a new invention.)

A. Listen to the information about inventions in the late twentieth century.
(CD3, Track 15)

• Invite students to comment on the pictures. Ask:

What does this thing do? Which of these things do you have at home? Are there any items you have never seen?

• The first time you play the audio, ask students to just listen. Point out the names at the bottom of the page and read them aloud. Then, play the audio a second time and have students write the inventor or company name under each picture. You may wish to pause the audio after each statement to give students time to copy the names.
• As you review the names of the inventors and companies as a class, ask students what information they remember about each invention.

---

14 Technology Today

Listen to the information about inventions in the late twentieth century. After you listen, write the name of the inventor or company under each invention.

anti-shoplifting device
Arthur Minasy
1965

747 Jumbo Jet
Boeing Company
1970

video games
Ralph Baer
1972

artificial heart
Robert Jarvick
1978

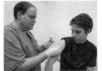
hepatitis B vaccine
Baruch Blumberg
1980

roller blades
Scott and Brennan Olson
1980

space shuttle
NASA
1981

personal computer
IBM
1981

minivan
Chrysler Corporation
1983

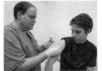
laptop computer
Sir Clive Sinclair
1987

digital camera
Apple Computer
1994

disposable cell phone
Randi Altschul
1999

Boeing Company	Randi Altschul	Sir Clive Sinclair	Ralph Baer
Robert Jarvick	NASA	Apple Computer	Scott Olson
Chrysler Corporation	Arthur Minasy	Baruch Blumberg	IBM

212 UNIT 14

Audio Script

A. Listen to this information about inventions in the late twentieth century. (CD3, Track 15)

People have always seen problems and tried to invent a way to solve them. In the late twentieth century, single individuals continued to invent helpful devices and machines. Many of the inventions have become so complex that groups of researchers or companies work together to design and manufacture them.

The first anti-shoplifting tag was invented in 1965 by Arthur Minasy. These tags made it difficult for people to steal items from a store.

In the late 1960s, the Boeing Company began to develop plans for a jumbo jet to carry more than three hundred people. The first 747 was built in 1970.

The first video games were invented by Ralph Baer. These first games were very simple, not like the colorful realistic games of today. Baer is called the "Godfather of Video Games."

The artificial heart was designed by Robert Jarvick in 1978. It was developed to keep a patient alive while waiting for a heart transplant.

In 1980, a hepatitis B vaccine was developed by Baruch Blumberg. Hepatitis B is a disease that attacks the liver and is often fatal. Today, hepatitis B vaccines are required by most public schools and colleges.

(Audio Script continues on page 257.)

Active Grammar: Passive Voice—Past Tense

Subject	be	Past participle	
The space shuttle	was	built invented	in 1976. by NASA.
747 jumbo jets	were	developed designed	in 1970. by Boeing.

A. Complete this information about the inventions on page 212. Use the passive voice.

1. The first anti-shoplifting device (invent) ___was invented___ by a consultant for the New York City Police Department, Arthur Minasy. These tags (attach) ___were attached___ to store merchandise. When a customer bought the item, the tag (remove) ___was removed___. The tag set off an alarm if a customer walked through the door without paying.

2. The Boeing 747 (design) ___was designed___ as a wide-body airliner for intercontinental flights. Eight hundred and thirty-seven of these (build) ___were built___ by Boeing. The runways of several major airports (extend) ___were extended___ in order to accommodate these larger planes.

3. The first family of personal computers (make) ___was made___ by IBM. The personal computer (develop) ___was developed___ by a team of engineers.

4. Before 1994, film ___was used___ (use) for photographs. The technology for digital imagery ___was developed___ (develop) by both NASA and by private industry. In 1994, the first digital cameras for the consumer market ___were introduced___ (introduce).

B. Answer these questions about the inventions on page 212. Use the passive voice.

1. When was the first artificial heart invented? It was invented in 1978.
2. Why was it invented? It was invented to keep a patient alive while waiting for a heart transplant.
3. By whom was the artificial heart invented? It was invented by Robert Jarvick.
4. When was the minivan introduced? It was introduced in 1983.
5. What consumer group was it designed for? It was designed for families.
6. By whom was the laptop computer invented? It was invented by Sir Clive Sinclair.
7. When was the disposable cell phone invented? It was invented in 1999.
8. When was the digital camera invented? It was invented in 1994.
9. When were roller blades invented? They were invented in 1980.
10. Why are they also called in-line skates? The wheels were placed in a line.

Technology Today **213**

Active Grammar: Passive Voice— Past Tense

A. Complete this information about the inventions on page 212.

• Review the grammar chart for past tense passives. Point out that the last column in the chart is used to give additional information about who did something or when it was done.

• Read the instructions and call students' attention to the base forms in parentheses. Then, go over the sample answer and have students complete the exercise individually. Review the answers with the whole class.

B. Answer these questions about the inventions on page 212.

Ask students to prepare their answers individually and then check them with a partner. To check the correct answers with the class, have different students write one sentence each on the board. As you review the answers, make any necessary corrections and answer any questions students may have.

Suggestion

Some students may feel that it's important to write out the answers to advanced grammar items like this. If this construction is confus-ing for some students to work with orally, have them prepare their answers to Exercise B in writing before checking them with a partner.

☀ Automotive Technology

A. Read this paragraph about the Model T.

• Ask students to cover the paragraph. Point to the picture and ask them to tell anything they already know about the Model T. Ask:

What company made the Model T? (Ford)
What year do you think it was invented? (1908)
What is important about the Model T? (It was cheap enough for lots of people to afford.)

• After students read the paragraph, review it orally with the class. Have students paraphrase each passive construction in their own words. For example, a paraphrase for *was developed* might be *was invented*.

Circle *A* for active voice or *P* for passive voice.

Remind students that a passive sentence must have the verb *be* plus a past participle. Students complete the activity on their own. Review the answers with the whole class.

Suggestion

As a review, you might wish to have students circle the verb *be* and underline the past participles in each sentence in the circling exercise.

☀ Automotive Technology

A. Read this paragraph about the Model T. The verbs in the passive voice are <u>underlined</u>.

The automobile **<u>was developed</u>** before 1900 and cars **<u>were already used</u>** in Europe on a limited basis. In America, Henry Ford **developed** a more affordable car in 1908 called the Model T. The first moving assembly line **<u>was installed</u>** in his factory in 1913. This **reduced** the cost and time of producing a car. A Model T car **<u>was assembled</u>** in 93 minutes and **cost** $850. By 1927, more than fifteen million cars **were** on the roads in America.

⟨Circle⟩ *A* for active voice or *P* for passive voice.

1. The first cars did not have windshield wipers.   Ⓐ P
2. People got out of their cars to clean their windshields.   Ⓐ P
3. The first windshield wipers were invented by Mary Anderson.   A Ⓟ
4. They were operated from the inside of the car.   A Ⓟ
5. The electronic ignition system was invented by Kettering and Coleman.   A Ⓟ
6. Before this, people turned a crank to start their engines.   Ⓐ P
7. Before 1929, people could not listen to the radio in their cars.   Ⓐ P
8. The first car radio was designed by Paul Galvin.   A Ⓟ
9. The radio was not installed at the automobile factory.   A Ⓟ
10. Car owners took their cars to a separate company for radio installation.   Ⓐ P
11. Turn signals were invented by Buick in 1938.   A Ⓟ
12. They were developed by a team of engineers.   A Ⓟ
13. Before this, people used their hands to signal a turn.   Ⓐ P

214   UNIT 14

B. Talk about each advance in car and traffic technology using the chart below. What did people do before each item was invented?

> The electronic ignition system was invented by Charles Kettering and Clyde Coleman in 1911. Before that, people turned a crank by hand in order to start their cars.

Invention	Inventor	Year
windshield wipers	Mary Anderson	1903
electronic ignition system	Charles Kettering and Clyde Coleman	1911
automatic traffic signal	Garrett Morgan	1923
car radio	Paul Galvin	1929
parking meter	Carlton Cole Magee	1932
turn signals	Buick	1938
car air-conditioning	Packard	1940
air bags	General Motors	1973

C. Complete the sentences about the inventions in the chart using the passive voice.

1. One of the first automatic traffic signals _____was developed_____ (develop) by Garrett Morgan.
2. He _____was issued_____ (issue) a patent in 1923.
3. Before this, many people _____were killed_____ (kill) in traffic accidents.
4. Three positions _____were featured_____ (feature) on this device: Go, Stop, and All-Direction Stop. The All-Direction Stop allowed pedestrians to cross safely.
5. Morgan's device _____was used_____ (use) until today's system of red, yellow, and green lights.
6. The first parking meters _____were installed_____ (install) in Oklahoma City.
7. They _____were met_____ (meet) with angry resistance by drivers.
8. Several of the first parking meters _____were destroyed_____ (destroy) by angry groups.
9. Air bags _____were invented_____ (invent) by General Motors.
10. Air bags _____were offered_____ (offer) as an option in 1973 Chevys.
11. For more than ten years, air bags _____weren't considered_____ (negative—consider) important by drivers. Now they are standard equipment in most cars.

B. Talk about each advance in car and traffic technology using the chart below.

- Read through the chart with the class. Answer any questions they may have about what the various inventions do.
- Complete this activity with the whole class. Students take turns telling who invented each device, when it was invented, and what people did before it was invented. Have students pause after each sentence so you can confirm the correctness of the sentence, or make a correction if necessary.

C. Complete the sentences about the inventions in the chart using the passive voice.

Students complete this activity individually and check their answer with a partner. Review the correct answers with the whole class.

D. Write these sentences about medical history and advances in medicine using the passive voice.

Review the instructions and sample answer before having students complete the activity individually. Have a different student write each sentence on the board. Review the sentences with the whole class, making corrections as necessary.

D. **Write these sentences about medical history and advances in medicine using the passive voice. The sentences are in the simple present tense or the past tense.**

1. In early times, the medicine man cured people.

   In early times, people were cured by the medicine man.

2. The Romans began the first hospitals.
   The first hospitals were begun by the Romans.

3. Germs cause many diseases.
   Many diseases are caused by germs.

4. Many years ago, hospitals did not sterilize equipment.
   Many years ago, equipment was not sterilized by hospitals.

5. Today, doctors and hospitals sterilize all equipment.
   Today, all equipment is sterilized by doctors and hospitals.

6. Sir Alexander Fleming discovered penicillin in 1928.
   Penicillin was discovered by Sir Alexander Fleming in 1928.

7. Bernard Fantus established the first blood bank in the United States in 1937.
   The first blood bank in the United States was established by Bernard Fantus in 1937.

8. Ian McDonald invented ultrasound in 1958.
   Ultrasound was invented by Ian McDonald in 1958.

9. Sound waves create pictures of internal organs.
   Pictures of internal organs are created by soundwaves.

10. Baruch Blumberg developed the hepatitis B vaccine in 1963.
    The hepatitis B vaccine was developed by Baruch Blumberg in 1963.

11. Most colleges require students to have the hepatitis B vaccine.
    Students are required to the hepatitis B vaccine by most colleges.

12. Doctors implanted the first artificial heart in Barney Clark in 1982.
    The first artificial heart was implanted by doctors in Barney Clark in 1982.

13. Doctors performed the first laser surgery to correct vision in 1987.
    The first laser surgery to correct vision was performed by doctors in 1987.

14. Doctors perform many operations on an outpatient basis.
    Many operations are performed by doctors on an outpatient basis.

A. Pronunciation: Compound nouns. Listen and repeat the names of these inventions.

1.	SAFety razor	6.	PARKing meter
2.	AIR conditioner	7.	CONtact lenses
3.	LIE detector	8.	SEAT belt
4.	MIcrowave oven	9.	LAser printer
5.	BALLpoint pen	10.	CELL phone

Note: The first word receives more stress than the second word.

Sit with a partner. Pronounce these inventions that are related to the computer.

1.	FLOPpy disk	6.	HARD drive
2.	KEYboard	7.	WEB page
3.	INKjet printer	8.	JOYstick
4.	LAPtop computer	9.	TOOLbar
5.	E-mail	10.	SOFTware

B. Questions in the passive. Read the examples in the box. Then, ask and answer questions about these inventions.

What's this?
By whom was it invented?
When was it invented?
What is it used for?

It's a pop-up toaster.
It was invented by Charles Strite.
It was invented in 1919.
It is used to toast bread.

Charles Strite–1919

King Gillette–1904

Ladislo Biro–1938

Chester Carlson–1949

Marion Donovan–1950

Zenith Electronics–1950

Technology Today **217**

A. Pronunciation: Compound nouns. (CD3, Track 16)

• Play the audio once while students only listen. Then, play it again and have students repeat each phrase. Point out that the first word (or first syllable of the first word) always gets strong stress.

• Ask students to say other two-word phrases aloud. Write each on the board, using capital letters for the word or syllable that gets the strong stress. For example: *TENnis racket, ENGlish book,* and *SOCcer team.* Then, have different students read aloud the list on the board.

Sit with a partner.

Students practice the words in pairs. After a few minutes of practice, call on different students to pronounce the words for the class. Correct pronunciation as necessary and have students repeat.

B. Questions in the passive.

• Discuss the instructions. Have two students role-play the sample dialogue. Answer any questions students may have. Explain that *by whom* is not often used in speech, and that it is a very formal grammatical form. Elicit the more common form of the *by whom* sentence in the sample dialogue. (*Who invented it?*)

• Students practice asking and answering the questions in pairs. Move around the room as they work offering help as needed.

C. More inventions.

You can begin the exercise by brainstorming a few inventions with the whole class. Then, have students complete their lists individually. As the pairs work together, they ask each other about the inventions on their partner's list.

D. Student to student dictation.

• Read and discuss the instructions. Point out the short answer lines at the left of each statement on this page and explain that both Student A and Student B will use these lines as their partner reads the questions on page 249 to them.

• Have students locate the sentences on page 249 and complete the activity in pairs. When they finish, the pairs exchange books and check each other's work.

Suggestion

Some students may enjoy researching and telling the class about an invention that has been important to them. For example, a student's parent might use a hearing aid or a student's child might use an asthma inhaler. They can use the Internet or the local library to get information and either read their reports to the class or display them in the classroom.

C. More inventions. List ten inventions in your classroom or that you have in your handbag or your backpack. Then, answer the questions about each invention.

1. ___(Answers will vary.)___   6. _____
2. _____   7. _____
3. _____   8. _____
4. _____   9. _____
5. _____   10. _____

1. What is the name of this invention?
2. How many years ago do you think it was invented?
3. What is it made of?
4. What is it used for?
5. What did people use before we had this invention?

Can you think of a problem or job you would like to solve? Can you think of a way to make your life or your work easier? Can you think of an invention that would save time in your life? Brainstorm some ideas for useful inventions.

| at home | at work | at school | in your car |
| at the airport | at the store | at the bank | at the supermarket |

D. Student to student dictation.

Student A: Turn to page 249. Read the questions.

Student B: Read each of these responses. Then, listen and write the number of each question next to the correct response. When you finish, change pages. Then, compare answers.

___5___ **a.** Because she had a heart attack.

___9___ **b.** Because there are heavy thunderstorms in the middle part of the country.

___1___ **c.** Because he had three car accidents and four speeding tickets.

___2___ **d.** Because she robbed a convenience store.

___4___ **e.** Because he didn't pay his rent for five months.

___6___ **f.** Because the boss has received several complaints about her work.

___8___ **g.** Because she has four credit cards already and she's maxed out on all of them.

___3___ **h.** Because we have a foot of snow on the ground.

___7___ **i.** Because you forgot her birthday.

___10___ **j.** Because they're repairing the bridge.

E. Listen to Hui-Fen describe school in Taiwan. Then, answer these questions.

1. Where was Hui-Fen educated? Taiwan
2. What were some of the rules in her school? Uniform, short-hair
3. How were students punished if they did not do their homework? Hands hit with a stick, stand with book on head
4. When were students allowed to date? College
5. What language is spoken at home in Taiwan? Taiwanese
   In what language are students educated? Chinese
6. When is school closed? Summer and winter vacations
7. What other information do you remember about Hui-Fen's education? (Answers will vary.)

F. Interview another student in your class. If possible, interview a student from another country. (Answers will vary.)

1. When were you born? Where were you born?
2. Where were you raised?
3. Were you educated in private school or in public school?
4. Were you involved in any after-school sports or activities?
5. Were you required to wear a uniform?
6. Were you allowed to date?
7. Was school ever cancelled? If so, why?
8. Was school closed in July and August?
9. What language was spoken in class?
10. What languages were taught?
11. Were students expected to stand when they answered a question?
12. How many hours of homework were you assigned?
13. Was homework given every night?
14. Were you kept after school if you didn't do your homework?
15. How often were exams given?

Write two things about your education and your partner's education that were the same. (Answers will vary.)

1. _____
2. _____

Write two things about your education and your partner's education that were different.

1. _____
2. _____

Technology Today **219**

E. Listen to Hui-Fen describe school in Taiwan. (CD3, Track 17)

Ask students to just listen the first time through. Then, play the audio a second time and call on different students to answer the questions.

F. Interview another student in your class.

• Ask students to read through the interview questions and ask about anything they don't understand. Then, have the pairs interview each other.
• Review the answers by having one pair present their interview to the class.

Write two things about your education and your partner's education that were the same.

Students complete the activity on their own.

Write two things about your education and your partner's education that were different.

Students complete the activity on their own. Then, the two compare what they have written about the similarities and differences in their educational backgrounds.

Audio Script

B. Listen to Hui-Fen describe school in Taiwan. (CD3, Track 17)

I am from Taiwan. I was born in Taiwan in 1963 and raised in the capital, that's Taipei. I attended public school. Most students in Taiwan are educated in public school. School in Taiwan is very strict and we had to follow many rules. First, we were required to wear a uniform. The girls wore a blue skirt and white blouse and the boys wore blue pants and a white shirt. I couldn't have long hair. Girls had to keep their hair above their shoulders. And the boys could only have hair one inch long. Very short!

We studied very hard. We went to school from 9:00 to 4:30 and we were assigned about three hours of homework. If we didn't do our homework, we were punished. Maybe the teacher hit our hands with a stick or we had to stand with a book on our head. We were given exams in the middle of the year and at the end of the year.

Boys and girls studied in separate classes. The only time we were together was for after school clubs and activities. Boys and girls were not allowed to date in high school. We were not allowed to call one another on the phone, either. Students began to date in college.

In Taiwan, our native language is Taiwanese. It's a spoken language, not a written language. When we begin school, we are expected to study, talk, and learn in Chinese, which is a new lan-guage for us. This is very hard for the students, especially when they begin school. Also, when we are in middle school, English is taught as a foreign language. By the time we finish high school, we can speak Taiwanese, Chinese, and English.

Vacations in Taiwan are similar to the United States. School is closed for two months in the summer and we have a one-month winter vacation in January or February, around the time of the Chinese New Year.

The Big Picture: Shopping

⚞ **A. Look at the pictures and listen** to a short history of some of the inventions and ideas that have made shopping easier.
(CD3, Track 18)

- Ask students to describe what they see happening in the pictures. You might use some questions like these:
  What are these people doing? Have you ever done this? When do you think this item was invented?
- As students listen to the audio the first time, you might have them point to each picture as they hear it described.

⚞ **B. Listen again.** (CD3, Track 18)

Tell students to write the dates and to take short notes in the right-hand column of the chart. They will not have time to write complete sentences. Review the correct answers orally with the class.

⚞ **A. Look at the pictures and listen to a short history of some of the inventions and ideas that have made shopping easier.**

⚞ **B. Listen again. Complete the chart.**

Invention	Date	How did this invention help people?
Catalogs	1872	Way to help customers view merchandise and order items.
Cash register	1884	People could receive an immediate printed receipt.
Shopping cart	1900s	Customers able to buy more items at one time.
Credit card	1950	Don't need to carry cash. Buy items and pay later.
Bar code (U.P.C.)	1973	Checkers scan each item and price appears on register.
Online shopping	1990s	Shopping is faster and more convient.

Audio Script

A. Look at the pictures and listen to a short history of some of the inventions and ideas that have made shopping easier.
(CD3, Track 18)

For many years, shopping was a simple process. A person went into a small local store, bought an item, and paid in cash. Another popular way of shopping was to buy merchandise from a traveling salesman. Many people lived far from the city, so salesmen traveled around the country by horse and wagon, showing the customers their merchandise.

In 1872, a traveling salesman named Aaron Montgomery Ward, had an idea to help his customers see more of his merchandise. Ward decided to print a catalog with pictures of the items that his company sold. The customers could look through the catalog and order the items they wanted. The first mail-order catalog was printed in 1872 and became an immediate success. Catalogs are still a very popular way to shop.

Before 1884, clerks kept money in the store in a drawer or cash box. When a customer bought a product, the clerk wrote a receipt by hand. In 1884, the first cash register was invented by James Ritty. People could receive an immediate printed receipt.

In the 1900s, stores were becoming larger, especially grocery stores. Customers were buying more items at one time. The owner of one of these grocery stores, Sylvan Goldman, had an idea. He put two baskets and wheels on a folding chair and the first shopping cart was invented. Goldman formed a company to design larger and better shopping carts.

(Audio Script continues on page 257.)

C. Which invention does each statement describe?

1. Before this invention, all receipts were handwritten. *cash register*
2. This invention was first used in 1974. *U.P.C. scanner*
3. With this advance in technology, it's easy to compare prices. *online shipping*
4. This idea was developed by a traveling salesman. *catalog*
5. This invention was designed by a grocery store owner. *shopping cart*
6. This advance was first used by business travelers. *credit card*

 D. Read the questions first. Then, listen again and answer the questions.

1. Why was a traveling salesman necessary? *Many people lived far from the city.*
2. How did Ward travel? *By horse and wagon.*
3. How did his idea help his customers? *They could look through the catalog and order items they wanted*
4. Where did store owners keep their money before 1884? *In a drawer or cash box.*
5. Was a receipt written or printed? *Written.*
6. How did the cash register make shopping simpler? *People could receive an immediate printed receipt.*
7. Why did customers need shopping carts? *They were buying more items.*
8. Who were credit cards first used by? *Business travelers*
9. What inventions are used by supermarket checkers? *U.P.C. and the U.P.C. scanner*
10. How does the bar code make their job easier? *The price appears on the register once the item is scanned.*
11. Why do small companies like online shopping? *It is an inexpensive way to advertise.*
12. How does online shopping save customers money? *They can compare prices.*

E. Complete the sentences. Verbs may be in the active or passive voice.

1. The first mail-order catalog (print) ____*was printed*____ in 1872.
   Customers (look) ____*looked*____ through the catalog
   and (order) ____*ordered*____ the items they wanted.

2. Before 1950, customers (pay) ____*paid*____ for their
   purchases with cash or by check. The first credit cards (issue)
   ____*were issued*____ to business travelers. With a credit card,
   people (negative—need) ____*don't need*____ to carry a lot of
   cash with them.

3. The first U.P.C. scanner (install) ____*was installed*____ in a
   supermarket in Ohio. Today, supermarket clerks simply (scan)
   ____*scan*____ each item. The price (appear)
   ____*appears*____ on their cash register's screen.

C. Which invention does each statement describe?

Students complete this exercise individually. Review the correct answers with the whole class.

 D. Read the questions first.
(CD3, Track 18)

Play the audio for the class, pausing after each section and then asking the related question or questions from this exercise. Repeat correct responses and call on a different student to correctly rephrase any incorrect responses.

E. Complete the sentences.

Students write their answers individually and compare them with a partner. Review the correct answers with the whole class.

Suggestion

Form two teams (or several sets of teams if you have a large class) and have an active/passive competition. The first person on Team A says a sentence that can be formulated in both active and passive voice. For example: *He gave me the book.* The first person on Team B must say the sentence correctly using the opposite form: *The book was given to me.* The person saying the first sentence can use either an active or a passive sentence. The person on the opposing team must always respond with the opposite form.

Reading: Cell-Phone Controversy

A. Before You Read.

• Point to the pictures and invite students to comment. Ask: *What is different about these two pictures?*

• Have students read the questions at the top to themselves. Then, have a class discussion based on their answers.

B. Vocabulary.

• Ask students to complete the matching activity individually and then check their answers with a partner. Review the correct answers with the class, answering any questions students may have about the meaning of either a vocabulary word or a word used in the definition.

• Students read the article all the way through on their own. Then, have them read it a second time, underlining any words or sentences they still don't understand. Review the reading, explaining new vocabulary to the class as necessary.

Reading: Cell-Phone Controversy

A. Before You Read. (Answers will vary.)

1. Do you own a cell phone? Is it a hand-held set or a hands-free set?
2. Do you talk on the phone when you are driving?
3. Does your state have any laws about the use of cell phones when driving?

B. Vocabulary. Match each word with its meaning.

_c_ 1. controversy	**a.** not permitted by law, not allowed
_e_ 2. relationship	**b.** the time it takes to react
_a_ 3. banned	**c.** disagreement or argument
_f_ 4. evidence	**d.** to put a limit on, to control
_g_ 5. distraction	**e.** connection or association
_h_ 6. to contribute	**f.** facts that prove something is true
_i_ 7. to perform	**g.** something that causes a person to lose concentration
_b_ 8. response time	**h.** to be part of the cause or the reason
_d_ 9. to restrict	**i.** to do, to act, to carry out instructions

Cell-phone technology was developed during the 1970s and 1980s. It was not until the 1990s that cell phones came into everyday use. In 1995, 24 percent of adults in the United States reported that they owned a cell phone. By 2002, that number grew to 64 percent. This little invention has produced a major **controversy**. What is the **relationship** between hand-held phones and accidents? Should there be a law against the use of hand-held phones by drivers?

In June, 2001, the governor of the state of New York signed the first law in the United States that **banned** hand-held phones by drivers. Violators are fined $100. At the ceremony, he was joined by individuals and families who had lost a loved one in an accident involving cell-phone use. New York is following the example set by other countries. The use of cell phones by drivers is banned in Portugal. In several other countries, including Italy, Poland, Spain, Slovakia, and Hungary, drivers are required to use hands-free sets.

The phone industry is fighting these laws. They say that there is not enough **evidence** to prove that cell-phone usage causes accidents. A study by the American Automobile Association (AAA), said that other **distractions** are more serious, such as eating, applying make up, or putting a CD into a CD player. In addition, less than 2 percent of all drivers involved in five thousand accidents reported between 1995 and 1999 said that they were distracted by their cell phone.

Other studies show that cell-phone use **contributes** to accidents. The National Police Agency of Japan reported that in 1997, 2,297 accidents were caused by drivers talking on cell phones. Another study in South Africa showed that one out of every four accidents was related to cell-phone usage.

A study at the University of Utah showed that all cell-phone use in cars is a distraction. Sixty-four drivers were asked to **perform** simple tasks, such as changing a radio station, listening to music, talking on a hands-free cell phone, and talking on a hand-held cell phone. Then, researchers measured their **response time** when they were braking or stopping a car. When people were using a cell phone, their responses were much slower. This was true of both hands-free phones and hand-held phones.

What can drivers expect in the years to come? More laws will be passed **restricting** the use of hand-held cell phones. Cell-phone manufacturers will continue to encourage cell-phone safety in their instructions. And cell-phone companies will advertise headsets, car speakerphones, and voice-activated dialing services. You can be sure that companies are busy today, inventing safer ways to use this new technology.

C. Looking at studies. Read each statement about a study in the reading. Then, (circle) T for True or F for False.

1. The American Automobile Association said that using a hand-held phone is more distracting than eating in a car. T (F)

2. AAA also reported that almost five thousand accidents were caused by cell-phone use. T (F)

3. Japan stated that 2,297 cell-phone users had accidents in 1997. (T) F

4. Only four accidents in South Africa were caused by cell-phone use. T (F)

5. A study at the University of Utah showed that hands-free cell phones are safer than hand-held cell phones. T (F)

D. Vocabulary. Use a vocabulary word from Exercise B to complete these sentences.

1. TV is a _____distraction_____ for children when they are doing their homework.

2. The museum _____restricts_____ the use of cell phones. They are limited to the lobby.

3. What is the _____relationship_____ between drinking and driving?

4. Poor weather conditions _____contribute_____ to many accidents.

5. The _____evidence_____ shows that the car's brakes failed.

6. There is an ongoing _____controversy_____ about how to spend taxes.

C. Looking at studies.

Students complete the exercise on their own and check their answers with a partner. Review the answers orally with the whole class.

D. Vocabulary.

Students complete the exercise on their own and check their answers with a partner. Review the answers orally with the whole class.

Writing Our Stories: An Opinion Letter

A. Read this letter from an annoyed customer to the owner of a popular restaurant.

- Have students read the letter to themselves. Call on a student to summarize what it says.
- Point out the first statement of the problem and have a student read it aloud. Then, have students restate in their own words some of the reasons the writer gave for her opinion. Point out the restatement of the opinion at the end of the letter.

B. Stating an opinion.

- Read the instructions and point out where the answers go on page 225. Then, have students copy the reasons on the correct lines and add a reason of their own.
- Review the original reasons students came up with. Write some of these on the board.

Writing Our Stories: An Opinion Letter

A. Read this letter from an annoyed customer to the owner of a popular restaurant.

25 Glen Street
Tampa, Florida 33615
March 3, 2003

Dear Mr. Lombardi,

opinion — Please consider a ban on cell phones at your restaurant. This past Friday evening, my husband and I were enjoying dinner at your restaurant when a woman at the next table received a cell-phone call. People at the nearby tables soon learned that she was annoyed at her sister for using her credit card. Her loud conversation continued for ten minutes. My husband and I were looking forward to a relaxing evening, a good dinner, and quiet conversation. We didn't pay $47.00 to listen to another customer's personal problems.

reasons

restatement of opinion — Please follow the example of several other restaurants in the city that have posted signs, "Cell-phone usage limited to emergencies only."

Sincerely,

Teresa Santiago

 B. Stating an opinion. Should drivers be able to use hand held-cell phones while driving? Write the following reasons under the correct heading on page 225. Add one more reason under each heading. (Answers will vary.)

a. Drivers need two hands on the wheel.
b. Drivers spend hours in traffic. Talking to friends gives them a way to pass the time.
c. There are not enough studies to prove that drivers using hand-held cell phones cause more accidents.
d. A person talking on the phone is concentrating on the conversation, not the road.

Drivers should be allowed to use hand-held cell phones:

1. _____

2. _____

3. _____

Drivers should not be allowed to use hand-held cell phones:

1. _____

2. _____

3. _____

C. An opinion letter. The legislature in your state is considering a law to ban the use of hand-held cell phones by drivers. Some legislators are in favor of the ban and others are opposed to it. Write a letter to your congressman or congresswoman stating *your* opinion. Follow this form: (Answers will vary.)

1. State your opinion in the first sentence.

2. Give two or three reasons for your opinion.

3. Restate your opinion in the last sentence.

D. Edit. Find and correct the mistakes in these sentences.

1. The accident was ~~causing~~ caused by a driver talking on a cell phone.

2. The driver ⌃was distracted when her cell phone rang.

3. Yesterday I ~~was seen~~ saw an accident.

4. She ~~was~~ bought a headset for her phone.

5. Hand-held cell phones are ~~ban~~ banned in New York State.

6. The man at the next table was ~~talk~~ talking on the phone.

7. The people in the theater ~~was~~ were annoyed when a cell phone rang.

8. She was ~~gave~~ given a ticket for driving while using a cell phone.

Looking at the Internet

Look at a few stores on the Internet. What do they sell? Are the prices cheaper or more expensive than stores in your area? How much is shipping? Bring in the home page of a store you like. Tell the other students about this site.

C. An opinion letter.
• Review with the class the instructions and discuss the format the letters must follow. Remind them that they can look back at the letter on page 224 to get ideas for their own letters.
• Have students write their letters in class or for homework. When you go over them, avoid discussing spelling or grammar errors for the moment, and focus on the correct use and placement of opinion statements and reasons within the letter.

D. Edit.
Have students complete this activity on their own. Review the correct answers with the whole class.

Suggestion

Some students may wish to write their own letters about a situation at their school they would like to see change. For example, they might write about the lack of parking spaces or the need for a water fountain on their floor. Help students correct their letters and encourage them to send them to the program director.

Looking at the Internet

You might want to suggest two or three items for students to research and see who can come up with the best price while shopping on the Internet. For example, a certain model of cell phone or a certain music CD.

Practicing on Your Own

A. Read and complete this article about advances in cardiology.

Students complete the activity individually. Check the answers with the whole class.

B. In your notebooks, write seven questions about this article.

To provide additional practice with the target structure, encourage students to include several passive voice questions.

Practicing on Your Own

A. Read and complete this article about advances in cardiology. Some of the verbs are active; others are passive. Choose the correct verb tense.

Heart disease is the number-one cause of death in the United States. For years, doctors have been developing tests, medications, and procedures to help patients with heart disease. In the most serious cases, a heart transplant (require) _____is required_____.

On December 3, 1967, Dr. Christian Barnard (perform) _____performed_____ the first heart transplant in Capetown, South Africa. The heart of an auto accident victim (transplant) _____was transplanted_____ into the body of Louis Washansky, a 55-year-old man. He (live) _____lived_____ for 18 days following the operation.

Since that day, over fifteen thousand heart transplants have been performed. The major difficulty in these procedures (be) _____was_____ the rejection of the new heart by the recipient's body's immune system. In 1969, an anti-rejection drug, cyclosponine, (discover) _____was discovered_____ by Jean-Francois Borel. Today, heart transplants (perform) _____are performed_____ throughout the world.

The first artificial heart (implant) _____was implanted_____ in Dr. Barney Clark in 1982. This mechanical heart (attach) _____was attached_____ by tubes and wires to a large machine. The heart (name) _____was named_____ the Jarvick-7 after its inventor, Dr. Robert Jarvick. Dr. Clark (live) _____lived_____ for 112 days. The next patient survived for 620 days. But research with the new heart (discontinue) _____was discontinued_____.

In July, 2001, a new artificial heart, the AbioCor®, (implant) _____was implanted_____ in Robert Tools, a 59-year-old grandfather with severe heart disease. Unlike the Jarvick-7, the AbioCor® is self-contained. A small battery pack (wore) _____was worn_____ around the waist. Mr. Tools (live) _____lived_____ for 151 days. The second recipient is still alive after 16 months. Studies are continuing with this new heart.

B. In your notebooks, write seven questions about this article.

Grammar Summary

▶ **1. Active and passive voice**

Active: The doctor **performed** the operation.

Passive: The operation **was performed** *by* the doctor.

In an active sentence, the subject (the doctor) performs the action.

In a passive sentence, the process (the operation), the product, or the action is emphasized. Use *by* to show the performer of the action. If the performer of the action is clearly understood, *by* is not necessary.

▶ **2. Uses of the passive voice**

a. We can use the passive when the subject receives the action.

The nurse **gave** him an injection. (active)

He **was given** an injection. (passive)

b. We can use the passive when the performer of the action is unknown or understood.

The patient **was admitted** to the hospital.

The operation **was performed** yesterday.

c. We can use the passive for general statements of fact.

Blood **is composed** of millions of cells.

▶ **3. Passive voice—Past tense statements**

Use *was* or *were* and the past participle to form the passive.

The patient	was	treated	at the hospital.
The patients	were		at the clinic.

▶ **4. *Wh-* questions**

When Where	was	the patient	treated?
By whom	were	the patients	

Grammar Summary

• Review the four grammar explanations and sample sentences with the class. Invite students to make up alternate sentences for each example in the chart. For example, in place of *The patient was admitted to the hospital,* a student might say, *I was admitted to college last week.*

• Answer any questions students may have about the grammar items.

• See the Grammar Summary Expansion on page 271 for a more complete explanation of these grammar points.

Unit 15
Country Music

Discuss what the person in the unit title art is doing. Ask:

• *Who is standing next to the number 15?* (A woman)
• *What is she doing?* (She's playing a guitar.)
• *How does this relate to the unit?* (The unit is about country music. Almost all country music uses guitars.)

A. Read the names of different types of music.

Read aloud the names of the types of music. Ask students to describe in their own words what each type of music is about. For any that students don't recognize, give your own simple definition. For example: *Gospel music started out in churches. The first gospel singers were African Americans.* If possible, bring to class photographs showing groups representing each type of music.

B. Look at the pictures.

• Ask students to look over the pictures and tell anything they know about the people they see. Respond by restating what students say in your own words. For example:

  S1: *Placido Domingo sings opera. I like him.*
  T: *Right. Placido Domingo is a famous opera singer.*

• Go back to the list of types of music in Exercise A and help students match as many of the musical types as possible to a singer in Exercise B.

Suggestion

Bring a recording of country music to class and play one or two songs. Country music songs often tell stories. Can they follow any of the meaning?

---

15 Country Music

A. Read the names of different types of music. Can you name a performer who plays each type of music? What's your favorite type of music?

rock and roll	classical	jazz	hip-hop
rhythm and blues (R&B)	country	salsa	rap
pop	heavy metal	opera	gospel

B. Look at the pictures. Which type of music is each performer known for?

Bob Marley

Enrique Iglesias

Faith Hill

Shakira

U-2

Celia Cruz

P. Diddy

Mariah Carey

Placido Domingo

Active Grammar: Adjective Clauses with *who*

A. Look at the people in the picture. Describe the country music fans. Complete the adjective clauses. (Answers may vary.)

The man **who is pointing to the boots** is asking, "Are you going to buy those boots?"
The man **who is standing in line** is asking, "How long have you been waiting?"

1. The girl who _is sitting on the ground_ is saying, "How many shows have you seen?"

2. The couple who _is sitting together_ is saying, "This is our tenth show."

3. The woman who _is in the wheelchair_ is saying, "I'm your biggest fan."

4. The woman who _is saying, "Hi! What's your name?"_ is signing autographs.

5. The woman who _is holding the camera_ is taking a picture of her friend.

6. The woman who _is looking at the boots_ is saying, "I only bought a few souvenirs."

B. In your notebook, write five sentences describing your classmates.

The student _who is sitting next to the window_ *is from* _____ .
(name of country)
(Answers will vary.)

A. Look at the people in the picture.

• Do this activity with the whole class. Invite students to make general comments about the people in the picture. For example, *That woman is in a wheelchair. That singer has a big guitar.*

• Then, read aloud the sample language under the picture and point out the adjective clauses with *who*. Ask students to make other comments about the people in the picture using adjective clauses with *who*.

• Students complete the sentences individually and check their answers with a partner. Review the correct answers orally with the whole class.

Suggestion

If students have any difficulty with word order in any of the adjective clauses, write them on the board so they can copy them in their notebooks for later study.

B. In your notebook, write five sentences describing your classmates.

Read the instructions and the sample sentence. Ask students to make up as many sentences about their classmates as they can in three minutes. Call on different students to say their sentences aloud. When there is an error in a student sentence, restate it in correct form and ask the student to repeat.

Active Grammar:
Adjective Clauses with *who, whom, which,* and *whose*

A. Underline the adjective clauses in the sentences below.

- Read the instructions and discuss the meaning of the terms *adjective clause, relative pronoun,* and *noun it modifies.* Use the marked up sample sentence to clarify what each term means.
- Point out the picture and ask students to share anything they know about Reba McEntire.
- Go over the different uses of the terms *who, whom, which,* and *whose.* Invite students to ask about any aspect of usage they don't understand.
- Students mark up the rest of the sentences on their own and compare their work with a partner. Review the correct answers orally with the class.

B. Listen: Country music.
(CD3, Track 19)

- Point to the map and help students locate where country music got its start in the United States. Have them name some of the states in that area if they can. (Tennessee, Georgia, and so forth)
- Have students read through the list of questions and ask about anything they don't understand. Then, ask them to just listen the first time you play the audio. The second time through, have them mark their answers.
- Review the correct answers with the whole class.

Active Grammar: Adjective Clauses with *who, whom, which,* and *whose*

A. <u>Underline</u> the adjective clauses in the sentences below. (Circle) the relative pronoun and draw an arrow to the noun it modifies.

> Adjective clauses begin with relative pronouns such as *who, whom, which,* and *whose.*
> **who**—replaces a person   **which**—replaces a thing
> **whom**—replaces an indirect object   **whose**—replaces a possessive
> Note: For more explanation and examples, refer to the Grammar Summary on page 243.

1. Reba McEntire, <u>(who) was country music's 1995 entertainer of the year,</u> made more money on her concerts than any other country star.
2. Reba McEntire, <u>(whose) songs are often about strong independent women,</u> has been in charge of her own career for some time.
3. McEntire, <u>(who) was forced to sound less country and more mainstream,</u> was not popular for the first thirteen years of her career.
4. McEntire's first husband, <u>(whom) she divorced in 1987,</u> did not promote her career well.
5. In 1982, McEntire had her first hit song, <u>(which) was titled "Can't Even Get the Blues."</u>
6. McEntire's fans, <u>(to whom) she often speaks after shows,</u> are at least 50 percent male.
7. In 2001, McEntire performed in a Broadway show, <u>(which) brought her new fans.</u>
8. In 2002, McEntire, <u>(whose) Broadway performance showed her comedic ability,</u> starred in her own TV show.

B. Listen: Country music. Listen to the history of country music. Then, (circle) *True* or *False* on the next page.

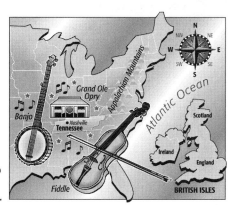

Audio Script

B. Listen: Country music. (CD3, Track 19)

The people who first sang the country sound in the United States lived over a hundred years ago in the Appalachian Mountains. These people sang all the time—while they were working, while they were doing laundry, while they were at church, or while they were taking care of their babies. People used to sing to make the work go faster. The music that they sang was very simple.

The music, which is called country music, came from the British Isles: Scotland, Ireland, England, and Wales. The people who immigrated to the United States moved to a land that was similar to their homeland. These people brought their music with them.

Two instruments were common in country music bands. The five-string banjo, which came from Africa, became popular in country music in the 1920s. The fiddle, which had early roots in Nashville, was the main instrument in country music until the 1930s. The fiddler, who carried the melody of the songs, was usually the main performer in country music bands. Banjos and fiddles are still popular in country music today, but other instruments such as electric guitars and keyboards are also used. Jimmy Rodgers and the Carter family, who first recorded in 1927, became the first superstars of country music.

1. Today's country music was originated by immigrants from the British Isles. (True) False

2. The people from Appalachia sang all the time. (True) False

3. People sang to make their work go more slowly. True (False)

4. Country music, which the Appalachians sang, was very complicated. True (False)

5. The banjo, which became popular among country musicians, came from South America. True (False)

6. The fiddle was the main instrument of country music. (True) False

7. The first superstars of country music recorded in 1947. True (False)

8. The Carter Family and Jimmy Rodgers, who all sang country music, became the first superstars of country music. (True) False

C. Relative pronouns. Fill in the correct relative pronoun from the box.

who	whose	whom	which

1. The music, ___which___ is called country music, came from the British Isles.

2. The people, ___who___ immigrated to this country, moved to a land that was similar to their native land.

3. Today's country music began in the Appalachian Mountains, ___which___ extend from the northeast to the south.

4. The music, ___which___ was very simple, was sung all the time.

5. The people, ___who___ immigrated from the British Isles, brought their music with them.

6. The fiddler, ___whose___ instrument was the main country music instrument until the 1930s, made people dance.

7. The fiddler, ___whom___ the community considered a very important part of the music, was necessary in every band.

8. The five-string banjo, ___which___ came from Africa, was used to play a different kind of music.

9. Jimmy Rodgers and the Carter family, ___whom___ a Virginia record company first recorded, were the earliest superstars of country music.

C. Relative pronouns.

• Review the uses of the four different relative pronouns using the information at the beginning of Exercise A on page 230. Answer any questions students may have.

• Students complete the fill-ins on their own and check their answers with a partner. Review the correct answers with the whole class.

D. Answer the following questions about you and your classmates.

Students answer the questions individually. Review the completed questions with the whole class. There will be a variety of different answers for most of the questions.

E. With a group of three or four students, complete the sentences.

• Review the sample answer with the class. Then, have the groups work together. Set a time limit, perhaps seven minutes.

• As you review each item in the exercise, have one person from each group read to the class the sentence that group came up with. Choose one sentence to write on the board as an example.

In your notebook, write five more sentences about your classmates.

Students can use the answers to Exercise E as a model for these new sentences. Encourage the class to use something other than the student's native country at the end of the sentence. Invite volunteers to read their sentences aloud to the class.

Suggestion

If some students find this work too challenging, suggest that they work with a partner. First the pair chooses a person to describe. Then, they make notes about two aspects of that person's life. For example: *Jill is very tall. Jill plays basketball on Sunday mornings.* Then, have them write the sentence together: *Jill, who is very tall, plays basketball on Sunday mornings.*

D. **Answer the following questions about you and your classmates. Write your answers on the blanks.** (Answers will vary.)

1. What musical instrument do you play? _____

2. Whom do you sit next to in class? _____

3. How long have you been in this country? _____

4. Who has a difficult work schedule? _____

5. Who has long hair? _____

E. **With a group of three or four students, complete the sentences. Use the information in questions 1 to 5 from Exercise D.** (Answers will vary.)

> **Who plays a musical instrument?**
> Sung Kul, **who is in a band**, is from Korea.
> Beata, **whom I sit next to**, is from Poland.

1. _____, who _____,
   (name of student)
   is from _____.
   (native country)

2. _____, whom _____,
   (name of student)
   is from _____.
   (native country)

3. _____, who _____,
   (name of student)
   is from _____.
   (native country)

4. _____, whose _____,
   (name of student)
   is from _____.
   (native country)

5. _____, whose _____,
   (name of student)
   is from _____.
   (native country)

In your notebook, write five more sentences about your classmates. Use adjective clauses that begin with *who, whom, which,* or *whose.*

A. Complete the sentences about country performer Tim McGraw. Use the information below.

a. Tim McGraw was born in Delhi, Louisiana.

b. He went to Nashville, Tennessee, in the early '90s to start a recording career because the country music industry is primarily located in Nashville.

c. In 1995, McGraw had a hit album.

d. He went on tour in 1996 and performed with Faith Hill.

e. McGraw and Hill married in October, 1996.

f. McGraw and Hill's first child was born in 1997.

g. The couple recorded a duet in 1998. McGraw and Hill's second child was born in the same year.

1. _Delhi, Louisiana_____ was the place where _Tim Mcgraw was born_____.

2. He went to _Nashville_____ where he _started a_____ _recording career_____.

3. _Nashville, Tennessee_____ is the city where the country music industry _is primarily located_____.

4. _1995___ was the year when McGraw _had a hit album_____.

5. In _1996___, when _he went on tour_____, he met his future wife, country performer Faith Hill.

6. _October_____ is the month when McGraw and Hill _got married_____.

7. _1997___ is the year when their _first child was born_____.

8. 1998 is the year when _the couple recorded a duet and they had their second child_.

B. Complete the sentences about your life. (Answers will vary.)

1. _____ is the place where I grew up.

2. _____ is the school where I _____.

3. I attend _____, where I study _____.

4. _____ is the year when I _____.

5. _____ is the year when my family and I _____.

6. I began to study English in _____ when I _____.

 Active Grammar: Adjective Clauses with *when* and *where*

A. Complete the sentences about country performer Tim McGraw.

Read and discuss the instructions. Then, have students complete the sentences on their own. Review the correct answers with the whole class.

B. Complete the sentences about your life.

Have students complete the sentences on their own and read them to a partner. Encourage students to correct each other's work. Invite several different students to read their sentences aloud to the class.

C. Musical preferences.

Students complete the activity individually. They will have a variety of different answers. Invite volunteers to share their lists with the class.

D. Rewrite your preferences from Exercise C.

• Review how to complete this activity. You may wish to have several different students use their preferences from Exercise C to complete the first sentence in different ways.

• Then, have them complete the exercise on their own and discuss their preferences with a partner.

E. Complete the questions on page 235.

• Have students complete the questions on their own. Then, ask a pair of students to role-play the sample conversation for the class.

• Partners then complete the activity together, taking turns asking and answering the questions. Review possible answers by inviting different pairs to present their conversations to the class.

C. Musical preferences. Complete the following sentences about your musical preferences. (Answers will vary.)

1. _____ is my favorite musician.
2. _____ is my favorite type of music.
3. _____ is my favorite musical group.
4. _____ is my favorite American performer.
5. _____ is my favorite radio station.
6. _____ is my favorite place to go dancing.

D. Rewrite your preferences from Exercise C. Then, discuss your preferences with a partner. (Answers will vary.)

1. _____, who is my favorite musician, is from
   _____.
   (name of country)

2. _____, which is popular in _____,
   (name of country)
   is my favorite type of music.

3. _____, which is my favorite musical group, plays
   _____.
   (type of music)

4. _____, whose music is _____, is
   (adjective)
   my favorite American performer.

5. _____, which is at _____ FM/AM,
   (letters of radio station)   (numbers)
   is my favorite radio station.

6. _____, which is located in _____,
   (name of club)   (name of city)
   is my favorite place to go dancing.

E. Complete the questions on page 235. Then, ask your partner your questions.

Do you know a *music store* where I can buy some country music?

Yes, I do. You should try the CD Den. It's on Broad Street.

1. Do you know a music store where _____(Answers will vary.)_____ ?
2. Do you know a movie theater where _____ ?
3. Do you know a dance club where _____ ?
4. Do you know a restaurant where _____ ?
5. Do you know a supermarket where _____ ?
6. Do you know an auto repair shop where _____ ?

F. Student to student dictation: Famous musicians.

Student A: Turn to page 250. You will only work on that page.
Student B: Read each sentence below to your partner. Then, listen to your partner's sentence. Use the information in both sentences and write a new, longer sentence with an adjective clause.

1. Elvis Presley was born in Mississippi.
2. Beethoven was first taught music by his father.
3. The Beatles first appeared in America in 1964.
4. Duke Ellington was a famous jazz composer.
5. Selena spoke English as her first language.
6. Mariah Carey is one of the best-selling artists of all time.

Write your new sentences.

1. Elvis Presley, who was born in Mississippi, sang and acted in movies .
2. Beethoven, who was a famous classical composer, was first taught music by his father .
3. The Beatles, who had two lead singers and song writers, first-appeared in America in 1964 .
4. Duke Ellington, who was a famous jazz composer, is still admired today .
5. Selena, who spoke English as her first language, became famous for her songs in Spanish .
6. Mariah Carey, who had a number one hit for ten years in a row, is one of the best-selling artists of all time .

F. Student to student dictation: Famous musicians.

• Read and discuss the instructions. Point out the blank lines on this page and explain that Student B will use these lines to answer as his or her partner reads the questions on page 250.
• Have students locate the sentences and blank lines for Exercise F on page 250. Explain that Student A will use these lines as his or her partner reads the questions on page 235.
• Have students complete the activity with their partners. When they finish, the pairs exchange books and check each other's work.

Write your new sentences.

Students write sentences containing the adjective clauses they came up with for Exercise F. Review the correct answers orally with the class.

☀ The Big Picture:
Fan Fair

A. Talk about the photographs of Fan Fair.

Ask students to describe what is happening in the pictures. You might use questions like these:

What are these people doing?
Who is this singer?
Why do you think country singers attend this fair?

B. Listen to the history of the world's biggest country music festival.
(CD3, Track 20)

Play the audio once and have students just listen. Then, point out the area where students can take notes and play the audio again. This time encourage them to take notes about what they hear. Remind them to focus on dates, numbers, and place names.

Suggestion

Bring to class recordings by some of the singers pictured on page 228 and play parts of their songs. Ask students to listen to each song and guess which singer is singing. If appropriate for your class, play the chorus of a song several times and ask students to write out the words. Have a student write the words on the board and discuss them with the class.

☀ The Big Picture: Fan Fair

A. Talk about the photographs of Fan Fair. What's happening?

B. Listen to the history of the world's biggest country music festival. Take notes of dates, numbers, and places.

> **Notes**
> - over 30 years ago-DJ convection
> - CMA & Grand Ole Opry-First Fan Fair-April, 1972-Nashville-50,000 fans
> - Moved to June-over 100,000 fans
> - 1982-Moved to Tennessee State Fairgrounds
> - 1974-Paul McCartney
> - 1992-Billy Ray Cyrus-600 reporters
> - 1996-Garth Brooks-Autographs-23 hours
> - 2001-Returned to Nashville
> - 2002-over 125,000 fans-445 performers
> - Order tickets online or by phone

236 UNIT 15

Audio Script

B. Listen to the history of the world's biggest country music festival. Take notes of dates, numbers, and places.
(CD3, Track 20)

Like other types of music, country music has loyal fans. But, different from other types of music, country music fans have an opportunity to meet many of their favorite performers in person. Every June, approximately one hundred and twenty-five thousand country music fans go to Nashville, Tennessee, for Fan Fair.

Over 30 years ago, there was an annual country music disc-jockey, or DJ, convention in Nashville. Many country performers used to attend the convention to promote their projects. Fans would go to Nashville hoping to see their favorite performers. Eventually, so many fans began showing up in Nashville that the Country Music Association and the Grand Ole Opry decided to have a festival just for the fans at a different time. Fan Fair was born.

The first Fan Fair was held in April 1972, in Nashville for four days. Some of country music's biggest stars attended. Booths were set up so that fans could take pictures with their favorite singers and get autographs. There was

(Audio Script continues on page 257.)

C. Use your notes in Exercise B on page 236 to complete the sentences.

1. _____125,000_____ fans attend Fan Fair, which is held in Nashville _____Tennessee_____.

2. The disc-jockey convention was over _____30_____ years ago.

3. Fan Fair began in _____1972_____.

4. Fan Fair is held in _____June_____, when the _____Weather_____ is better.

5. _____50,000_____ fans attended the first year.

6. _____100,000_____ fans attended the following year.

7. Paul McCartney, who is a former _____Beatle_____, attended Fan Fair in _____1974_____.

8. Billy Ray Cyrus brought more than _____600_____ reporters in 1992, when he introduced a new _____country line dance_____.

9. Fan Fair, which is now attended by over _____125,000_____ fans, has more than _____445_____ performers.

10. Tickets can be bought _____seven_____ months ahead of time.

D. Listening for details. Read the following questions. Then, listen again to find the answers.

1. Why did the Country Music Association (CMA) and the Grand Ole Opry start Fan Fair? They started Fan Fair for the fans to hear the performers.

2. What did fans do at the first Fan Fair? They took pictures with their favorite singers and got autographs.

3. Why was the date changed to June? The date was changed because of the weather.

4. Where was Fan Fair moved to? The Tennesse State Fairgrounds.

5. Why was it moved? It was moved because so many fans and performers attended.

6. What are some of the surprises that happen at Fan Fair? Paul McCartney attended, Garth Brooks signed autographs, over 600 reporters attended to cover Billy Ray Cyrus.

7. How many fans attended Fan Fair in 2002? 125,000

8. Where is Fan Fair held today? Nashville

9. How can fans purchase tickets? Online or by telephone

10. Why do fans return to Fan Fair every year? For the new surprises and activities.

E. A summary. Use your answers to Exercises B, C, and D to complete the summary of the story in your notebook. The first sentence has been started for you.

The Country Music Association began Fan Fair in...

C. Use your notes in Exercise B on page 236 to complete the sentences.

Ask students to complete the sentences on their own. If they missed any key information in their notes on page 236, play the audio again so they can find the answers they need. Review the completed sentences with the whole class.

D. Listening for details. (CD3, Track 20)

Have students review the questions before you play the audio again. Have them write their answers after each question line in their books. Review the answers with the class.

E. A summary.

Ask students to write their summaries on their own in class. As they work, move around the room offering help as needed. Invite one or two students to read their completed summaries to the class.

☀ Reading:
Shania Twain

A. Before You Read.

• Point to the picture and invite students to tell anything they know about Shania Twain. Have them read the five questions. Then, have them locate by scanning, underlining, and numbering the answers. Review the answers orally with the class.

• Ask students to read the passage on their own. When they finish, ask them to point out any sentences they don't understand. Invite other students to restate them in their own words, or do this yourself. Answer any other questions students may have about the passage.

Suggestion

Before assigning Exercise A, you may wish to review how to scan a reading passage. Remind students to:

1. keep in mind the fact or answer they are looking for as they scan.
2. move their eyes quickly through the reading.
3. continue reading without stopping on individual words or sentences until they find the information they are looking for.

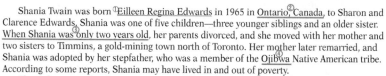

A. Before You Read. Scan the reading to find the answers to the questions. Underline and number the answers.

1. What is Shania Twain's original name?
   Eilleen Rengina Edwards
2. Where was she born?
   Ontario, Canada
3. When did her parents divorce?
   When Shania was only two years old.
4. What is the name of Shania's stepfather's Native American tribe? *Ojibwa*

5. Is she married or single? *Married*

Shania Twain was born ①Eilleen Regina Edwards in 1965 in Ontario,② Canada, to Sharon and Clarence Edwards. Shania was one of five children—three younger siblings and an older sister. When Shania was only two years old, her parents divorced, and she moved with her mother and two sisters to Timmins, a gold-mining town north of Toronto. Her mother later remarried, and Shania was adopted by her stepfather, who was a member of the Ojibwa Native American tribe. According to some reports, Shania may have lived in and out of poverty.

Shania began performing at a young age. Her mother, whose desire for her daughter to succeed was very strong, took the young singer to many different bars, clubs, and other venues to perform. In high school, Shania joined a local band, with which she performed regularly.

After high school, Shania moved to Toronto, where she continued singing. At age 21, however, her parents were killed in a car crash, and Shania had to take over the role of parent to her younger siblings. Taking care of two teenage brothers and a sister was overwhelming at times. Suddenly, she had to pay bills, keep food on the table, and earn a living. Singing helped Shania to pay the bills.

In 1991, Shania went to Nashville, the home of the country music industry. In 1993, she recorded *Shania Twain*, her first CD. In 1995, her next CD, *The Woman in Me*, which had eight hit songs, sold more than ten million copies. Her third CD, *Come on Over*, was also successful and had another hit song.

Shania and her producer husband, Robert Lange, married in 1993 after a nine-month relationship. Before Lange met Shania, he had already successfully produced albums for rock-and-roll performers. Lange was also the person who produced *The Woman in Me*.

After finishing her 2000 world tour to promote her CD, which was the best-selling album by a female singer, she decided to take a break from performing. She went back to Switzerland, where she and her husband currently reside. In August 2001, they had a son, whom they named Eja. After September 11th, Shania decided to put more emphasis on her family and extended her break until the fall of 2002. Her reappearance in the music world put her face on magazine covers and country music publications. She also began to promote her new album, *Up*, on TV shows.

Some critics say that Shania was not disadvantaged growing up, and she is using her adopted father's Native American heritage to promote her career. Her talent, however, is not in dispute.

B. Scan the reading. (Circle) *True* or *False*.

1. Shania is the oldest child in her family.   True   (False)
2. Shania became responsible for her siblings when she was a teenager.   True   (False)
3. Shania has been singing in public since she was very young.   (True)   False
4. Sharon Edwards encouraged her daughter to sing.   (True)   False
5. Shania's parents were killed in an airplane crash.   True   (False)
6. Shania stopped singing after her parents were killed.   True   (False)
7. Her first CD was titled *The Woman in Me*.   True   (False)
8. Her second CD sold more than ten million copies.   (True)   False

C. Chronological order. Put the following events in order from 1–9.

_5_ **a.** Shania became the "mother" to her siblings.
_9_ **b.** She recorded *The Woman in Me*, which was produced by Robert Lange.
_2_ **c.** Shania's mother remarried.
_7_ **d.** She recorded her first CD.
_3_ **e.** She began to perform in public.
_1_ **f.** Shania's parents divorced.
_6_ **g.** She moved to Nashville.
_8_ **h.** She married Robert Lange.
_4_ **i.** Her parents were killed.

D. Complete the adjective clauses based on the reading.

1. In 1991, when Shania ___went to Nashville___, she began looking for a record contract.
2. *The Woman in Me*, which ___sold more than ten million copies___, had eight hit songs.
3. In 1993, Shania married Robert Lange, who ___produced "The Woman in Me"___.
4. Shania, whose awards include ___best-selling album by a female singer___, won the 2000 Entertainer of the Year Award from the Country Music Association.
5. After finishing her 2000 world tour, her first child, whom she ___named Eja___, was born.

B. Scan the reading.

Ask students to study the list of questions carefully and be sure they understand each one. Suggest that students then read one question at a time and then scan the reading until they locate the information and record the answer in their books. Review the answers with the whole class.

C. Chronological order.

Students can do this exercise in three steps.

a. They can try numbering the events in chronological order without looking back at the story.
b. Then, they look back and check their work.
c. Finally, they can check their answers with a partner.

D. Complete the adjective clauses based on the reading.

Ask students to complete the exercise on their own and check their answers with a partner. Review the correct answers orally with the class.

Suggestion

Bring a recording by Shania Twain to class and play it. Ask students how they liked her music.

Writing Our Stories: My Autobiography

A. Read Armin's time line of his life in the United States.

• Ask students to read through the time line and underline any words they don't know. Review the time line with the class, explaining any underlined words.

• Ask some simple comprehension questions based on the time line. For example:

T: *When did he first come to the U.S.?*

S1: *In July, 1993.*

T: *Did he enroll in English class before or after he started selling phone cards?*

S1: *He enrolled in English classes before he started selling phone cards.*

B. Read Armin's autobiography, which is based on the time line.

Ask students to read the autobiography all the way through without stopping. Ask: *Is there anything you don't understand about what you read?* Invite students to answer each other's questions if possible.

C. Make a time line.

• Have students quickly jot down ideas that they may want to include in their life stories. Tell them not to worry about writing complete sentences or putting their ideas in the correct order. Emphasize that the purpose of this part of the exercise is just to get the ideas down on paper.

• Then, ask students to use these ideas, and any others that come to them, to create their time lines.

Writing Our Stories: My Autobiography

A. Read Armin's time line of his life in the United States.

Time Line

July 1993	came to the United States
Aug. 1993	began to promote soccer games in local parks
Jan. 1995	enrolled in English class
Sept. 1995	started selling phone cards
Oct. 1995	quit promotion business
Aug. 1995	bought 10,000 phone cards to sell
Nov. 1995	became successful phone card salesman
July 4, 1996	opened business as distributor
July 1998	entered a partnership with phone card makers
Now	has two offices and a very successful business

B. Read Armin's autobiography, which is based on the time line.

In July, 1993, I emigrated to the United States with my wife and children. We didn't know anyone, but in my country, I used to be a promoter. I tried to continue the same business in this country.

Soccer was popular among the immigrants here, so I began to promote soccer games in the local parks. I arranged for close-circuit TV broadcasts of the games because people were very interested in soccer games, especially professional games between South American teams.

In 1995, a friend of mine told me about phone cards. I offered to sell them for him even though I didn't know anything about phone cards. I was a good salesman and sold more and more cards because I had confidence in myself and my abilities. In October, the promotion business, which wasn't stable, was finished. Sometimes I had no work for two months, so I decided in August to quit the promotion business and to concentrate on selling phone cards. I bought 10,000 cards, which I was able to sell in a short time. In November, 1995, my sales were excellent, and business was strong, so I decided to become a distributor of phone cards.

In July, 1996, I opened an office as a phone card distributor. Many people wanted to sell phone cards, so my business grew quickly. Two years later, I was able to enter a partnership with phone card makers. Today, I have two offices with nine employees and a very successful distribution business, which sells cards in over 5,000 stores.

C. Make a time line. Choose six to ten significant events in your life. Write the year and a phrase about the event on a time line. Use Exercise A as an example. (Timelines will vary.)

D. In your notebook, write your autobiography. Use the information in your time line.

E. Run-on sentences. Read the paragraph and correct the run-on sentences. Rewrite the paragraph in your notebook.

> **A *run-on sentence* looks like this:**
>
> **Incorrect:** The Dixie Chicks won the Entertainer of the Year award and Music Video and Vocal Group of the Year and then they won Album of the Year.
> **Correct:** The Dixie Chicks won the Entertainer of the Year award, Music Video of the Year, Vocal Group of the Year, and Album of the Year. Then, they won Album of the Year.
> **Incorrect:** The 35th Annual Country Music Association Awards had 1.2 million more viewers than in 2000 because it changed to a different time the host was Vince Gill.
> **Correct:** The 35th Annual Country Music Association Awards had 1.2 million more viewers than in 2000 because it changed to a different time. The host was Vince Gill.

> Vincent Grant Gill was born in 1957, in Oklahoma his father *(His)* was a judge and his mother was a homemaker when he went to *(When)* high school he was already busy performing in a band he played *(He)* the banjo and guitar. After he graduated from high school he started his professional career. He got a recording contract with a record company, where he scored one of his first solo country hits and he *(He)* moved to a different company in 1989 and won "Single of the Year" award with "When I Call Your Name."

F. Edit. Find and correct the mistakes.

1. The singer ~~who his~~ *whose* music I like has written many hit songs.
2. Lyle Lovett, to whom |was married| Julia Roberts|, has acted in movies.
3. Placido Domingo is a famous tenor, ~~whose~~ *who is* known worldwide.
4. Faith Hill, ~~whom~~ *who* is married to another country singer, is one of the most popular female country singers.
5. Shania Twain is married to her producer |with him| ~~she~~ *she* lives| in Switzerland.
6. The Beatles toured all over America, where |many fans| they had|.

Looking at the Internet

It is easy to find information about your favorite performers on the Internet. Search the Internet to find facts about your favorite musician or singer. Put the name in quotation marks to make sure that you find the person you're looking for. One thing to remember is that fans have Web sites, too. Some of those Web sites may not have the most accurate information. Search for the official Web site. Tell your classmates a few interesting facts you found.

D. In your notebook, write your autobiography.

• Have students look back at the autobiography in Exercise B. Ask them to point out words and phrases that are used to connect events in the person's life. Write these words and phrases on the board. (Examples: *In June 1998, After working in the shop for two years, In January 2000, In May of 2000, A few months later*)

• Have students use their time lines as an outline as they write about themselves. Suggest that they use the life story in Exercise B, including connecting phrases like those they just found, as a reference as they write their autobiographies.

E. Run-on sentences.

• Read the sample sentences and discuss what constitutes a run-on sentence:

a. Using *and* to connect several ideas, instead of using commas after each idea, and a comma and the word *and* before the last idea in the sentence.
b. Running two complete sentences together with no punctuation, instead of ending the first with a period and beginning the second with a capital letter.

• Have students correct the sentences in the paragraph and check their answers with a partner. Have different students put parts of the paragraph on the board. Review (and correct if necessary) the use of punctuation and capitalization using the sample on the board.

F. Edit.

Have students complete this activity on their own. Write the correct answers on the board.

Looking at the Internet

Invite students to print out pictures, if possible, to add interest to their presentations. They might also play part of a song by the person they choose to research.

Practicing on Your Own

A. Relative pronouns.

Ask students to complete the exercise and check their answers with a partner.

B. Combining sentences.

Ask students to read the instructions and look at the sample sentence. Answer any questions they may have. Then, have them complete the activity individually. Review the correct answers with the class.

Suggestion

For additional practice with adjective clauses, you might have students see how many sentences they can write about the person they researched for the Internet activity on page 241 using adjective clauses with *who*, *whose*, and *whom*. Invite volunteers to read their sentences to the class.

Practicing on Your Own

A. Relative pronouns. Circle the correct relative pronoun.

1. Nashville, **who / which / whom** is located in Tennessee, is known as Music City.

2. For many years, the headquarters of country music has been Nashville, **when / where / which** many of the singers live.

3. Two music producers, Owen Bradley and Chet Atkins, created the Nashville Sound, **whom / which / where** was a more popular and sophisticated sound.

4. Chet Atkins, **whom / who / which** some people say is the most recorded solo artist, built a billion-dollar business and recording center.

5. The idea of the Nashville sound was born **which / when / where** Bradley and Atkins wanted to compete with more popular music.

6. Sixteenth Avenue, **which / where / when** a popular country radio station was started, is called Music Row.

7. After World War II, **which / where / when** people needed some entertainment, the Grand Ole Opry recruited talent to perform country music.

8. Patsy Cline, **which / whose / who** music was produced by Owen Bradley, became one of the most talented Nashville stars.

B. Combining sentences. Read each pair of sentences. Then, combine them into one longer sentence with an adjective clause. Use *who, whose, which, whom, where,* or *when.* Write the sentences in your notebook.

1. Patsy Cline died young. Patsy Cline sang the song "Crazy."
   Patsy Cline, who sang the song "Crazy," died young.

2. Johnny Cash is one of the most famous country singers. Johnny Cash likes to wear black. Johnny Cash, who likes to wear black, is one of the most famous country singers.

3. Reba McEntire has performed in a Broadway musical. Reba McEntire is a popular country music singer. Reba McEntire, who is a popular country singer, has performed in a Broadway musical.

4. John Lennon was successful after leaving the Beatles. His wife, Yoko Ono, sang with him, too. John Lennon, whose wife, Yoko Ono, sang with him, was successful after leaving the Beatles.

5. The five-string banjo was first used in Africa. The five-string banjo became a popular country music instrument. The five-string banjo, which was first used in Africa, became a popular country music instrument.

6. Disco music was popularized in the late 1970s. In the late 1970s, the movie *Saturday Night Fever* was a big hit. In the late 1970s, when disco music was popularized, the movie *Saturday Night Fever* was a big hit.

7. Placido Domingo is a famous tenor. Many other artists have performed with him. Placido Domingo, who has performed with many other artists, is a famous tenor.

8. Trisha Yearwood has earned many awards. Her career started over ten years ago. Trisha Yearwood, whose career started over ten years ago, has earned many awards.

242 UNIT 15

Grammar Summary

> **1. Adjective clauses** An adjective clause describes a noun. It can describe a subject or an object.

The man **who is sitting next to the door** is from Spain.

> **2. *Who* and *which* clauses** *Who* and *which* can replace a subject.

The man is singing a song. ⟨The man⟩ *who* is wearing a cowboy hat.

The man **who is wearing a cowboy hat** is singing a song.

Country music is very popular. ⟨Country music⟩ *which* started in the Appalachians.

Country music, **which started in the Appalachians**, is very popular.

> **3. *Whom* and *which* clauses** *Whom* and *which* can replace an object. *Whom* is often used with a preposition. *Whom* is more formal than *Who*.

Many country music performers have attended Fan Fair. The fans admire the ⟨performers.⟩ *whom*

Many country music performers, **whom the fans admire**, have attended Fan Fair.

> **4. *Whose* clauses** *Whose* shows possession. It replaces possessive nouns and pronouns.

Shania Twain sings to sold-out audiences. ⟨Her⟩ *whose* latest CD was a hit.

Shania Twain, **whose latest CD was a hit**, plays to sold-out audiences.

> **5. Restrictive versus non-restrictive adjective clauses** There are two types of adjective clauses—restrictive clauses and non-restrictive clauses.

> **a.** A **restrictive clause** is necessary to understand the sentence; therefore, no commas are necessary.

> 1. The man is from Spain. *Which man do you mean?*

>   The man **who is sitting next to the door** is from Spain.

> 2. Providence is the city. *What do you mean?*

>   Providence is the city **where I went to college**.

> **b.** A **non-restrictive clause** requires commas because the clause contains extra information. The sentence is understandable without the clause. A non-restrictive clause often describes a specific person, place, or thing.

> 1. Tim McGraw began his career in the 1990s.

>   Tim McGraw, **who is married to Faith Hill**, began his career in the 1990s.

> 2. Nashville is the home of country music.

>   Nashville, **which is located in Tennessee**, is the home of country music.

• Review the five grammar explanations and sample sentences with the class. Invite students to make up alternate sentences for each example in the chart. For example, in place of *The man who is wearing a cowboy hat is singing a song*, a student might say, *The students who study the most get the best grades*.
• Answer any questions students may have about the grammar items.
• See the Grammar Summary Expansion on page 272 for a more complete explanation of these grammar points.

Appendix A

Unit 4: Comparisons—Global and Local
Page 59

D. Student to student dictation.

Student A: Read sentences 1–6 to Student B. Student B will circle the number of the family that matches the description.

1. The son is as tall as his father.

2. The daughters are older than the son.

3. The sister isn't as old as her brother.

4. This family is as big as family number 1.

5. The mother is older than the father.

6. The son is much taller than the daughter.

Change pages. Student A will turn to page 59.

Student B: Read sentences 1–6 to Student A. Student A will circle the number of the family that matches the description.

1. The son's hair is as red as his mother's.

2. The father is as tall as the mother.

3. The son is the same age as the daughter.

4. This family is the largest.

5. The daughter is one year younger than her brother.

6. The father isn't as old as the mother.

H. Student to student dictation.

Student A: Read questions 1–5 to Student B. Student B will write the questions in the correct space.

1. Who cooked when you were growing up?

2. Who taught you how to cook?

3. Do you watch cooking programs on TV?

4. Is your kitchen big enough for you?

5. What kind of cooking classes did you take before now?

Change pages. Student A will turn to page 73.

Student B: Read questions 6–10 to Student A. Student A will write the questions in the correct space.

6. Does your husband like to cook?

7. What classes did you take together?

8. What was the first dish that you cooked?

9. How does your husband like your food?

10. Why did you decide to go to cooking school?

D. Student to student dictation.

Student A: Read the sentences to Student B.

1. You haven't been coming to work on time.

2. I haven't been feeling well.

3. It's been making a strange noise.

4. They've been running for two hours.

5. I've been having pains in my stomach.

6. It's been leaking oil.

7. They've been drinking a lot of water.

8. We've been receiving complaints about your work.

Change pages. Student A will turn to page 104.

Student B: Read the sentences to Student A.

1. It's been overheating in traffic.

2. I've been having trouble sleeping.

3. The fans have been cheering.

4. You've been making a lot of mistakes in your paperwork.

5. I haven't been eating right.

6. You haven't been getting along well with your coworkers.

7. It hasn't been running smoothly.

8. Roger has been in the lead for 30 minutes.

D. Student to student dictation: Good News / Bad News

Student A: Listen to Student B talk about the weekend. Be a good listener. Give an appropriate response. Use *must have* and an adjective from the box.

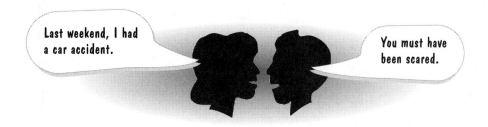

Last weekend, I had a car accident.

You must have been scared.

have / car accident

excited	pleased	surprised	disappointed	frustrated
scared	exhausted	thrilled	proud	worried

Student A: Turn to page 155.

Student B: Listen to Student A talk about the weekend. Be a good listener. Give an appropriate response. Use *must have* and an adjective from the box.

C. Student to student dictation.

Student A: Read these excuses to Student B. Student B will copy them.

1. Every time I start to study, my kids interrupt me.

2. I wanted to get up early, but I forgot to set my alarm clock.

3. I want to walk a mile after work, but I'm too tired when I get home.

4. I need to get a cavity filled, but I hate to go to the dentist.

5. I've decided to buy a computer, but I don't know which one to choose.

Student A will now turn to page 166.

Student B: Read these excuses to Student A. Student A will copy them.

1. I'd like to save $100 a month, but I love to shop at the mall.

2. I would love to travel, but I can't afford to.

3. I need to study more, but the boss often asks me to work overtime.

4. I decided to clean the basement, but there was a great movie on TV.

5. I know we need to make a will, but I don't understand legal matters.

Unit 14: Technology Today   Page 218

D. Student to student dictation.

Student A: Read the questions.

1. Why was his car insurance canceled?

2. Why was she arrested?

3. Why is school closed today?

4. Why was he evicted from his apartment?

5. Why was she taken to the hospital?

6. Why was she fired?

7. Why was she hurt?

8. Why wasn't her credit application approved?

9. Why was the plane delayed?

10. Why is the road closed?

Change pages. Student A will turn to page 218. When you finish, compare your answers.

F. Student to student dictation: Famous musicians

Student A: Work on this page only! Read each sentence below to your partner. Then, listen to your partner's sentence. Use the information in both sentences and write a new, longer sentence with an adjective clause.

1. Elvis Presley sang and acted in movies.

2. Beethoven was a famous classical composer.

3. The Beatles had two lead singers and songwriters.

4. Duke Ellington is still admired today.

5. Selena became famous for her songs in Spanish.

6. Mariah Carey had a number-one hit for ten years in a row.

Write your new sentences.

1. _____

   _____

2. _____

   _____

3. _____

   _____

4. _____

   _____

5. _____

   _____

6. _____

   _____

Unit 1: Education
Page 8, Exercise A.

(CD1, Track 2)

Lizzy: Hi, I'm Lizzy. Sophie and I are complete opposites. She's a morning person, but I'm a night owl. I rarely go to bed before 2 A.M., so I don't get up until noon. I take all afternoon classes. I don't care about keeping my things in order. I can always find my things, even if I have to look on the floor or under the bed. Sophie hates that. She's really neat. My favorite subjects are literature, writing, and art. I love to write and I love to draw. I think I'll major in art history or English literature. I have a computer, but I almost never use it. I prefer to write everything by hand. I only use the computer to type my papers, which are sometimes late. I often have to talk to my professors about my late papers. Sophie is completely different from me, but she's a great roommate.

Page 12, Exercise A.

(CD1, Track 4 *continued*)

Like most other universities, U.T.S.A. offers many academic areas. Students can major in the liberal arts, sciences, or technical fields. Here are just a few of the possible majors: accounting, art history, biology, criminal justice, engineering, and international business.

U.T.S.A. offers many facilities and student services to help the students be successful in their college studies. There are 800 computers available on campus. For students who need extra help or preparation for their college courses, there is a learning center. At the learning center, students can work with tutors to get free help with their homework and talk to counselors about their problems at school. When the students aren't studying, they can take advantage of the many extracurricular activities. There are athletic teams for both men and women. And, there are many student organizations that cover many different interests from drama and theater to science.

To help prepare freshmen or new students for college life, many universities, including U.T.S.A., offer orientation programs. The orientation programs introduce students to life on a college campus, tell students where to go for academic help, and inform students of the many fun activities that are available.

Unit 2: Colonial Times (1607–1776)
Page 27, Exercise A.

(CD1, Track 8 *continued*)

Eric: After school, I played soccer with my brothers and my cousins.

Oscar: How about the summer? What did you do in the summer?

Eric: In the summer, we used to work in the fields with my father.

Oscar: Did you go on vacation?

Eric: We never went on vacation. My mother said that we didn't need a vacation because we lived in the country. A few times each summer, my Mom packed a big lunch and we drove to the ocean.

Oscar: Did you see your relatives a lot?

Eric: All the time. There was always something to celebrate: a birthday, a wedding, or a holiday. We all used to go to my grandparents' house. My mother and aunts used to cook inside and the men barbecued a pig outside. My grandmother always made the desserts. They were wonderful—cakes and rice pudding and *mazamorra morada*.

Page 28, Exercise B.

(CD1, Track 10)
B. Note taking. Listen and complete this outline about the life of Benjamin Franklin.

Benjamin Franklin was born in Boston, Massachusetts, on January 17, 1706. At that time, school was not required and Franklin only attended school for two years. For the rest of his life, he continued to read and study on his own, and he even learned five foreign languages. At the age of 12, he began to work at his brother's printing office and learned quickly. By the age of 17, he was an excellent printer. Franklin then moved to Philadelphia in 1728, and at the young age of 22, he opened his own printing shop in that city. He published a newspaper, the *Pennsylvania Gazette*. He knew that many people could not read well, so his publications had many cartoons and pictures.

Benjamin Franklin was respected in Philadelphia and he helped to improve everyday life for the people in the city. In 1732, he started the first public library in America so that people could borrow and read books. In 1736, he helped to organize the first fire department in Philadelphia because most of the houses were wood and there were many fires. Benjamin Franklin was also postmaster in Philadelphia and he helped to set up the routes for the delivery of mail. He also spoke to the officials of the city and encouraged them to pave the streets of the city.

Franklin was also an inventor. He was always asking questions and trying to improve everyday life. At the time, colonial fireplaces sent black smoke throughout the house. Franklin invented a stove that used less wood and gave off more heat. When he was postmaster, he invented the odometer to set up mail routes throughout the city. Franklin wore glasses and became tired of taking his glasses off to see far away, so he invented bifocals. Franklin also experimented with electricity and realized that lightning is a form of electricity. He invented the lightning rod to help protect homes during lightning storms.

As the years passed, Franklin became a leader in the city and in the country. He signed the Declaration of Independence, which stated that the 13 colonies were a free and independent nation. He served as minister to France during the war with England. When he returned, Franklin signed the Constitution, which established the new government.

Benjamin Franklin died on April 17, 1790, and was buried in Philadelphia.

Unit 3: Family Matters
Page 44, Exercise B.

(CD1, Track 13 continued)
Tom: Yes.

Mediator: OK, now, you have two cars. The minivan is paid off. You have a new car and the payments on that are $300 a month for two more years.

Tom: No, the payments are for just one more year.

Mediator: OK. Let me change that information. Tom, your retirement account is up to $40,000.

Tom: Right.

Mediator: You still have all of the furniture in the house to decide about and you have a lot of electronic equipment, including a big screen TV, a stereo, and a new computer. Did I forget to list any assets?

Tom: We have a dog, a Labrador retriever. He's five years old.

Mediator: We definitely have to decide who will keep the dog.

Mediator: Anything else?

Tom: No.

Amy: No.

Page 45, Exercise D.

(CD1, Track 14 continued)
Tom and Amy: No.

Mediator: You have two cars. Tom is in sales and depends on his car. Tom, the new car is yours, and you'll make the rest of the payments on it. Amy, you'll keep the minivan.

Amy: What about the insurance on the cars?

Mediator: You'll each pay your own insurance. You've agreed on the furniture and electronic equipment.

Amy: Yes, I'll keep all the furniture in the house.

Tom: I'll take the electronic equipment.

Mediator: You have agreed on joint custody of the children.

Amy: They'll live with me during the week and continue in their same schools.

Tom: Yes, and they'll live with me on the weekends.

Mediator: Amy, the children will live with you in July and, Tom, they'll live with you in August. Joint custody also means that you have to make all major decisions about the children together. Tom, you will pay child support of $300 a month for each child. That's $600 a month for the children. In addition, for three years you'll pay Amy $400 a month for alimony. This will help with expenses until she can get some more education and some experience at work. Also, Tom, you put in a lot of overtime. All the money that you make in overtime is yours.

Tom: You forgot Rocky.

Mediator: Oh, yes. Tom, we all agreed that you will keep the dog.

Unit 4: Comparisons— Global and Local
Page 60, Exercise B.

(CD1, Track 17 *continued*)

Luncheonette. My mom worked there as a waitress part-time. There was a department store downtown, too. It was the tallest building in town, about three floors. It had everything, and I knew everyone who worked there.

Every Saturday afternoon, my siblings and I could go to the movie theater. There was one movie theater, and it showed only one movie all day. It closed late, at about 10:00. At night, we could ride our bikes home alone. I thought I lived in the best town in the world. Unfortunately, in my second year of high school, my dad sold our orchard and we moved away.

Last year, after 25 years, I went back for my elementary school reunion. What a difference! My parents' old house was surrounded by an entire development of houses. Because of all the new housing, there were many new people in the community. There were two new elementary schools, a new middle school, and the high school was renovated to accommodate 1,000 high school students. Because of the economy, almost all of the farms disappeared, and instead, there were many businesses: factories, a computer manufacturer, and a large pharmaceutical company. And, there's a large shopping mall with 50 stores on the highway. People shop there from all over the area, so traffic is much heavier than it used to be.

Downtown was so different! I didn't recognize it! There was a parking garage where the department store used to be, and there were five traffic lights to control the traffic. The mayor and the sheriff still share the same building, but there's a brand-new post office next to City Hall. It has 10 employees! There are many tall buildings. Some of them have 20 floors! The only thing that was the same was Millie's Luncheonette. The waitresses were older, but they were still as friendly as I remember them.

Unit 5: Leisure Activities
Page 70, Exercise A.

(CD1, Track 19 *continued*)

coffee shop nearby and talk about what's new with our fish and what new fish we've bought. You'd be surprised to know that keeping an aquarium is a lot of work. I have to change the water regularly and check the water chemistry. I also have to make sure that none of my new fish decide to eat my other fish. But watching my fish is very relaxing after a hard day at work.

(CD1, Track 20)

Yelena: After I retired, I was bored, and I needed something to do. I live in a senior citizen's apartment building, and one day I saw two men playing chess. It brought back memories for me. My father taught me to play chess when I was a child, and I even joined the chess team in high school, but when I was in university, I didn't have any time for chess. Now that I'm retired, I'm playing again. Chess is a game for people who like to think. I'm getting older, and I need to keep my mind sharp. I play every evening, and tomorrow I'm going to start teaching my grandson how to play.

Page 74, Exercise 1.

(CD1, Track 21 *continued*)

L: I get them from many different places. My wife and I go to yard sales, garage sales, and toy shows. Sometimes my friends find something and give it to me. My father and my brother have gotten things for me, too. Once I even got a poster from the parking lot attendant where I park my car every day.

W: That's quite a collection you have. Do you have a favorite object?

L: It's hard to pick a favorite, but I really like a talking toy from 1949.

W: Is there anything in particular that you're looking for now?

L: Well, there's a 1950s cookie jar that I've been looking for.

W: If I find it, I'll let you know.

L: Thanks.

Unit 7: Sports
Page 105, Exercise A.

(CD2, Track 9 continued)

Reporter: Are you going to continue with your tennis?

Robert: Uh-huh. I'm going to be a professional tennis player when I'm older.

(CD2, Track 10)

B. Listen to this interview between Anna and a reporter.

Reporter: Congratulations! You took first place in the competition.

Anna: I'm so excited!

Reporter: No one was surprised when you won today. Your movements are beautiful to watch.

Anna: Thank you. I have a great coach. She's the best!

Reporter: How long have you been working with Ms. Koshevaya?

Anna: For five years now.

Reporter: You've been working with a new choreographer this year, too.

Anna: I really like her. We've been doing a new routine. Last year, I was working with another choreographer, but her style didn't work for me.

Reporter: We hear that you have been practicing the triple jump.

Anna: I've been practicing, but I'm not ready to try it in competition yet. Maybe next season.

Reporter: Thank you, Anna. We wish you the best.

Unit 8: Changes
Page 122, Exercise A.

(CD2, Track 15 continued)

or a side dish. And we're going to order a big cake for dessert.

Gloria: How about decorations?

Angela: We're not going to get too crazy with the decorations. But we have bought some colorful tablecloths and paper products and plastic utensils. There was a big sale after July 4 and we got everything at a good price.

Gloria: Angela, you're not going to try to do everything yourself, are you? You need time to talk to people and have fun yourself.

Angela: This time, I was smart. I have already hired two people to help us. One is going to cook on the grills and the other is going to help serve and clean up.

Gloria: What a great idea! Angela, let me know if there's anything I can do. I'd be happy to do anything you need.

Angela: Thanks, Gloria. If I think of anything, I'll call.

Page 124, Exercise B.

Conversation 4 (CD 2, Track 19)

A: You've heard about Paul, haven't you?

B: No. What about Paul?

A: He's just been promoted.

B: Promoted?

A: Yup. To assistant sales manager.

B: You've got to be kidding! He's got the worst sales record in the company. He hasn't made a sale this month.

A: I know. But it helps when your cousin is the head of the sales department.

B: That explains it.

Conversation 5 (CD2, Track 20)

A: You know Mary Johnson, don't you?

B: Yeah. We used to take the bus together.

A: Well, guess what?

B: What?

A: She's going out with a man twice her age!

B: Twice her age? Let's see. I guess Mary's about 35.

A: That's what I guess. And this guy, he must be about 70.

B: What's the attraction?

A: Money. I've heard that he has lots of it!

B: Well, I hope she's happy.

Conversation 6 (CD2, Track 21)

A: Have you heard about Grandpa?

B: No. Is he OK?

A: Okay? Well, first he's a bought a new convertible.

B: A new convertible? He's 70!

A: He's 72. And he's dyed his hair red.

B: Red? No more gray for Grandpa!

A: And he left yesterday.

B: He left?

A: Yes, he's left on a cross-country trip!

B: Good for him!

Unit 9: Job Performance
Page 140, Exercise B.

(CD2, Track 28 *continued*)

Mr. Davis: You are great with customers—friendly, respectful, complimentary. You enjoy sales and you are an effective salesperson. This is your number one strength.

Katie: Thank you. I really like to work with the customers.

Mr. Davis: Unfortunately, you have made several mistakes on your transactions, like entering the wrong price on the register and forgetting to enter in the sales price. You've overcharged some customers and they've complained. You've undercharged other customers and the store has lost money. You had several problems during our sale last week.

Katie: I know. When we're busy, I sometimes make mistakes.

Mr. Davis: I've decided to have Ms. Nickerson retrain you on our sales transactions procedures. Are you available next Saturday?

Katie: Yes.

Mr. Davis: Do you have any comments about your evaluation?

Katie: No. I like working here a lot. I don't understand why I've had problems with the transactions. I'll be more careful, you'll see.

Page 141, Exercise C.

(CD2, Track 29 *continued*)

Mr. Davis: You've been helpful with the customers and your sales are average. I think at times you could use more effective sales techniques. If a customer seems to like a necklace, be more complimentary. Say, "That really looks nice with your hair color," or "That would look perfect with a black evening dress."

Amy: I'll try.

Mr. Davis: Amy, you've had one serious problem—taking messages. When you answer the phone, you've taken the wrong information several times. For example, you've written down incorrect phone numbers and wrong addresses. This has caused problems because I haven't been able to return calls.

Amy: I'm not too good on the phone.

Mr. Davis: From now on, I want you to repeat everything back to the caller to double-check all the information. Do you have any comments on your evaluation?

Amy: No. I really enjoy working here.

Unit 10: Regrets and Possibilities
Page 156, Exercise A.

Conversation 2 (CD2, Track 36)

Mr. D.: The last time we talked, Miguel, your classes were not going well.

Miguel: You can say that again. I was failing everything.

Mr. D.: We talked about the people you could've asked for help and the things you should've done to improve. Do you want to talk about that today?

Miguel: Yeah. I'm doing a little better. I got a C+ in math last semester.

Mr. D.: Your instructor must've been pleased.

Miguel: She was.

Mr. D.: Did you see a tutor?

Miguel: No, I didn't. I could've, but when I talked to my math instructor, she volunteered to give me some extra help. She also showed me a computer program in the learning center that could help me.

Mr. D.: Great. Now, how about your English class? Have your grades improved?

Miguel: Well, you know I can speak very easily, but writing's really hard for me.

Mr. D.: Do you go to the writing center for tutoring?

Miguel: I've been once.

Mr. D.: That's not enough, Miguel.

Miguel: I know, but I didn't like the tutor.

Mr. D.: Now, Miguel, there must've been another tutor who could've helped you.

Miguel: Yeah, I guess I'll go back and try again. By the way, I got the part-time job at the bookstore. Thanks for telling me about it.

Mr. D.: How's the job?

Miguel: Great! I have to work two nights a week and all day on Saturday. I get discounts on everything. It's easy. I help customers find books and other things.

Mr. D.: That's wonderful, Miguel.

Miguel: Thanks, Mr. D. I couldn't have gotten the job without your help.

Mr. D.: That's my job, Miguel. Now, go to the writing center.

Unit 11: Let's Get Organized
Page 172, Exercise A.

(CD3, Track 3 continued)

Diana: Hi.

Alex: Diana, it's Alex.

Diana: Hi, Alex. Are you still at school?

Alex: Uh-huh. I'm here with Carlos and Mia. We're at the library now and we're studying for the math test tomorrow. Why don't you come over here and study with us? This math is really difficult and it's helpful to work together.

Diana: I don't know. I think I'll study alone this time.

Alex: If you want to meet before class, we could go over a few of the problems.

Diana: OK. The test is at 10:00. Can we meet in the cafeteria at 9:00?

Alex: Sure. See you then.

Diana: Hello.

Katie: Hi, Diana. It's me, Katie. I'm going to the mall. They're having a big sale on shoes at Gabby's. Want to come?

Diana: A shoe sale? You know, I need a pair of black boots.

Katie: I'm getting in my car now. I'll pick you up in ten minutes. OK?

Diana: I have a math test tomorrow. I really should study.

Katie: Don't worry. We won't stay that long. I'll see you in a few minutes.

Diana: Well, sure.

Unit 12: Becoming a Citizen
Page 180, Exercise A.

(CD3, Track 4 continued)

spoke to Marco in English and asked him a few questions about United States history. He also asked Marco to write a few sentences in English. Before having her interview, Luciana was very nervous because her English was not strong. The interviewer spoke slowly and asked her to name the president, the vice president, and the governor of the state. She had no problems with those questions or with writing three sentences in English.

Three months later, Marco and Luciana received their approval letters. At their swearing-in ceremony, one hundred men and women from thirty different countries recited the Oath of Allegiance to the United States together, and then, they signed the oath. They received a copy of a letter from the president of the United States, congratulating them and telling them about their rights and responsibilities as citizens.

Page 188, Exercise B.

(CD3, Track 10 continued)

Well, there's an empty seat on the City Council, and John has decided to run for the seat. At first, he complained about spending so much time campaigning and shaking hands, but now he's looking forward to giving interviews and meeting other people in town. My wife, Andrea, is good at organizing people, so she has a group of neighbors and other volunteers at our house almost every night. They've been talking about having a voter registration drive. It's important to get the vote of everyone that we can. So, they're thinking about setting up registration tables in front of the library, the high school, the mall, and the supermarkets. We're not worried about spending too much money because John knows many people who have insisted on donating services like vans to get people to the polls on election day, envelopes for mailings, and printing services for signs.

John's wife, Kathy, is anticipating doing a lot of work for the campaign and after the campaign. She quit working temporarily in order to support John's campaign. Kathy's in charge of getting volunteers to make phone calls to voters. She's reminding people to vote. Our children are interested in helping, too. They're making signs and stuffing envelopes.

And I surprised myself. I'm interested in helping John write his speeches. Back in my country, I was very involved in local politics, but until now, I haven't been involved here. Now I'm enjoying helping John practice for next month's debate. I am pretending to be one of his opponents or one of the reporters who will be asking John the tough questions.

A campaign is a lot of work, but it's worthwhile, too.

Unit 14: Technology Today
Page 212, Exercise A.

(CD3, Track 15 *continued*)

Roller blades were designed by Scott Olson and his brother Brennan. Instead of having four wheels, positioned like the wheels on a car, the wheels were placed in a line. This is why roller blades are also called in-line skates.

NASA is the National Aeronautics and Space Administration. The first space shuttle was launched by NASA in 1981. It orbited the globe in less than two hours.

Many engineers and researchers were involved in the invention of the personal computer. The first personal computers were manufactured by IBM in 1981.

The first minivan was designed and built by Chrysler Corporation in 1983. The minivan was designed to be a family car and was an immediate success.

The laptop computer was invented by Sir Clive Sinclair in 1987. Today, laptop computers are slowly replacing desktop computers in popularity.

The digital camera is another invention that involved many people and ideas. One of the first easy-to-use digital cameras was introduced by Apple Computer in 1994.

The disposable cell phone was invented by Randi Altschul in 1999. Do you have this new invention?

Page 220, Exercise A.

(CD3, Track 18 *continued*)

Up until this time, people paid for their purchases by cash or check. In 1950, the first credit card was issued. At first, credit cards were used by business travelers for restaurant and hotel bills. By the 1960s, many companies were offering these cards. People did not need to carry so much cash. They could buy items and pay later. Another idea that was developing at this time was the idea of a bar code. At the time, stock clerks had to put a price on every item. The clerk rang up each item on the cash register, punching in the price of each item by hand. Store owners, especially the owners of large supermarkets, asked about a method of automatically reading information about products during checkout. Several inventors worked on the idea, but there was not a standard on how to identify each item. The Uniform Pricing Code, known as the U.P.C., was invented in 1973. In 1974, the first U.P.C. scanner was installed in a supermarket in Ohio. It was no longer necessary to put the price on every individual food item. Now supermarket checkers simply scan each item and the price appears on the register.

In the 1990s, another form of shopping became popular, online shopping. The Internet offers an inexpensive way for companies to advertise their products to a worldwide audience. Customers can look at pictures of products, check prices, and place their orders over the Internet. This has made shopping fast and convenient. Customers are able to easily compare prices from several different companies.

Can you think of other inventions and ideas that have made shopping easier? Can you think of an invention that would help you with your shopping?

Unit 15: Country Music
Page 236, Exercise B.

(CD3, Track 20 *continued*)

live entertainment, and barbecue and beverages. About fifty thousand fans attended. The first Fan Fair was so successful that planning began almost immediately for 1973. The date was changed to June, when the weather would be better. Over one hundred thousand fans attended the second Fan Fair.

Every year brought so many performers and fans to Fan Fair that, in 1982, it was moved to the Tennessee State Fairgrounds. Fan Fair stayed at the fairgrounds for another nineteen years.

One of the reasons that Fan Fair has stayed popular is because of the unexpected. In 1974, former Beatle Paul McCartney attended. In 1996, Garth Brooks, who made a surprise appearance, signed autographs for 23 hours. In 1992, more than six hundred reporters from Europe, Asia, and South America went to cover the appearance of a popular star, Billy Ray Cyrus, who had introduced a new country line dance. Movie and television stars and professional athletes have also visited Fan Fair. When a popular football star attended, even some of the country performers got in line for his autograph.

In 2001, Fan Fair returned to downtown Nashville as the World's Biggest Country Music Festival. But, the biggest crowd attended Fan Fair 2002. Over one hundred and twenty-five thousand fans attended to see some of the 445 performers.

As you can imagine, fans who want to attend Fan Fair must plan ahead. They can buy tickets online or by telephone as early as seven months ahead of time. The ticket packages include four days of live performances. Every year there are new surprises and activities for the fans, which keep them coming back year after year.

Grammar Summary Expansion

1. Present continuous tense

Yes/No questions	
Are they **studying** now?.	No, **they're not. They're sleeping.**
Is she **drinking** soda?	Yes, she **is**.

Wh- questions	
What **is** he **reading**?	He **is reading** the newspaper.
Who **is studying** math?	The students **are**.
Where **are** you **going**?	I **am going** home.
Why **are** they **running**?	They **are running** to a 9:00 class.

2. Simple present tense

Yes/No questions	Affirmative	Negative
Do you speak English?	Yes, I **do**.	No, I **do not (don't)**.
Does he know Alice?	Yes, he **does**.	No, he **does not (doesn't)**.

Wh- questions	
Where **do** you **live**?	I **live** in Chicago.
How often **do** we **go** swimming?	We **go** swimming every week.
When **does** she **study**?	She **studies** at night.
How much **does** he need?	He **needs** five dollars.

3. *Who* questions

Questions	Short Answers
Who **plays** soccer?	I do.
Who **has** two sisters?	He does.

4. Adverbs of frequency

- Adverbs of frequency come before most verbs.
  *I **always go** to bed early.*
- Adverbs of frequency come after the verb *be*.
  *I **am never** tired in the morning.*

5. Nonaction verbs

- Nonaction verbs usually take the present tense form.
  *I **need** a new car.*
  *My brother **owns** three cars.*
- Nonaction verbs are often related to the senses (*see, smell*), emotions (*like, hate*), and mental action (*believe, know, want*).
  *I **see** the taxi now.*
  *They **want** chocolate ice cream.*

1. Past tense

- Regular past tense verbs end in *–ed*
  Pablo **arrived** at 2:00. We **walked** ten miles on Saturday.
- A list of irregular past tense verbs is on page 273.
  We **had** toast for breakfast. **I went** to the movies last night.

2. Past time expressions

(See list on Student Book page 35.)

3. Past tense: *Be*

Statements
Franklin **was** an inventor.
The Pilgrims **were** from England.

Yes/No questions	Short Answers
Was Franklin from Philadelphia?	Yes, he **was**.
Was Franklin a teacher?	No, he **wasn't**.
Were some Native Americans friendly?	Yes, they **were**.
Were the Pilgrims' settlements large?	No, they **weren't**.

Wh- questions	
Where was the first Pilgrim settlement?	It **was** along the eastern coast of the U.S.

4. Past tense verb forms

Statements	
I arrived at 6:00.	(regular)
You **left** at 9:00.	(irregular)

Yes/No questions	Short Answers
Did they plant corn?	Yes, they **did**.
	No, they **didn't**.
Did she wear a long dress?	Yes, she **did**.
	No, she **didn't**.

Wh- questions	
What ocean did they cross?	They **crossed** the Atlantic Ocean.
Where did tobacco grow?	It **grew** in Virginia.

5. *Used to*

(See explanation on Student Book page 35.)

1. The future tense

- Future tense has two forms: *will* and *be going to*. Both forms talk about future actions and plans.
  *I **will** see you after class. **I'm going to** take math next term.*
- *Will* is also used to express promises and predictions.
  *I **will** help you with your homework. I think it **will** rain later.*

2. Present continuous tense: Future meaning

Note

The present continuous tense can have future meaning.
*Gina **is arriving** tomorrow night.*

3. Future time expressions

(See list on Student Book page 51.)

4. Future

be + going to	will + verb
I'm **going to leave** tomorrow.	I **will call** you Thursday night.
Are you **going to study** tonight?	**Will** you **study** math?
When **are** you **going to have** lunch?	What **will** you **eat**?

5. Future time clauses

- With future time clauses, the verb in the main clause is in the future tense, and the verb in the time clause is in the present tense.
  *We **will buy** a new car when we **have** enough money.*
- When the time clause comes at the beginning of a sentence, it is followed by a comma.
  *If we **save** enough money, we**'ll get** a sports car.*

1. Comparative adjectives

Note

Comparative adjectives compare two people, places, or things.

My math class is **harder than** my science class.
My science class is **less difficult than** my math class.
My science class is **more interesting than** my math class.
In fact, my science class is **much more interesting than** my math class

2. Superlative adjectives

Superlative adjectives compare three or more people, places, or things.

The library is **the largest** room in the school.
The cafeteria is **the most modern** room in the school.

3. Comparing nouns

- Use *more + than* and *fewer + than* to compare count nouns.
  *There are **more colleges** in New York **than** in Miami.*
  *There are **fewer men** in my English class **than** women.*
- Use *more + than* and *less + than* to compare noncount nouns.
  *There is **more water** in the Atlantic Ocean **than** in Lake Michigan.*
  *There is **less rain** in Hawaii **than** in Florida.*

4. *As* + adjective + *as*/not *as* + adjective + *as*

Note

You can use (*not*) *as* + adjective + *as* to compare two people or things.

I am **as tall as** my father.
My mother is **not as tall as** my father.

5. *As many* + noun + *as; not as many* + noun + *as, as much* + non-count noun + *as*

Note

Use *as many* + count noun + *as, not as many* + count noun + *as*, and *as* much + non-count noun + *as* to compare nouns.

Mr. Bridge has **as many students** *as* Mrs. Green.
I do**n't** have **as many friends as** you do.
Mr. Bridge gives **as much homework as** Mrs. Green.

1. *Yes/No questions*

- *Yes/No questions with* be *are formed by reversing the subject and verb.*
  She is *married.* **Is she** *married?*
  They were *at home.* **Were they** *at home?*
- *Yes/No questions with* have *and other verbs require the use of the helping verb* do *or* did.
  We have *a small car.* **Do we have** *a small car?*
  He had *a test yesterday.* **Did he have** *a test yesterday?*
  He studies *every day.* **Does he study** *every day?*

2. *Who* questions

Who is leaving early.	I am.
Who has long hair?	He does.

3. *Whom/Who*

- Most of the time *who* is used to refer to the object in a sentence.
  Who *are you having dinner with tonight?*
- In very formal situations, *whom* is used to refer to the object in a sentence.
  Whom *are you having dinner with tonight?*
  With whom *are you having dinner tonight?*

4. *Whose* questions

Whose is used to talk about one or more possessions.

Whose car is that?
Whose shoes are those?

5. *Wh-* questions

(See examples on Student Book page 83.)

6. Tag questions

- Tag questions use a helping verb in the same tense as the verb in the main part of the sentence.
  You **knew** *some nice people at school,* **didn't** *you? (past)*
  He **is** *a good painter,* **isn't** *he? (present)*
  We **will** *leave soon,* **won't** *we? (future)*
- If the main verb is affirmative, the tag is negative; if the main verb is negative, the tag is affirmative.
  You **have** *a new computer,* **don't you***?*
  She **doesn't live** *in California,* **does she***?*

1. *Have to* and *must*

Note

Have to and *must* show necessity.
You **have to** have a license to drive in this state.
I **must** study for the test tomorrow.

2. *Don't have to/doesn't have to/Didn't have to*

Note

Don't have to/doesn't have to/didn't have to show that something isn't necessary.
You **don't have to** wear a coat in the summer.
She **didn't have to** buy lunch because she brought it from home.

3. *Must not* and *Cannot*

- *Must not* and *cannot* show that an action is against the law or against the rules.
  You **must not** drive if you have been drinking alcohol.
  A twelve-year-old **cannot** drive a car in this country.
- *Must not* is rarely contracted to *mustn't*.

4. *Can*

Note

Can show ability or possibility. *Cannot* shows the opposite.

Ability:	She **can** drive very well.
Inability:	She **can't** speak Chinese.
Possibility:	I **can** play tennis this afternoon if you're free.
Impossibility:	I **can't** play tennis this afternoon because I have to work.

5. *Should*

Note

Should is used to give advice. *Shouldn't* is used to tell people what not to do.
You **should** stop smoking.
You **shouldn't** eat so much sugar.

6. *Had better/Had better not*

Note

Had better and *had better not* are used to give a warning that if you do (or don't do) something, an unpleasant result will follow.
You **had better** drive more slowly, or you will have an accident.
I **had better not** buy an expensive car, or I will have no money to pay the rent.

1. Present perfect continuous

Note

The present perfect continuous talks about actions that started in the past, continue into the present, but aren't complete yet.
*I **have been reading** for an hour and a half.*
*We **have been living** here since 2001.*

2. *For* and *since*

Note

For shows an amount of time and *since* tells when an action started.
*They **have been playing** soccer **for** two hours.*
*We **have been watching** this game **since** 2:00.*

3. *Yes/No* questions

Questions	Short Answers	
	Affirmative	Negative
Have you **been waiting** long?	Yes, I **have**.	No, I **haven't**.
Has she **been studying** Spanish?	Yes, she **has**.	No, she **hasn't**.

4. *How long* questions

How long have you been watching TV?	*For* an hour.
How long has he been sleeping?	*Since* 9:00 last night.

1. Present perfect

Note

The present perfect tells about actions that started in the past, continue into the present, but aren't complete yet.

*I **have known** Celia for two years.*
*We **haven't watched** TV since Friday night.*

2. Statements

See examples of present perfect statements on Student Book page 131.

3. *Yes/No questions*

Questions	Short Answers	
	Affirmative	Negative
Have you **lived** here for many years?	Yes, I **have**.	No, I **haven't**.
Has she **played** tennis every day this week?	Yes, she **has**.	No, she **hasn't**.

1. *How many* questions

We often use the present perfect with how many.

How many jobs **have** you **had?**	**I have had** six jobs.
How many movies **have** you **seen** this week?	**I have seen** three.

2. Repeated past actions

Note

The present perfect describes:
- Repeated past actions.
  *I've **been** late to work three times this week.*
- Past actions that may happen again.
  *I've **eaten** two hot dogs so far, but I may eat another one.*

3. Past actions

Note

The present perfect can be used to show that we are more interested in *what* the action is than *when* it happened.
*They **have bought** an expensive new car.*
*She **hasn't spoken** to her husband about the problem.*

4. Present perfect with adverbs

Note

Many different adverbs are used with the present perfect.
*I **have finished** my exams **at last**!*
*I **have finally finished** my exams.*

1. *Should have*

Note

Should have shows that a person has a regret about a past action.
*I **should have** stayed home yesterday. I didn't get anything done at work.*
*I **shouldn't have** gone to the beach this morning. It was raining.*

2. *Might have/may have/could have*

- *Might have, may have,* and *could have* describe past possibilities.
  *He **might have** left early. I'm not sure.*
  *I **may have** written the phone number on a piece of paper and lost it.*
  *They **could have** been sleeping when you called.*
- *Could have* can also describe a past choice and *couldn't have* can describe a past impossibility.
  *I **could have** gone to Hawaii, but I went to Florida instead.*
  *You **couldn't have** seen Anna in New York last week. She was in California.*

3. *Must have*—Probability and deduction

Note

Must have can describe a probability or deduction based on a past event.
*You **must have** been really tired after running ten miles.*

4. *Must have*—Expressing sympathy or empathy

Note

Must have can express sympathy.
*You couldn't go to your daughter's wedding? You **must have** felt terrible!*

5. *–ing* versus *–ed* adjectives

Note

Adjectives with *–ing* describe things and adjectives with *–ed* describe people.
*That was an **exciting** soccer game. The fans were really excited.*
*The test was **tiring**. I was very **tired** after studying for it.*

1. Verb + infinitive

Note

Only certain verbs follow the pattern verb + infinitive.
*I **plan to attend** college next year.*
*We **try to get** to class on time every day.*
(See list on Student Book page 179.)

2. Verb + object + infinitive

Note

Only certain verbs follow the pattern verb + object + infinitive.
*I **advise you to study** for the test tomorrow.*
*The teacher **asked me to use** a pen, not a pencil.*
(See list on Student Book page 179.)

3. *Be* + adjective + infinitive

Note

Only certain adjectives follow the pattern *be* + adjective + infinitive.
*It **is stressful to work** seven days a week.*
*It **was impossible to get** to class on time.*
(See list on Student Book page 179.)

1. Verb + gerund

Note

Only certain verbs follow the pattern verb + gerund.
*I **don't mind driving** you home.*
*We should **practice speaking** English every day.*
(See list on Student Book page 181.)

2. Preposition + gerund

Note

Only certain verbs follow the pattern preposition + gerund.
*I closed the door carefully **before locking** it.*
*She handed in the test **without checking** the answers.*
(See list on Student Book page 183.)

3. Verb + preposition + gerund

Note

Only certain verbs follow the pattern verb + preposition + gerund.
*We **concentrated on learning** the new vocabulary words.*
*We **thought about playing tennis**, but we decided not to.*
(See list on Student Book page 184.)

4. *Be* + adjective phrase + gerund

Note

Only certain verbs follow the pattern *be* + adjective phrase + gerund.
*We **were worried about arriving** late.*
*He **is capable of running** ten miles in half an hour.*
(See list on Student Book page 184.)

1. Active and passive voice

Note

The passive voice follows the pattern *be* + past participle.
*The students **are tutored** each week.*
*My car **is parked** on the street.*

2. Uses of the passive voice

Note

The pasive voice is used
- When we want to emphasize the action.
  *The exam **is finished** at 10:00.*
- When we don't know who performed the action
  *My car **is stolen**.*
- To make general statements of facts.
  *Rice fields **are found** in many parts of Japan.*

3. Passive and *by*

Note

By can be used in a passive sentence to tell who performed the action.
Passive: The new president of the company is selected ***by* the board of directors.**
Active: The board of directors select the new president of the company

4. Questions

Notes

Passive voice questions follow the pattern *be* + subject + past participle.
Are *cars manufactured* in China?
Is *Spanish taught* in your school?

1. Active and passive voice

Note

In a passive sentence, the focus is on the process, the product, or the action, not on the performer of the action.
*Today more and more cars **are manufactured** in China.*
*The package **was given** to the delivery driver.*

2. Uses of the passive voice

Note

The passive voice is used
- When the subject receives the action.
  *The winning ticket **was sold** on Monday.*
- When we don't know who performed the action.
  *The window **was broken** sometime last night.*
- To make general statements of fact.
  *Fish **are found** in the sea.*

3. Passive voice—Past tense statements

Note

Past tense passives follow the pattern Subject + *was/were* + past participle.
*My car **was stolen** from in front of my house last Thursday.*

4. *Wh-* questions

Note

Past tense passive *Wh*-questions follow the pattern *Wh*-word + *was/were* + subject + past participle.
Where was** this book **printed?
***By whom were** you **greeted** when you arrived?*

1. Adjective clauses

Note

An adjective clause describes the subject or the object in a sentence.
*The book **which I bought yesterday** cost $25.*
*I lost the book **which I bought yesterday.***

2. *Who* and *which* clauses

Note

Adjective clauses with *who* and *which* can describe a subject.
The woman was 36 years old. The woman won the race.
*The woman **who won the race** was 36 years old.*

The movie was very good. I saw the movie last night.
*The movie **which I saw last night** was very good.*

3. *Whom* and *which* clauses

Note

Adjective clauses with *whom* and *which* can describe an object.
The famous singer lives in California. I met the famous singer.
*The famous singer **whom I met** lives in California.*

That red shirt is beautiful. You bought the shirt on sale.
*That red shirt, **which you bought on sale,** is beautiful.*

4. *Whose* clauses

Note

Adjective clauses with *whose* show possession.
Garth Brooks is very successful singer. His manager is his wife.
*Garth Brooks, **whose manager is his wife,** is a very successful singer.*

5. Restrictive versus non-restrictive adjective clauses

Notes

- Adjective clauses which contain information that is required in order to understand the sentence are called *restrictive adjective clauses*.
  *The woman **who is leaving the room** is my sister.*
- Adjective clauses which merely add extra information to a sentence are called *non-restrictive adjective clauses*. We put a comma before and after non-restrictive clauses.
  *Madonna, **who now has two children,** plans to move back to the United States.*

Irregular Verbs

Simple form	Simple past	Past participle
be	was/were	been
bear	bore	born
become	became	become
begin	began	begun
blow	blew	blown
break	broke	broken
bring	brought	brought
build	built	built
buy	bought	bought
catch	caught	caught
choose	chose	chosen
come	came	come
cut	cut	cut
dig	dug	dug
do	did	done
drink	drank	drunk
drive	drove	driven
eat	ate	eaten
fall	fell	fallen
feel	felt	felt
fight	fought	fought
find	found	found
fly	flew	flown
forbid	forbade	forbidden
forget	forgot	forgotten
get	got	got/gotten
give	gave	given
go	went	gone
grow	grew	grown
hang	hung	hung
have	had	had
hear	heard	heard
hit	hit	hit
hold	held	held
hurt	hurt	hurt
keep	kept	kept
know	knew	known

Simple form	Simple past	Past participle
lay	laid	laid
leave	left	left
lend	lent	lent
lose	lost	lost
make	made	made
meet	met	met
pay	paid	paid
prove	proved	proven
put	put	put
quit	quit	quit
read	read	read
ride	rode	ridden
rise	rose	risen
run	ran	run
say	said	said
see	saw	seen
sell	sold	sold
send	sent	sent
set	set	set
sew	sewed	sewn
show	showed	shown
sing	sang	sung
sit	sat	sat
sleep	slept	slept
speak	spoke	spoken
spend	spent	spent
split	split	split
steal	stole	stolen
stick	stuck	stuck
sweep	swept	swept
take	took	taken
teach	taught	taught
tell	told	told
think	thought	thought
understand	understood	understood
wear	wore	worn
win	won	won

Skills Index

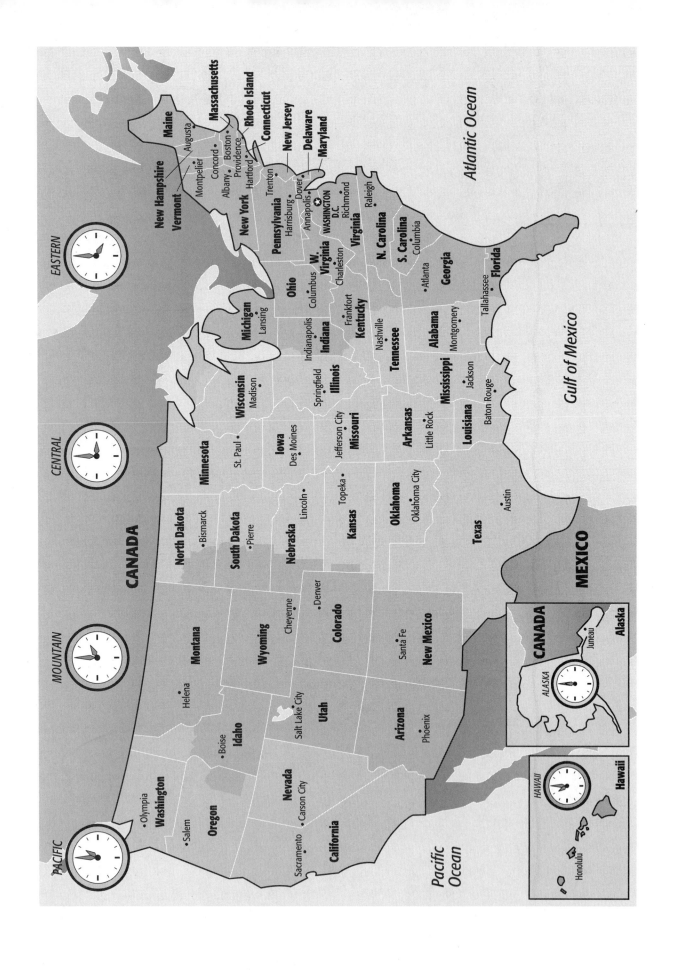